DA CAPO PRESS SERIES IN
ARCHITECTURE AND DECORATIVE ART
General Editor: ADOLF K. PLACZEK
Avery Librarian, Columbia University

Volume 33

The Life of Pierre Charles L'Enfant

The Life of
Pierre Charles L'Enfant

BY

H. Paul Caemmerer

DA CAPO PRESS • NEW YORK • 1970

A Da Capo Press Reprint Edition

This Da Capo Press edition of *The Life of Pierre Charles L'Enfant* is an unabridged republication of the first edition published in Washington, D.C., in 1950. It is reprinted by special arrangement with the estate of the author.

LMS

Library of Congress Catalog Card Number 71-87546
SBN 306-71381-0

Published by Da Capo Press
A Division of Plenum Publishing Corporation
227 West 17th Street, New York, N.Y. 10011

Manufactured in the United States of America.

The Life of Pierre Charles L'Enfant

The Heart of the Nation, Washington, D. C.

The Life of Pierre Charles L'Enfant
Planner of the City Beautiful
The City of Washington

BY

H. PAUL CAEMMERER, PH.D.,

Secretary, National Commission of Fine Arts
Member, International City Managers' Association

Based on Original Sources

"Few men can afford to wait a hundred years to be remembered. It is not a change in L'Enfant that brings us here. It is we who have changed, who have just become able to appreciate his work. And our tribute to him should be to continue his work."

From the Address of the Honorable Elihu Root,
Secretary of State, at the dedication of the L'Enfant
Tomb, Arlington National Cemetery, on May 22, 1911.

NATIONAL REPUBLIC PUBLISHING COMPANY
WASHINGTON, D. C.
1950

In fancy now beneath the twilight gloom,
Come, let me lead thee o'er this second Rome,
Where tribunes rule, wher dusky Davi bow,
And what was Goose Creek once is Tiber now.

This jam'd metropolis, where fancy sees
Squares in morasses, obelisks in trees;
Which second-sighted seers e'en now adorn
With shrines unbuilt and heroes yet unborn.

—Thomas Moore, 1804.

FOREWORD

It is fitting that a book on the life of Pierre Charles L'Enfant, architect-engineer, the planner of the Capital of the United States of America, should be prepared for publication in 1950—the year which marks the one hundred fiftieth of the establishment of the seat of the Government in the City of Washington.

In the years that have passed since 1791, when L'Enfant was commissioned by President Washington to prepare a plan for the new capital of this Nation, a city has been developed at the confluence of the Potomac and the Anacostia Rivers which enjoys the distinction of continuous growth predicated upon a notable plan conceived more than a century and a half ago.

The story of the life of the man who prepared this plan for the City of Washington is fascinating. L'Enfant was born and educated in France, came to these shores early in the American Revolution, was commissioned an officer in the Continental Army, and subsequently rendered distinguished service as an architect and engineer before embarking upon the crowning accomplishment of his career, the plan for Washington in the District of Columbia.

The report of the McMillan Park Commission of 1901 on the District of Columbia stated that "so extensive a composition, and one containing such important elements, does not exist elsewhere;" and so the distinguished artists of the McMillan Commission, Daniel H. Burnham, Charles F. McKim, Augustus Saint-Gaudens, and

Frederick Law Olmsted, Jr., builded more secure the basic plan for the Nation's Capital laid down by L'Enfant one hundred ten years earlier. Since 1910 the National Commission of Fine Arts, joined by the National Capital Park and Planning Commission in 1926, have successfully guided the development of Washington along the lines of the L'Enfant plan of 1791.

The author of this volume, Dr. H. Paul Caemmerer, is a recognized authority on the history of Washington as his books, *Washington, the National Capital* (1932), *A Manual on the Origin and Development of Washington* (1939), and *Historic Washington* (1948), attest. After careful research, which took the author to France in 1948, Dr. Caemmerer has faithfully recorded the life-story of one to whose memory we owe a full measure of gratitude for having established the distinguished monumental pattern of the Capital of this Nation.

GILMORE D. CLARKE,
Chairman,
The National Commission of Fine Arts.

Washington, D. C.,
June 14, 1949.

CONTENTS

ix

ILLUSTRATIONS

Introduction

THE CITY OF WASHINGTON is undoubtedly the best known city in the United States, since it is our National Capital. It belongs to the people of the country by virtue of the Constitution of the United States, which provides for a Federal District. Today our National Capital is also recognized as the most beautiful city in the United States, and considering the trend of events and of their effect on our capital city, the profound interest manifested by government establishments in the development of the city, esthetically, and in accordance with the highest standards of city planning, we can scarcely realize what a marvelous city this will be 50 or 100 years hence. And in all this work we should not forget the services rendered by patriotic citizens and organizations, who have given valiant service to make this capital city ever greater and more beautiful.

Yet with all it is of the highest interest to note that, to quote Thomas Adams, eminent city planner of this country . . .[1]

"Washington owes its beauty, primarily, to the fine qualities of the ground plan that was made for it in 1791. The spacious environments of its buildings, their setting and approaches, and their reciprocal relationships are major elements in the splendor of its structures. The plan was a product of that combination of statesmanship and technical skill which has always distinguished great enterprise in the field of city building. The foresight and driving force of President Washington [and let us not forget in the earliest days there were times when it was the will of Washington alone that kept the capital city here] joined with the

---

[1] Thomas Adams, **Outline of Town and City Planning,** Russell Sage Foundation, New York, 1935, pp. 125-126.

xvii

practical idealism of Thomas Jefferson and the art of Major Pierre L'Enfant, created the groundwork on which the capital city of the United States has been built."

Thus, considering the fundamental importance of the L'Enfant Plan in contributing to the beauty of the City of Washington, and the fact that such recognition was given by the Nation in having the remains of Major L'Enfant brought, in 1909, to the Rotunda of the United States Capitol to lie in state, and then placed on the eastern hill of Arlington National Cemetery to overlook the city he planned, the writer felt some eight years ago that the life of the author of that Plan deserves to be made known to the people of this country. The occasion was a Lecture he gave here in the year 1941 at the University Women's Club entitled, The Sesquicentennial of the L'Enfant Plan of 1791. Also as an Officer and Past President of the Columbia Historical Society further opportunity was given to become thoroughly familiar with L'Enfant's work in our National Capital. Furthermore, after having visited fully two dozen national capitals in various parts of the world in as many years, the writer has always come back with the conviction that there is no more beautiful capital than the City of Washington. Today, after a mere one hundred and fifty years, Washington is a city of fully one and one-half million inhabitants, including the metropolitan area, and a beautiful World Capital.

Information concerning the ancestry of Pierre Charles L'Enfant, facts concerning his youth, his training as an artist, and sources of his inspiration are described in Chapter I. The greater part of the information is from original sources consulted by the writer during the course of research in France, the assistance of Monsieur

Abel Doysié, of Paris, information from members of the staff of the Bibliothèque Nationale and of the Archíves Nationales, Paris, the Director of the Gobelin Tapestries, as also suggestions from Mr. Welles Bosworth, architect, of Vaucresson, France, who designed the L'Enfant Tomb in the Arlington National Cemetery, and who gave him a photograph of the competition drawing; and a Memorandum from Colonel R. Trutat, Service Historique de L'Armée, Paris, concerning Pierre Charles L'Enfant. The Conservateur of the Palace at Versailles, supplied the photograph of the large painting by the elder L'Enfant on exhibition there, and the Conservateur Musée des Beaux-Arts, at Tours, Monsieur Boris Lossky, the two photographs of water color paintings, of Amboise and Chanteloupe, on exhibition there. The writer was also in conference with Dr. Waldo G. Leland, Director Emeritus of the American Council of Learned Societies, concerning L'Enfant.

Chapter II is devoted to an account of "L'Enfant with Other French Officers Enters the American Service." For much of the information contained therein the writer is indebted to Miss Elizabeth Kite, Historian, formerly of the Library of Congress, and author of the well-known book, *L'Enfant and Washington*.

We note in this chapter that L'Enfant was but 22 years of age when he became interested in the independence of the American colonies as one of about thirty officers; and with the help of Beaumarchais, who also provided much needed military supplies, definite aid was brought to the patriot army in America that culminated in the victory at Yorktown.

Chapter III describes L'Enfant's varied and interesting experiences as an officer of the War of Independence that took him from Valley Forge to the Staff of General Washington, being promoted by Congress to the brevet Major. He was the "artist of the American Revolution." The letters by L'Enfant to General vonSteuben (copies of which are in APPENDIX B) were secured by courtesy of the New York Historical Society, and were translated by Mrs. V. M. Thatcher of the Department of State. Dr. Ernst Correll, Graduate Language Examiner of the American University, was also helpful to the writer in this matter.

Chapter IV relates to L'Enfant's services to the Society of the Cincinnati as the designer of their medal and diploma. For information on the subject the writer is indebted to present members of the Society and the writings of them as indicated, particularly to President General Bryce Metcalf, who read the article; also to Secretary General Francis A. Foster. L'Enfant's devotion to his father and mother whom he visited while abroad in the interest of the Society is set forth in a letter of September 10, 1787, which is printed by courtesy of the Historical Society of Pennsylvania. (Appendix C, p. 423)

Chapter V is devoted to that period in the life of L'Enfant from the time of his discharge as an Officer of the American Revolution, in 1783, and the subsequent years when he resided in New York City, during which he rendered conspicious architectural service in St. Paul's Chapel, and in remodeling Federal Hall for the first inauguration of President Washington in 1789. For information concerning L'Enfant's work at St. Paul's Chapel the writer is particularly indebted to Mrs. Buchanan Henry, one of its members, who herself made it the subject of considerable research and published her finding in an article entitled *L'Enfant and St. Paul's Chapel,* in the *Trinity Parish Herald* for October and November, 1947. The writer is grateful to Columbia University (Avery Library) for a copy of papers by Mr. William Hindley, an architect of New York City, relating to houses alleged to have been built or restored by L'Enfant in New York City, and to Mr. Gardner Osborn, Custodian of the Federal Hall Museum, to whom Mrs. Hindley gave her husband's interesting collection of papers and prints relating to Federal Hall.

For much of the information concerning the work of L'Enfant in remodeling Federal Hall, the writer is indebted to the New York Municipal Reference Library, as also to the New York Historical Society, which has in its collections a part of the balcony that the hand of General Washington must have touched after he took the Oath of Office as the first President of the United States of America on that memorable April 30, 1789; also to Gardner Osborn, Curator of the Federal Hall Memorial, National Park Service, Department of the Interior, above mentioned.

Soon after the inauguration ceremonies, Major L'Enfant became interested in the proposed permanent seat of Government of the newly established Republic, and thus on September 11, 1789, he addressed a letter to President Washington applying for the appointment to prepare the Plan, which is described in CHAPTER VI. As to the type of Plan he had in mind for the future capital city, his words are indeed prophetic, when he states that . . .

" . . . The plan should be drawn on such a scale as to leave room for that aggrandizement and embellishment which the increase of the wealth of the Nation will permit it to pursue at any period, however remote . . ."

That is exactly what happened, for after one hundred years, in 1901, the L'Enfant Plan was restored (after having been neglected for many years) and adapted to the entire District of Columbia. This work was undertaken by the McMillan Park Commission of 1901, and furthered by the National Commission of Fine Arts, established in 1910. Since the year 1926, by authority of Congress, the principles of the L'Enfant Plan have been extended beyond the District of Columbia by the National Capital Park and Planning Commission, which cooperates with similar Commissions in both Maryland and Virginia in planning for the Metropolitan Area of Washington.

For detailed information concerning the writings of L'Enfant as pertaining to the Plan which he designed, the writer is much indebted to the Staff of the Library of Congress, in particular to Dr. Luther Evans, Librarian, and to Dr. St. George L. Sioussat, until recently Chief of the Division of Manuscripts, as also to Mr. John Beverley Riggs, Assistant of that Division; to Miss Elizabeth Kite, and the Institut Français de Washington, for permission to quote from her book, heretofore mentioned, entitled *L'Enfant and Washington;* and to The Columbia Historical Society, Dr. F. Regis Noel, President, which during a period of somewhat over fifty years has through its *Records* published in its 49 volumes, in great detail, most valuable information concerning the L'Enfant Plan and its application in the founding, growth and development of the City of Washington.

Chapter VII relates the difficulties encountered by L'Enfant in endeavoring to carry his Plan forward, and his resignation by March, 1792, after but a year of intense activity concerning it.

Chapter VIII relates L'Enfant's achievements in other localities. Soon after leaving Washington, L'Enfant was called by Alexander Hamilton, Secretary of the Treasury, to plan the first "Industrial Center" at Paterson, New Jersey. For a copy of the Plan of Paterson, 1792, the writer is indebted to D. Stanton Hammond, President of the Passaic County Historical Association.

There is also indication, from a letter from Alexander Hamilton, to L'Enfant which appears in this volume (page 123) that Hamilton wanted L'Enfant to design our United States coins.

Thereupon L'Enfant went to Philadelphia and became architect of the never-completed-mansion of Robert Morris; for information on the subject the writer is indebted to The Art Jury, of Philadelphia, Miss Grace G. Haupt, Executive Secretary, and to the Public Library of Philadelphia, which furnished a photograph of the building. For other information concerning services rendered by L'Enfant in Philadelphia, the writer wishes to express his grateful appreciation to the American Philosophical Society and to the Pennsylvania State Historical Society, whose headquarters are in Philadelphia; as also to Mr. Harold E. Eberlein, author and historian of Philadelphia, for information concerning Fort Mifflin, Pa.

Coming back to Washington in 1800, L'Enfant made his home with friends. The events of this and subsequent years, until his death in 1825, are described in Chapter IX.

In 1812 L'Enfant declined an appointment offered by Secretary of War Eustis as professor of civil and military engineering in the newly established Military Academy at Westpoint. Secretary of State Monroe urged acceptance. L'Enfant set forth his reasons for not accepting the appointment in a lengthy letter that he wrote to Secretary of War Eustis (Appendix G, p. 445, original in the National Archives), while Monroe urged acceptance, (See page 449).

However, during the war of 1812, L'Enfant rendered useful service on Fort Washington along the Potomac, near Mount Vernon; for information on the subject the writer is grateful to his friend Delos Smith, architect, and to the National Park Service, Department of the Interior, Washington. For information concerning the friendship shown him by the "Glover Family," as well as a print of the portrait drawn by L'Enfant of Charles Glover, the writer is grateful to his great-grandson Col. Charles C. Glover, Jr., of the Riggs National Bank. L'Enfant died June 14, 1825, on the estate of William Dudley Digges, at "Green Hill" in Prince Georges County, Maryland. A picture of an etching of his resting place under the cedars at Green Hill, the writer was pleased to receive from the artist, Minnie L. Briggs Raul. For details concerning L'Enfant's last days at the home of the Digges's the writer is grateful to Miss Elizabeth Kite, who points out that while L'Enfant got into trouble with the Carroll family when he contended for the L'Enfant Plan of 1791, it was the Carroll-Digges family that befriended him when in need both at Warburton (the old name of Fort Washington) and at Green Hill. Thanks is due to Mr. John J. Cunningham, Educational Director of the National Sculpture Society, for information concerning the L'Enfant Chair, and to Hon. F. Lammot Belin, of Georgetown, for a picture of it.

Chapter X, entitled, "The Nation Honors L'Enfant," relates the movement that resulted in giving national recognition to the distinguished services rendered by Pierre Charles L'Enfant, and his reinterment in the Arlington National Cemetery with full military honors. For the photograph of the original competition drawing of his tomb, as well as a description of it, the writer is profoundly grateful to its architect, Mr. Welles Bosworth, of Vaucresson, France.

Chapter XI is a brief summary of "The Development of the L'Enfant Plan." For detailed information on that subject the writer is indebted to the Report of the McMillan Park Commission of 1901, edited by Dr. Charles Moore, who subsequently became a member of the National Commission of Fine Arts, in 1910, and served as its chairman for a period of 22 years, from 1915 to 1937. During a period of more than 20 years the writer served under Dr. Moore and through him became inspired as to the services rendered by L'Enfant to the City of Washington. In addition, information received by the writer from members of the National Commission of Fine Arts generally, in support of the L'Enfant Plan and in making our National Capital a beautiful city, worthy of the Nation, has been a constant source of inspiration in this work.

Chapter XII relates the influence of the L'Enfant Plan on other cities. They include Detroit, Buffalo, Indianapolis, Medellin, Colombia, S. A., and Canberra, Australia; Ottawa, Canada, is the most recent to be added to the list. While not adopting the L'Enfant Plan in its entirety, numerous cities of the United States have nevertheless been inspired by the achievements of the City of Washington, particularly its wide and shaded streets, its parks and reservations, its monuments that recall the history of the Nation, and its public buildings with proper landscape setting. More than twenty of our state capitols followed the type of our national capitol building.

For most of the aerial photographs the author is very grateful to Capt. A. E. Nesbitt, Director of the Fairchild Aerial Surveys, Incorporated, and to others as indicated.

In the Appendix will be found in particular the Memorials of L'Enfant, written from and after 1800, and taken from the *Records of the Columbia Historical Society.* A careful reading of them will show that they contain much descriptive material concerning his Plan for the City of Washington, which during these past 150 years has grown to what is destined to become the most beautiful capital city of any Nation in the world. The Appendix also contains copies of numerous letters written by L'Enfant that gave information concerning his life.

In closing, the writer wishes to thank authors and publishers for permission given to quote from books as cited and to add the names of several individuals not heretofore mentioned who rendered assistance for which he is grateful. Among these are Madame S. Briet, Conservateur Adjoint, Bibliothèque Nationale, Paris, and her assistant, Madame Calve; Mrs. Henry W. Howell, Jr., Librarian, of the Frick Art Reference Library, and to Mr. Harry B. Tucker of the Vestry of St. Paul's Chapel, New York; to Prof. F. V. Murphy, F. A. I. A. Dean, College of Architecture, Catholic University of America, to Mr. Meredith B. Colket, of the National Archives, and Curator of the Columbia Historical Society and to Mr. Herbert Post and his staff of the *National Republic* for the care and interest manifested in the publication of this volume.

H. PAUL CAEMMERER.

Washington, D. C.
October, 1948.

Chapter I

PIERRE CHARLES L'ENFANT was born in Paris
on August 2, 1754, the son of Pierre L'Enfant, who
was Painter in Ordinary to the King in his manufacture
of the Gobelin tapestries. It is of record that he was
baptized the next day in the Church Royale of the Parish
of Saint Hippolytus, one of the oldest Catholic churches
in Paris, destroyed during the French Revolution. Its
exact location would be No. 8 rue Saint Hippolyte, near
the Gobelins. The painter, whose wife's name was
Marie Charlotte Leullier, had for his specialty landscapes
and battle scenes; that is, he was a "battle-front painter,"
and his large paintings are devoted to that subject.

It appears that L'Enfant descended from a family of
artists. Jean L'Enfant, pastelliste et graveur, born at
Abbeville in 1615 and who died in Paris in 1674. He thus
lived during the reign of Louis XIV, and achieved distinction as a painter, whose portraits were executed in an
"harmonious and agreeable" style.

Pierre L'Enfant, the father of Pierre Charles, was born
at Anet, in 1704, on a farm which he bequeathed to his
children. Anet is a picturesque town which one passes
on the way from Paris to Chartres. In his youth Pierre
was a pupil of Parrocel. As a young man he served on

1

Siege of Tournai May 14, 1745, by Cozette based on painting by Pierre Charles L'Enfant in the Palace at Versailles

the battlefield by painting scenes that he witnessed. In 1744 the Count d'Argenson, War Minister, attached two painters of battles to the Bureau of Geography, at his Ministry, Lapeignat and Marin, with a salary of 2400 livres per annum each. In 1746 Lapeignat was replaced by L'Enfant, who followed the campaigns of 1746–1747 in Flanders, drawing on the spot the towns besieged — Tournay and Fribourg, the taking of Menin, and the battlefield of Fontenoy, Lawfeld, and Rocoux. He was kept from 1748 to 1758 by Count d'Argenson, who made him draw paintings of sieges first destined for his residence at Neuilly and later on placed in the chateau des Ormes. In 1758 the Marshal de Belle Isle, then War Minister, dismissed these artists, but Berthier, who supervised them, suggested to have them retained to decorate the "Hotel de la Guerre" (War Ministry) at Versailles, which was agreed upon. He employed them eight years. It is stated in an article by Charles Hirschauer on Jean Baptiste Berthier (Revue d'l'Histoire de Versailles et de Seine et Oise, Versailles 1930, pp. 137–51):

> "On avait cru bon de donner un certain apparat á la salle d'audiences (de l'Hotel de la Guerre) oú le public etait admis. C'est dans cette piéce qu'on pourait admirer les tableaux peints par Cozette sur des compositions de L'enfant aujourd'hui exposées dans la galerie basse du Palais, ou dans notre musée Houdon. C'etaient la Bataille de Lawfeld, le Siege de Fribourg, le Bataille de Rocoux, les Sieges de Menin, de Ypres et d'Anvers, la Surprise de Gand, le Couitat de Melle, le Siege de Tournai, et la Bataille de Fontenoi." [1]

There are also two paintings by Pierre L'Enfant at the Museum at Tours, watercolors, a panoramic view of the Chateau d'Amboise, one of the largest and most imposing, in the chateau country of the Loire, the other a perspective of Chanteloup. It so happened that on the day the writer visited Tours to see these paintings, the Con-

---

[1] It had been thought proper to give a somewhat stately appearance to the audience-chamber (of the War Ministry), where the public was admitted. The pictures painted by Cozette from some of the L'Enfant compositions, now on display in the Palace's lower gallery or in our Houdon museum, could be admired in this room. They were the Battle of Lawfeld, the Siege of Fribourg, the Battle of Rocoux, the Siege of Menin, Ypres and Antwerp, the Surprise of Ghent, the Battle of Melle, the Siege of Tournai, and the Battle of Fontenoy.

Manufacture Nationale des Gobelins, La Cour Colbert

Photograph by the Author

The Gobelin Manufacture (main building), Paris

servateur du Musée, M. B. Lossky, had received a letter inquiring whether there was any relationship between Pierre L'Enfant, the painter, and the author of the Plan of Washington. Of course Monsieur Lossky was informed that the relationship was that of father and son, and received information concerning Pierre Charles and his career in America that was much appreciated.

In the year 1745 Pierre became an Academician. There is on record the Action of the Royal Academy of Painting and Sculpture, 1648–1793, published by Anatole de Montaiglon, Book VI, page 17, as follows, on the subject:

> "Today, Saturday, October 30, 1745, Reception to M. L'Enfant, painter of talent, native of Anet near Dreux, who has presented to the Academy the painting which has been ordered for his reception, of which the subject represented a Country Market. The votes were taken as usual. The Company received the said Sir L'Enfant Academician to sit in the assembly, enjoy privileges, honors and prerogatives permitted by the rules of the Academy, which he promised to maintain."

The Archives de la Seine, Paris, shows that Pierre L'Enfant married Marie Charlotte Lullier on November 12, 1748.

Pierre-Charles was not an only child — he had a sister and a brother. In August, 1754, Pierre asked for more rooms at the Gobelins so as to be able to take his children along with him. This was granted, according to records that designate him as "Director of the Manufacture of the Gobelins, Paris." Thereupon, L'Enfant applied to Marigny for alterations. This he agreed to in a letter to d'Isle dated February 23, 1755:—

> I have received, Sir, with your letter of April 4 (estimating the expense at 400 livres) the memoir of Sir L'Enfant which you have returned to me. I consent that he make the changes in his lodging mentioned in his memoir

and of which you gave account of the condition; nevertheless that they will be done at his expense and by the workmen of the builders.

"On November 27, 1758, Pierre Joseph Lenfant, aged 6 years, died, son of Pierre Lenfant, painter du Roi, and Marie – Charlotte Lullier, witness Charles Cozette, painter du Roi aux Gobelins (Nouvelle Archives de l'Art francais, 1897, p. 48)." Cozette was a distinguished painter of the period, and friend of the L'Enfant family.

By decision of February 1st, 1769, Pierre L'Enfant was granted a salary of 2400 francs on the "Extraordinary of War" and on October 1st, 1776, Count de Saint Germain gave him an equal sum of 2400 for his retreat, half transferable to his eventual widow. He was not allowed to work for the public. The eight years at Versailles he

Photograph by the Author

Rue St. Hippolytus, Paris

spent working on two paintings for the "Salon of the Ministry of War," as stated in his Memoir to Count de Saint Germain, dated April, 1776, in which he mentions what is still due him for his works; thus would he establish his son and daughter whom he did not wish to leave without any kind of fortune.

According to information from the Frick Art Reference Library, New York City, there is a portrait of Pierre L'Enfant in the National Museum at Stockholm, of which a picture appears in this volume, but no original portrait of his son Pierre Charles has been discovered.

Pierre Charles's mother, Marie Charlotte Lullier (thus spelled by her) was the daughter of François Mathieu Lullier, officer of the Queen and Commissioner of the Marine, and of Charlotte Boquet. She was born on July 3, 1729, and baptized on the 5th in the church Saint Louis at Versailles, by Laroche, priest of the Congregation; godfather Jacques François Guerin, officer of the King and of the Queen, living at Paris in the Parish Saint Louis; godmother, Madam Marie Lebrun, daughter of M. Lebrun, officer of the King, of the parish Notre Dame of Versailles. On September 28, 1738, the mother of Pierre Charles was granted an annual gratuity of 300 livres on the funds of the Marine, on account of her father's services.

Thus it is evident that the ancestors of Pierre Charles L'Enfant were people of culture, from whom he inherited those fine qualities which manifested talent and good taste, and found him (to quote the late Dr. Charles Moore) "always a gentleman." But now we come to some facts that require us somewhat to reconstruct for ourselves the hitherto accepted story of the early life of

Pierre L'Enfant
1704-1787

By Charles Parocel, Original in the National Museum Collection,
Stockholm

Pierre Charles. For, because of the meagre information available concerning his early life, during the past 40 or 50 years, some misleading conclusions have become more or less fixed concerning him. These must now be reconstructed in the light of thorough research and investigation which the writer has conducted during the past eight years. Thus, for example, because it has been stated that L'Enfant "possessed a commission of lieutenant in the French colonial troops," it was thought he had been in the military service of France, and therefore stationed at various posts where as an army officer he was occupied in constructing fortifications (one of his specialties in America); also because in 1789 he was architect of Federal Hall in New York City, it has been assumed that L'Enfant acquired his knowledge of architecture while a student of engineering, of which architecture was considered a branch in those days.

But it can now be stated with certainty that L'Enfant never was an officer in the French Army prior to his coming to America, and that a brevet was given him in 1777 to protect him in case he should be taken prisoner by the British on his way to America.

Also these researches have made this highly interesting discovery (in what remains of the archives of the Académie Royale de Peinture et de Sculpture after the Revolution of 1789 — part of which are in the Archives Nationales and part in the library of the Ecole des Beaux Arts) that Pierre Charles L'Enfant had been from September 1771 on, a student of the Academie Royale de Peinture et de Sculpture *under his father*. This capital piece of information as regards his earlier years has escaped all previous historians, including Jusserand.

*Vue du Chateau de Chanteloup et de la Ville d'Amboise,
Musée de Tours*

*Vue de la Ville et de Chateau d'Amboise Pierre L'Enfant, 1762
Musée de Tours*

It is therefore evident that as a student of the Royal Academy of Painting and Sculpture, L'Enfant became a student of THE FINE ARTS in a comprehensive sense. While learning to draw battle scenes from his father, he also learned from him the art of drawing fortifications. It is of record in the Bibliothèque de l'Ecole des Beaux Arts (Ms. 543, Memoire, plan des etudes qui se font a L'Académie Royale de Peinture et de Sculpture" XVIII Century, by Nulst) that:

"They admitted pupils from all nations; painters, sculptors, engravers. Every month there was a competition for the prize of drawing from the model. Every three months there was an exhibition of drawings and sculpture in view of prizes: 3 silver medals distributed every year by the Directeur General des Bátiments. The first Saturday of April there was a competition for the grand prix de peinture et de sculpture; a subject from the Old Testament to be drawn on the very day.

"The best drawers executed on the next day a new subject from the Old Testament. Then they had three months to execute their paintings or bas-reliefs in closed lodges. After being examined by the officers, the best were exhibited to the public for 8 days in one of the rooms of the Academy. Then the Officers and Academicians passed their judgment. The four prizes (gold medals) were handed by the Directeur General des Batiments du Roi before all the school. The first prizes of painting and sculpture went to Rome after spending three years in the new school founded in the Louvre by the King. Then they spent three years at the Académie de France at Rome. On their return they showed their works to become 'agrées' and then academicians."

Pierre Charles does not appear among the "agrées." Up to the age of 25 the students paid every week for the models, but the sons of Academicians had not to pay that fee. Among the subjects dealt with were perspective and anatomy.

For practical information and instruction in landscape architecture, Pierre Charles L'Enfant had but to see the work of the greatest French Landscape Architect, André LeNôtre. LeNôtre's work at Versailles expressed the

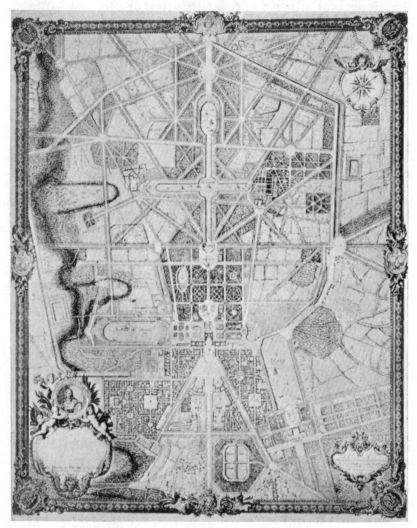

The Plan of City and Park of Versailles

power of France and the magnificence of the reign of Louis XIV in the great formal gardens that surrounded his palace, embellished with terraces, fountains and water basins. We are told that flat lands extended for miles and were incorporated in the palace grounds. The effect of great extent, with recognizable unity and variety of open and wooded areas, was produced and here employed for the first time on so great a scale as to be a memorial to LeNôtre today, even after the lapse of centuries. This formal design was in the "grand manner" that extended its influences all over Europe, including London, Rome and St. Petersburg. Thus we can understand the source of his visions when L'Enfant was blamed, as he often was, for seeing and trying to do things "en grand" or "in the large." LeNôtre brought his genius to bear and marked the beginnings in the development of architecture with landscape architecture. He had great influence on city planning for a long period. A saying of his time was that he who was able to design a park could easily draw a plan for a city. In Paris LeNôtre designed the Gardens of the Tuilleries, covering 56 acres, under Louis XIV. Though added to and altered afterwards, they retain the main outlines of the original plan even now. Placing terminal motives at the end of long vistas, and the location of public buildings in relation to their landscape settings, were typical features that gave beauty to LeNôtre's designs, and we see them demonstrated in L'Enfant's Plan for the City of Washington.

LeNôtre's gardens are still the admiration of the world. Versailles, Fontainebleau, Vaux-le-Vicomt, St. Cloud, Chantilly, the Terrace of St. Germain, have never

*Versailles by Patel, 1668
from Musée de Versailles*

The Mall and Fountains of Versailles, by Le Nôtre

The Louvre, and the Gardens of the Tuilleries, Paris

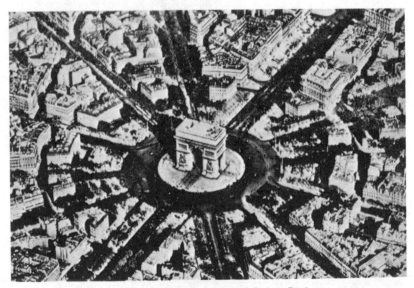

L'Arc de Triomphe et Rond Point, Paris

been surpassed in design or elegance and in sumptuousness. They were planned as landscape settings for palace or chateau and were enjoyed by those who attended great fetes or social gatherings. Charles II employed LeNôtre to design the royal parks in England. Thus he made the design for St. James Park about 1670. He was in the prime of life and undoubtedly influenced Sir Christopher Wren in his design of London made subsequent to the great fire of 1666. For as we see in that plan, LeNôtre planted avenues forming rays, diverging from a central point and extending far out into open country, a fashion followed by the nobility sometimes beyond the limits of their purses.

Pope Innocent XI was enchanted with the plans of Versailles, as well as with the personality of their creator. But since the topography of hilly Italy was so essentially different from the plains of France, LeNôtre neither gave nor received inspiration from his Italian visits. LeNôtre's influence spread to still other countries. It is evident in a marked degree at the palace of Schoenbrun, near Vienna.

The gardens directly planned by LeNôtre, or based on the principles laid down by him, are innumerable. But to Americans LeNôtre had even a greater claim than comes from his gardens. Colbert, LeNôtre, Blondell and the Academy of Architects of Louis XIV planned the great avenues of Paris which in the fullness of time were to make that city the orderly, well articulated, magnificent city which it became under Baron Haussmann during the days of Napoleon III. It is difficult for us to realize that when about 1672 Paris was planned as a unit —-as a work of art — the great axis LeNôtre drew from

The Champs Elysées, Paris

Terrace at St. Germain, near Paris, by Le Nôtre

*The Verniquet Map of Paris, 1796, showing walls and plan of development
to that time. (1792 was declared the year I.)*

the Garden of the Tuilleries even to Neuilly began in a congested medieval walled city. The wretched living conditions of Paris, of that day and later, Victor Hugo describes vividly in his *Notre Dame de Paris*. From the centuries-old civic center of Paris the great central axis extended through open fields with scarcely a dozen buildings in its entire course to the *rond point* of the Place de l'Etoile, located in an apple orchard. The Place de la Concorde was planned by Gabriel in 1763 (when L'Enfant was nine years of age). And it was during the decade before L'Enfant drew his Plan of the City of Washington that Verniquet, with the help of sixty engineers, measured medieval Paris by torchlight and laid down definitely the dominant lines drawn by the planner of Louis XIV. It was published in 1796 and was said to be the finest city plan prepared before the nineteenth century; it showed a series of great avenues to encircle the city following the outer ring walls. For this volume the writer secured a print of it from the Bibliothèque Nationale. Following the great Revolution of 1789, a committee of artists undertook to develop a plan for the reconstruction of Paris. This work received even more attention in the reign of Napoleon Bonaparte, who planned many new streets and laid out the Rue de la Paix and part of the Rue de Rivoli, that is the western portion.

City planning had developed into an art, and its influence on other countries has been well expressed by Luc Benoist in his *Versailles,* 1947, p. 72, as follows:

"Mais, dans ces examples, il ne s'agit aprás tout que des residences, princieres et des jardins oú l'on peut ne voir que l'imitation passagére d'une mode. Il est beaucoup plus important de montrer une ville entire, comme Carlsruhe, construite sur le modéle de Versailles.

"Mieux encore, il est necessaire de mettre en pleine lumière que ce

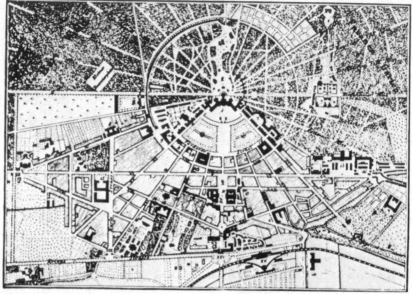

Courtesy Bibliothèque Nationale
Map of Carlsruhe

Photograph by the Author
*Rue de la Reine, Versailles, 1948. The Musée Houdon is the
Building at the Left*

Compiegne, Avenue de Beaumont, by Le Nôtre

meme esprit commande la naissance de deux villes nouvelles, capitales de deux puissantes nations, la Russie et l'Amerique.

"Car c'est un Français LeBlond qui donne á Pierre-le-Grand le plan de Pétersburg, comme ce fut un autre Français le major L'Enfant qui donna celui de Washington, deux capitales politiques concues d'un seul coup comme Versailles et dont le dessin réunit comme celui de cette ville, les avantages du plan rayounant et ceux du plan rectangular, les conditions de la stabilité et celles d'un developpement indefini." [2]

From all this we may feel convinced that L'Enfant did no mere copying of Old World city plans when he was sent by President Washington in March 1791 to this locality, the future District of Columbia, first to make a preliminary sketch and then a Plan for our National Capital. His work represents what we may well term "a stroke of genius" for, as subsequent pages will show, the leading features of his Plan were presented to President Washington in June 1791, and by December 13th of that year the completed Plan was exhibited in the Halls of Congress. But first, L'Enfant was to enlist and then render valiant service in our War of Independence, the story of which is told in the following two chapters.

---

[2] But, after all, these examples deal only with princely residences, and gardens in which one sees only the temporary imitation of a fashion. It is much more important to show a complete city, like Carlsruhe, built on the pattern of Versailles.

Moreover, it is necessary to clarify the fact that this same spirit presides at the birth of two cities, capitals of two powerful nations, Russia and the United States.

For a Frenchman, Le Blond, conceived the plan of Petersburg for Peter the Great, as did another Frenchman, Major L'Enfant, that of Washington, two political capitals conceived at one stroke—like Versailles—and whose design unites, as in this city [of Paris] the advantages of the diagonal avenues and the rectangular plans, creating conditions of stability and possibilities of unlimited growth.

Chapter II

PIERRE CHARLES L'ENFANT, at twenty-two, a
Lieutenant of Infantry in the French Colonial
troops, was one of the first officers to offer his services to
the American cause for Independence. This took place
early in August, 1776, though it was September 11th of
that year when the agreement was signed between Phil-
ippe-Charles-John Baptist Tronson DuCoudray, Adju-
tant of Artillery, with some thirty or more commissioned
and non-commissioned officers of engineers, artillerymen,
miners, trained laborers, and Silas Deane, at that date
commercial and political agent of the Committee of
Secret Correspondence (a commission granted by Congress on November 29, 1775). Silas Deane had arrived
in Paris July 6, 1776.

When news of the uprising against British aggressions
in the Colonies reached France the attention of people
everywhere was attracted, wondering what the outcome
would be. The recent loss of Canada through the fall of
Quebec, in the notable victory of Wolfe over Montcalm,
whetted French interest. The French army was shat-
tered in that War, known in America as the French and
Indian War, in which George Washington received his

25

early training. The Navy had been destroyed when in
1754 England attacked the French fleet. Especially
young men of the nobility were cut off from hope of winning glory — so dear to the heart of every Frenchman —
among embattled hosts, for their young King Louis XVI,
who came to the throne in May, 1774, not yet twenty
years old; he, however, was peacefully minded, and
showed no signs of interest except in internal reforms,
which he pursued with ardor.

In the meantime his Minister of Foreign Affairs, the
Comte de Vergennes, was biding his time. He agreed
with the King that internal reforms were badly needed to
improve the lot of the people of France, but he never
ceased to point out that unless his Country was respected
among sister nations real prosperity for France could
never be attained. The turning point came when on
April 22, 1776, Louis XVI gently led by Vergennes, encouraged by two Ministers of War and Navy, but above
all influenced by the sage counsels of his uncle, Charles
III of Spain, whom he revered, signed his "apprové" to
a BILL ordering the French Navy rebuilt, and the most
up-to-date equipment for the Army.

A thrill as of new life went throbbing through the entire Nation of France, broadening the outlook and bringing fresh hope and encouragement to every class among
the French. First of all the wheels of industry were set
going. As soon as orders could be issued, horsemen went
galloping out in all directions to every factory, port, ar-
senal and fortress over the land. Foreign Embassies began to wake up, but the French Minister was prepared
for them. Calm, self-possessed, the Comte de Vergennes
made it clear that every nation had a right, even much

more, a duty to herself and her neighbors, to be prepared at least for self-defense, which all the world knew was not the case at present with his royal Master, whose acts at the time were altogether governed by his steadfast desire for lasting peace at home as well as among peoples.

In the meantime much had happened on the other side of the Atlantic, following an Act by the British King George III, who on August 23, 1775, had mounted the Throne and issued a PROCLAMATION calling the meeting of the Continental Congress in Philadelphia a *Rebellion* and the leaders *Traitors*. France had the news sent immediately by its Ambassador at the British Court, but it took more than two months for the same news to reach America. A *Proclamation Broadside* of George III reached Boston and came into the possession of General Washington, who sent it in a packet dated November 2 to the President of Congress. He received it the 8th. On November 9th a *Resolution of Secrecy* was signed by every member, while Congress stopped all other proceedings, to decide what was to be done. On November 29th, Benjamin Franklin, Benjamin Harrison, John Dickinson, John Jay, and a fifth who could not serve and who was replaced by Robert Morris, were named on the Committee of Secret Correspondence (it was the same Committee that sent Silas Deane to France a few months later).

When the Comte de Vergennes learned of the act of George III, being a man endowed with clarity of vision, he foresaw the inevitable reaction of the leaders in Congress; that is, instead of the Proclamation intimidating them, it would force them to break with England or else, supinely, to accept whatever the King's whim meted out to them — something unthinkable. In order to know positively what attitude the leaders in Congress would take an *unofficial observer,* Archand de Bonvoulier, whose brother was a friend of the French Ambassador at the British Court, set out, with *oral instructions* only, on September 9th, on a vessel bound for Philadelphia, arriving early in December. Through a Frenchman, M. Daimons, City Librarian, Bonvoulier was introduced to Benjamin Franklin, and through the latter brought to a meeting of the Secret Committee. "Sound heads" he called them, in his *Report* which was sent through a merchant at Antwerp to the Ambassador at London, so that it reached the Comte de Vergennes March 3, 1776. From the moment of receiving the Report of Bonvoulier, the Minister's confidence in the integrity of the American Cause was fixed. Nine days later, March 12th, with the consent of the King, Vergennes sent a copy of a document he composed, called CONSIDERATIONS, to the Ministers of War, Navy and Finance, while a similar copy was sent to the King of Spain. In this document Vergennes asked, after a lengthy exposition of attendant facts —

" . . . whether it would be advisable to give secret aid to the *insurgents* in munitions and in money since the presupposed utility would justify the small sacrifice, and no reason of dignity or equity deters us."

In reply to this question the Ministers of War and Navy answered immediately. Turgot, the Philosopher, took time to compose his negative answer. He drew up a document taking the opposite view, basing his objections partly on the low state of the finances of France, which impressed the King. However, the response of Spain was altogether encouraging so far as the new idea went. Spain wished only that her cooperation might remain un-

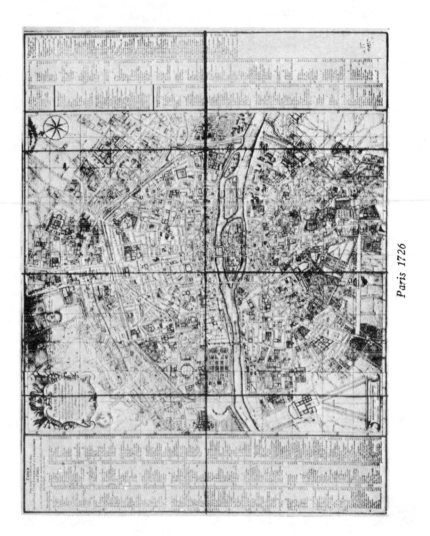

Paris 1726

*Statue de Pierre Augustin Caron de Beaumarchais, 1732-1799.
Rue St. Antoine, Paris*

known, as Charles III offered to *double* any sum France might think wise to devote to such a project.

From the beginning of the resistance manifested in the Colonies toward British interference in what was considered internal affairs, the most interested observer was one Caron de Beaumarchais, a brilliantly gifted Frenchman residing temporarily in London — 1774-1776, son of a watchmaker, whose real name was Pierre August Caron, the story of whose elevation and sudden fall from the heights of affluence and social prestige, through the jealous envy of associates whom he surpassed, reads like a thrilling romance.

Beaumarchais made important connections while in England, and his presence there became very valuable to the French Foreign Minister. Beaumarchais foresaw the gravity of the conflict arising between England and her colonies in America and the advantages that might result from it for France. He felt it important not to neglect the opportunities, and to this end hurled a succession of warnings at the Foreign Minister Vergennes, saying —

" . . . You cannot maintain peace unless at any price you prevent its being made between England and America . . . and the only way to prevent it is to aid the Americans with supplies that will balance their forces with those of England. . . . "

After many hesitations Vergennes became convinced. With the understanding that Beaumarchais would assume all "risks and perils of the undertaking," there was established *The House of Roderigue Hortales et Cie.*, in the Hotel de Hollande, rue Vielle du Temple, under color of commerce, but sending to the Colonists in America arms and munitions. Under title of a subsidy he obtain-

Hotel de Hollande

ed a million livres from Vergennes, June 10, 1776, and another from Spain, August 11th.

From the beginning obstacles of every kind had to be overcome, such as protests from the British Ambassador, rivalries among American agents, the intervention of administrative departments. Then there were also material dangers besetting the enterprise, such as the menace of English sloops of War, weak protection of the French fleet in guarding the rights of private ventures and the difficulties encountered in hiring vessels, to recruit the necessary crews, securing reliable officers, and continually guarding the necessary secrecy to make the enterprise succeed.

But Beaumarchais was not to be discouraged by any number of difficulties. M. Marsan, in his little volume *Beaumarchais et les Affaires d'Amérique,* states,

"One finds Beaumarchais showing himself in all natural impulses so characteristic of him — his taste for dramatic intrigue, his activity, his adaptability, his enthusiasm, his brilliancy and wit . . .

"During the last months of 1776, using all the caution and discretion possible, he had collected in the different ports convoys . . . cannon . . . , guns . . . tons of powder . . . Tents . . . clothing and some fifty or more officers to go out with these things, all under the direction of Du-Coudray, a high officer in the French Artillery. . . . " (Fully 25,000 guns and as many tents, also ammunition.)

Just as Beaumarchais, so also DuCoudray is of primary importance in a study of the life of L'Enfant; and there is abundant source material concerning him in the Manuscript Division of the Library of Congress, as well as in the superb collection of European sources found in the famous *Benjamin Franklin Stevens Facsimiles,* and in the huge volumes of Henri Doniol, a monumental work entitled *La Participation de la France à L'Etablissement des Etats-Unis,* where DuCoudray is shown in all his complexity of situation and character.

Charles Philippe John Baptist Tronson DuCoudray, well born, an artilleryman of genius, Precepter of the Duke d'Artois, brother of Louis XVI, had powerful backers. In 1776, active in the distribution of the new arms, replacing those of earlier date, he became indispensible to Beaumarchais and Silas Deane in collecting the old arms for the American service, which the Minister of War, the Comte de St. Germain, was glad to sell at bargain prices. They were to be sent, as was supposed, to the French West Indies for the Colonial Troops of His Majesty, but really to what the French Government called "the Insurgents." Endless diffiiculties had to be overcome in securing ships for the service, which had to be hired at exorbitant prices, as America had none she could send herself to obtain the supplies. Three of these ships, *the Romaine, the Andromade,* and the largest, *the Amphitrite,* were ready in the harbor at Havre by December, 1776, to set out. The officers going to America were crowded on the last named vessel, and were given not only passage money but also sums sufficient to enable them to live and procure necessary equipment after reaching America, all which funds, with their commissions signed by Silas Deane, were in the custody of DuCoudray, who was in command and had obtained powers superior to the Captain of the vessel. This last concession had been made so as to placate this high officer, grown sullen and proud since his *contract* which made him a Major General in the American Army.

Beaumarchais was at Havre going about under the name of *Durand,* but overwhelmingly busy seeing that everything was in order, everybody happy, hoping all the time they could set out before the British spies (some of them Americans, even privateer captains in the American pay as well as subsidized by the British), who had begun to swarm in all the ports, could find out what was going on. The *Amphitrite* had hardly left the "roadstead" when orders from the Minister of the Navy (at the insistence of the British Ambassador, Lord Stormont, who had learned from the spies about the stores being sent out), forced the *Romaine* and the *Andromade* to unload their entire cargoes; and such officers as had not been able to get on the *Amphitrite* were turned adrift.

At this critical juncture for France, confusion worse confounded was spread abroad, for every French Minister was assailed by the British Ambassador as implicated in the shipment of arms that everyone suspected were being sent to the Americans, though bound for the French West Indies. As a matter of fact, none was in any way responsible, except M. de Vergennes, who, however, from the beginning had given the positive warning to Beaumarchais that if noise went out, the Government would always act against him as an enemy and with the utmost severity, and that he had nothing to depend upon but his own ingenuity; but certain vague hopes of aid, financial, or the equivalent, were accorded to him in case he should be faced with downright bankruptcy.

To make matters worse at this crucial moment for France and America, news reached Paris (and Havre, evening before the sailing of the *Amphitrite*) that the famous old American philosopher, Dr. Benjamin Franklin, had landed at Brest on the 4th of December, 1776. He came in an American vessel, the *Reprisal*, that had captured a British privateer and dragged it along with them to Brest. Luckily for Beaumarchais and his great business of getting secret aid to the Insurgents, this news sent the whole world of spies and emissaries somersaulting in the air, not knowing which way to turn their penetrating powers of vision, to discover what else might now be set going! The only two people who seemed to have remained calm were M. de Vergennes and Beaumarchais. The latter, ordered by the Minister of War to unload his vessels, immediately complied, which satisfied the Minister, who, busy elsewhere, did not notice that the resourceful Secret Agent lost no time in having his two vessels painted an entirely different color and each renamed: the first became THE SEINE, and the second THE AMELIE, both of which were quietly reloaded and sailed away unnoticed to the French West Indies. One of them, *The Seine,* was captured by the British, the only one of Beaumarchais' ships that was lost out of his entire fleet. For the Secret Agent to be calm was manful, but what about the cost of all this rehandling, as well as outright loss? No one paid any heed, and all Beaumarchais could do was to bide his time, struggling ahead against all reverses, past, present and to come. It was estimated that in twelve months Beaumarchais dispatched to America 8 shiploads of warlike stores valued at 6 million francs.[3]

Scarcely was his back turned on Havre than to his dismay Beaumarchais found DuCoudray, making use of his superior command over the Captain, compelled the latter to turn on his course and enter the port of Lorient where he left the vessel secretly, and rushed back to Paris where

---

[3] Parton, **Life of Franklin,** p. 1196. See also Wharton, **U. S. Revolutionary Correspondence,** Vol. I, p. 62.

he hid himself. DuCoudray's real motive was to procure through his protectors a new commission from Franklin, whose position he knew would out-rank that of Silas Deane. We do not need to follow his movements, except to say, having obtained his wish, he managed to slip away on a vessel bound for the West Indies, when Beaumarchais, furious, forbade his going out on any one of his vessels. Most of his officers followed DuCoudray, since he had their papers and money. There were some that managed to get on other vessels, but subsequently most of them joined their chief, finally arriving in Philadelphia, where they presented themselves to the Congress.

There were three or four of DuCoudray's most experienced officers who remained on the *Amphitrite* and sailed in it to America. For these DuCoudray seems to have provided, though he had someone write Silas Deane begging for recommendations to Congress for those of them who were scattered, assuring their being able to join his train, wherever and whenever it might be again assembled. By one of these officers he sent a letter dated from Paimboeuf, in February, 1777, a vicious letter, denouncing Beaumarchais to the Americans as an adventurer who wanted the credit of the aids sent, while it was he, DuCoudray, who was responsible for everything. The letter was written when, to his fierce anger, he found Beaumarchais was able to prevent him to again take command of the *Amphitrite* (that sailed, according to a document signed by Beaumarchais and found among the Robert Morris Papers) and it seems to point to L'Enfant's having gone out on the *Amphitrite* after all, since the same document shows that the *Mercury* had already sailed on February 5th, before Beaumarchais' letter to

Paris, ce 10 février 1777.

Si vous avez fini les affaires que je vous ai recommandées par ma dernière, mon cher Francy, partez et venez ici. Je voudrais bien être sûr que M. Ducoudrai a emporté ou a laissé à quelqu'un les commissions de ses officiers et leur argent. Car d'être parti en gardant le bien et l'état de tout le monde est une si grande audace ou folie que rien ne pourrait l'excuser. On dit ici que, fuyant la colère des ministres, il est parti furtivement de Paris pour Bordeaux à dessein de s'y embarquer sous un nom inconnu⌐. Il pourrait bien ne pas mieux réussir dans ce plan que dans tous les autres. Quoi qu'il en soit, sachez juste l'état de tout le monde et surtout celui de M. Lenfant, car on me l'a bien recommandé. Il m'a écrit et paraît dans un grand besoin, vous pourriez lui laisser quelques louis s'il n'y a pas moyen de nettoyer [*sic*] ce que sont devenus ses gratifications et appointemens. Sauf à reprendre quand on en aura des nouvelles.

Nous nous occupons de procurer aux gens de bonne volonté leur passage, mais sans bruit. Pour les gens bruyans ou indiscrets, nous ne les regretterons pas s'ils restent en France.

Revenez dès que vous le pourrez.

Quotation from Letter by Beaumarchais, Mentioning L'Enfant

de Francy was written, allowing some *louis d'or* to be given him. The *Amphitrite,* having a cargo value of 979,483 livres, left Lorient on February 15, 1777, and arrived at Portsmouth, New Hampshire, on the 20th or 21st of April. Specifically the cargo consisted of 4,000 muskets, 80 barrels of gun powder, 8,000 pairs of boots, and 3,000 woolen blankets, also several engineer and artillery officers.[4]

The records show that Lieut. L'Enfant was left stranded without papers or money at Nantes, but no explanation of how it came about; though in America he eventually joined the train of DuCoudray, as is proven from his name on the list of officers presented to Congress after the accidental drowning of their Chief in September, 1777. Also L'Enfant had been mentioned by vonSteuben as one of his aids in a memorial presented to Congress, which was in session at York, Pa., at the time.

But it is evident from one of DuCoudray's lengthy Memoirs sent to Congress during the summer of 1777 that he resented L'Enfant leaving his train and appealing directly to Beaumarchais. We learn of this appeal through M. Marsan, who quotes the letter of Beaumarchais written to his Secretary, de Francy, who at the time, early in 1777, was busy at Nantes sending out both the *Mercury* and the *Amphitrite* for his chief, Beaumarchais. The letter states:

"Paris, February 10, 1777.

"If you have finished the business that I recommended to you in my last, my dear Francy, leave and come here. I must be very certain if M. DuCoudray has taken with him or left with someone the officer's commissions and their money. Because to have left and taken with him the rank and the belongings of everybody is an audacity or madness that nothing could excuse . . . Whatever the facts may be try to find out the exact state of everybody and especially of M. Lenfant, who has been highly recommended. He has written me and seems to be in great need. If you cannot find what has become of the moneys given him, you might let him have some *louis* [twenty franc pieces] to be returned if his own funds turn up.

"It's our affair to make possible the passage [to America] of those of

---

[4] Memoires du Comte de Moré (Chevalier de Pontigbaud) Paris, 1898, p. 86.

good-will, but without publicity. As for noisy and indiscrete persons we shall not regret if they are left behind in France. . . . "

It seems probable that someone had directly appealed to Beaumarchasis regarding L'Enfant, since DuCoudray calls him "a creature of B."

The first mention of DuCoudray after his arrival in America is in a letter of General Washington from Headquarters, Camp Middlebrook, May 31, 1777, to the President of Congress announcing his arrival at Camp, though Washington had not had any conversation with him, but ventured to suggest that great caution be exercised in dealing with the General. He says:

"Headquarters, Middleboro, May 31, 1777.

"Sir: Monsieur Coudré is just arrived in Camp, and proposes to set out tomorrow for Philadelphia . . . I find an idea prevails that there is an agreement between Mr. Deane and him, that he shall have the chief command of the artillery . . . Supposing Monsr. Coudré to have made such an arrangement, the case is of great difficulty, and which in my opinion is worthy of the most delicate consideration in Congress . . . From the recommendations we have had of him, I am obliged to esteem him of high character, and of great knowledge in what he professes . . ."

Elsewhere General Washington admits that the Americans are sadly lacking in this branch of military science, which, however, he says, is not to be wondered at. Early in July the greater part of DuCoudray's men were employed on the defenses of the Lower Delaware, serving under him or General Knox, to prevent the British from taking possession. Some of his officers performed amazing feats, though as yet they were only acting as volunteers, while Congress struggled with the problem of deciding how to adjust matters with our own high officers, who would all have resigned had a foreigner been placed over them, regardless of their qualifications. All the while DuCoudray was bombarding Congress with letters and memorials, most of which can be found in the Papers of the Continental Congress (P. C. C. — the greater part in Vol. No. 156).

It is in one of these Memorials, in which DuCoudray explains the special qualifications of certain of his officers that he takes exception to two — des Epinier and L'Enfant; the first, a nephew of Beaumarchais and the second "a creature" of his. "The latter has indeed some talent," he says, "for drawing figures, . . . but nothing of use for an engineer."

To digress briefly, had DuCoudray not been drowned while crossing the Schuylkill to join General Washington at the Battle of the Brandywine, one wonders what actually would have happened, so curious and complex a character he turned out to be after he lost his head on being made a Major General by Silas Deane. Deane knew no such power had been given him when sent over by the Secret Committee. But DuCoudray alone was the one officer who could without noise or difficulty provide the arms, munitions, clothing, etc., from the stores accumulating in the Department of War after the King ordered the Army equipped with new material. To secure his services in this work, Deane and Beaumarchais realized he would have to be given a high rank and be allowed to go to America with the men whom he chose to take with him. Deane had no money, so it was Beaumarchais that financed it all, expecting surely to be repaid by the Americans. At the time, the middle of August, 1776, when he had just been given the million promised by Spain (this was added to Beaumarchais' capital for his Commercial House of Roderigue Hortales and

Co., established after the King had given his *apprové,* as before noted, to replenish the War and Navy Departments of France with new material) things looked bright, and the American's need was so great that both men plunged deeper and deeper into the work of supplying the Americans.

Chapter III

L'Enfant's Services as an Officer in the American
Revolution. With Washington at Valley Forge
and Pulaski at Savannah

*I*T MAY BE SAID at the outset that Lieut. Pierre
Charles L'Enfant won his "spurs" during the American Revolution by his loyalty to the Cause for which he
enlisted. Unlike Lafayette, who represented the nobility
of France, and who had been named Major General
(before he was 20 years of age) by Silas Deane — which
Congress and General Washington accepted in spite of
his youth — L'Enfant served as a volunteer whose future
prospects were uncertain until his services were accepted
by Congress.

The first mention of L'Enfant in the Journals of Congress is found under date of October 4, 1777, five days
after the assembly came together at York, Pennsylvania,
when driven from Philadelphia by Washington's defeat
at Germantown and the British army's threat of immediate occupation of the City. DuCoudray had been
drowned by his horse jumping with him into the Schuylkill when crossing with his men to join General Washington at the Battle of the Brandywine, September 15 or
16. On September 17, 1777, L'Enfant with six others
were accorded $100 pay. On November 7th, twenty-
seven officers, twelve sergeants of artillery, and a work-

Pierre Charles L'Enfant

man, each according to rank, were given certain sums of money under the heads of *Pay, Traveling expenses, Passage and traveling expenses to Paris*. L'Enfant's account reads: "427 pay — $100 traveling expenses and 900 francs for the trip home." — evidently up to this date he was without hope of finding a place in the Continental army, though already two or more of the higher ranking officers had obtained this goal. A week later he with five others received additional sums — he received 600 livres as back pay that should have been given him before leaving France.

Thereupon we hear of L'Enfant at Valley Forge. We know indirectly that during the winter of 1777–1778 Lafayette established for himself headquarters at a farmhouse a short distance outside of the Valley Forge Camp, a mile or more diagonally across the Park from Washington's Headquarters.[1] Here such Frenchmen as were not attached to the Continental Army were always welcome guests, though none of them was likely to stay long at a time, for they were always on the lookout for engagements of one kind or another. We know that L'Enfant had joined himself to the Baron von Steuben, in fact had become one of the Baron's aides as heretofore stated. General von Steuben had come over in Beaumarchais's ship *La Flammande*, that left Marseilles September 25, 1777, reached Portsmouth, New Hampshire, on December first and left Boston on January 14, 1778, to appear before Congress at York, Pa. He brought with him an interpreter, young Peter S. Duponceau, who remained with him, and with whom L'Enfant was afterwards associated (Duponceau also remained in America, married

---

[1] Memoirs of Comte de Moré Pontgibeaud.

into the Livingston family, and became a well-known lawyer in Philadelphia).

Von Steuben had been an officer under Frederick II of Prussia (called Frederick the Great). He was of great service to General Washington at Valley Forge, where he set himself to train the raw recruits so they might become fit for service in the field. He was much liked, even by them, though he was a strict disciplinarian. He and Duponceau lived at another farmhouse near that of Lafayette, so in this way it probably came about that so early in his military career we hear the name of L'Enfant associated with that of Washington. His gift as an artist, his clearness at catching likenesses, made him welcome among his brother officers. He assisted von Steuben, who had become Inspector General of the Army, as disciplinarian. During dreary days at Valley Forge, L'Enfant would draw pencil portraits of his fellow-officers — one we know of General Washington, at the request of Lafayette, who wanted also a painted portrait. Concerning this General Washington wrote Lafayette from Fredericksburg, New York, on September 25, 1778:

"Could I have conceived, that my Picture had been an object of your Wishes, or in the smallest degree worthy of your Attention, I should, while Mr. Peale was in the Camp at Valley Forge, have got him to have taken the best Portrait of me he could, and presented it to you; but I really had not so good an opinion of my own worth, as to suppose that such a compliment would not have been considered as a greater instance of my Vanity, that a mean of your gratification; and therefore when you requested me to set for Monsr. Lanfang [Pierre Charles L'Enfant] I thought it was only to obtain the outlines and a few shades of my features, to have some Prints struck from."[2] [The sketch seems lost as a careful search has failed to discover it.]

Also, according to information that the writer received

---

[2] Writings of Washington, Bicentennial Edition, United States Government Printing Office, Vol. 12, p. 501.

from Mr. Gene Holcomb, of the Office of Chief of Engineers, "Mrs. Green, the vivacious wife of General Nathanael Green, whose hospitable entertaining was considered among the few blessings of the place, quickly came to appreciate the engaging young Frenchman, with courtly manners. She particularly was pleased when he did a fashionable miniature of her in oils."

In the meantime much had happened. Even before the arrival of Beaumarchais' ship *LaFlammande*, had come the victory of Saratoga — that may truly be said to be due to the *Secret Aid* permitted by the French King Louis XVI and his Minister Vergennes, carried out successfully by Beaumarchais and the neglected American Commissioner Silas Deane. News of the victory of Saratoga reached Paris December 4, 1777. Behind Secret Aid, which served as a useful screen, the actual French Government never ceased working toward an Alliance with the Americans, backed, they knew, by the King of Spain, though he never actually joined in the movement.

News of the Alliance had reached Congress sitting at York, Pa., on the afternoon of Saturday, May 2nd, brought by a man on horseback, Simeon Deane, brother of Silas, who bearing copies of the great document, had been sent on a fast sailing frigate *Le Sensible* that had landed him at Casco Bay on April 16th. Then followed one of the most dramatic rides in history; down the coast to Boston, spreading the news as he dashed along. General Heath in command at Boston detailed General McDougal to accompany Deane, so now two riders dash together across Massachusetts, crossing the Hudson at West Point, circling around British held New York City, on to Bethlehem, Pennsylvania. Here the two riders

separate: McDougal heads for the Commander-in-Chief
at Valley Forge; Simeon Deane for Congress protected
behind the Susquehanna at York, Pa. Solemnly, yet
with quickened strokes, the bell of the old Court House
is tolled, calling the adjourned Congress together to hear
the great news! Monday, May 4th, the Treaties are ratified and a messenger sets out on May 5th, to Valley
Forge, where Washington has been given timely notice
to prepare for the great Celebration which the Continental Army is to carry out as soon as the news of the ratification by Congress arrives.

In connection with the Celebration, it is a joy to note
that the first mention of the name of L'Enfant by General Washington occurs at Valley Forge in that remarkable Address, under the caption of "After Orders" for
May 5, 1778, which begins:

> "It having pleased the Almighty ruler of the Universe propitiously to
> defend the Cause of the United American States and finally by raising up
> a powerful Friend among the Princes of the Earth to establish our Lib-
> erty and Independence upon lasting foundations, it becomes us to set
> apart a day for gratefully acknowledging the divine Goodness and cele-
> brating the important Event which we owe to his benign interposition."

First of all everyone is ordered to attend Divine Service where the several Chaplains, after offering thanksgiving, announce the news and the Order of the Day to
the man. Imagine the joy of L'Enfant — almost a year
before he is actually given by Congress the rank and back
pay, to learn that his Commander calls him "Captain
Lanfan," having assigned him to serve the Baron deKalb,
who commanded the second line, when the entire Army
will Huzza, "Long Live the King of France" with all that
is to follow in the way of celebration! What would one
not give to find the letter the young officer wrote home

to his parents after the event? How glad and thankful he must have been that he had decided to serve as a volunteer, now that his King had recognized American Independence (A few letters have survived of our own soldiers as well as of a few Frenchmen). L'Enfant is regarded by some as the founder of the Corps of Engineers and the author of their motto "Essayons,"[3] though the Office of the Chief of Engineers and the Military Academy at West Point do not confirm this.

Von Steuben had been entrusted by General Washington with the training of the troops almost since his arrival at Camp not later than early February. In May that same year he had been named Major General by Congress, while an entirely new Department in the Army was created for him, that of Inspector General of the Troops. This meant a prolonged and intensive study, whose objective was the creation of an American Army with definite regulations adapted to conditions of life in a country as yet unformed, in no way like anything that existed in Europe, a work for which Congress rightly judged von Steuben was to prove himself admirably fitted. As aids in the work he chose four subordinates, whom he found at Camp — Col. Fleury, one of DuCoudray's most expert officers, who had won great fame on the Delaware and later on the Hudson; Walker (undoubtedly an American); L'Enfant, and Duponceau, who had accompanied von Steuben to America on the *Flammande*. The group seem to have worked together late summer, fall and early winter in Philadelphia. In Frederick Kapp's *Life of Baron von Steuben*, Col. Fleury and Captain Walker are spoken of as Assistants (the lat-

---

[3] See **The American Engineers In France**, by William B. Parsons, D. Appleton Co., 1920, p. 363.

ter translated, what was written in bad French by von
Steuben, into English), while "De l'Enfant drew the
plans"[4] and "Duponceaux acted as Secretary to von Steuben. . . . " They left Valley Forge soon after the British
Army under Sir William Howe left the City, fearing precisely that the French King would send over a fleet to
back up his Alliance with the Americans, now known by
everybody.

With this removal to Philadelphia, L'Enfant's experience of the American way of life can truly be said to have
begun, although it was to an almost totally ruined and
devastated city they came. Prices were terribly high,
food scarce, and feelings greatly embittered by the unnecessary destruction of property made by the British
before evacuation. Practically all so-called "Tories,"
among whom were some prominent citizens, left with
the Army of Howe, though some were detained as prisoners. Public execution by order of the State (for one
must not forget that Philadelphia was the State Capital
as well as the seat of the Continental Congress) were going on all summer. News of the French Alliance coming
in May, following the demonstration at Valley Forge,
changed the attitude of many people in that city; but it
came much too late to save the men who had cooperated
with Howe; living so contentedly in Philadelphia in ease
and luxury while the "patriots" starved and froze at Valley Forge. One can imagine the deep and permanent
faith in the future of America that had already begun to
take root in the heart and mind of L'Enfant as he found
himself chosen to aid so distinguished and trained a vet-

---

[4] The "Plans" mentioned were for the **Regulations, Order and Discipline
for the Army of the United States,** prepared by von Steuben, with the aid
of assistants of whom L'Enfant was one (the designer) and published in
1779. (Original copy in the Rare Book Room, Library of Congress.)

REGULATIONS, &c.

CHAPTER I.

Of the Arms and Accoutrements of the Officers, Non-commiffioned Officers, and Soldiers.

THE arms and accoutrements of the officers, non-commiffioned officers, and foldiers, fhould be uniform throughout.

The officers who exercife their fanctions on horfeback, are to be armed with fwords, the platoon officers with fwords and efpontoons, the non-commiffioned officers with fwords, fire-locks, and bayonets, and the foldiers with fire-locks and bayonets.

A 3   CHAPTER

In CONGRESS, 29th March, 1779.

CONGRESS *judging it of the greateft importance to prefcribe fome invariable rules for the order and difcipline of the troops, efpecially for the purpofe of introducing an uniformity in their formation and manoeuvres, and in the fervice of the camp :*

ORDERED, *That the following regulations be obferved by all the troops of the United States, and that all general and other officers caufe the fame to be executed with all poffible exactnefs.*

By Order,

JOHN JAY, PRESIDENT.

Atteft.

CHARLES THOMPSON,

Secretary.

A 2

Courtesy Rare Book Room,

Page from "Army Regulations" by von Steuben, 1779

Page from "Army Regulations" by von Steuben, 1779

eran as von Steuben in what amounted to being the definitive creation of a *Regular Army* that would remain a bulwark of the Republic that was to be created following the united victory of French and American armies, assisted by the French Navy, the first detachment of which

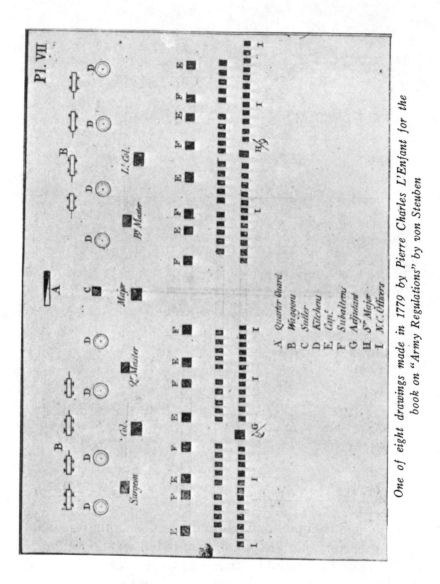

One of eight drawings made in 1779 by Pierre Charles L'Enfant for the book on "Army Regulations" by von Steuben

arrived at the mouth of Delaware Bay early in July, 1778, bringing the first Foreign Minister ever received in the Western Hemisphere, Conrad Alexandre Gerard, a Frenchman given that honor by Louis XVI, since it was he who had successfully carried the negotiations that led to the Treaties of Amity and Commerce, followed by the Alliance, which he signed along with Benjamin Franklin, Silas Deane and Arthur Lee, February 6, 1778.[5]   One can well believe that L'Enfant lost nothing, that Sunday July 12, of all the excitement which attended the arrival in Philadelphia of the Minister with his train, who was met at Chester, on debarking from the frigate *D'Estaing* detached from his Fleet, by a delegation from the Congress, and taken to lodge temporarily in the mansion so recently evacuated by Sir William Howe.   No word, of course, has come down of how L'Enfant conducted himself on the occasion, so it must be left to the imagination to penetrate into his joy.

Congress during this time, and that which followed, was indeed overwhelmed with an infinite diversity of matters requiring attention and did nothing until early in April, 1779, in actually giving L'Enfant the rank promised in February, 1778, to von Steuben for him.   A Report of the Board of War for the 2nd of April, 1779, reads:

> "The Board have been witness of the great diligence and attention of Colonel Fleury, Captains Walker, L'Enfant and Duponceaux, during the Baron Steuben's having been employed in forming the regulations of his Department.   Notwithstanding the Baron's superior knowledge of his subject, there were subordinate assistants necessary, which were with great attention and labor afforded him by these gentlemen. . . . "

[5] The building in which that Treaty was signed, and thus marked by a tablet, is the monumental building at the left looking north from the Place de la Concorde, as shown on page 148.

Along with the above announcement the Board sent the following letter from von Steuben in their behalf:

"March 30, 1779

"Gentlemen:

"The officers who assisted me in composing the regulations for troops having remained near six months for this purpose in this expensive City, I owe these gentlemen as I think a duty to desire that the Board mention these services to Congress who, I doubt not, will make them some recompense.

"If you think Congress would be at loss what sum to offer them I think that the following:

To Coll. Fleury   1000 Dolls.
    Captain Walker   600   "
    Capt. L'Enfant   500   "
    Capt. Duponceau   400   " would be sufficient.

"I would also take the liberty of requesting that M. L'Enfant's Commission may be given him agreeable to a promise given on my first arrival at Yorktown, repeated by the President Laurens the 18 February, 1778. You will see by the annexed extracts that the affair was put off till the arrangement was made; since it has not been mentioned.

"I am with great respect, Gentlemen,
    Your most obedient most humble servant,
      (Signed) Steuben"

The Journals of the Continental Congress, in quoting part of the letter do not name the number of dollars they would give each "assistant," but say that they are of the opinion that "Mons. L'enfant" be appointed a Captain in the Corps of Engineers in the service of the United States, to have rank from the 18th day of February, 1778.

To anticipate, finally on May 2, 1783, Congress appointed L'Enfant a brevet Major in the same service. General Washington expressed his appreciation of L'Enfant's service by letter of March 4, 1782. (*Printed on Page* 64).

It is of interest to note here that, in tracing the career

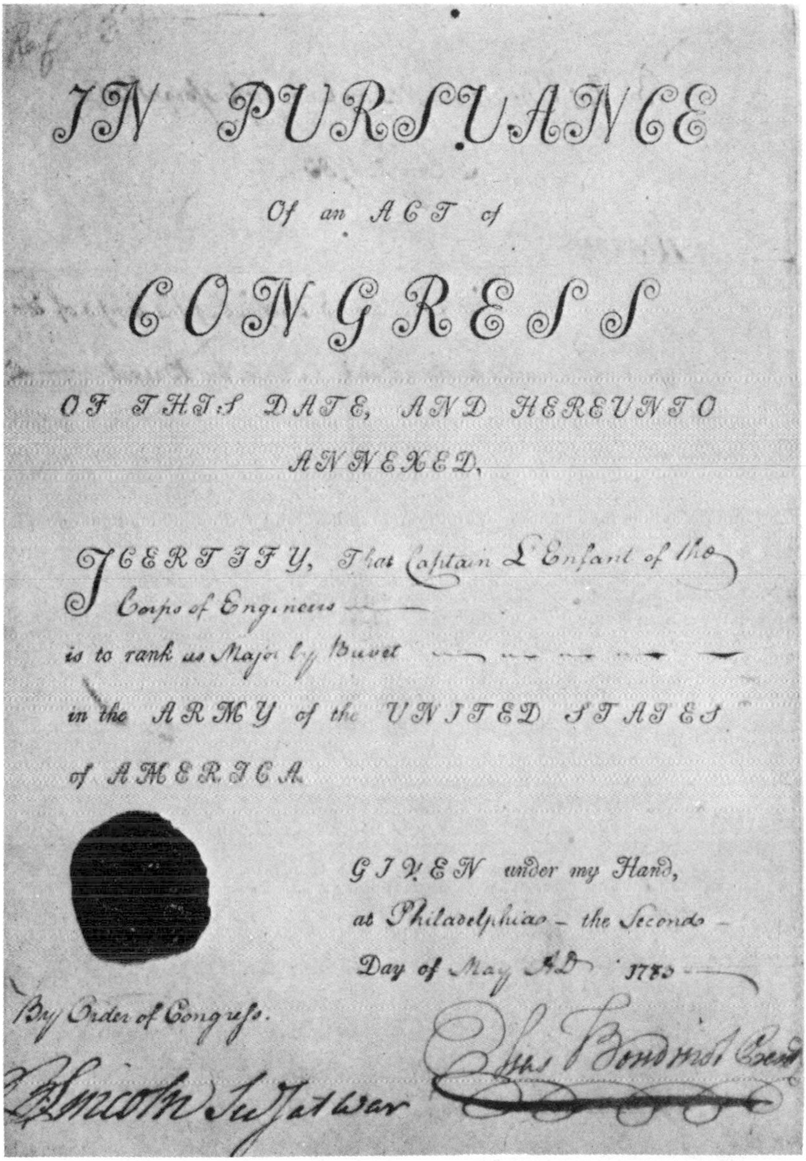

IN PURSUANCE

Of an ACT of

CONGRESS

OF THIS DATE, AND HEREUNTO ANNEXED,

I CERTIFY, That Captain L'Enfant of the Corps of Engineers
is to rank as Major by Brevet
in the ARMY of the UNITED STATES of AMERICA.

GIVEN under my Hand,
at Philadelphia — the Second
Day of May AD 1783

By Order of Congress.

B Lincoln Secy at War

Elias Boudinot Presd

Courtesy Library of Congress

L'Enfant's Commission as Major by Brevet

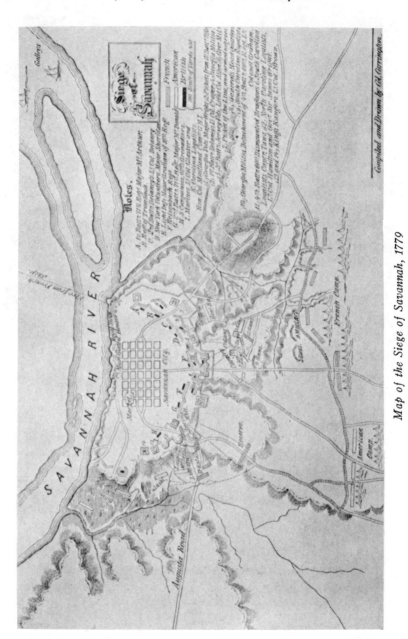

Map of the Siege of Savannah, 1779

of Pierre Charles L'Enfant, there are few lapses. He was a courageous young officer. From the above letter by von Steuben we note that he stayed in Philadelphia "six months" after the American Army had come from Valley Forge to take possession of the city. Very probably L'Enfant might have remained in that popular city had he wished. But he wanted to be where he felt there was real opportunity for service. ˙ Thus we find him by the fall of 1779 taking a valiant part in the Siege of Savannah with General Pulaski, and severely wounded in the same battle in which Pulaski gave his life for the Cause of American Independence.

THE SIEGE OF SAVANNAH

Savannah was invested on August 23, 1779, by the combined forces of General Lincoln, which included those of Count Pulaski and his Legion and Count d'Estaing and his powerful fleet of 22 ships of the line and 11 frigates. For three weeks the siege was vigorously carried on. Then d'Estaing grew impatient and feared a dangerous autumnal hurricane. To reduce the town by a regular siege would perhaps have required several weeks more and it was accordingly thought best to try to carry it by storm. On the 9th of October a terrific assault was made in full force. Some of the outworks were carried and for a moment the Stars and Stripes and the Fleurs-de-Lis were planted on the redoubts. But British endurance and the strength of the position at last prevailed. The Americans and French were totally defeated, losing more than 1,000 men, while the British in their sheltered position lost but 55. The gallant Pulaski

was among the slain and d'Estaing received two severe
wounds.

Captain L'Enfant was one of the soldiers who fought
valiantly in the Siege of Savannah. Lossing, in his
"Field Book of the Revolution," states:

> "A council was held and when his [D'Estaing's] engineers informed
> him that it would require ten days more to reach the British lines by
> trenches, he informed Lincoln that the siege must be raised forthwith, or
> an attempt be made to carry the place by storm. The latter alternative
> was chosen, and the work began on the morning of the following day
> [October 9]. To facilitate it, the *abatis* were set on fire that afternoon
> by the brave Major L'Enfant and five men, while exposed to heavy volleys
> of musketry from the garrison, but the dampness of the air checked the
> flames and prevented the green wood from burning."[6]

In later years L'Enfant describes his experiences at
this period in a letter to General Washington, as follows:

"Philadelphia, February the 18th, 1782.
"Sir:
"A strong desire of convincing your excellency of the
sentiments which have ever actuated me since I have had
the honour to serve the United States induces me to address this to you and I flater myself you will perceive that
my sole ambition has Been to merite in your opinion and
to owe to you the favor of Congress. I have never therefore embraced those opportunities which the success of
other stronger offered of soliciting Congress — but on the
contrary have submitted in silence to the advancement of
persons who were inferior to me in Rank — a very late
instance may Be cited in the promotion of a much younger Capt. of Engineer than my-self, I mean *Monsieur
Rochefontaine* promoted to a majority at his returne
from York-town, it is true that having been prisoner of

---

[6] **Lossing's Field Book of the Revolution,** Harper & Brothers, N. Y., 1860,
Vol. II, p. 531.

war these 19 months past I had no share in the honors
of last campagne and therefor should not complain if
a younger officer by particular service merits promotion,
nor do I mention it by way of complaint — it is not my
intention to intimate anything to the disadvantage of
those gentlemen who have been so happy as to obtaine
the favor of Congress — But your *Excellency* will permit
me to observe that tho a foreigner I have never pretended
to derive any advantage therefrom to the prejudice of
any American officer, nor would I now sollicit for the
commission of major if I thought an individual officer
would thereby be injured. — attached to no particular
line it is seldom an officer of engineer can Roll in duty
with the officer of Regiments; the Corps of artillery is
that with whom we seem to have the most connexion,
but this Corps was formed so long before ours and has
so many officers that to Roll for promotion with them
would be extremely injurious to us and if it is agreed
that promotion should take place alternatively in the
two corps it will give weight to my pretention, for in the
Corps of Engineers there has been no general promotion
since its formation but several in the artillery.

"It was not till after I had scrupulously weighed
every objection that might offer that I determined to
address your *Excellency* on this subject—I pretend not
to any preference to my Brother officer when I say that
in five years that I have served the United States I have
sought every oppurtunity and neglected none that offered
to distinguish myself by love for the Service.

"in february 1778 I was honored with the commission
of capt. Engineers and By leave of congress attached to
the Inspector general. from this moment I have made

every possible effort to employ for the public benefit the little theoretical knowledge I had acquired by study— having finished that campagne By working five months successfully during the winter of 1778 and 1779 and seeing no appearance of an active campagne to the northward, my whole ambition was to obtaine leave to attend the Southern army, where it was likely the seat of war would be transferred. I arrived at Charles-town at the moment when *general provot* retired from before it, and hastened to join the army but finding very little to do in the Corps I belonged to I obtained leave to join the light infantry under *Lt. Col. laurence.* his friendship furnished me with many opportunities of seeing the enemie to advantage, and determined me to accept the offer he made me of a majority in the corps he expected to Raise. But he Being disappointed in his expectation I remained attached to the Corps of Engineers leaving every opportunity to follow the light Infantry when anything offered, and in this manner I passed the campaign in *georgia.*

"the affair at Savannah was I thought a glorious opportunity of distinguishing myself, what had I not promised myself from the success. I thought I might expect advancement in this country and even in france, having everything to hope for from the favor of *monsieur le comte d'Esting.* my disappointment was compleat. I have however this satisfaction to have been among troops who among the distresses of that unfortunate day acquired of much glory of it they had Been crowned with success. It is without partiality to say that never were greater proof of true valor exhibited than at the assault at Savannah, never was there a more favorable moment for the troops of this Continent.

"there my military career was for a time stopped by a wound I received that day which detained me in my bed to january, 1780 — my weak state of health did not permit me to work at the fortification of Charlestown, and when the enemy debarked I was still obliged to use a crutch, being thereby prevented from doing duty as an Engineer I determined to obtain advantage of skirmishing with the enemy Before they approached the town. the 30th march again afforded me some hope, the major who commanded the light infantry being wounded by fire I was supplied his place till the party returned to town, which was not without having successfully opposed the parties sent by the enemy to reconnoitre the work, when it was important to gain time. from this moment till the reduction of the place I flater my-self *general lincoln* will say that I attached my-self wherever I could render the best service.

"I shall not make a merite of having on every occasion (despised?) danger for the common cause — sensible of the duty of an officer, and jalous of my professional honor I have done nothing with a lucrative view. my ambition was to gain the general esteme of the army and particularly to merite the approbation of your excellency. I have hitherto defered every sollicitation, always hoping for some happy occasion my captivity deprived me of showing in the Reduction of yorktown. I dare however promise myself to much justice from *your excellency* as to compare the merit of several unfortunate company with the good fortune of those who happened to be at york.

"it is not long since *Lt. Col. Laurence* renewed to me the offer of a majority in the corps he expect to Raise in caroline. But when I considere the many difficulty which attend the raising of this Corps and the instability of such a Corps when Raised, and contrast this with the advantage I may probably derive from serving in the Corps of Engineer the next campagne I do not hesitate to prefer the latter. Especially as I flatter my-self your Excellency will not oppose my promotion to a majority — a promotion for which I am the more sollicitous as such a mark of your esteme with one doubly advantageous to me by giving countenance to the protection of my friends in Europ.

"I shall be happy if this succinct account of my conduct and of my motive for this address should meet your Excellency approbation. it is not the ————— eclat of a ————— procured by intrigue that I am ambitious of obtaining it if thru your approbation of my conduct I wish for promotion and it is on this principle I have taken the liberty to address this to you at the same time I beg you you to believe that what ever may be your sentiments on this subject I shall pay the most implicit obedience to them—and that nothing can lessen my zeal for the Service and the profound respect with which

I have the honour to be

your Excellency

your most obedient

and most humble servant,

P——L'Enfant

Capt. of the Corps of Engineers

his Excellency general Washington"

General Washington sent the following letter in reply:

Courtesy Library of Congress

L'Enfant's Certificate of Parole

"Philadelphia, March 4, 1782.

"Sir:

"I have been favored with a Letter from you of the 18th feby. I am sensible how disagreeable it is to have an inferior Officer promoted over your head, and am sorry it is not in my power to remedy it. The promotion of Major Rochefontaine was a matter in which I had not the least interference, it took place soly on the recommendation of General Duportail, who I believe represented to Congress that it was the practice of all Nations after a successful Seige to promote the Engineers who had contributed to the Success.

"Your Zeal and active Services are such as reflect the hightest honor on yourself and are extremely pleasing to me and I have no doubt they will have their due weight with Congress in any future promotion in your Corps, I am.[7]

To Captain Pierre Charles L'Enfant."

L'Enfant was to have his wish fulfilled in about a year, for as heretofore stated we find that he was commissioned Brevet Major in the Corps of Engineers by Congress on May 2, 1783.

In the Journals of the Continental Congress (Vol. 24 [1783] pp. 323-24) published by the Government Print-Printing Office, 1906, we find the following:

"Friday May 2, 1783

"On the report of a committee consisting of Mr. (Theodorick) Bland, Mr. (Alexander) Hamilton and Mr. (Richard) Peters, to whom were referred a memorial of Major Villefranche and Captain L'Enfant and a memorial of Lieutenant Colonel Cambray.

"The Committee (Mr Theodorick Bland, Mr. Alexander Hamilton, Mr. Richard Peters) to whom were referred the letters of the Commander in Chief of the ———— and ————, together with the memorials of Major Villefrance and Capt. L'Enfant beg leave to report, —

"That the long and meritorious services of those two officers in the important department in the army in which they have acted and the proofs which they have produced of the commander-in-chief's entire and perfect approbation of their conduct, as well as from his own observation, as the testimonials of other General Officers under whom they have more immediately served with distinguished skill and bravery, entitles them to

---

[7] In the writing of Benjamin Walker, in the Papers of the Continental Congress No. 78, XIV, fol. 535. The draft, which is also in the writing of Walker, is dated March 1.

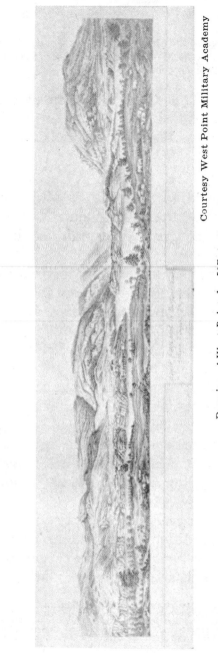

Drawing of West Point, by L'Enfant

Courtesy West Point Military Academy

the notice of Congress and the promotion which they have requested as the most important reward for their services and strongest proof Congress can give of their approbation: . . . . "

"RESOLVED, That Capt. L'Enfant of the Corps of Engineers be promoted to the rank of Major in that corps to take rank as Major from the date of this resolution.

"RESOLVED,—that Captain L'Enfant of the said Corps be promoted to the rank of Major by brevet."

L'Enfant received from King Louis XVI a pension of 300 livres with the grade of captain in the provincial troops of France.

L'Enfant, being paroled, took no part in the Siege of Yorktown, in October, 1781. Through the aid of General Rochambeau he was exchanged for a Hessian soldier. Probably he returned from the South by boat to join Washington's Army in New York. For we find that at West Point is a sketch by L'Enfant of the encampment of the Revolutionary Army in the Highlands on the Hudson, with an inscription by General Knox, "By Major L'Enfant, Engineer, 1780." Of its authorship there can be no doubt, but the date must be placed after L'Enfant's return to the North. General Washington and his Army were at Newburg, New York, the winter following Yorktown.

Thus L'Enfant served as the "Artist of the American Revolution," in addition to performing general military duties befitting his rank.[8] Whenever something in any way connected with art was wanted during the War or

---

[8] It is believed that in the summer of 1783, L'Enfant accompanied General von Steuben on an expedition to the forts on the American frontier, which were still occupied by the British to secure their evacuation, but, as General Washington reported to the President of the Congress the mission was unsuccessful. (See Writings of Washington, Bicentennial Edition, Vol 27, p.p. 123-124.)

for years after the War, he was appealed to; if not to sketch portraits, it would be to design banquet halls, a residence, an insignia, a pageant, a fortress, or a city to be planned. L'Enfant had many accomplishments, and with an overflow of ideas and few competitors his services were constantly in demand.

Fraunces Tavern, built in 1719, Broad and Pearl Street, New York City

Chapter IV

L'Enfant and the Society of the Cincinnati

THE SOCIETY of the Cincinnati was organized to perpetuate the aims of the American Revolution; also to perpetuate the friendships between the officers "formed under the pressure of common danger" and forming "one Society of Friends to endure as long as they shall endure. ...."[1] It was named in honor of the famous Roman General Lucius Quinctius Cincinnatus, who, when called upon, left his farm and after winning a decisive victory for his countrymen refused all honors and returned to his home and plow.

It seems the idea originated with Major General Knox, Chief of Artillery under General Washington. A preliminary meeting of officers was held May 10, 1783, and on the 13th a committee met in the Verplanck Mansion, the headquarters of General von Steuben, at Fishkill, New York, and adopted the "Institution" as it was called.

In 1783 there were 5,795 officers eligible to join the Society and 2,269 did so. A "branch" of the Society was formed in each of the thirteen Original States and one in France. Its membership was restricted to male lineal descendants or collateral relations of Revolutionary heroes, with a limited number of honorary individuals. Succession in the Society was made hereditary.

---

[1] Bryce Metcalf, Extract from **The Institution of The Society of the Cincinnati,** (1938) p. 1.

Insignia of the Society of the Cincinnati designed by L'Enfant

At the first meeting of the Society of the Cincinnati, held on June 19, 1783, over which Major General von Steuben presided, the Society elected General Washington President-General. At that meeting also a letter from Major L'Enfant was presented by the presiding officer, together with a design of the medal and order, containing the emblems of the Society. The letter is of great interest, since it gives us not only the views of L'Enfant, the artist, concerning the design for the Insignia of the Society of the Cincinnati, but also gives splendid advice concerning medals, saying *"A medal is a monument to be transmitted to posterity. . . ."*

Philadelphia, 10th June, 1783

To Baron de Steuben:

"My General: Immediately on receiving your letter on the 20th May, which I met by accident at the Post Office, on the 7th inst., I set myself about the plan of the medal. I send you both faces of the design, which I have made large, so that you may better judge of them. In the execution they can be reduced to a convenient size, which on account of the precision required in the design, ought not to be less than a dollar, the subject being too complex to admit of its being properly detailed in a smaller compass

"I have not made it oval, agreeably to your desire, as such a form is not proper for a medal; besides, it can be done in the execution, if the idea should be persisted in of having the order in that form, to which, however, I think any other preferable. I also believe and hope that you will be persuaded of this, and endeavor to convince the gentlemen of it who compose the committee for forming the Institution, and to whom I beg you to communicate the following observations:

"A medal, whether round or oval, is considered, in the different states of Europe, only as the reward of the laborer and the artist, or as a sign of a manufacturing community, or religious society; besides the abusive custom prevailing particularly in Germany and Italy, of sending to France mountebanks, dancers and musicians, ornamented in this manner, renders it necessary to distinguish this Order by a form which shall be peculiar to itself, and which will answer the two-fold purpose of honoring those invested with it, and making itself respected for its simplicity, by such as may be in a situation minutely to examine its different parts.

"Not that I suppose one form or another will change the opinion of a republican people accustomed to think; I only say, that in an Institution of this sort, the main design should be to render it respectable to everybody and that it is only in appealing to the senses that you can engage the attention of the common people, who have certain habitual prejudices which cannot be destroyed. A gentleman already invested with any European Order would be unwilling to carry a medal, but if flattered by receiving a mark of distinction from a respectable society, he should do it, the manner of it would by no means increase the value of the Order. On the contrary, giving it a new and particular form will be adding a recommendation to its real value, and engage those invested with it to wear it in the same manner, as their other Military Order, which is the surest means of putting it at once upon a footing with them.

"The bald eagle, which is peculiar to this continent, and is distinguished from those of other climates by its white head and tail, appears to me to deserve attention.

"I send you two essays which I have made, and desire one of them may be adopted instead of the medal. In one, I make the eagle supporting a star with thirteen points in the centre of which is the figure of the medal, with its inscription, as well in front as on the reverse. A legend might be added in the claws and go round the neck of the eagle, with a particular inscription, or the contour of the medal transferred there. In the other, I have made simply the eagle, supporting on its breast the figure of the medal, with a legend in his claws and about the neck, which passes behind and sustains the reverse. I would prefer the latter, as it does not resemble any other Order, and bears a distinct character; nor will it be expensive in its execution. The first device, although more complex, would not be so dear as people might imagine, especially if the execution of it should be committee to skillful persons, which would not be the case any more than with the medal, but by sending it to Europe, where it would not take up a great deal of time, nor be so expensive to trust the execution of it here to workmen not well acquainted with the business.

"*A medal is a monument to be transmitted to posterity* (italics added) and, consequently, it is neccessary that it be executed to the highest degree of perfection possible in the age in which it is struck. Now, to strike a medal well, is a matter that requires practice and a good die; and as there is not here either a press proper for this work, nor people who can make a good die, I would willingly undertake to recommend the execution of the Medal, the Eagle, or the Order, to such persons in Paris as are capable of executing it to perfection.

"So far from proposing to change the oval medal into an eagle, on which should be impressed the medal, I do not pretend to say medals cannot be made. On the contrary, my idea of the subject is that silver medals should be struck, at the common expense of the Society, and distributed one to each member, as an appendage to a diploma of parchment, whereon it would be proper to stamp the figure of the medal, the eagle, or the star, in its full dimensions, and properly colored, *enjoining on the Members to conform to it,* though leaving them the liberty, provided it be at their own expense, of having it made of such metal and as small as they please, without altering any of the emblems. It seems to me by no means proper that the Honorary Members should wear the Order in the same manner as the Original Members; it would be necessary that they should wear the Medal, the Star, or the Eagle, round their necks, and the Original Members at the third button-hole. "These remarks, I beg you, my General, to have translated and submitted to the gentlemen concerned. I shall be obliged to you to let me know the issue of this letter, and their decision upon it.

"I have, etc., etc., etc.,
L'ENFANT."

N. B. The head and tail of the eagle should be silver, or enamelled in white, the body and wings gold, the medal on its breast and back enamelled in the same color as the legend; sprigs of laurel and oak might be added in the wings enamelled in green; the star should be pointed in gold, or enamelled in blue and white; those who would be at the expense might, instead of white, have diamonds. The riband, as is customary in all orders, should be watered."[2]

Favorable action was taken by the Society in this matter by the adoption of the following Resolution:

"*Resolved,* That the bald eagle, carrying the emblems on its breast, be established as the order of the Society, and that the ideas of MAJOR L'ENFANT, respecting it and the manner of its being worn by the members, be adopted. That the order be of the same size, and in every other respect comformable to the said design, which for that purpose is certified by the BARON DE STEUBEN, President of this Convention, and to be deposited in the archives of the Society, as the original, from which all copies are to be made. Also, that silver medals, not exceeding the size of a Spanish milled dollar, with the emblem, as designed by MAJOR L'ENFANT, and certified by the President, be given to each and every member of the Society, *together with a diploma, on parchment, whereon shall be impressed the exact figures of the order and the medal, as above mentioned; anything in the original Institution, respecting gold medals, to the contrary notwithstanding.*"

A Resolution of thanks was adopted by the Society, in appreciation of his "ingenuity" in preparing the designs as follows:

"*Resolved,* That the thanks of this Convention be transmitted by the President, to MAJOR L'ENFANT,

---

[2] Edgar Erskine Hume, **General Washington's Correspondence Concerning The Society of the Cincinnati,** The Johns Hopkins Press, Baltimore (1941), pp. 11-13.

Diploma of Membership of the Society of the Cincinnati by L'Enfant

for his care and ingenuity in preparing the aforementioned designs, and that he be acquainted that they cheerfully embrace his offer of assistance, and request a continuance of his attention in carrying the designs into execution, for which purpose the President is desired to correspond with him."

(See APPENDIX C for translation of letters by L'Enfant concerning the subject. The originals of these letters are in the Archives of the New York Historical Society, p. 422).

As heretofore indicated, for the insignia appeal had been made to the "Artist of the Army," Pierre Charles L'Enfant, as usual, to design an eagle and also the *Diplome* or Certificate of Membership of the Cincinnati. At the time L'Enfant was desirous of returning to France to visit his family, particularly to see his aged father, and he received permission to be absent from his Corps "for the purpose of going to France on his own affairs," and to transact some business for the Society. A letter from General Washington to Major General Henry Knox on the subject reads as follows:

"Rocky Hill, October 16, 1783

"Dear Sir:

"Major Shaw not returning so soon as I imagined, and the subject of your Letter of the 28 September not admitting much delay I take the opportunity of the Post to reply to it.

"On referring to the Institution of the Society of the Cincinnati I find that the Chevr. de la Luzerne, the Sieur. Gerard, the Count D'Estaign, de Barras and De Grasse, the Chevalier DesTouches, and the Count de Rochambeau, with the Generals and Colonels of his Army, are to be presented with the Order of the society.

"As it is however proper that these Gentlemen should be made acquainted with the nature of the Society, I propose to write to each of those above named (except Chevalier de la luzerne who was written to in the first instance) and inclose them a Copy of the Institution, at the same time informing them, that Major L'Enfant is charged with the execution of the Order, and has directions to furnish them from the first that are finished.

"I· propose also to inclose a Copy to the Marquis de la Fayette, and request him to take the signature of such of the French Officers in our service, who are entitled and wish to become Members, to receive their Months pay and deliver them the Orders on their paying for them.

These Letters Major L'Enfant will carry with him, and deliver to each of those Gentlemen, and must be directed to deliver them the Orders so soon as they are compleat, delivering them to Count Rochambeau for the Officers of his Command, who will receive them of him, and to the Marquis de la Fayette sufficient for the French Officers in our Service, who become Members.

"I inclose to you the permission for Major L'Enfant to go to France, and a Certificate of his being a Member of the Society; however before he setts off, I think it should be well explained, and understood by him, that the Voyage is not undertaken for the Society, but that their business is committed to him, only in consequence of his going there on his own affairs and consequently he is not to be paid any Expense of the Voyage or his Stay, but only such Extra Expences as might be incurred by any person residing in France, who transacted the same business for the Society; these are my sentiments, if they accord with yours and the rest of the Gentlemen, and he accepts these conditions, I think the sooner he sets out, the better.

"I will be obliged to you to make out his instructions comprehending the objects I have mentioned above, and such other as you may think necessary, and to make the necessary arrangement with him respecting the funds to be furnished. I am told subscriptions have been paid in by those who wish to have Orders. I propose taking seven, for which the money is ready at any time, and it may not be amiss in this place to inform you, that it has always been my intention to present the Society with 500 Dollars; if any part of this is necessary, and can with propriety be applied in this business I have no objection.

"Major L'Enfant might also be directed to receive from the Marquis the Months pay of the French Officers in our service who become members.

"I must request you to procure Six or seven Copies of the Institution to be made out neatly, to transmit to the Gentlemen above mentioned; Major L'Enfant can bring them on with him.

"I intend immediately to write to the Commanding Officer of each of the State Lines who have not yet made known their intentions respecting the formation of their State Societies, pressing them to a determination for as I wish to adapt the place of the general Meeting to the convenience of all until I know which of the States form the Society I cannot fix it. With great regard."[3]

The letter above referred to, which was sent to Comte de Grasse, Comte D'Estaing, Comte de Barras, Chevalier Destouches, and Sieur. Gerard reads as follows:

"Rockyhill, in New Jersey, October 29, 1783.
"Sir: The Officers of the American Army, to perpetuate those friendships which have been formed during a time of common danger and distress, and for other purposes mentioned in the Institution, did before their seperation associate themselves into a society of Friends under the name of the Cincinnati; and having done me the honor to elect me their President General, it becomes a pleasing part of my duty to acquaint you, that the society have done themselves the honor to enroll your name among their Members.
"Major L'Enfant, who will have the honor to deliver you this Letter, is charged by the Society with the execution of their Order in France, and has directions to furnish you with one of the first that are compleated, and so soon as the Diploma can be made out, I shall do myself the honor to transmit it to you. With the greatest consideration, respect, etc[4]

The letter to Comte de Rochambeau varied slightly from the foregoing letter, stating, "The society have done themselves the honor to consider You and the Generals and Colonels of the Army you commanded in America, as Members." After the word "compleated" is the sentence, "He is also directed to deliver to You the Orders for the Gentlemen of Your Army before mentioned which I must take the liberty to request You to present them with in the name of the Society."

General Washington commissioned L'Enfant to avail himself of an opportunity to order from some good Paris jeweller the eagles to be worn by the members of the Society of the Cincinnati, and wrote to Major L'Enfant as follows:

---

[3] **Writings of George Washington,** Bicentennial Edition, Vol. 27, pp. 194-196.
[4] Ibid, p. 210.

I do hereby certify that Mr. L'Enfant of the Corps of Engineers in the service of the United States has acquired by his service during the War the right of being acknowledged a Member of the Society of the Cincinnati, and having obtained permission to return to France on his own private Affairs. he has at the same time undertaken to transact some necessary business relative to the Order of the said Society:

Given under my hand this 16th day of October 1783

G. Washington Presid't Gen'l

Scribner Sons, New York, 1917, p. 147.

L'Enfant's Certificate of Membership

"October 30, 1783.

"Sir: Herewith you will receive 250 Dollars in bank notes, with which you will please to procure for me eight of the bald eagles. One of which if there shall appear (upon conversing with gentlemen, better acquainted in these matters than I am) no improperiety in it, or any deviation from the intention of the Order. May not only be finished in a masterly manner but ornamented in an elegant, tho' not in a costly Stile. If, on the contrary, it should be thought best to have no difference between any of them, in the decorations (for I do not mean to depart in the smallest degree from the forms of the Order) then seven will be sufficient for me, as the ornamental one would only have been used on extra occasions.

"I have in the Letter you are charged with to the Marquis de la Fayette, requested him to send me, by the earliest opportunity, a sett of Silver plated ware; but as there is not only a possibility but a probability, that he may have left Paris for this country before you get there, or may be absent on some other ocassion, I beg, in that case, that you would open my letter to him, and comply with the contents of it, if you can do it conveniently. Wishing you a pleasant passage, and a prosperous voyage, I am,[5]

To the Marquis de la Fayette, General Washington wrote as follows:

"Rocky Hill, October 30, 1783.

"Sir: I do myself the honor to transmit You herewith a Copy of the Institution of the Cincinnati, a Society formed by the American Officers before they separed and retired to private life.

"The principles of the society the purposes for which it was form'd and the qualifications necessary to become Members will fully appear by the Institution. Should any of the Foreign Officers who are qualified by serving three years in our Army wish to become Members, I must take the liberty to request You to let them sign the Institution and pay the necessary sum into Your hands.

"Major L'Enfant who will have the honor to deliver You this, has undertaken to get the Order of the society executed in France. He has directions to deliver you one of the first that are compleated, and You will please also to call on Him for as many as You may want. Major L'Enfant will inform You the price of them; the Diploma shall be forwarded as soon as they can be made out. I am, etc."[6]

L'Enfant, while in Paris, helped organize the French branch of the Society of the Cincinnati. As to this we

---

[5] Ibid, pp. 213-214.
[6] Ibid, pp. 214-215.

are told by M. Jusserand[7] that "L'Enfant sent to Washington glowing accounts of the way the idea had been welcomed in France, and told him of the first meetings held, one at the house of Rochambeau. Rue de Cherche-Midi, for officers in the French service, and another at the house of Lafayette, Rue de Bourbon, for French officers who held their commissions from Congress, both groups deciding thereupon to unite under Admiral d'Estaing as president-general [December 18, 1783, Rochambeau papers]." The concession to organize in France was granted by the King, Louis XVI.

On December 25, 1783, Major L'Enfant wrote to President Washington from Paris, reporting that he had forwarded to Counts d'Estaing, de Rochambeau and de-Grasse, and to the Marquis de Lafayette, the letters placed in his care and that he had called upon a number of officers of France, resident in Paris, who "might from their services and rank be considered as fit for the Cincinnati." L'Enfant stated in part—

"It is not less flattering to me to be able to inform Your Excellency of the success of my mission, and of the high appreciation which the French Nation entertains in general of the American Army for thus honoring an illustrious part of our Army with such flattering distinction.

"One single conversation with the French officers would at once convince you how thoroughly they appreciate in their hearts those brotherly sentiments which make them take so deep an interest in the happiness of America.

"This Institution, which they with reason consider as a monument erected to Republican virtues, as the fundamental basis of a cordial union between the different States, as a new tie which assures the duration of that reciprocal friendship which France has evinced to America, cannot be looked upon in too advantageious a light.

"The permission which this powerful Monarch, the Most Christian King, has already given to his subjects to wear in his dominion the Order of the Society of Cincinnati, is not only a strong mark of his deference,

---

[7] J. J. Jusserand, **With Americans of Past and Present Days,** Charles Scribner's Sons, New York, 1917, p. 147.

but also an unmistakable proof of the sentiments of His Majesty towards America."

On the same day, December 25, 1783, Major L'Enfant wrote also to Major General Baron de Steuben and said:

"It is with greatest satisfaction that I acquaint you with the success of the Cincinnati in France. The difficulties have been removed which could have been opposed to the admission of the Order into France, where they are accustomed to tolerate no foreign Order. His Majesty, desires of giving to the Americans a proof of the friendship which he wishes to maintain with them, in his Council, has permitted his officers to wear this badge with the other Orders of his kingdom . . . Here in France they are more ambitious to obtain the Order of the Cincinnati than to be decorated with the Cross of St. Louis . . . ."

It was on January 7, 1784, that Count de Rochambeau wrote to M. le Marechal de Segur, Minister of War, informing him of a voluntary subscription of 42,000 (out of a desired 60,000) livres made at a preliminary meeting by the principal general officers and colonels who had served in the Army; the King's approval was solicited. Louis XVI was so much interested in the whole proceeding that he signified his assent at once in order that it could be conveyed to Count de Rochambeau without the usual delay of formal transmission through office channels.

After making their subscription the members who attended the preliminary meeting on January 7, 1784, adjourned until January 16, 1784. On that date the officers reassembled at the same place formally to assume the insignia of the Order of the Cincinnati. At the same time those French Army Officers, who had served in the United States under commissions from the Continental Congress and who happened to be in Paris, assembled at the hotel of the Marquis de Lafayette, in the Rue de Bourbon, and, after informally considering several ap-

plications from other Frenchmen who had served in like
manner, proceeded in a body to the hotel of the Count de
Rochambeau to unite with the order French Cincinnati
in session there.   Major L'Enfant was present at these
meetings, and was authorized to inform President General Washington of this proceeding.   A second meeting
was held on March 8, 1784, which also L'Enfant attended.

During the intervening weeks L'Enfant had been busy
with jewelers who were to make the Eagles for the Cincinnati.   The designs were engraved on a copper plate
in Paris under Major L'Enfant's direction.[8]   But here
again, to quote M. Jusserand, "What proved for L'Enfant one of his chief qualities, as well as one of his chief
defects, was that, whatever the occasion, he ever saw
things 'en grand.'   It had been understood that he would
pay the expenses of the journey and that the Society of
the Cincinnati would only take charge of those resulting
from the making of the Eagles.   His own modest resources had been, as General Duportail testified, freely
spent by him during the War for the good of the Cause,
and little enough was left him.   Nevertheless, he wrote
to Alexander Hamilton 'Being arrived in France, everything there concurred to strengthen the sentiment which
had made me undertake the voyage, and the reception
which the Cincinnati met with soon induced me to appear in that country in a manner consistent with the dignity of the Society of which I was regarded as the representative.' "   He spent without counting: "My abode at
the court produced expenses far beyond the sums I had
first thought of."   He ordered the Eagles from the "best"
artists, who rivaled each other for the honor of working

_____
[8] Hume, op. cit. p. 45.

for the Society (See undated memoir May, 1787, in the Hamilton papers, Library of Congress) but wanted, however to be paid; and a letter to Rochambeau, written later, showing him grappling with the problem of satisfying Duval and Francastel of Paris, who had supplied the Eagles on credit and to whom the large sum of 22,303 livres [or about $4,000] were still due. These money troubles caused L'Enfant to shorten his stay in France. While there he had the pleasure of seeing his aged father again.

L'Enfant returned by way of Havre and was back in New York City on April 29, 1784. On the same day L'Enfant wrote to President-General Washington stating that, "the French Cincinnati unanimously considered that those officers who served in Count d'Estaing's 'Co-operating Army' of proper grade were equally entitled with those of the 'Auxiliary Army' to original membership." He also communicated the views of the French Cincinnati as to the advantages resulting from being organized as a State Society "similar to that of the Regular Lines of the Continental Army," and solicited concurrence of the General Society in this behalf. (See letter Appendix C, p. 423).

The first meeting of the General Society of the Order of the Cincinnati was held in Philadelphia in May, 1784, President-General Washington, who had come from Mount Vernon, presided, and submitted the several communications and reports that he had received, which were read.

The Society took note of L'Enfant's financial problem and "Resolved that, in consideration of services rendered by Major L'Enfant, the general meeting make arrangements for advancing him the sum of $1,548.00, being the amount of the loss incurred by him in the negotiation for a number of Eagles, or orders, of the Cincinnati."[9]

On May 10, 1784, Major L'Enfant addressed President General Washington and the General Society of the Cincinnati, then in Session, as follows:

> "As the reading of the several letters of thanks and petitions, which are now before you, may easily convey to you an idea of the high consideration which the Cincinnati enjoy in Europe, give me leave, in the name of all my Countrymen, to assure you of their sincere and heartfelt gratitude.
>
> "No pledge of friendship can be dearer to them than that which they have received at the hands of the Society of the Cincinnati.
>
> "I am particularly charged by them with supporting the several demands which have been addressed to you . . . The captains of His Majesty's ships, who all have the rank of Colonel, have no doubt acquired your fovor, by their repeated services in the different squadrons of Messieurs d'Estaing, deGrasse, deBarras, deVaudreil, and Destouches, and they hope that you will pay some attention to their demands.
>
> "Several captains of frigates, who are designated by the Minister of France, as having had particular commissions on the American Coast, have acquired a title to be distinguished from those of the same rank who have not rendered the same services.
>
> "It is in order to enable you to attain the object which you have proposed to yourselves that the French General officers have recommended the above gentlemen to your illustrious Assembly. It is with the same view that the Counts d'Estaing and deRochambeau have recommended to your favor the particular services of some land officers, who, on account of those services and of their wounds, have been promoted since the War to the rank required by our Institution. . . . "

On the 13th of May, 1784, the General Society approved certain amendments and alterations to the Institution, which were thereupon embodied in an "Amended and altered Institution," and directed to be submitted to the respective State Societies in the United States and in France for ratification.

---

[9] See L'Enfant's letter to Rochambeau, June 15, 1786, Rochambeau papers, Library of Congress.

The Society of the Cincinnati in France was thus officially recognized as on the same basis as the other State Societies, and governed by the same principles, and consisted of original, hereditary and honorary members.

The Society of the Cincinnati describes the "Badge of Membership" as follows:

" 'The Badge of Membership,' generally known as the Eagle, consists of a bald eagle in gold, with the head and tail enameled white, holding in its talons laurel branches, enameled green, that continue upward round its head, bearing on its breast a medallion, enameled a deep blue and bordered with white, showing three' Roman senators presenting Cincinnatus with a sword and other military ensigns, while his wife stands at the door of their cottage, near which are a plow and other instruments of husbandry. Surrounding the medallion is the legend: OMNIA RELINQUIT SERVARE REMPUBLICAN. The medallion on the reverse shows the sun rising over a city with open gates and vessels entering the port, while Fame crowns Cincinnatus with a wreath inscribed VIRTUTIS PRAEMIUM. Below are hands joined supporting a heart, with the motto ESTO PERPETUAL. Around the whole SOCIETAS CINCINATORUM INSTITUTA A. D. 1783.

"The eagle is suspended by a blue ribbon edged with white, emblematical of the union of the United States of America. It is worthy of mention that the Eagle is permitted to be worn on the uniform of the United States and French army and navy.

"At the first general meeting of the Society, in May, 1784, General Washington received from the Count d'Estaing, president of the Society in France, the Eagle of the Order elaborately set in diamonds as a gift to him on behalf of the French Navy. This jewel, which Washington wore on occasions of ceremony connected with the Society, was transmitted by his heirs to successor as President General, Major General Alexander Hamilton, whose widow in turn presented it to Major General Charles Cotesworthy Pinckney on his accession to office. At a meeting of the General Society in 1811 it was voted that this jewel should be considered as 'appurtenant to the office of President General', and each succeeding incumbent has so worn it.

"The diplomas of membership, based upon a design by Major Charles Pierre L'Enfant, the distinguished French engineer who planned the city of Washington, were from a plate engraved by the celebrated LeVeau in Paris, but the text was added in Philadelphia by another noted engraver, Robert Scott. The design is elaborate and symbolical in nature, and among other features shows the flag of the Society and the obverse and reverse of its seal. Diplomas issued to original members were signed by General Washington as President General and countersigned by the Secretary General, Major General Knox. Members today have the privilege of obtaining from the Secretary General, for a designated sum, diplomas struck from the same plate and authenticated by the two general officers holding the offices mentioned.

THE ORDER OF THE PURPLE HEART

The Order of the Purple Heart, a badge of military merit as originally established by General Washington, on August 7, 1782, is said to be according to a design by Pierre Charles L'Enfant. It was then known as the Badge of Military Merit. It was reestablished on February 22, 1932, in connection with the George Washington Bicentennial Celebration, while General Douglas MacArthur was Chief of Staff.

The original badge was awarded for "extraordinary fidelity or essential service in war or in peace." The Washington decoration, worn over the left side, was a heart in purple cloth or silk edged, with narrow lace or binding. The revised design follows the original one in shape and color, but is made in enamel, with a reverse as well as an obverse. It ranks below the Distinguished Service Cross and the Distinguished Service Medal. Under the Order of February 22, 1932, the Purple Heart is "Awarded to Army personnel who, as a result of enemy action, receive wounds necessitating treatment by a medical officer."

General MacArthur submitted the revised design to the National Commission of Fine Arts, and the Commission approved it.[10]

---

[10] Twelfth Report of the Commission on Fine Arts, 1929-1934 p. 124.

FETE IN PHILADELPHIA

While L'Enfant was still in the Army, his services were requested to aid in celebrating the birth of the Dauphin, by designing a Hall that was built in Philadelphia for that purpose. Request was made of General Washington by letter as follows:

"Newburgh, April 27, 1782

"Sir:

"I have the Honor to receive your Excellency's Favor of the 22d instant pr Captain leEnfant.

"I beg your Excellency to be assured that I feel myself happy in an Opportunity at any Time to gratify your Desires; more particularly so on the presetnt Occasion, which I view as diffusive of the most sensible Joy to the allied Nations of France and America.

"I most chearfully comply with your Excellencys Request for Capt. L'Enfant to return to Philadelphia, and to remain in that City for the Time you mention; and hope he will approve himself of great Utility to your Designs. With the highest Sentiments, etc.[11]

The "Fete" is described in a letter by Dr. Benjamin Rush, reported in the Pennsylvania Magazine, Vol. XXI, page 257, as follows:

"FETE — Monday July 15, 1782

"Hundreds crowded daily to see a large frame building which he (the Minister of France) had erected for a dancing room on one side of the house (the Minister of France occupied the house of John Dickinson on Chestnut Street). This building, which was sixty feet in front and forty feet deep, was supported by large painted pillars and was open all around. The ceiling was decorated with several pieces of neat paintings emblematic of the design of the entertainment. The ground contiguous to this shed was cut into beautiful walks and divided with cedar and pine branches into artificial groves. The whole, both the buildings and walks, were accommodated with seats. Eleven hundred tickets were distributed.

"On one side of the room were provided two private apartments where a number of servants attended to help the company to all kinds of cool and agreeable drinks with sweet cakes, fruit and the like.

"Between these apartments and under the orchestra there was a private room where several Quaker ladies, whose dress would not permit them

---

[11] The original is in the writing of Johnathan Trumbull, jr., which is in the **Paris Archives, Aff. Etrang. Mems. et Docs. E. U. Vol. 6.**

to join the assembly were indulged with a sight of the company through a gauze curtain."

The Fete given by Count Luzerne was one of a series of celebrations (the most outstanding) to mark the birth of the Dauphin. We are told that crowds came to look at the building while under construction. It was ornamented with the arms of the United States and France and with many other emblems. At night it was brilliantly lighted within and without. The boughs of the trees in the grove around it were converted into arches and hung with glass lamps. It is said that in addition to the 1,100 invited guests there were an estimated 10,000 persons that looked on through the palisades. Both General Washington and Count deRochambeau and their aides, bearing the laurels of Yorktown, were present at this brilliant festival.

LAND BOUNTY

As is well known the soldiers who served in the American Revolution were rewarded generally by bounties of land. Among these was also Major L'Enfant, but whether or not he ever profited by it is not known.

Concerning this matter, the following is an extract of a letter received by the writer from Mr. Thomas M. Owen, Jr., Chief, Division of Veterans' Records, of the National Archives.

"Washington, D. C.
"November 28, 1945

"L'Enfant, Charles Peter,
"BL Wt. No. 1335-300 acres.

"On a register of *Land Warrants Issued Prior to November, 1800,* which is in the National Archives, it is shown that military bounty Warrant No. 1335 for 300 acres was issued November 30, 1789, on account of the military service of 'Charles Peter L'Enfant' as Captain of Engineers, Revolutionary War. There are, however, no papers on file relating to the application for this bounty land as such records were destroyed by fire in the War Department in November 1800."

L'ENFANT AND HOUDON'S VISIT TO THE UNITED STATES

In October, 1785, occurred Houdon's brief but notable visit to the United States to secure measurements and make a life mask of General Washington, at Mount Vernon, for the statue which the State of Virginia wanted of its illustrious citizen. The visit must have been particularly pleasant to L'Enfant, to whom the sculptor could bring news of his co-Academician, the old painter of the Gobelin Manufacture.

An unpublished letter of L'Enfant to Charles Thomson, Secretary of Congress, sitting then in New York, gives a number of details on Houdon's stay in America. The Continental Congress, by an Act of 1783, had decided on securing an equestrian statue of George Washington (the location for which was noted later on the L'Enfant Plan at the intersection of the Capitol-White House axes, near where the Washington Monument stands today), but did not know what its cost would be. On behalf of Houdon, who knew no English, L'Enfant wrote to Thomson that M. Houdon could not "properly hazard to give any answer relating to the cost of the General's equestrian statue"; that there are a great many ways of making such work and Congress must say which it prefers; that a book is on a vessel soon expected, bringing Dr. Franklin's baggage. The book belongs to M. Houdon and in which particulars as to the "performance of several statues which have been created in Europe are mentioned, together with their cost." Houdon had ardently expected to secure the commission for this equestrian statue. It was Thomas Jefferson, our Ambassador to France at the time, who had definitely arranged with Houdon for his coming to America; he complimented himself on having made a good bargain with Houdon for the Virginia statue, and the hope was

Statue of George Washington by Houdon
Capitol, Richmond, Virginia

expressed that arrangements might be made by Congress for the equestrian statue. In fact Jefferson sent a communication to Congress dated July 8, 1786, stating that Houdon was asking the sum of 600,000 livres and 10 years for execution of the work (a livre was worth a shilling or about 25c, which would be $125,000 for the equestrian, not an exorbitant price for such a statue). But it was very costly when we recall that at the time the American dollar was not worth a continental. And to anticipate, it was not worth more than a "continental" — about 2½ cents — until the agreement with Hamilton and Jefferson was reached in 1790 on the question of the funding bill, that is Congress agreeing to take over the debts of the States incurred during the War, about $20,000,000, partly for land claimed in the eastern half of the Mississippi Valley and ceded by them to the Government, and the location of the National Capital on the banks of the Potomac.

Thus Houdon returned to Paris a somewhat disappointed man, and instead of the equestrian of 1783 we have the Washington Monument in the form of an obelisk today. However, Houdon made busts of Washington, Jefferson, Franklin, John Paul Jones, Robert Fulton, Joel Barlow, and after four years the notable portrait statue of General Washington, life size according to exact measurements, was completed and sent to Richmond, being a reminder also of the time when there was no sculptor in this country. Copies of them can be seen at the Houdon Musée, rue de la Reine, Versailles. It is interesting to note also how earnestly the leaders of the Nation tried to secure the best in the way of art for the newly established country. Certainly Houdon was at the time the most outstanding sculptor in Europe, and we are told that he held a commission to make a statue of Peter the Great in abeyance pending his visit to America. Again, when it came to preparing a Plan for the National Capital, a real artist was appointed, and, when the time came for securing Government buildings for the Federal District, designs for monumental and beautiful buildings were selected.

We shall have occasion to refer to this later, but to digress a moment, since the matter is of great interest, it may be stated here that we are much indebted to Thomas Jefferson in this matter. For in 1785 he (in response to request for advice) had recommended to the

Mount Vernon, Virginia

authorities in Virginia a classical building resembling the Maison Carrée at Nismes, and in 1792, as Secretary of State and the first Superintendent of Public Buildings, he arranged a competition for the Capitol and the President's House, and again favored classical designs.

Major Pierre Charles L'Enfant
(Redrawn from a wood cut)

Chapter V

L'Enfant as a Practicing Architect
of New York City

WHILE living in New York City, L'Enfant displayed his artistic gift in designing the altar piece and very probably the staircases of St. Paul's Chapel to be described subsequently. Also, when in the autumn of 1787 Caffieri's monument to General Montgomery was placed under the portico of St. Paul's facing Broadway, L'Enfant was asked to devise a means of concealing the rough stone work of the back, which was visible from within through the great east window behind the altar. There is a reference in L'Enfant's Memorial[1] that in New York he lived "in style." Also there is a tradition that he was married, but careful search at the appropriate New York State Record and City Bureau Record offices, as also Paris, (see page 5), have disclosed no proof of this.

The following year, as will be related more fully subsequently, L'Enfant helped in the exciting Federalist campaign to secure the vote for the adoption of the Constitution by the State of New York by devising pageantry for a grand, artistic, historical and especially political procession. It took place on July 23, 1788, and was a grand affair, "with artillery salute, trumpeters, foresteers, Christopher Columbus on horseback, farmers,

---

[1] See page 375 and 389 of Memorials, Appendix A.

St. Paul's Chapel, New York City, Erected 1766

gardeners, the Society of the Cincinnati in full uniform, brewers, butchers, tanners, and furriers exhibiting an Indian in native costume loaded with furs notwithstanding the July heat. The chief attraction was a ship entitled HAMILTON presented by the ship carpenters, mounted on wheels, a perfect frigate of 32 guns with its crew, and firing salutes on the way. The confectioners surrounded an immense Federal cake."[2] Following the judges and lawyers were three carrying the new Constitution, elegantly engrossed on vellum. L'Enfant's particular contribution to the occasion was a dome, under which sat the President, members of Congress, and other persons enjoying a grand banquet with numerous guests. The dome was surmounted by a figure of Fame, with a trumpet proclaiming a new era holding a scroll, emblematic of the three great epochs of the War: Independence, Alliance with France, and Peace.

Whether or not the pageant was helpful is not known definitely. Doubtless it was, for three days later the New York Convention, which had been in session a month, adopted the Federal Constitution by a majority of two, and the State became the eleventh of the Union.

L'ENFANT'S WORK AT SAINT PAUL'S CHAPEL

Saint Paul's Chapel dates from pre-Revolutionary times. It is related by Mrs. Buchanan Henry (Margaret Elliman Henry) a member of Saint Paul's, that "It is the oldest public building on Manhattan Island with its original structure, in fact, the only contemporary colonial, Georgian building. It was built as a chapel through

---

[2] Martha J. Lamb, **History of the City of New York**, 1881.

the efforts of the Vestry of Trinity Church,"[3] who in the
Spring of 1763 appointed a committee to select "a proper
and convenient Lott of Ground whereon to erect a New
Church." A field of wheat on rising ground on the corner
of Partition (Fulton) Street was chosen and approved.
The cornerstone was laid May 14, 1764, and the build-
ing was dedicated October 30, 1766. It was used as a
chapel by King's College in the year 1786 (the present
Columbia University), which was located at Murray
Street. The chapel became closely associated with the
British Government, and the British did not hesitate
to bury their dead and erect memorials in the Chapel
grounds. It was used by Lord Howe as a British Military
Chapel.

Saint Paul's recalls St. Martin's in the. Fields, and it
is interesting to note that its architect, McBean, was a
pupil of James Gibbs, who was in turn a pupil of Sir
Christopher Wren, the architect of that famous structure.

During the Great Fire of September 21, 1776, which
destroyed the lower part of New York City, Saint Paul's
was saved and a service of thanksgiving for its preservation was held there. The chapel has always been a place
of worship. In the years 1786-1788 Pierre Charles
L'Enfant worked to adorn and beautify the building. He
designed the "Glory" over the altar, chiefly to conceal
the Italian monument to General Richard Montgomery,
which was visible through the hand-hammered glass of
the windows. This represented the Shekinah, Mount
Sinai, lightning and clouds, the Tables of the Law,
Jehovah in Hebrew in the Triangle above, symbolizing
Deity, and all leading down to the New Testament Altar,

---

[3] See Appendix I.

Courtesy Judson Hayward, Photographer, New York

The Reredos of St. Paul's Chapel, designed by Pierre Charles L'Enfant

the Law of Love. He added the gold garlands to the pulpit and clerk's desk in the manner of Grinling Gibbons. As related by Mrs. Henry, "There is a strong probability that he also designed the curved stair cases so deftly fitted into the East vestibule, originally sacristies." After the Inauguration on April 30, 1789, President Washington, accompanied by his entire official family, repaired on foot from Wall Street to Saint Paul's and occupied the pew on the north aisle for solemn service. Here he worshipped regularly (until 1790) and the pew is still preserved.

THE GREAT SEAL OF THE UNITED STATES

Mrs. Henry related to the writer that it is believed that L'Enfant designed the Great Seal of the United States. The reverse of the Seal, with its Pyramid, is similar in its Old Testament symbolism to the "Glory," a connection. in his mind, God's All-Seeing Eye over the Nation as well as the Church.

When he returned to New York, after his work in the preparation of the Plan for the City of Washington, he did work on various mansions similar to the stairs at the east end of the Chapel.

THE GENERAL MONTGOMERY MONUMENT
ST. PAUL'S CHAPEL, NEW YORK

The Daily Advertiser for November 22, 1787, contained the following information:

> The Monument erected to the memory of Gen. Montgomery (on the Broadway side of St. Paul's Chapel) has received the following elegant

ornamental addition designed by ·Major L'Enfant, the gentleman to whom we are indebted for superintending its original erection. "Hymen extinguishing his torch, mourns over his tomb." From behind the pyramid rises a Sun with 13 rays, which enlightens the quarter of a terrestial globe, emblematic of America. Above the whole is the American eagle flying from E to W carrying in his talons a starry curtain, in which the globe appears to have been wrapped.

It is quite evident from an inspection of the monument today, or a photograph of it, that the ornamentation referred to above is not now a part of the monument, which is also known as a "Cenotaph." It has been described as follows:

From an altarpiece supported by two brackets rises a broken column, on which rests a cinerary urn. On one side of the column is a military trophy, joined by a branch of cypress; on the other are the emblems of liberty, with a palm branch. Under the altarpiece, between the two brackets is an escutcheon and a white marble tablet for the inscription.

The monument was ordered by Congress, by Resolution adopted on January 25, 1776, in appreciation of the gallant service rendered by General Richard Montgomery, in the attack on Quebec, made by the Continental forces. The sum of £300 sterling was appropriated, and the securing of the monument was entrusted to Dr. Benjamin Franklin. Franklin arrived in Paris a few days before Christmas, 1776, and selected for the work Jean Jacques Caffieri, one of the principal artists in France. Caffieri worked on it the following year and the model was exhibited at the *Salon* for 1777. The monument was completed a year later, and, because of dangerous transportation facilities, it was decided to ship the monument in care of Joseph Hewes, of Edenton, North Carolina. It appears from a letter of Franklin that it was intended to place the memorial on the wall of the State House at Philadelphia. Years passed, and on June 1, 1784, Con-

Interior of Saint Paul's Chapel, New York City
(Perfect Example of Georgian·Architecture)

Portico of St. Paul's Chapel Facing Broadway
Showing the General Montgomery Monument

gress adopted a Resolution to have the monument sent to New York City, with authority that it "be erected in such part of the state as the Legislature of that state may judge proper." The New York Legislature gave the monument to the City of New York and the City Council authorized its erection, in April 1787, at St. Paul's Chapel.

EDIFICES AROUND NEW YORK BY MAJOR L'ENFANT

From notes by William Hindley, Avery Library, Columbia University,—

1. The old Erasmus Academy at Flatbush, built 1787. By the Flatbush connections he was ordered to build many houses in the flatlands in the modern manner, an example is the "Cortelyou Home." See Metropolitan bulletin for October 1927.

2. In the same year (1787) L'Enfant built for Joshua and Comfort Sands, now 31 Front Street, Brooklyn, a mansion facing the East River 50' x 50'. This mansion corresponds in detail with the row of houses on Greenwich Street, New York, Nos. 2 to 10.

3. L'Enfant duplicated the Lefferts farmhouse and he made it in the modern manner. It is now in Prospect Park, Brooklyn. It has a square-head door (rounded for the most part with echo moulding in the ceiling) in the Andrews Room. Center piece with 16 stars.

(In the Lady Moody house there is a L'Enfant mantel placed there after the War.)

(In New York Saint Paul's Chapel, Trinity Parish, there is the first work. There are many monuments in Trinity and St. Paul's church yard by L'Enfant.)

4. State Street, overlooking Battery Park was the situation of some of the finest mansions by him. No. 9 State Street with a splendid edifice, a palace of 24 rooms with an extension designed in the modern manner by L'Enfant for Carey Ludlow.

The southern part of Greenwich Street built on filled in ground and supported by wood piling was called the "Millionaire's Row," erected about 1790, a trifle earlier than the magnificent City Hotel. These houses have the same characteristics as the house or mansion at 31 Front St., Brooklyn, by L'Enfant.

5. The present Gracie Mansion at Hell Gate is formed of an addition added to an original mansion. The origi-

Jumel Mansion, 160th Street and St. Nicholas Avenue, New York City,
Built 1765

nal faced the East River and was the work of Major
L'Enfant. Here again all the mantels are L'Enfant's and
the typical entrance door details repeated in the mantels.
The present Hall has a wood mantel, lent by Garvey, also
the work of L'Enfant.

6. The residence of Duncan Phyfe in Parton (Fulton)
Street, was also by Major L'Enfant. Also the home of
Major Philip Howe, near City Hall. Possibly also the
home of John Jacob Astor, near St. Paul's.—(7)

8. Rufus King Mansion at Jamaica is the work of
L'Enfant, now minus its ornamental doorway as at Lef-
fert's, Gracie and Sans. King House is very much as it
was at the time Rufus lived in it.

9. The Magnificent Prince Mansion at Flushing is by
Major L'Enfant.

10. The Jumel Mansion, which was in the midst of the
War, was restored by L'Enfant, added to and made mod-
ern. The Octagon Room was added by L'Enfant. (See
P. W. A. publication and records)

11. Van Cortland Park Mansion was restored by L'Enfant, also

12. Manor House at Croton River.

13. The Crosby Mansion in the Bronx, Throggs Neck,
is the work of L'Enfant. (It was a common practice of
L'Enfant to use emblems)

14. Alexander Hamilton Mansion, designed by L'Enfant, has a fine wood mantel in the basement.

In New Jersey (see article in the Architectural Record,
"Some Early Dutch Houses," by John T. Boyd, Jr., in
No. 11) Zabriski House, Hopper House, splendid mantel

Van Cortland Park Mansion, Broadway and 242nd Street, New York City,
Built 1748

of the Westervelt House; the third article gives 8 mantels
by L'Enfant.

Note also "Hasta" (spearhead) Gate, and lamps in
Bowling Green, which faced the Custom House.

L'Enfant as a Decorator and Furnisher, Feb. 2, 1939.

". . . No great epoch occurred without great men were there and great
events taking place, between 1784 and 1820; these events and personalities
occupied the stage. After reading the life of John Jacob Astor by Smith
I learnt that Astor was the New York agent for his kinsmen in London,
who were makers of musical instruments, using the best class of cabinet
work obtainable (all know his interest in furs). Astor and L'Enfant came
here the same year 1784 (on the latter's return trip from Paris for the
Cincinnati) with similar objects, to establish themselves. The one by a
profession, the other in business. It need surprise no one that eventually
they became attached and friendly. L'Enfant often visited Astor's store

and display rooms, and the two became interested in Duncan Phyfe's cabinet work. L'Enfant was connected with Trinity and the aristocracy of New York. In L'Enfant's first period he was the lion-architect of this city, his voice was listened to and work poured in upon him from every direction.

"Duncan Phyfe˙ needed L'Enfant and he paid a gruelling price for his eminence. The military architect L'Enfant was an exacting man—dealing with all these fabrications of cabinets in New York, for he depended upon them for his clients. The Lord help that man who did not comply with his standard of excellence, and so L'Enfant gave Phyfe many headaches, but Phyfe had sense and bore with L'Enfant; for while he exacted from him he also brought business and saved him many times when otherwise he might have been ruined. This country has never seen better ware than those made 1784 to 1820."

THE PARADE IN NEW YORK CITY TO HONOR THE

CONSTITUTION

When the debates for the adoption of the Federal Constitution, were at their height, during the Convention held at Poughkeepsie in the summer of 1788, there was held in New York City on July 23d of that year a remarkable parade, civic in character, in support of it, under the direction of Major L'Enfant. It was a great event in the history of the city, which at that time had a population of about 35,000, and extended from the Harbor northward not much beyond Wall Street. Fulton Street, about six blocks further north on Broad Way, where St. Paul's Chapel was located, was then in the suburbs.

The parade was an expression of animated joy of the people of New York City upon the Founding of the Federal Constitution and the establishment of the Republic. It was a precursor of torchlight processions and fireworks that are these days prominent features in presidential and other political campaigns in cities throughout the

United States. All classes of people, including Members
of Congress, as well as notables from foreign countries,
took part in it. "The costumes and implements of many
mechanical trades were featured. Banners elaborately
painted with symbols and mottos appropriate to the several trades were displayed. During the procession cabinet makers on a platform drawn by horses constructed a
cradle and a table. The blacksmiths likewise forged an
anchor; and the sail-makers made sails. A printing press
complete with cases and other typographical implements,
and with compositors and pressmen at work, struck off
hundreds of copies of a song, and an Ode entitled "Ode
for the Federal Procession upon the Adoption of the New
Government." The painted banner carried by the Pew-
terers is now owned by the New York Historical Society.
Bands of music were also in the Procession. The outstanding feature was the federal ship "Hamilton." There
was also Columbus in his ancient dress on horseback.
Two bullocks had been roasted and after the Parade a
sumptuous feast was served. In the evening a very in-
genious transparent piece of painting representing General Washington was exhibited, and at Wall Street 13
Stars enclosed in a Circle were shown, ten brilliantly for
those States that had ratified the Constitution, New York
half obscure, and North Carolina and Rhode Island
obscure.

OLD CITY HALL

Public Buildings were few. The City Hall stood on
the northeast corner of Wall and Nassau Streets, having
been erected in 1700. When Congress assembled in New
York in 1785, the city authorities gave up the use of the

Photograph Courtesy of Gardner Osborn, Curator

Federal Hall Prior to Restoration

greater part of it to that body.[4] The main hall or "Congress Chamber" was at the east end of the second floor. On an elevated platform on the south side stood the President's chair, lined with red damask silk and over it a crimson canopy fringed with silken cords. The chairs of the members were mahogany richly carved and trimmed with red Morocco leather. In front of each chair stood a small bureau table. The walls were hung with portraits of Washington and the king and queen of France. The Mayor's office was on the first floor, the Common Council chamber at the west end of the second floor. Upon the adoption of the Federal Constitution by the several States, or in the fall of 1788, the "City Fathers" resolved to make the entire buliding available to the use of the new Government and Major L'Enfant was entrusted with the work of remodeling it. Thereafter it was known as the "New Federal Hall" and was regarded the most imposing structure in the country.

In the fall of the year 1788 the Continental Congress, which had moved to New York City on January 11, 1785, was meeting in one rather large room fitted up by L'Enfant in the old City Hall on Wall Street, near Broad Way, and the City Council in another part of the building. When the problem was presented of making adequate room for the Congress of the newly established Government of the United States of America, to begin on March 4, 1789, the City Council decided to make the entire building available for the "New Government." Public spirited gentlemen advanced $32,000 out of $65,000 spent to remodel the building and it became known as "Federal Hall."

The work was placed in charge of Major L'Enfant. The Minutes of the Common Council of the City of New York (1784–1831, Vol. I, p. 404) for Tuesday, 30th September, 1788, under the heading Pierre Charles L'Enfant Alters City Hall, reports the following:

"Your Committee appointed on the 17th Inst. to consult the Delegates of this State in Congress & such other Gentlemen as they might think proper & to report what Alterations & Repairs are necessary to the City Hall for the accommodation of the Gen'l. Government Do report that they have consulted the said Delegates & other Gentlemen on the subject & that they have procured a Plan (Executed by Major L'Enfant) on the Additions, Alterations & Repairs necessary to the City Hall which in their

[4] It is said that L'Enfant had something to do with fitting up the chamber of the "Congress of the Confederation", for as heretofore stated he was practicing architect in New York City at the time.

FEDERAL HALL
The Seat of CONGRESS

Design of Federal Hall and the Inauguration of President Washington, April 30, 1789. Artist: Peter Lacour. Engraver Amos Doolittle, New Haven, 1790. Original Owned by I. N. P. Stokes

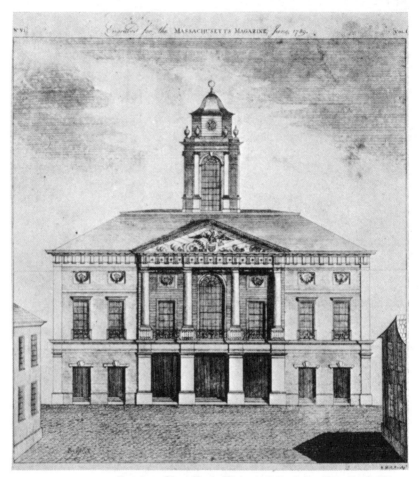

N.° VI.   *Engraved for the* MASSACHUSETTS MAGAZINE, *June,* 1789.   Vol. I.

Federal Hall, Engraved for the Massachusetts Magazine, June, 1789,
Design by Hill

Opinion is well calculated to answer the purpose & which they do recommend to be adopted by the Board.

"September 30, 1788.

> Wm. W. Gilbert
> M. Millet
> Geo. Janeway"

At the same meeting Major L'Enfant was nominated one of five Commissioners "to purchase the Materials & superintened the said Business. . . ."

The following is a description of Federal Hall as it appeared in *The Massachusetts Magazine* for June, 1789 (as well as a drawing of the building attributed to Charles Bulfinch, who became the distinguished architect of New England, and who was that year, 1789, in New York on his wedding trip and witnessed the Inauguration of George Washington):

"The citizens of New York, desirous of testifying their attachment to the new national government, and of making their city the place of the permanent residence of the Federal Legislature, have enlarged and repaired their city Hall, and made it a convenient and elegant structure, worthy of the respectable body for whose use it is designed.

"This building is situated at the end of Broad Street, where its front appears to great advantage. The basement story is Tuscan, and is pierced with seven openings; four massy pillars in the center support four Doric columns and a pediment. The frieze is ingeniously divided to admit thirteen stars in the metopes; these, with the American Eagle and other insignia in the pediment, and the tablets over the windows, filled with the 13 arrows and the olive branch united, mark it as a building set apart for national purposes.

"After entering from Broad Street, we find a plainly finished square room, flagged with stone, and to which the citizens have free access; from this we enter the vestibule in the center of the pile, which leads in front to the floor of the Representatives' room, or real *Federal Hall*, and through two arches on each side, by a public staircase on the left, and by a private one on the right, to the Senate chamber and lobbies. This vestibule is paved with marble; is very lofty and well finished; the lower part is of a light rustic, which supports an handsome iron gallery; the upper half is in a lighter stile, and is finished with a sky light of about twelve

Corner of the Old Gallery at the New York Historical Society

Fragment of the Railing of the Balcony of Federal Hall, Where President Washington Was Inaugurated

by eighteen feet, which is decorated with a profusion of ornament in the richest taste. Passing into the Representatives' room, we find a spacious and elegant apartment, sixty one feet deep, fifty-eight wide, and thirty six high, without including a coved ceiling of about ten feet high. This room is of an octangular form; four of its sides are rounded in the manner of niches and give a graceful variety to the whole. The windows are large and placed sixteen feet from the floor; all below them is finished with plain wainscot, interrupted only by four chimneys; but above these a number of Ionic columns and pilasters, with their proper entablature, are very judiciously disposed, and give great elegance. In the pannels between the windows, are trophies carved, and the letters U. S. in a cypher, surrounded with laurel. The speaker's chair is opposite the great door and raised by several steps; the chairs for the members are ranged semicircularly in two rows in front of the speaker. Each member has his separate chair and desk. There are two galleries which front·the speaker; that below projects fifteen feet, the upper one is not so large, and is intended to be at the disposal of the members for the accommodation of their friends. Besides these galleries, there is a space on the floor, confined by a bar, where the public are admitted. There are three small doors for common use, besides the great one in the front. The curtains and chairs in this room are of light blue damask. It is intended to place a statue of Liberty over the Speaker's chair, and trophies upon each chimney.

"After ascending the stairs on the left of the vestibule, we reach a lobby of nineteen by forty eight feet, finished with Tuscan pilasters; this communicates with the iron gallery beforementioned, and leads at one end to the galleries of the Representatives' room, and at the other to the Senate chamber. This room is forty feet long, thirty wide, and twenty high, with an arched ceiling; it has three windows in front, and three back, to correspond to them; those in front open into a gallery twelve feet deep, guarded with an elegant iron railing. In this gallery our illustrious PRESIDENT, attended by the Senate and House of Representatives, took his oath of office, in the face of Heaven, and in presence of a large concourse of people assembled in front of the building.

"The *Senate chamber* is decorated with pilasters, &c., which are not of any regular order; the proportions are light and graceful, the capitals are of a fanciful kind, the invention of Major L'Enfant, the architect; he has appropriated them to this building, for amidst their foliage appears a star and rays, and a piece of drapery below suspends a small medallion with U. S. in a cypher. The idea is new and the effect pleasing; and although they cannot be said to be of any antient order, we must allow that they have an appearance of magnificence. The ceiling is plain, with only a sun and thirteen stars in the center. The marble which is used in the chimnies is American, and for beauty of shade and polish is equal to any of its kind in Europe. The President's chair is at one end of the room, elevated about three feet from the floor, under a rich canopy of crimson damask. The arms of the United States are to be placed over it. The chairs of the members are ranged semicircularly, as those in the Representatives' room. The floor is covered with an handsome carpet, and the windows are furnished with curtains of crimson damask. Besides these rooms, there are several others, for use and convenience; a library, lobbies and committee rooms above, and guard rooms below. On one side (which we could not shew in the plate) is a platform, level with the floor of the Senate chamber, which affords a convenient walk for the members, of more than two hundred feet long, and is guarded by an iron railing.

"We cannot close our description without observing that great praise is due to Major L'Enfant, the architect, who has surmounted many difficulties, and has so accommodated the additions to the old parts, and so judiciously altered what he saw wrong, that he has produced a building uniform and consistent throughout, and has added to great elegance every convenience that could be desired.

"The exertions of the workmen ought not to pass unnoticed, who effected so great a work, in an unfavourable season, in the course of a few months."

The Gazete of the United States pronounced Federal Hall to be "on the whole superior to any building in America," and that the general appearance of the front was "truly august."

A most interesting letter is one dated the 11th of June, 1789, from David Humphreys, Secretary to the President, telling L'Enfant that Mrs. Washington was desirous of seeing the Federal building. The letter reads as follows:

"Sir: Mrs. Washington having postponed an engagement she had for Saturday next, is desirous of seeing the Federal Building on that day. I have therefore taken the liberty of informing you and of inquiring the hour which will be most convenient in all respects for making the visit.

"I have the honor to be, sir,

Your most obedt. and most humble servt.

D. Humphreys

Thursday morning,
11th June, 1789,
Major L'Enfant."

L'Enfant experienced great joy and satisfaction at the inspection of Federal Hall by the wife of his beloved General.

On October 12, 1789, the Common Council, in acknowledging Major L'Enfant's architectural and decorative services, conferred on him the freedom of the city and ten acres of land near the city (in the region where now Third Avenue crosses 68th Street). The Minutes of the Meeting of Common Council state:

"The following Resolutions were then unanimously agreed to by the Board, viz.:

"Whereas Major Pierre C. L'Enfant having at the request of the citizens furnished a Plan for altering and improving the City Hall so as to render it suitable for the reception and accommodation of the Congress of the United States, generously undertook to superintend and direct the Work; And in the Execution thereof hath displayed a highly distinguished Degree of Skill & Taste in Architecture & hath moreover exerted uncommon Zeal & Industry in accomplishing the said Design, notwithstanding the unfavorable Season in which it was undertaken. And the said Hall from His Talents & Exertions hath become a signal Ornament of this city and a Monument of the Munificence of the Citizens——

"Resolved therefore that the Thanks of this Board be presented to the said Major L'Enfant for his eminent Services in forming and executing the said Plan and that the Freedom of this city be presented to him under the Common Seal of the Corporation as a Proof of this esteem.

"Resolved also that this Corporation as a further proof of their Sense of the Services of the said Major L'Enfant in the premises convey to him in fee a Lot of their common Land containing the quantity of Ten Acres in such place as shall be agreed upon by a Committee of this Board. Ordered that Ald. Bayard & Messrs. T. Van Zandt & Janeway be the Committee to fix on the place for locating the said Lot as aforesaid."

The "testimonial" was transmitted to Major L'Enfant by letter, as follows:

"New York Office of Mayoralty,
13th October, 1789.

"Sir: It is with very great pleasure that I present to you the enclosed Testimonial of your distinguished merit and services, in behalf and by the unanimous order of the Corporation. While the Hall exists it will exhibit a most respectable monument of your eminent talents as well as of the

munificence of the citizens. With my best wishes for your happiness and prosperity, I have the honor to be—with great esteem,
"Sir, Your most obedient servant,

Jas. Duane, Sec."

"Major L'Enfant.

"At a Meeting of the Common Council held on Wednesday, 30th of December, 1789,—The Committee appointed to report to the Bd. the proper part of the Common Lands to locate the ten Acres to be granted to Major L'Enfant for his Services in the Improvements to the City Hall reported that the ten Acres of the Common Lands between the Land of David Provoost decd. & the Post Road be assigned for the Purpose, which was agreed to by all the members present except Mr. Recorder.

"Ordered that one of the City Surveyors lay out the said Ten Acres & that the Clerk prepare the Draft of Grant accordingly.

"At a meeting of the Common Council held on April 6, 1790 the Clerk presented to the Board a Map or Survey of the 10 Acres of Common Lands to be granted to Major L'Enfant agreeable to the Resolution of the Board of the 12th of October & 30th December last, which was approved by the Board—Beginning at the north corner of the Lane of the two Roods wide leading from the Post Road to the farm of Davie Provoost decd—containing Ten Acres of Land. Ordered that the Clerk prepare the Draft of a Grant accordingly."

"Minutes of April 16, 1790.

"The Clerk according to order presented the Draft of a Grant to Major L'Enfant for the ten Acres of Common Lands, which was read, approved & ordered to be engrossed.

"Minutes of meeting of Common Council, Friday, April 30, 1790.

"It being suggested to the Board that Major L'Enfant declined accepting of a Grant of the 10 Acres of the Common Lands, which the Board have determined to grant to him, Whereupon it was ordered that the Clerk communicate this to Major L'Enfant & report his answer to the Board & that in the meantime the engrossing of the Grant ordered on the 16th instant be suspended."

The Clerk on May 10, 1790, wrote to Major L'Enfant on this subject. A reply from him was read at a meeting of Common Council held May 14, 1790:

"New York, May 11, 1790.

"Sir: In answer to your Request of yesterday I will acknowledge herein that the Idea suggested of a disinclination in me to accept of a Grant of the ten Acres of Common Land, your Letter allude (s), is perfectly agreeable with my Sentiments and Disposition to refuse the Gift.

I am Sir your Most Obdt. Servt.

P. C. L'Enfant

Mr. Robt. Benson."

Almost ten years elapsed before this matter again came to the attention of the "City Fathers" of New York. At a meeting of the Common Council held on Monday, January 19, 1801, we find the following recorded in their Minutes:

"A letter from Thomas Morris, Esq., to Mr. Mayor on the subject of compensation to Major L'Enfant for his Services in planning & rebuilding the City Hall for the accommodation of Congress agreeable to the Resolution of this Board on the 12th October 1789 was read & it was determined that on Major L'Enfant's making application himself the same would be taken into consideration."

At a meeting of the Common Council held on Monday, 26th January, 1801, the following is recorded in the Minutes of that meeting:

"A memorial of Major P. Charles L'Enfant claiming compensation for Services in planning & directing the Improvements made to the City Hall for the accommodation of the Congress of the United States in the year 1789 was read & the Board on considering the subject determined to allow Major L'Enfant seven hundred & fifty dollars in full discharge of all further Claims against this Board for or on account of his said Services & that Mr. Mayor issue his Warnt. on the Treasurer for payment thereof accordingly."

L'Enfant was informed of this action by the Common Council, but he considered the amount inadequate and declined to accept it, as is indicated in the Minutes of Common Council held on Monday, February 16th, 1801, as follows:

"On reading a Letter from Elias Kane to the Clerk covering a Letter from Major L'Enfant to Mr. Kane, in which the Major signifies his unwillingness to accept the allowance made him by this Board on the

26th Ult. for his Services in planning & directing the Improvement to the City Hall for the accommodation of Congress in 1789, & requesting this Board to reconsider the subject & make him a greater Allowance, the Board determined not to reconsider the subject."

Nearly twenty years passed. The vicissitudes of fortune left L'Enfant a poor man, and of money owing him he now hoped for compensation for services rendered thirty years before. Thus we find in the Minutes of the Common Council of the City of New York, February 28, 1820, the following Record:

A petition from Peter Charles L'Enfant addressed to His Honor, the Mayor, stating the services rendered by him in devising the plan & superintending the erection of the Old City Hall, for which he received no compensation, altho' a grant of Ten Acres of land in the outward was on 9th October, 1789, voted to him & praying the Corporation to take his case into consideration, was read and referred to the Finance Committee.

That Committee, at a meeting of Common Council held April 17, 1820, rendered a long report giving a résumé of the facts as above stated in this matter and made an adverse recommendation on L'Enfant's request.

Owing to the speed with which the building was remodeled and the quarrels between the architect and the contractor, bad work resulted, and in a few years Federal Hall was torn down. On March 15, 1712, a Mr. Jennings bought the material for $425 to make way for the commercial development of the city. Congress moved to Philadelphia in 1790, and the Wall Street site was used for other purposes. This created some dissatisfaction on the part of some citizens of New York. It was expressed in the following piece of doggerel from one of the newspapers of the day, entitled,

The Waiting Girl in New York, to Her Friend in Philadelphia
"Well Nanny, I'm sorry to say, since you writ us

The Congress and court have determined to quit us
And for us, my dear Nanny, we're much in a pet,
And hundreds of houses will be to be let.
Our streets, that were quite in a way to look clever,
Will now be neglected, and nasty as ever,
Again we must fret at the Dutchified gutters.
And pebble-stone pavements, which wear out our trotters.
My master looks dull, and his spirits are sinking;
From morning till night he is smoking and thinking,
Laments the expense of destroying the fort,
And says you great people are all of a sort.
He hopes and he prays they may die in a stall,
If they leave us in debt for Federal Hall.
In fact, he would rather saw timber, or dig.
Than see them removing.to Connogocheague,
Where the houses and kitchens are yet to be framed,
The trees to be felled, and the streets to be named."

The Government purchased the site on December 2, 1816, for a custom house and from 1832 to 1833 additional ground was purchased for $270,000. For this site Ithiel Town, architect, built a new Custom House in the classical style of the Parthenon (this being in the Greek Revival period), and was completed in May, 1842. In 1862 it was occupied as a subtreasury. On November 25, 1883 (the centennial anniversary of the Establishment of Peace and the evacuation of troops from New York) the Chamber of Commerce marked the event by presenting to the Government the large bronze statue of George Washington, by J. Q. A. Ward, to mark the spot where George Washington took the oath of office as First President of the United States on April 30, 1789. On May 26, 1939, the Sub-treasury building was declared a national historic site by the Secretary of the Interior, and the Federal Hall Memorial Association adopted plans for a museum in the building. Congress has authorized the erection of a similar statue of George Washington on the

Capitol Grounds in Washington, to commemorate the Sesquicentennial of the first inauguration of President Washington.

A mural painting in the New York Historical Museum gives us a picture of the scene (painted by Keith Shaw Williams),—Washington, with his hand on the Bible and Chancellor Livingston administering the Oath. Also there can be seen at this Museum today part of the railing of the portico of Federal Hall from which Washington acknowledged the enthusiastic acclaim of the multitude.

As heretofore stated, Charles Bulfinch, then a young man who had recently returned from Europe, was one of the onlookers. When he returned to Boston he brought with him a sketch of Federal Hall, which was published in the Massachusetts Magazine of June, 1789, and was widely copied.

L'ENFANT AND UNITED STATES COINS

It was Thomas Jefferson who recommended the decimal system for our United States Coinage, and legislation provided for the same was enacted soon after the inauguration of President Washington.

Many artists have had a part in designing coins for our Government during the past 150 years, but it seems that the first who was asked to design a coin is L'Enfant.

On May 24, 1791, Alexander Hamilton, the first Secretary of the Treasury, wrote to L'Enfant about the design for a United States coin; stating,

"My dear Sir:

"I received in due time your letter of the 8th of April, an early acknowledgment of which has been postponed by the hurry of business.

"I thank you much for the full communication you have made me concerning the intended seat of Government and will be obliged by a

Letter from Alexander Hamilton to L'Enfant, Suggesting
"Devices for the Coin."

continuance of your observations and such further information as the progress of your operations may render interesting.

"You will not forget, I hope, the devices for the coin. As soon as your imagination shall have fixed upon any thing I shall be glad to know it.

With very great regards, I remain
always your friend &
obed. serv.

A. Hamilton."

However, because L'Enfant had proceeded on his mission that was to make him world famous, namely, to make the Plan for the National Capital of the United States of America, he gave up all other activities during that period.

Broad Street and Federal Hall, 1797

L'Enfant's Letter of Application, First Page, September 11, 1789

Chapter VI

Preparation of the L'Enfant Plan and Founding the City of Washington

A MONG the numerous problems of the first Congress in 1789 was the question of establishment of a seat of Government or a National Capital. During the period of the Continental Congress and the subsequent period of the Congress of the Confederation, from 1774 to 1789, Congress had met in eight different towns and cities,— Philadelphia, Baltimore, Lancaster, York, Princeton, Annapolis, Trenton, and New York City, part of the time pursued by the enemy and part of the time attacked by disgruntled soldiers. It was found difficult for Members of Congress to find adequate quarters, and it was always a problem to move records and files. Thus it developed that Congress wanted a home of its own. The Constitution of the United States provided for a Federal District ten miles square (Art. I, Sec. 8, Par. 17)

On September 11, 1789, while yet the idea of locating a capital city was still unsettled, L'Enfant wrote to President Washington, asking to be employed to design the Capital of "this vast empire." The nations of Europe wondered at the probable future of the new Republic. Visualizing the future, L'Enfant wrote:

"New York, Sept. the 11th, 1789.
"Sir: The late determination of Congress to lay the Foundation of a city which is to become the Capital of this vast Empire, offer so great an occasion of acquiring reputation, to whoever may be appointed to conduct

127

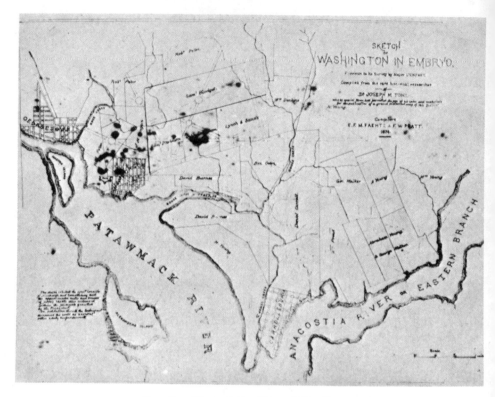

Location Plan of the City of Washington

the execution of the business, that Your Excellency will not be surprised that my Ambition and the desire I have of becoming a usefull citizen should lead me to wish a share in the undertaking.

"No nation perhaps had ever before the opportunity offerd them of deliberately deciding on the spot where their Capital city should be fixed, or of combining every necessary consideration in the choice of situation— and altho' the means now within the power of the country are not such as to pursue the design to any great extant it will be obvious that *the plan should be drawn on such a scale as to leave room for that aggrandisement & embellishment which the increase of the wealth of the Nation will per-*

mit it to pursue at any period however remote (Italics supplied)—viewing the matter in this light I am fully sensible of the extant of the undertaking and under the hope of the continuation of the indulgence you have hitherto honored me with I now presume to sollicit the favor of being Employed in this Business.

"And now that I am addressing your Excellency, I will avail myself of the occasion to call to your attention an object of at least equal importance to the dignity of the Nation, and in which her quiet and prosperity is intimately connected.   I mean the protection of the Sea Coast of the United States—this has hitherto been left to the individual States and has been so totally neglected as to endanger the peace of the Union for it is certain that any insult offered on that side (and there is nothing to prevent it) however immaterial it might be in its local effect, would degrade the nation and do more injury to its political interests than a much greater depradation of her Inland frontiers   From these considerations I should argue the necessity of the different quays and Sea ports being fortified at the expense of the Union, in order that one general and uniform system may prevail throughout, that being as necessary as an uniformity in the dicipline of the Troupes to whom they are to be Intrusted.

"I flatter Myself your Excellency will excuse the freedom with which I impart to you my ideas on this Subject indeed my confidence in this Business arises in a great measure from a persuasion that the subject has already engaged your attention.

"having had the honor to belong to the Corps of Engineer acting under your orders during the late war, and being the only officer of that corps remaining on the Continent I must confess I have long interested myself with the hope of a reappointment a hope which was encouraged by several individuals of the former Congress—and now when the Establishment of a truly federal Government renders every post under it more disirable. I view the appointment of Engineer to the United States as the one which could possibly be most gratifying to my wishes and tho' the necessety of such an office to Superintendent & direct the fortification necessary in the United States is sufficiently apparent the advantages to be derived from the appointment will appear more striking when it is considered that the Sciences of Military and Civil architecture are so connected as to render an Engineer Equally Serviceable in time of Peace as in war, by the employment of his abilities in the internal improvement of the Country.

"Not to intrude any longer on your patience and without entering on any particular relating to my private circumstances of which I believe you are sufficiently informed I shall conclud by assuring you that ever animated as I have been with a desir to merite your good opinion nothing will be wanting to compleat my happiness if the remembrance of my former services connected with a variety of peculiar circumstances during fourteen years residence in this Country can plead with your Excellency in Support of the favour I Sollicite.

"I have the honor to be with a
profound respect
your Excellency
Most humble and
obeident Servant,
P. C. L'Enfant"[1]
"The President of the United States."

Thus the letter, in addition to being an application for appointment to make a plan for the "Federal City," also points out the importance of having adequate sea coast defenses. As to this it may be stated, L'Enfant was to have a share in this work, which will be described in a subsequent chapter.

It might be inferred from the letter above quoted that L'Enfant knew more about the controversy in the Halls of Congress on the subject of location of the Seat of Government than we know today. It was at its height, that we know. The question of size of the Federal District had been settled by the Constitution—it was to be ten miles square. Now the question of location predominated,—the question of "exclusive jurisdiction" to be exercised by Congress had been generally conceded.

The discussion was finally limited to two sites: first, a location on the banks of the Potomac at least as far south as Georgetown, Maryland, which was favored particularly by the Southern members of Congress as being the geographical center of the United States; second, a site on the Delaware River near the falls above Trenton, which Pennsylvania, Delaware, and the other States nearby favored. But on the whole it was deemed very important during the First Congress to give the national

---

[1] Copy in the L'Enfant-Digges-Morgan Papers, Library of Congress.

capital a central location along the Atlantic coast. Southern members led by Richard Bland Lee and James Madison, of Virginia, argued for consideration of the question by Congress before adjournment, and recommended the Potomac River site near Georgetown.   Amidst much dis-

Courtesy of the George Washington University

The Planning of Washington
By Garnet W. Jex, 1931

The site represents a plot of fairly high ground, approximately at Washington Circle, which is at the intersection of Pennsylvania Avenue and Twenty-Third Street, Northwest.   The painting measures 7 feet by 5 feet. Near President Washington is L'Enfant holding his map.   Among others in the group are the District Commissioners Thornton, Carroll and Stuart; James Hoban; Andrew Ellicott; and two assistants of L'Enfant, Isaac Roberdeau and Benjamin Banneker.

cussion, maneuvering, and disappointment the question
of location was finally resolved into the consideration of
two locations, one at Wright's Ferry, Pennsylvania, near
the falls of the Susquehanna, and the other at Georgetown, Maryland, near the lower falls of the Potomac.
General Washington was familiar with that location,
since in 1784 he became president of the Potomac Company, which had for its purpose the development of trade
and commerce with the West,—and indeed this had led
to the call of the Constitutional Convention of 1787.
Madison argued for the advantages of a central location
of a seat of government, since thereby the people living
near to it would be better informed as to the laws of the
Government, and added "If it were possible to promul-
gate laws by some instantaneous operation it would be of
less consequence in that point of view where the government might be placed."

About six months after the beginning of the second
session of the first Congress, which convened in New
York in January, 1790, the residence bill was taken up
again.   By that time Baltimore had raised about thirty
thousand pounds or about $69,000, offering to provide
accommodations for Congress—as it had done during the
winter of 1776.   Now after nearly fourteen years it had
grown to be a town of 13,000 people.   The House adopted
an amendment naming Baltimore, but the Senate laid
this aside and proceeded to consider a bill naming a site
on the Potomac River between the mouths of the Eastern
Branch (where the City of Washington is today) and the
Conococheague—about 80 miles up the river.

The burning question before Congress at the time was
a bill for funding of the public debt and the assumption

of debts incurred by the States during the Revolutionary War, amounting to about $20,000,000. Alexander Hamilton as the first Secretary of the Treasury had recommended the funding of both forms of indebtedness in obligations of the United States. His aim was to restore the value of the worthless continental dollar[2] but it was pointed out that the assumption of State debts by the Government would result in most benefits to the northern States where there was most of the trade, while mostly agriculture was in the South. The "anti-assumptionists" had succeeded in defeating the measure in the House of Representatives and they rejoiced in their victory. Thus we come to the famous compromise proposed by Hamilton about the middle of June, 1790, when in consideration of locating the capital on the banks of the Potomac he hoped to secure enough votes to secure the enactment of the funding bill. To pass the funding bill he needed five votes in the House and one in the Senate.

Jefferson, who was living on Maiden Lane, relates in his "Anas" of an interview on this subject at the time with Hamilton. It took place on the sidewalk in front of the residence of the President, and resulted in Jefferson giving a dinner, at which an agreement was reached to give votes for the funding bill in consideration of the capital being placed in Philadelphia temporarily for ten years, and then permanently on the Potomac. Jefferson relates two Virginia members, Alexander White and Richard Bland Lee, changed their votes in favor of the funding bill, "but White with a revulsion of stomach almost convulsive."

---

[2] A pound of tea sold for $90; a pair of shoes for $100; a barrel of flour for $1,500 in paper money.

Thus by the Act of July 16, 1790, it was definitely decided that the seat of government should be on the banks of the Potomac. And of the "funding bill," which also became a law, whereby the value of a dollar was re-established, the great statesman, Daniel Webster, said in later years of Hamilton, "He smote the rock of national resources, and abundant streams of revenue gushed forth."

As to the exact location of the Capital City, it is said the loftiest minds in Congress were swayed by the judgment of George Washington in this matter. They agreed with him that America should establish the precedent of a nation locating and founding a city for its permanent capital by legislative action, and the boundaries of no other city were ever fixed with more certainty. Washington might have selected any point above the mouth of the Eastern Branch for a distance of 80 miles (that is some 20 miles beyond Harper's Ferry), but it is believed he wanted the federal city established on the Potomac at the head of navigation. He was intimately acquainted with the location and we find him referring to it in letters to his friends. At his request, the Act of 1790 was amended by Congress on March 3, 1791, to include the town of Alexandria, Virginia, and thereby dividing more equally the land comprising the District of Columbia in Maryland and Virginia. This was his "home town"; it marked the beginning of his distinguished career. In those days Alexandria had a good harbor.

Thereupon arose the question of design for the federal city. Pursuant to the application received, President Washington chose Pierre Charles L'Enfant, "the artist of the American Revolution," for this work. No better choice could have been made. L'Enfant applied his ability to the task with enthusiasm; the approbation of "his General" gave him supreme satisfaction.

In accordance with directions from President Washington, Major L'Enfant proceeded to Georgetown for the purpose of making a sketch of the area proposed for the Federal City that would enable him to fix locations on the spot for public buildings. He arrived on March 9, 1791. L'Enfant carried with him a letter of instructions from Secretary of State Jefferson, as follows:

"Sir: You are desired to procéed to Georgetown where you will find Mr. Ellicott employed in making a survey and Map of the Federal Territory. The special object of asking your aid is to have a drawing of the particular grounds most likely to be approved for the site of the Federal town and buildings. You will therefore be pleased to begin on the Eastern branch and proceed from thence upwards, laying down the hills, valleys, morasses and waters between that and the Potomac, the Tyber, and the road leading from Georgetown to the Eastern branch and connecting the whole with certain fixed points on the map Mr. Ellicott is preparing. Some idea of the height of the lands above the base on which they stand would be desirable. For necessary assistance and expense be pleased to apply to the Mayor of Georgetown who is written to on the subject. I will beg the favor of you to mark to me your progress about twice a week, say every Wednesday and Saturday evening, that I may be able in proper time to draw your attention to some other objects which I have not at this moment sufficient information to define."

The *Maryland Journal and Baltimore Advertiser* of March 18, 1791, reported Major L'Enfant's arrival in Georgetown as follows:

"GEORGETOWN (Patowmac) March 12.

"Wednesday [March 9] evening arrived in this town Major Longfont, a French gentleman employed by the President of the United States to survey the lands contiguous to Georgetown, where the Federal City is to be put. His skill in matters of this kind is justly extolled by all disposed to give merit its proper tribute of praise. He is earnest in the business and hopes to be able to lay a plan of that parcel of land before the President on his arrival in this town."

L'Enfant reported to Secretary of State Jefferson, promptly:

"Friday, March 11, 1791.

"Sir: I have the honor of informing you of my arrival at this place where I could not possibly reach before Wednesday last and very late in the evening, after having travelled part of the way on foot and part on horseback leaving the broken stage behind.

"On arriving I made it my first care to wait on the Mayor of the town in conformity with the direction which you gave me. He appeared to be much surprised and he assured me he had received no previous notice of my coming nor any injunction relating to the business I was sent upon. However next day—yesterday morning—he made me a kind offer of his assistance in procuring for me three or four men to attend me in the surveying and this being the only thing I was in need of, every matter has been soon arranged. I am only at present to regret that an heavy rain and thick mist which has been incessant ever since my arrival here, does put an insuperable obstacle to my wish of proceeding immediately to the survey. Should the weather continue bad, as 'there is every appearance it will, I shall be much at a loss how to make a plan of the ground you have pointed out to me and have it ready for the President at the time he is expected at this place. I see no other way, if by Monday next the weather does not change, but that of making a rough draft as accurate as may be obtained by viewing the ground in riding over it on horseback, as I have already done yesterday, through the rain, to obtain a knowledge of the whole. I—[rode] from the Eastern branch towards Georgetown up the heights and down along side of the bank of the main river and along side of Goose and Rock creeks as far up as their springs.

"As far as I was able to judge through a thick fog, I passed on many spots which appeared to me really beautiful and which seem to dispute with each other who (*sic*) commands the most expensive prospect on the water. The gradual rising of the ground from Carrollsburg towards the ferry road, the level and extensive ground from thence to the bank of the Potomac as far as Goose Creek—present a situation most advantageous to run streets and prolong them on grand and far-distant points of view. The water running from springs at some distance into the creeks appeared also to me possible to be conducted without much labor, so as to form ponds for watering every part of that spot. The remainder part of that ground towards Georgetown is more broken. It may afford pleasant seats, but, although the bank of the river between the two creeks can command as grand a prospect as any of the other spots, it seems to be less commendable for the establishment of a city, not only because the level surface it presents is but small, but because the hights from beyond Georgetown absolutely command the whole.

"No part of the ground between the Eastern branch and Georgetown can be said to be of a commanding nature; on the contrary it appears on first sight as being closely surrounded. However, in advancing towards the Eastern branch these hights seem to sink as the waves of a tempestuous sea, and *when considering the city on that grand scale on which it ought to be planned* it will appear that the only hight would unavoidable [italics added] . . . . mean for bettery in it, a small town easily to be comprehended in the limits of such a one as ___ _____ and be rendered by a proper care in the appropriation of the buildings that may be there erected, a means of protection and security. Such, Sir, are the few remarks which I have been able to make in a journey when the badness of the weather much impeded my progress. I hope, therefore, for your indulgence in hazarding to communicate them to you.

> "I have the honor to be
> with very great respect."

Jefferson replied to L'Enfant on March 17th, as follows:

"SIR: Your favor of the 11th instant has been duly received. Between the date of that and the receipt of the present, it is probable that the most important parts of the ground towards the Eastern branch will have been delineated. However, whether they have or not, the President will go within two or three days, and would wish to have under his eye when at Georgetown, a drawing also of the particular lineaments of the ground between Rock Creek and the Tyber; you are desired immediately on the receipt of this, to commence the survey of that part, beginning at the river, and proceeding towards the part back of that till his arrival. If the meanders of those two creeks and of the river between them should not have been laid down either by yourself or by Mr. Ellicott, it is desired that Mr. Ellicott should immediately do this while you shall be employed on the interior ground, in order that the work may be as much advanced as possible on the arrival of the President, and that you will be so good as to notify this to Mr. Ellicott.

"I am with great esteem, Sir, your most obedt. humble servt.

> "Th. Jefferson.

"P. S. There are certainly considerable advantages on the Eastern branch; but there are very strong reasons also in favor of the position between Rock Creek and Tyber, independent of the face of the ground. It is desired that the proper amount should be in equilibrio between the two places till the President arrives, and we shall be obliged to you to endeavor to poise their expectations."

By this postscript, should L'Enfant have had occasion

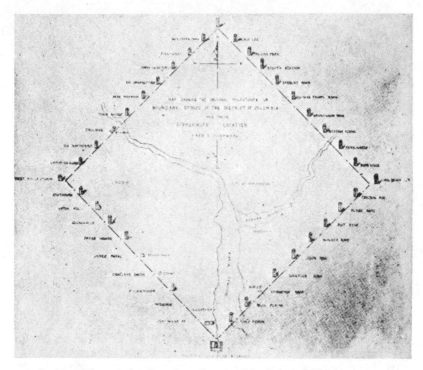

Map of the Boundary Stones, District of Columbia

to show it, the landholders, it was thought, could be thrown in doubt. Nevertheless, it took argument by President Washington himself, when he arrived at the end of the month, to culminate the transaction with them.

On March 20, 1791, L'Enfant wrote another letter to the Secretary of State:

"Sir: On the 17th the change in the weather at last having permitted me to proceed to the Eastern branch, I did on the afternoon of that day, Sat., [set] about the survey. But the variety of the weather has been such since as has impeded my progress. I have only been able this day, to lay down of that part which lay between the Eastern branch and the Tiber so much as included Jenkin's Hill and all the water course from round Carroll point up to the ferry landing; leaving for a better time swampy parts which were rendered absolutely impassable by the heavy rain which overflowing all the low ground determined me to confine myself on the high land. I expected to have before this day attempted to lay down some part of those laying between the Tiber and Rock Creek had not a fall of snow and stormy wind which succeeded for these three days past prevented me.

"I hope tomorrow will prove more favorable for me to proceed laying down those parts which you prescribe in your letter which [I] this moment receive from Mr. Ellicott, who brought it himself to me, and shall according to your direction join his endeavors to mine in running as much as possible of the water course as may serve to connect the whole of our different surveys together.

"I have the great honor to be
with great respect Sir,
Your most humble and most obedient servant,
(Signed)   P. C. L'Enfant."

The Secretary of State, Mr. Jefferson, on March 11th, prepared for the President a memorandum of matters to be considered at Georgetown; together with a form of proclamation dated March but the day blank. This proclamation was upon the basis that the lands near Georgetown would be selected. It reads in part:

"I do hereby further declare and make known, that the highest summit of the lands in the town heretofore called Hamburg within the said territory, with a convenient extent of grounds circumjacent, shall be appropriated for the Capitol for the accommodation of Congress, and such other lands between Georgetown and the stream heretofore called the Tyber, as shall on due examination be found convenient and sufficient, shall be appropriated for the accommodation of the President of the United States for the time being and for the public offices of the government of the United States. And I do hereby direct the said commissioners accordingly."

"The part within the ([]) being conjectural, will be to rendered conformable to the ground when more accurately examined."

With the memorandum and proclamation was a rough plat of the city, in part, to be. It placed the President's House at the old Naval Hospital site (where we are told

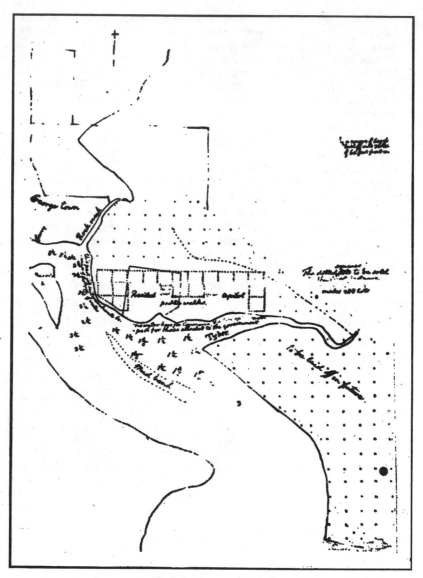

Jefferson's Plan for the Federal City

Washington hoped he might have a house some day, and where he bought lots for a University) and the Capitol eastward at about Fifteenth and E Streets.

We are told that real estate speculation in the eastern sections of the future city caused Jefferson to make his sketch for establishing the city in the western part but on a very small scale, comprising not more than 1500 acres, whereas President Washington felt the city should be four times as large. It seems, however, Washington preferred to have L'Enfant begin his surveys in the eastern section of the city adjacent to the Anacostia, in the hope that land owners in the western part might be persuaded to be more reasonable in the price of land. Washington was informed by his agents of their intention to offer Mr. Burnes as high as twelve or eighteen pounds, namely from $32 to $48 an acre, but should he ask 25 pounds or $67 an acre they would wait for further instructions. To prevent delay Washington agreed to that amount and $67 an acre was the amount specified in the agreement subsequently made.

In the meantime President Washington had begun his triumphal tour through the South. In Maryland he was escorted by his Excellency Governor Howard and the Honorable Mr. Kilty: Washington's Diary for March 28-30, 1791, reports:[3]

"Monday 28th. Left Bladensburgh at half after six, and breakfasted at George Town about 8:—where, having appointed the Commissioners under the Residence Law to meet me, I found Mr. Johnson one of them (and who is Chief Justice of the State) in waiting—and soon after came in David Stuart, and Danl. Carroll Esqrs. the other two. A few miles out of Town I was met by the principal Citizens of the place and escorted in by them; and dined at Suter's tavern (where I also lodged) at a public dinner given by the Mayor and Corporation—previous to which I exam-

[3] J. C. Fitzpatrick, The Diaries of George Washington, Houghton Mi%in Co., Vol. IV, p. 152

ined the Surveys of Mr. Ellicott who had been sent on to lay out the district of ten miles square for the federal seat; and also works of Majr. L'Enfant who had been engaged to examine and make a draught of the grds. in the vicinity of George Town and Carrollsburg on the Eastern branch making arrangements for examining the ground myself tomorrow with the Commissioners.--

"Tuesday, 29th.

"In a thick mist, and under strong appearance of a settled rain (which however did not happen) I set out about 7 o'clock, for the purpose above mentioned, but from the unfavorableness of the day, I derived no great satisfaction from the review.

"Finding the interests of the Landholders about George Town and those about Carrollsburgh much at variance and that their fears and jealousies of each were counteracting the public purposes and might prove injurious to its best interests, whilst if properly managed they might be made to subserve it, I requested them to meet me at six o'clock this afternoon at my lodgings, which they accordingly did.

"To this meeting I represented that the contention in which they seemed engaged, did not in my opinion comport either with the public interest or that of their own; that while each party was aiming to obtain the public buildings, they might by placing the matter on a contracted scale, defeat the measure altogether; not only by procrastination but for want of the means necessary to effect the work;—That neither the offer from Georgetown or Carrollsburgh, separately, was adequate to the end of insuring the object. That both together did not comprehend more ground nor would afford greater means than was required for the federal City; and that, instead of contending which of the two should have it they had better, by combining more offers make a common cause of it, and thereby secure it to the district, other arguments were used to show the danger which might result from delay and the good effects that might proceed from a Union.

"Dined at Colo. Forrest's today with the Commissioners and others." [(whose residence was at 3348 M Street).]

"Wednesday, 30th.

"The parties to whom I addressed myself yesterday evening, having taken the matter into consideration, saw the propriety of my observations; and that whilst they were contending for the shadow they might loose the substance; and therefore mutually agreed and entered into articles to surrender for public purposes, one half of the land they severally possessed within the bounds which were designated as necessary for the City to stand with some other stipulations, which were inserted in the instrument which they respectively subscribed.

"This business being thus happily finished and some directions given to the Commissioners, the Surveyor and Engineer with respect to the mode of laying out the district—Surveying the grounds for the City and forming them into lots—I left Georgetown. dined in Alexandria and reached Mount Vernon in the evening."

The following is the Agreement between the Government and the Proprietors:

AGREEMENT BETWEEN THE GOVERNMENT AND THE PROPRIETORS

"We, the subscribers, in consideration of the great benefits we expect to derive from having the Federal city laid off upon our lands do hereby agree and bind ourselves, heirs, executors and administrators, to convey in trust to the President of the United States, or Commissioners, or such a person or persons as he shall appoint by good and sufficient deeds in fee simple, the whole of our respective land which he may think proper to include within the lines of the Federal city, for the purposes and on the conditions following:

"The President shall have the sole power of directing the Federal City to be laid off in what manner he pleases. He may retain any numbers of squares he may think proper for any public improvements or other public uses, and the lots only which shall be laid off shall be joint property between the trustees on behalf of the public and equally divided between the public and the individuals as soon as may be after the city shall be laid off.

"For the streets the proprietors shall receive no compensation, but for the squares or lands in any form which shall be taken for the public buildings or any kind of public improvements or uses, the proprietors whose lands shall be so taken shall receive at the rate of £25 per acre [Maryland currency value $66.67] to be paid by the public.

"The whole wood on the lands shall be the property of the proprietors and should any be desired by the President to be reserved or left standing, the same shall be paid for by the public at a just and reasonable valuation, exclusive of the £25 per acre to be paid for the land on which the same shall remain.

"Each proprietor shall retain the full possession of his land until the same shall be sold and occupied by the purchasers of the lots laid out thereupon, and in all cases where the public arrangements as the streets, lots, etc., will admit of it, each proprietor shall possess his buildings and other improvements and graveyards, paying to the public only one half the present estimated value of the land, on which the same shall be or £12 10 sh per acre; but in cases where the arrangements of the streets, lots, squares, etc., will not admit of this, and it shall become necessary to remove such buildings, etc., the proprietors of the same shall be paid the reasonable value thereof by the public.

"Nothing herein contained shall affect the lots any of the parties to this agreement may hold in the town of Hamburgh or Carrollsburg.

"In witness whereof we have hereunto set our hands and seals this 30th day of March in the year of our Lord, 1791.

Here follow the signatures of the 19 original proprietors.[4]

This was one of the most remarkable real estate transactions ever consummated for the Government.

The land not taken for streets and public reservations was laid out in building lots, and apportioned equally between the Federal Government and the original owners. In this way, without advancing a dollar and at a total cost of $36,000, the Government acquired a tract of about 540 acres for public buildings and parks in the heart of the city. For laying out the streets 3,606 acres in all were taken. Of 20,272 building lots, one-half, or 10,136 were assigned to the Government—apportioned on the basis of every other lot in a square.

Within a few days the President wrote to Major L'Enfant as follows:

"Mount Vernon, April 4th, 1791.

"Sir: Although I do not conceive that you will derive any material advantage from an examination of the enclosed papers, yet, as they have been drawn under different circumstances, and by different persons, they may be compared with your own ideas of a proper plan for the Federal City, under the prospect which now presents itself. For this purpose I commit them to your private inspection until my return from the tour I am about to make. The rough sketch by Mr. Jefferson was done under an idea that *no* offer, worthy of consideration, would come from the Land holders in the vicinity of Carrollsburg from the backwardness which appeared in them; and therefore was accomodated to the grounds about George Town. The *other* is taken upon a larger scale, without reference to any described spot.

"It will be of great importance to the public interest to comprehend

---

[4] See **Manual on the Origin and Development of Washington,** by the author, 1939.

as much ground (to be ceded by individuals) as there is any tolerable prospect of obtaining from them:—although it may not be *immediately* wanting, it will nevertheless increase the Revenue; and of course be beneficial, not only to the public but the individuals also hereafter inasmuch as the plan will be enlarged, and thereby freed from those blotches which otherwise might result from not comprehending *all* the lands that appear well adapted to the general design—& which in my opinion are those between Rock Creek, Potomac River, & the Eastern branch & as far up the latter as the turn of the Channel above Evens' point;—thence including the flat back of Jenkins' height;—thence to the Road leading from Georgetown to Bladensburg as far Easterly along the same as to include the branch which runs across it, somewhere near the exterior of George town Session.—thence in a proper direction to Rock Creek at, or above the ford, according to the situation of the ground."

President Washington informed Secretary of State Jefferson of the proceedings on March 30th, with instructions that the information be published:

"Mount Vernon,
"31 March, 1791.

"Dear Sir: Having been so fortunate as to reconcile the contending interests of Georgetown and Carrollsburg and to unite them in such an agreement as permits the public purposes to be carried into effect on an extensive and proper scale, I have the pleasure to transmit to you the enclosed proclamation, which after annexing the seal of the United States, and your counter-signature, you will cause to be published.

"The terms entered into by me on the part of the United States, with the landholders of Georgetown and Carrollsburg, are that all the land from Rock Creek along the river to the Eastern Branch, and so upwards to, or above the Ferry, including a breadth of a mile and a half, the whole containing from three to five thousand acres, is ceded to the public on condition that when the whole shall be surveyed and laid off as a city (which Major L'Enfant is now directed to do), the present proprietors shall retain every other lot; and for such part of the land as may be taken for public use, for squares, walks, etc., they shall be allowed at the rate of twenty five pounds per acre, the public having the right to reserve such parts of the wood on the land, as may be thought necessary to be preserved for ornament; the landholders to have the use and profits of all the grounds until the city is laid off into lots * * *

"With great regards and esteem, I am,"

On April 4, 1791, L'Enfant wrote to Jefferson as follows:

"Sir: I would have reproached myself for not having written to you as regularly as you desired. I should were it not for circumstances to which you will I doubt not attribute this seeming neglect in approving of the considerations which made me give the whole of my time to forwards as much as possibly could be the business I had to perform. Great as were my endeavors to that end it *still* remained unfinished at the moment of the President arrival at this place where I could present him no more but a rought drawing in pencil of the several surveys which I had been able to run—nevertheless the President indulgent disposition making him account for the difficulties encountered, I had the satisfaction to see the little I had done agreeable to his wish—and the confidence with which he has been pleased since to Honor me in ordering the survey to be continued and *the delineation of a grand plan for the local distribution of the city* (italics inserted), to be done on principle conformable to the ideas which I took the liberty to hold before him as the proper for the Establishment being to highly flatering to my Embition to fail exerting the best of my hability. it shall be from this moment my endeavor to answer the president expectations in preparing those plans and having them ready for the time of his return from the Southern tour.

"I shall in the meantime, Sir, beg for every information respecting all what may in your judgment appear of most immediate importance to attend to as well as relating to every desirable Establishment which it will be well to foresee, although delaying or perhaps leaving the Execution thereof to a natural succession of time to Effect.

"the number and nature of the publick building with the necessary appendix I should be glad to have a statement of as speedily as possible—and I would be very much obliged to you in the mean time if you could procure for me whatever map may fall within your reach—of any of the differents grand city now Existing such as—for example—as london—madry [Madrid]—paris—Amsterdam—naples—venice—genoa—florence, together with particular maps of any such sea-ports or dock-yards and arsenals as you may know to be the most compleat in their Improvement, for, notwithstanding, *I would reprobate the Idea of Imitating and that contrary of Having this Intention it is my wish and shall be my endeavor to delinate on a new and original way the plan the contrivance of which the President has left to me without any restriction soever* (italics inserted)—yet the contemplation of what exists of well improved situation iven the parallel of these with deffective ones, may serve to suggest a variety of new Ideas and is necessary to refine and strengthen the Judgment particularly in the present instance when having to unite the useful with the comodious and agreeable viewing these will by offering means of comparing enable me the better to determine with a certainty the

propriety of a local which offer an Extensive field for combinations.
"I have the Honor to be, with great respect,[5]
　　　Your most humble and most obedient servant,
　　　　(Signed)　P. C. L'Enfant"

The above letter indicates that, while L'Enfant aimed to produce an original plan for the Federal City, adapted to the topography, nevertheless he endeavored to secure ideas from plans of great cities of Europe that might be found possible of adaptation.

To this letter sent by L'Enfant, Jefferson forwarded his notable reply and plans of a number of cities that he had secured, evidently, while our Minister to France.[6]

"Philadelphia, Apr. 10, 1791.

"Sir: I am favored with your letter of the 4th inst. and in compliance with your request I have examined my papers and found the plans of Frankfort-on-the Mayne, Carlsruhe, Amsterdam, Strasburg, Paris, Orleans, Bordeaux, Lyons, Montpelier, Marseilles, Turin and Milan, which I send in a roll by this post. They are on large and accurate scales having been procured by me while in those respective cities myself. As they are connected with the notes I made in my travels & often necessary to explain them to myself, I will beg your care of them and to return them when no longer useful to you, leaving you absolutely free to keep them as long as useful. *I am happy that the President has left the planning of the Town in such good hands and have no doubt it will be done to general satisfaction. (italics added.)* Considering that the grounds to be reserved for the public are to be paid for by the acre, I think very liberal reservations should be made for them, and if this be about the Tyber and on the back of the town it will be of no injury to the commerce of the place, which will undoubtedly establish itself on the deep waters on the Eastern branch and mouth of Rock Creek; the water about the mouth of the Tyber not being of any depth. Those connected with the Government will prefer fixing themselves near the public grounds in the center, which will also be convenient to be resorted to as walks from the lower and upper town.— Having communicated to the President before he went away such general ideas on the subject of the town as occurred to me, I make no doubt that, in explaining himself to you on the subject, he has interwoven with his own ideas such of mine as he approved; for fear of repeating therefore what he did not approve, and having more confidence in the unbiased

---

[5] Original in the Manuscript Division, Library of Congress.
[6] L'Enfant-Digges-Morgan Papers, Library of Congress.

Place de la Concorde, Paris

state of his mind than in my own, I avoid interfering with what he may have expressed to you. *Whenever it is proposed to prepare plans for the Capitol I should prefer the adoption of some one of the models of antiquity which have had the approbation of thousands of years; and for the President's house I should prefer the celebrated fronts of modern buildings which have already received the approbation of all good judges.* (italics added) Such are the Galerie du Louvre, the Gardes meubles;[7] and two fronts of the Hotel de Salm. But of this it is yet time enough to consider."

In this connection it is interesting to recall Jefferson's celebrated letter to Governor James Madison of Virginia, in 1785, when the Building Committee of Richmond requested of Jefferson, then in Paris, advice as to a design for their proposed capitol building. Jefferson recommended a building in imitation of the little Roman temple at Nismes, which he stated was "superior in beauty to anything in America and not inferior to anything in the world." With the result that the Capitol Building at Richmond stands as the first classical building in the United States.

During the succeeding two months there was considerable argument among the landholders with the Commissioners of the District of Columbia (Thomas Johnson, David Stuart, and Daniel Carroll) regarding the amount of land to be taken over by the Government and the location of parts of it. This came to a crisis in connection wtih the execution of deeds of conveyance. Some hesitated and this threatened to disorganize the entire future proceedings. Washington heard of it while in the far South and it caused him considerable chagrin, for he had mentioned the fact and taken delight in it that beginnings were being made on the future federal city. Thus

[7] See location of the "Gardes Meubles" (furniture store) in picture, page 148. That portion of the building (once a palace) is now occupied in part by the Hotel Crillon—next to it, at left, is the American Embassy.

Washington sent back the hint that if the landowners would not comply with their agreement of March 30th there were other locations for the federal city that could be considered. It seemed this had the proper effect, for by the end of June the deeds of conveyance were ready.

Also, in the meantime, both L'Enfant and Ellicott had proceeded in their work on the basis of the agreement of March 30th. Ellicott was making a survey of the boundary lines of the "Ten Miles Square" and L'Enfant was at work on a more complete map of the city, which he proposed to bring to the attention of President Washington on his return from the South, the latter part of June. On April 15, 1791 the Commissioners of the District of Columbia met at Alexandria and accompanied by Ellicott "and a large concourse of spectators," proceeded to Jones Point and dedicated the first Boundary Stone. This is still in place and was made the occasion of a "re-dedication" by the Commissioners of the District of Columbia on April 15, 1941, to mark the 150th anniversary. That portion of the District of Columbia lying in Virginia was ceded back to that State by Act of Congress in the year 1846, a time when the L'Enfant Plan had been well nigh forgotten and the people residing in the Virginia portion felt they were being neglected with public improvements. However, in accordance with a decision by the United States Supreme Court, the Government owns the land up to the high water mark of the Potomac River.

We are informed by President Washington that he returned to Mount Vernon on Sunday, June 12th, and that from the 13th to the 27th, while inspecting his farms he also received many visitors. One of these visitors was

Major L'Enfant, who brought with him a "progress map"
of the Federal City, and a long report, dated June 22d, as
follows:

"Georgetown, Jun 22—1791

"Sir.　In framing the plan here anexed, for the for the intended Federal City I regreted much being indered by the shortness of time from making any particular drawing of the several buildings—squars—and every other improvement which the smallness of the scale of the general map together with the hurry with which I had it drawn could not admit of having so correctly lay down as necessary to give a perfect Idea of the effect of the whole in the execution.

"My whole attention was given to the combination of the general distribution of the grand local as to an object of most immediate moment and of importance to this I yielded every other consideration and have in consequence to sollicite again your Indulgence in submitting to you my Ideas in an incomplete drawing only correct as to the situation and distance of objects all of which were determined after a local well ascertained having for more accuracy had several lines run on the ground cleared of the wood and afterwards measured with posts fixed all along, to serve me as certain bases from after the which I might arrange the whole with a certainty of making every part fit to the various grounds.

"having first determined some principal points to which I wished making the rest subordinate 1 next made the distribution regular with streets at right angle *north-south* and *east west* but afterwards I opened others on various directions as avenues to and from every principal places, wishing by this not merely to contrast with the general regularity nor to afford a greater variety of pleasant seats and prospect as will be obtained from the advantageous ground over the which the avenues are mostly directed but principally to connect each part of the city with more efficacy by, if I may so express, making the real distance less from place to place in menaging on them a reisprocity of sight and making them thus seemingly connected promot a rapide stellement over the whole so that the most remot may become an adition to the principal while without the help of these divurgents communications such setlements if at all attempted would be languid, and lost in the Extant would become detremental to the main establishment.

"Several of these avenues were also necessary to effect the junction of of several out road which I concluded essential to bring central to the city in rendering these road shorter as is done with respect to the bladensburg and Eastern branche Road made above a mile shorter besides the advantage of their leading from the direction given immediately on the warfs of georgetown without passing the hilly ground of that place whose agrandissement it will consequently check . . .

"across the tiber of above were the tide water come lay certainly the elligible spot to lay the Foundation of an establishment of the nature of the one in view, not because this point being central is most likely to diffuse an Equallity of advantages trough the whole territory and in turn to devise, a benefit propotional to the rise of its value but because the nature of the local is such as will made everything concur to render a settlement there prosperous—there it will benefit of the natural jalousie which most stimulate establishments on each of its opposed limits it will become necessarily the point of reunion of both and soon become populouz. a canal being easy to open from the eastern branch and to be lead across the first settlement and carried toward the mouth of the tiber where it will again give an issue into the Potowmack and at a distance not to far off for to admit the boats from the grand navigation canal from getting in, will undoubtedly facilitate a conveyance most advantageous to trading Interest it will insure the storing of marketts which, as lay down on the map, being erected all along the canal and over grounds proper to shelter any number of boats will serve of Mart Houses from were when the city is grown to its fullest extent the most distant markets will be supplied at command.

"to these advantages of first necessity to consider to determine the seat of a City is added that of the propositions which there offer and the which are the most suceptible of any within the limits of the intended city of leading to those grand improvements of publique magnitude and as may serve as models for all subsequent undertaking and stand to future ages a monument to national genious and munificence.

"After much menutial search for an elligible situation, promoted I may say from a fear of being prejudiced in favour of a first opinion I could discover no one so advantageously to greet the congressional building as is that on the west of Jenkins heights which stands as a pedestal waiting for a monument, and I am confident, were all the wood cleared from the ground no situation could stand in competition with this. some might perhaps require less labour to be rendered agreeable but after all assistance of arts none ever would be made so grand and all other would appear but of secondary nature.

"that were I determine the seat of the presidial palace, in its difference of nature may be view of advantageous to the object of ading to the sumptuousness of a palace the convenience of a house and the agreeableness of country seat situated on that ridge which attracted your attention at the first inspection of the ground on the west side of the tiber entrance it will see 10 or 12 miles down the Potowmack front the town and harbor of Alexandria and stand to the view of the whole city and have the most improved part of it made by addition to those grand Improvements for which the ground in the dependenly of the palace is to proper.

"fixed as expressed on the map the distance from the Congressional House will not be to great as what the activity of business may be no message to nor from the president is to be made without a sort of

decorum which will doubtless point out the propriety of committee waiting on him in carriage should his palace be even contigious to Congress.

'-'to mak however the distance less to other officers I placed the three grand Departments of State contigous to the principle Palace and on the way leading to the Congressional House the gardens of the one together with the park and other improvement on the dependency are connected with the publique walk and avenue to the Congress house in a manner as most form a whole as grand as it will be agreeable and convenient to the whole city which form the distribution of the local will have an early access to this place of general resort and all along side of which may be placed play houses, room of assembly, accademies and all such sort of places as may be attractive to the learned and afford diversion to the idle.

"I proposed continuing the canal much further up but this being not to be effectual but with the aid of lock, and from a level obtained of the height of the spring of the tiber the greatest facility being to bring those waters over the flat back of Jenkins I gave the more readily a preference to avail of this water to supply that part of the city as it will promot the execution of a plan which I propose in this map, of leting the tiber return in its proper channel by a fall which issuing from under the base of the Congress building may there form a cascade of forty feet heigh or more than one hundred waide which would produce the most happy effect in rolling down to fill up the canall and discharge itself in the Potowmack of which it would then appear as the main spring when seen through that grand and majestic avenue intersecting with the prospect from the palace at a point which being seen from both I have designated as the proper for to erect a grand Equestrian figure.

"in the present unimproved state of the local it will appear that the height were is marked that monument dose intercept the view of the water from the palace and in fact it is partly the case but it most be observed that having to bound the entrance of the tiber at the breadth of a canal of 200 ft. which is the utmost breadth that can be preserve to avoid its being drained at low water. it will require much ground to be trown in to feel up, and at least as much as will enable to levell that point of heigh ground between the tiber and P Yong House to almost a level with the tide water and of course to procure to the palace and all other houses from that place to congress a prospect of the Potowmack the

which will acquire new swithess being laid over the green of a field well
level and made brilant by shade of few tree artfully planted
"I am with respectfull submission
"Your most humble & obedient servant,
                                    "P. C. L'Enfant."[8]

To the President of the United States.

There is no record of any comment on this "progress
map" by President Washington, while discussing the subject with Major L'Enfant at Mount Vernon. However,
we find several comments as to the map in Washington's
diary for June 29th. One June 27th Washington states
that he left Mount Vernon "before six o'clock" for an
appointment with the District Commissioners at nine
o'clock and a conference with "the Proprietors of those
Lands on which the federal City was. proposed to be
built," to explain to them the present situation of matters
"and the consequences of delay in this business," whereupon "they readily waived their objections and agrd. to
convey to the utmost extent what was required." Then,

"Tuesday—28th. Whilst the Commissioners were engaged in preparing
the Deeds to be signed by the Subscribers this afternoon, I went out with
Majr L'Enfant and Mr. Ellicot to take a more perfect view of the ground,
in order to decide finally on the spots on which to place the public buildings and to direct how a line which was to leave out a Spring (commonly
known by the name of Cool Spring) belonging to Majr. Stoddard should
be run."

"Wednesday—29th. The Deeds which remained unexecuted were to be
signed today and the Dowers of their respective wives acknowldged ac-
coring to Law. This being accomplished, I called the several subscribers
together and made known to them the spots on which I meant to place
the buildings for the P: and Executive departments of the Government—
and for the Legislature of Do. A Plat was also laid before them of the
City in order to convey to them general ideas of the City but they were
told that some deviation from it would take place—particularly in the
diagonal streets or avenues, which would not be so numerous; and in the
removal of the President's house more westerly for the advantage of

---

[8] Records of the Columbia Historical Society, Vol. 2, pp. 32-37.

higher ground—they were also told that a Town house, or exchange wd. be placed in some convenient ground between the spots designed for the public buildgs. before mentioned,—and it was with much pleasure that a general approbation of the measure seemed to pervade the whole."[9]

On the following day, Thursday, the 30th, Washington noted, "The business which brot. me to Georgetown being finished and the Comrs. instructed with respect. to the mode of carrying the plan into effect, I set off this morning a littel after 4 O'clock, in the prosecution of my journey towards Philadelphia. . . ."

Thereupon the building site for the city took on intense activity. The surveyors were busy marking lines for streets and avenues, trees were cut down, and foundations for buildings were dug. Numerous brick-kilns were built for the making of brick on the spot for the new buildings. There is nothing of record as to any other further developments during the succeeding six weeks. The diaries of Washington from July 5, 1791 to September 30, 1794, are unfortunately missing. However, we do know that L'Enfant devoted more time to perfecting his Plan for the Federal City, embodying the criticisms of President Washington. On August 18, 1791, Secretary of State Jefferson writing from Philadelphia, sent the following significant letter to L'Enfant:

"Sir: The President had understood for some time past that you were coming to Philadelphia & New York, and therefore has delayed mentioning to you some matters which have occurred to him. Will you be so good as to inform me by return of post whether it is still your purpose to come this way, & when, that the President may thereon decide whether he will communicate his ideas by letter, or await your coming to do it by word. If you are detained by laying out the lots you had better not await that, as a suggestion has been made here of arranging them in a particular manner which will probably make them more convenient to the purchasers, and more profitable to the sellers.

'Diaries of Washington, op. cit. Vol. IV., p.p. 199-201.

"A person applied to me the other day on the subject of engraving a map of the Federal territory. I observed to him that if yourself or Mr. Ellicott[10] chose to have this done, you would have the best right to it—do either of you intend this? If you do I would suggest to you the idea of doing it on a square sheet to hang upwards, thus the outlines being N.W. N.E. S.E. S.W. the meridians will be vertical as they ought to be; the streets of the city will be horizontal and vertical, & near the center, the Potomac and the Eastern branch will be nearly so also; here will be no waste in the square sheet of paper. This is suggested merely for your consideration.

"I am with much esteem Sir, Yours etc.
Thomas Jefferson."

L'Enfant having arrived in Philadelphia a few days before August 27th, was asked to call upon the President" . . . . about 5 o'clock or from that to 6 . . ." on that date. He was also invited to dine at Mr. Jefferson's "with him and Mr. Madison alone at half after three tomorrow" (dated Wednesday August 31).

To quote Elizabeth S. Kite, in her *L'Enfant and Washington,* pages 66-72, *passim.*

"In journeying to Philadelphia, L'Enfant had two very definite objects in view: to arrange for the engraving of his 'Plan' and to request the President to call a conference in order that certain important points might be discussed for carrying it out. In order for the distinctive character of the 'Plan' to be maintained, L'Enfant felt it imperative that there be from the very start a simultaneous development of all the salient features of the city; moreover he had very cogent reasons for desiring the sale of lots to be deferred. The Memoir which accompanied the 'Plan' contained a detailed account of his ideas on these different heads.

"Owing to the length of the Memoir and its tediousness the ideas contained in it are given here in condensed form.[11]

"Georgetown August 19, 1791.

"Sir: The hight of my ambition is gratified in having met with your approbation in the project of the plan which I now have the honor of presenting to you *agreeable to your direction* [italics added]. There still

---

[10] L'Enfant noted in pencil, "What right could this man have thereto?" From the unpublished letters among the L'Enfant Papers in the Library of Congress.

[11] **Institut Francais de Washington,** Historical Documents, The Johns Hopkins Press, Baltimore, 1929.

remains the fulfillment of the wish to see the execution of the plan effected to the full attainment of your object.

"I shall here beg permission to fix for a moment your attention on a matter which I conceive to be most important for the advancement of the business.

"The annexed plan shows the advancement that has been made since your visit.

"The business has proved more tedious than at first thought owing to the multiplicity of operations in order to determine the acute angles and intersecting lines with exactness. In this process many difficulties have been encountered on account of the felled timber lying in every direction which the proprietors wish to preserve and are unwilling to remove.

"As matters stand—the sites assigned to the Congress House and the President's palace exhibit a sumptuous aspect and claim already the suffrage of crowds of visitors, serving to give a grand idea of the whole. Nevertheless it is greatly to be desired that more be done to render the sale favorable as the beauties of the locality are lost in a chaos of felled timber without the possibility of being able to judge of the relative advantages to be derived from intended improvements, even after inspecting a map.

"The grand avenue connecting the palace and the Federal House will be magnificent, with the water of the cascade [falling] to the canal which will extend to the Potomac; as also the several squares which are intended for the Judiciary Courts, the National Bank, the grand Church, the play house, markets and exchange, offering a variety of situations unparalleled for beauty, suitable for every purpose, and in every point convenient, calculated to command the highest price at a sale.

"But, as I observed before, a sale this fall is premature, for the land will not bring a tenth part of what it will later. Besides a sale before the general plan is made public and before the whole continent has been notified, will fail through lack of numbers. It will be confined to a few individual speculators who will not be interested to improve the lots; besides the low sale in the first instance may prove injurious to subseqent ones by serving as a precedent. Moreover I apprehend the underselling of lots, far from promoting a speedy settlement will rather disgrace the whole business.

"It will, I am convinced, favor a scheme already encouraged in consequence of the small deposit required, of designing men who, in Georgetown in particular, are more active than ever . . . to cross the operation of the plan adopted, and with others . . . to engross the most of the sale and master the whole business . . .

"So far it has been impossible to make equal division of property between the individual owners and the public . . . they not having returned the survey of their possessions as was repeatedly required of them and which they declined to do until disputes aroused among them respecting the boundary are settled. This precludes for some time proceeding with the work of separation and will prevent devising a mode to effect those lots which will be found laid across the lines of two or three different territories.

"I am convinced it will not delay providing for the necessary accommodation of Congress if we proceed to develop the establishment on the Eastern branch of the proposed canal and the other parts . . . provided that a due attention is given to carrying on in every part those improvements which combine convenience with charm in the outlying situations, as these are meant to lead to the sumptuousness of the more central. When I say 'provided due attention is given' and though I indulge the idea of soon seeing the establishment become the wonder of all—yet I am sensible of the check its progress may receive and am well persuaded that individual exertion will wait on the spirit in which the public business is conducted.

"It being essential to begin well and considering that a relaxation in the forward movement is always more injurious than delay in moving . . . I conceive it important not to confine the building idea to erecting a Congress House and a President's palace . . . other exertions are necessary to set going and to enlarge private undertakings.

"If we are to make of this city a fact it will be indispensable to consider every part of the proposed plan as essential . . . and however unconnected they may appear at first every part should go forward with a proportional degree of despatch.

"Whatever will advance mercantile interests should be pushed with the greatest activity; as the canal from the Tiber to the Eastern branch which is absolutely necessary in order to insure a speedy settlement of that part and to help convey the material to the two grand edifices.

"*The making of the public walk from under the Federal House to the Potomac and connected with the palace* . . . will be productive of equal advantages with the foregoing as it *will give to the city from the very beginning a superior charm over most of those of the world* [italics added] as it will likewise be an improvement over all in point of convenience of distribution . . . After bringing the various squares to their intended shape, leveling every grand avenue and principal street . . . and extending the improvements in a way to attract settlements thereon, there will be no necessity of hastening to encourage them to chuse the best situations, which it may be well to preserve until the great rise in their value makes it worth the sacrifice.

"These ideas . . . which met with your approbation at the beginning, having directed my attention to devising a plan of distribution of localities has made me consider the idea of appropriating several squares to be allotted to each of the several states and also the making a free donation to every particular religious society of ground for a house of worship. A move from which infinite advantage must result.

"Betwixt the two edifices, the streets from the grand avenue to the palace and towards the canal will be proper for shops . . . which undoubtedly will increase in a short time to a number sufficient to meet the needs of every one . . .

"Methods so out of the ordinary for developing a town will presumably meet with your opposition and be objected to by others. As it may effect public speculation in public property many will decide against the idea . . . but confident that in the end this system will prove best able to promote real prosperity, I feel the more encouraged to submit my ideas thereon to your judgment.

"As to the means necessary to secure the success of the system I will observe that however extensive, proportioned to the magnitude of the undertaking, yet I consider the property at your disposal fully proportioned to the object—if attention is given to managing it.

"15,000 lots will fall in the share of the public as half of the property left for improvements after deduction is made for streets and for ground appropriated to public uses. These lots will be of various sizes from 66 feet to 37 in front and from 4 to 7 in an acre. The sum that will arise must be immense but as I observed before—only if it is cautiously managed. For if the most valuable lots are offered on low terms, it would in my opinion prove as destructive to the attainment of the grand object as would a timorous survey tending to lessen the planned measurements . . . For to look upon the property at this moment as a source of supply and to use it to defray the first expenses would be to destroy the capital from the very beginning.

"From these considerations, and viewing the matter in this light, being persuaded that money is the wheel to give motion to the machine . . . I shall now call your attention to the advantages which may be expected from borrowing a sum on the credit of the property itself.

"Under the facility of a loan there would be no hurry to dispose of lots, and it would then be possible to appropriate a sum to each particular object so that all could progress regularly and at the same time.

"Thus every improvement could be completed without restraint of petty saving, and every private undertaking could be assisted where a reciprocity of benefit would ensue. This mode of proceedure I venture to assert, would in the end bring three to one for the money expended and would raise the reputation of the undertaking to a degree of splendor and greatness unprecedented that would in turn increase the population, develop commerce and in a short time raise the city to one of the first the world contains.

"In this manner, and in this manner only, I conceive the business may be brought to a certainty of success. *It was my wish to delineate a plan*

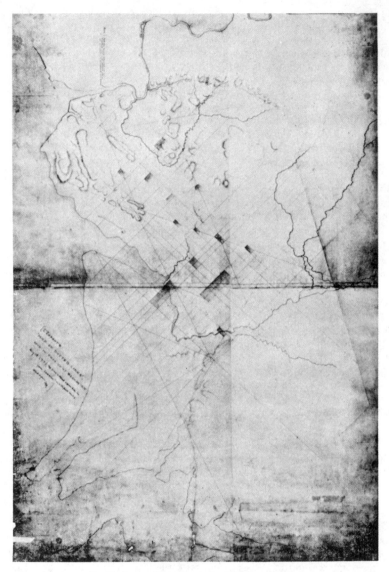

Preliminary Sketch of the L'Enfant Plan

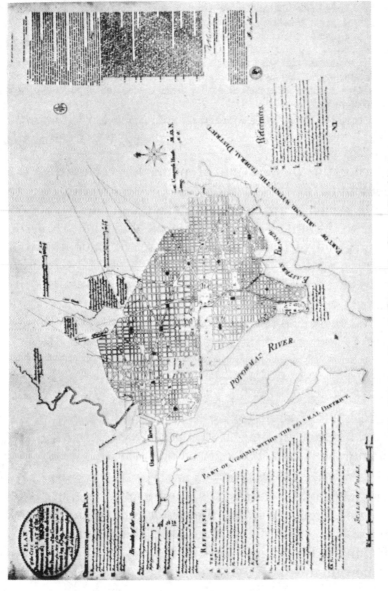

The L'Enfant Plan of 1791 for the City of Washington

wholly new and which combined on a grand scale will require more than ordinary exertions but not more than is within your power to procure. And as I remain assured you will conceive it essential *to pursue with dignity an undertaking of a magnitude so worthy of the concern of a grand empire,* [italics added] I have not hesitated to express myself freely, realizing that the nation's honor is bound up in its complete achievement and that over its progress the nations of the world, watching with eyes of envy, themselves having been denied the opportunity, will stand as judge.

"I have the Honor to be with respect and submission, Your, etc.

(Signed) P. C. L'Enfant."[12]

During the preparation of plans for celebrating the Bicentennial of the Birthday of George Washington in 1932, a sketch drawing was discovered among papers relating to Mount Vernon, and Col. Lawrence Martin, former Chief of the Division of Maps of the Library of Congress, contended that this sketch, a print of which is published herein, (page 160) was the one submitted by L'Enfant to President Washington on August 19, 1791, referred to in the above quoted Memorial. The Report of the Librarian of Congress for the year 1934 contains a report by Col. Martin concerning the sketch, and it is included in the Appendix D of the volume, page 428). The writer takes the view that this sketch was submitted to President Washington by L'Enfant during his visit at Mount Vernon, in June, 1791, heretofore referred to; and it would thus seem but natural that the sketch was left with "Mount Vernon papers".

In view of the detailed character of L'Enfant's Memorial of August 19, 1791, the writer concurs in the views expressed by Miss Kite that the "Plan" presented by L'Enfant to President Washington on that date "is the one now in the possession of the Map Division of the

---

[12] Ibid.

Library of Congress . . ." It is the plan which was prepared for the engraver and contains the copious notes of
L'Enfant explaining the Plan (Published by the *Gazette
of the United States,* Philadelphia, January 4, 1792), as
follows:

"PLAN OF THE CITY, INTENDED FOR THE PERMANENT SEAT
OF GOVERNMENT OF THE UNITED STATES, PROJECTED
AGREEABLE TO THE DIRECTION OF THE PRESIDENT OF
THE UNITED STATES, in pursuance of an ACT of CONGRESS
passed the SIXTEENTH DAY OF JULY MDCCXC, ESTABLISH-
ING THE PERMANENT SEAT on the banks of the POTOMAC.
Peter Charles L'Enfant.

Observations Explanatory of the Plan

"I. The positions for the different Grand Edifices, and for the several
Grand Squares or Areas of different shapes as they are laid down, were
first determined on the most advantageious ground, commanding the most
extensive prospects, and the better susceptible of such improvements as
the various intents of the several objects may require.

"II. Lines or Avenues of direct communication have been devised, to
connect the separate and most distant objects with the principal, and to
preserve through the whole a reciprocity of sight at the same time. Attention has been paid to the passing of those leading avenues over the
most favorable ground for prospect and convenience.

"III. North and South lines, intersected by others running due East and
West, make the distribution of the city into streets, squares, etc., and
those lines have been so combined as to meet at certain given points with
those divergent avenues, so as to form on the spaces "first determined,"
the different Squares or Areas which are all proportional in magnitude to
the number of avenues leading to them.

Breadth of the Streets

"Every Grand transverse Avenue, and every principal divergent one,
such as the communication from the President's House to the Congress
House etc. are 160 feet in breadth and thus divided:

10 feet of pavement on each side	20
30 feet of gravel walk planted with trees on each side	60
80 feet in the middle for carriage way	80
	160 feet

"The other streets are of the following dimensions viz.
Those leading to public buildings or markets   130
Others   110

"In order to execute the above plan, Mr. Ellicott drew a true Meridional line by celestial observation, which passes through the area intended for the Congress House, this line he crossed by another due East and West, which passes through the same area. These lines are accurately measured, and made the bases on which the whole plan was executed. He ran all the lines by a transit instrument and determined the acute angles by actual measurement, and left nothing to the uncertainty of the compass.

REFERENCES

"A. THE equestrian figure of GEORGE WASHINGTON, a Monument voted in 1783 by the late Continental Congress.

"B. An historic Column—also intended for a Mile or itinerary Column, from whose station (a mile from the Federal house) all distances of places throughout the Continent to be calculated.

"C. A Naval itinerary Column, proposed to be erected to celebrate the first prize of a Navy and to stand a ready Monument to consecrate its progress and achievements.

"D. This Church is intended for national purposes, such as public prayer, thanksgiving, funeral orations etc., and assigned to the special use of no particular Sect or denomination, but equally open to all. It will be likewise a proper shelter for such monuments as were voted by the late Continental Congress for those heroes who fell in the cause of liberty, and for such others as may hereafter be decreed by the voice of a grateful Nation.

"E. Five grand fountains intended with a constant spout of water. N. B. There are within the limits of the City above 25 good springs of excellent water abundantly supplied in the direst season of the year.

"F. Grand Cascade, formed of water from the sources of the Tiber.

"G. Public walk, being a square of 1200 feet, through which carriages may ascend to the upper Square of the Federal House.

"H. Grand Avenue, 400 feet in breadth, and about a mile in length, bordered with gardens, ending in a slope from the houses on each side. This Avenue leads to Monument A and connects the Congress Garden with the

"I. President's park and the

"K. well-improved field, being a part of the walk from the President's house of about 1800 feet in breadth, and ¾ of a mile in length. Every lot deep-colored read with green plots, designates some of the situations which command the most agreeable prospects, and which are the best calculated for spacious houses and gardens, such as may accomodate foreign Ministers etc.

"L. Around this Square and all along the

"M. Avenue from the two bridges to the Federal House, the pavement on each side will plass under an Arched way under whose cover Shops will be most conveniently and agreeably situated. This street is 160 feet in breadth and a mile in length.

The Squares colored yellow, being fifteen in number, are proposed to be divided among the several States of the Union, for each of them to improve, or subscribe a sum additional to the value of the land; that purpose and the improvements around the Square to be completed in a limited time.

The center of each Square will admit of Statues, Columns, Obelisks, or any other ornament such as the different States may choose to erect: to perpetuate not only the memory of such individuals whose counsels or Military achievements were conspicuous in giving liberty and independence to this Country; but also those whose usefulness hath rendered them worthy of general imitation, to invite the youth of succeeding generations to tread in the paths of those sages, or heroes whom their country has thought proper to celebrate.

The situation of these Squares is such that they are the most advantageously and reciprocally seen from each other and as equally distributed over the whole City district, and connected by spacious avenues round the grand Fedreal Improvements and as continguous to them, and at the same time as equally distant from each other, as circumstances would admit. The Settlements round those Squares must soon become connected.

This mode of taking possession of and improving the whole district at first must leave to posterity a grand idea of the patriotic interest which prompted it.

"Those figures colored red, are intended for the use of all religious denominations, on which they are to erect places of worship, and are proposed to be allowed to them in the manner as those colored yellow to the different States in the Union, but no burying grounds are to be admitted within the limits of the City, an appropriation being intended for that purpose without.

"N.B. There are a number of squares or areas unappropriated, and in situations appropriate for Colleges and Academies and of which every Society whose object is national can be accomodated.

"Every house within the City will stand square on the Streets, and every lot, even those on the divergent avenues will run square with their fronts, which on the most acute angle will not measure less than 56 feet and many will be above 140 feet."

The Plan of L'Enfant as above outlined, by himself, stamps him for all time as the author of the Plan for the City of Washington and as one of the world's greatest city planners. It must be studied as a whole to be appreciated. And while it was originally intended to acquire approximately 6400 acres, it will be noted that approximately 16 square miles are inscribed in the L'Enfant Plan,—an area about 4 miles square. L'Enfant states the whole "internal content of the district . . . was surveyed in the most minutial (sic) way by the most laborious operations (which no ordinary surveyor of land is called upon to understand)."[13]

Following the submission of the Plan for the Federal City by Major L'Enfant to President Washington, Secretary of State Jefferson thereupon wrote to the Commissioners of the District of Columbia, as follows:

"August 28, 1791

"Gentlemen: Your joint letters . . . as also Mr. Carroll's . . . have been duly received.   Major L'Enfant having also arrived here and laid his plan of the Federal City before the President, he was pleased to desire a conference of certain persons, in his presence, on these several subjects. It is the opinion of the President in consequence thereof that an immediate meeting of the Commissioners at Georgetown is requisite, that certain measures may be decided on and put into a course of preparation for a commencement of sale on the 17th of Octob. as advertised.   As Mr. Madison and myself, who were present at the conference, propose to pass through Georgetown on our way to Virginia, the President supposes that our attendance at the meeting of the Commissioners might be of service to them, as we could communicate to them the sentiments developed at the conference here and approved by the Presidnt. . . . time and distance oblige me to take the liberty of proposing the day of meeting, and to say that we will be in Georgetown on the evening of the 7th or morning of the 8th of next month. . . .

"I have the honor to be etc. etc.,

"(Signed) Th. Jefferson."

---

[13] See L'Enfant Memorial.   L'Enfant Papers, Library of Congress Vol. II, 319-22.

After the meeting above referred to, on September 8th, the Commissioners wrote to Major L'Enfant, as follows:

"Georgetown, September 9, 1791.

"Sir: We have agreed that the Federal district shall be called the 'Territory of Columbia' and the Federal city the 'City of Washington.' The title of the map will therefore be, A Map of the City of Washington, in the Territory of Columbia.

"We have also agreed the streets to be named alphabetically one way and numerically the other, the former divided into north and south letters, the latter into east and west numbers, from the Capitol. Major Ellicott, with proper assistance, will immediately take and soon furnish you with soundings of the Eastern Branch, to be inserted in the map. We expect he will also furnish you with the direction of the post road, which we wish to have noticed on the map . . . ."

"We are, Sir, etc.

"Th. Johnson
"D. Stuart,
"Danl. Carroll."

Here ended we may say the first chapter in the history of the Plan of Washington. It was a creative work of art, and we arrive at this conclusion not only from an examination of the Plan itself, but from an understanding of the letters and other documents set forth in this chapter. Indeed we must admit that the salient points in the Plan of Washington were fixed when L'Enfant reported to President Washington on June 22, 1791. We note particularly the location of the Capitol and the President's House, the Mall and the point of intersection of the axes (near where the Washington Monument stands today).

In the following chapter we shall relate the story of having the Plan of Washington engraved. This led to difficulties, which increased as the succeeding months passed by, and as we shall see, by March, 1792, L'Enfant leaves the work officially, having devoted simply one year, but a year of intensive work, on it. Others, more than a dozen, attempted to change, and possibly even improve, the Plan of L'Enfant. Nevertheless it has retained its essential features throughout the period of its history since 1791.

Chapter VII

PART I

COMPLETION OF THE L'ENFANT PLAN

*T*HE TROUBLES which were going to disappoint L'Enfant so greviously began when the Commissioners of the District of Columbia, in a letter dated September 9, 1791, requested that "10,000 of the maps to be struck on the best terms, and as soon as possible, leaving what number the President pleases subject to his order, one half the residue to be left in Philadelphia, subject to our order for the expenses." While in Philadelphia, L'Enfant had arranged with a French engraver, M. Pigalle, to make an engraving of the plan before October, when the District Commissioners wished to use prints of it in connection with a sale of lots. To his great disappointment M. Pigalle failed in the production of the engraving. L'Enfant wrote to the President's secretary, Tobias Lear, on October 3d, and received the following reply:

"Philadelphia, October 6, 1791.

"Sir: By the post of today I had the pleasure to receive your letter of the 3d instant; and agreeably to your request I immediately called upon Mr. Pigal, who to my great surprise and mortification, informed me that he had not been able to get the plate of copper for the engraving of the federal city, till two days ago, and that, in consequence thereof, it would not be in his power to have a single plate struck off sooner than the last of this month. I pointed out to him, in the strongest manner, the great disappointment, and probable detriment which would be caused by his not having fulfilled his engagement. He appeared fully sensible of it, and expressed the utmost concern, at it; but protested that it was not a

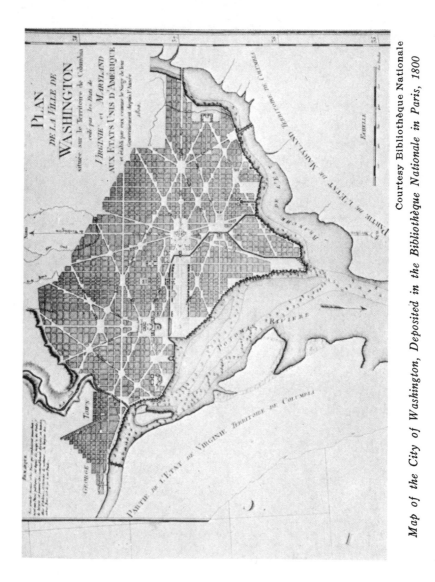

Map of the City of Washington, Deposited in the Bibliothèque Nationale in Paris, 1800

fault of his; he said he has spared no pains to get a plate suitable for the business, and had been deceived in the time of having it prepared for him, altho' he had used every means in his power to get it in time.   He put into my hands the enclosed letter for you, which he says is upon the subject, and requesting to have your large draft of the City, as he does not think that which he has is sufficiently accurate.   I shall call upon him again in the morning and will press him, if it is possible to get some done from the draft which he has—and in almost any manner, before the sale, as I am sensible of the great inconvenience you will suffer by being disappointed.   Nothing in my power to have it effected shall be left undone.

"I am, Sir,
          With great respect & esteem,
                    Your most Obdt. Servt.
To Major P. C. L'Enfant.   Tobias Lear"[1]

At the sale of lots there were no copies of the plan to aid the buyers, but Washington was satisfied that L'Enfant was not to blame for this deficiency.   While the President lauded L'Enfant's ability, it provoked him when he heard that at the sale L'Enfant took care "to prevent the exhibition of the general plan at the spot where the sale was made."

"L'Enfant purchases a lot.   Situated West side 17th St.
                    between H and I Streets, N. W.
"At a public sale of lots in the City of Washington, Peter Charles L'Enfant of Georgetown, Maryland, became purchaser of Lot number thirty in square number one hundred & twenty seven for the consideration of ninety-nine pounds Current Money of Maryland, on the terms and conditions published at same . . . .

                    Wm. Johnson, D. D. Stuart, Danl. Carroll, Commrs."[2]

L'Enfant explained subsequent developments of the plan in one of his Memorials:

"At that time too the particular plan and copper plates by me prepared for engraving in the month of August '91 in Phila. had (by reason of the multiplicity of my other avocations at Washington) been unavoidably delayed and lodged in the best place of safety, into the hands of the Presi-

[1] Records of the Columbia Historical Society, Vol II. p. 156.
[2] Ibid p. 157.

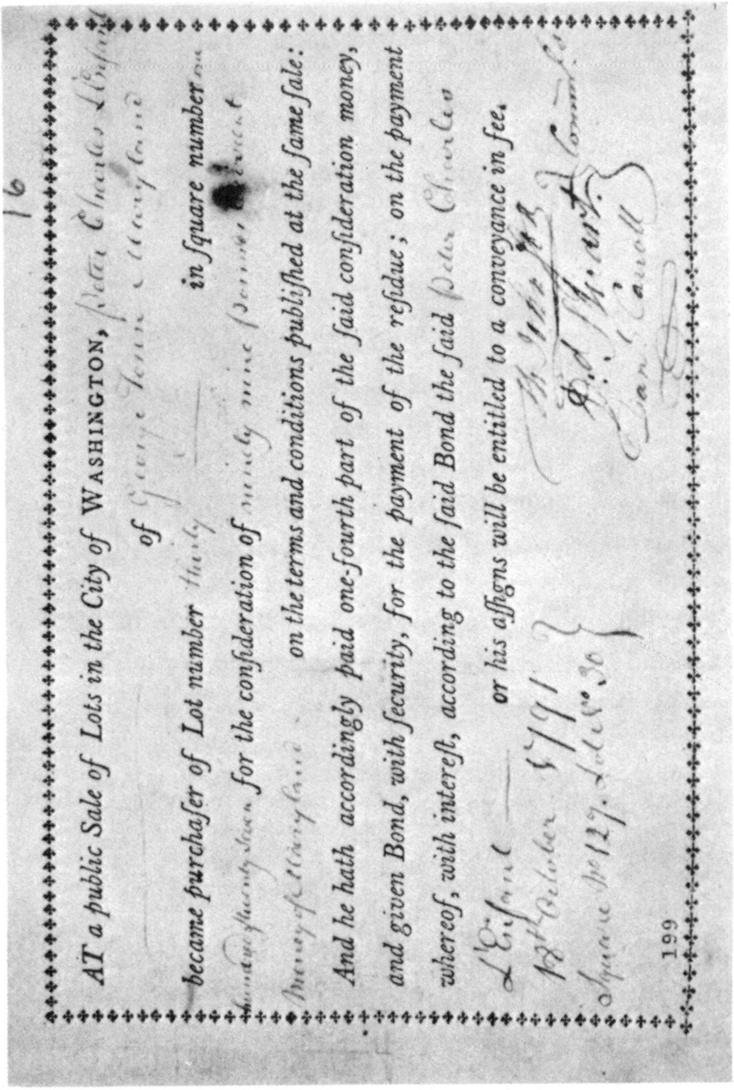

AT a public Sale of Lots in the City of WASHINGTON, Peter Charles L'Enfant

of George Town Maryland

became purchaser of Lot number thirty in square number

for the consideration of

on the terms and conditions published at the same sale:

And he hath accordingly paid one-fourth part of the said consideration money,

and given Bond, with security, for the payment of the residue; on the payment

whereof, with interest, according to the said Bond the said Peter Charles

L'Enfant or his assigns will be entitled to a conveyance in fee.

18th October 1791

Square No 127. Lot No 30

Th. Johnson
Dd Stuart
Danl Carroll
Commissioners

199

Certificate of Sale of Lot to L'Enfant

dent, as is shown in documents No. 1. But although thus protected a number of my drawing copies had been made therefrom without my knowledge such as were seen in both houses of Congress hanging on the Walls in December '91. Others were sent to Europe, viz., to Portugal and even to Petersburg in Russia. The Commissioners by means of an agent at Phil. in a surreptitious way procured the aforesaid plan prepared for engraving as shown by document No. ____, and having effected the engraving prevailed on the President himself to cause the publication whereby having obtained the number of copies they wanted and becoming ultimately possessed of the copper plate they deemed themselves disengaged from the obligation of paying me the value of 10,000 copies, which they had before in an affected manner requested of me as the document No. ___ , which No. proves . . ."

The details of what happened at the sale are best told by L'Enfant himself, who wrote the same evening to Mr. Lear, calling attention to the purchase of a lot desired by Mr. Lear. The following is L'Enfant's letter:

"Georgetown, October 19, 1791.

"Dear Sir: The sale of this day having been directed on one part of the city where I thought a lot might suit your purpose, I gave charge to a friend of mine and your countryman, Mr. Cabott, to bid upon your account and am happy he has been able to obtain the lot I had pointed his attention upon at a much lower price than any of the like have sold for—. This lot is situated on a south exposition—near public square to that of the President and on a direct avenue from the palace to Government . . .

"As far as the sale has gone it has been middling good considering the excessive badness of the weather which much lessened the concurrences, but however pretty large may be the sum it will procure, I cannot say I am otherwise pleased with it, but inasmuch as it set the business in a proper train and will undoubtedly give the whole property a value—as is essential to facilitate a loan being made adequate to the work in contemplation.—This sale upon the whole, far from promoting private building as is necessary to make a city and insure the main object will only be making the sacrifice of a number of lots—the loss of which I the more regret on account of their sale having not been conducted with moderation. A reservation of intermedial lots I thought would be expedient and expected the Commissioners would have considered it so—but they apparently being reduced by bids have lost sight that the consequences of a sale of the whole lots on the one fronts of a square (sic) may in the event prove injurious by diverting from their hands the only means they could secure for forcing at a future time improvements there where the individual proprietor may be interested in delaying them.

"Happily the few squares where the lots have been sold, and the small number of other squares that are in readiness for a sale are so situated as to lessen in a great measure the inconveniency of their remaining 'as will probably be the case' for ages unimproved—otherwise I should reckon this apparent Success a misfortune. The advantageous price obtained for a number of lots, the less advantage in their local being wholly owing to the care I took to prevent the exhibition of the general plan at the spot where the sale is made must convince that enabling individuals to then compare the situation offered for sale with many others apparently more advantageous would have depreciated the value of those lots that sold the most high. This being sufficiently evidenced by the events and acknowldged by every individual concerned 'in the property' the judiciousness of my measure makes me hope the Commissioners would themselves acknowledge the propriety of it were not a mistaken motive for resentment in my opposition to them to interest in their selling contrary to their better judgment. The President himself, considering the advantage which resulted from the attention of bidders being confined on the detached plot of the selected situations of each square where a lot was offered for sale—without having in hand any means to compare them with other situations, will the less regret the picture of the plate I had endeavored to procure—and I rest upon your friendship to convince him from the circumstances known by you, how much I regretted the disappointment. Now respecting to this object, I am most at a loss what to determine as I consider that this plate, intended only for the sale now becomes useless . . . it cannot be completed with that accuracy necessary to make it a map worth sending abroad unless the work is conducted under my eyes, which could not be done until I return to Philadelphia after matters here shall assume winter aspect. If you could advise me what I am to do respecting this I will think it a favor and in the mean while will be obliged to you if you will demand from the engraver every drawing he may have made, and the copper plate he may have begun, to prevent his going forward on private acrount. He received from me $30.00 on account which must be above any claim he can make after having failed in delivering the plate as requested. Pardon for the trouble I am giving you.

"I am Sir,

With great consideration your,

"P. S. Mr. _____ who pressed me for a drawing of the city will probably apply to you for the small draft which with the outlines the engraver has taken from the big map, may enable him to have a copy made answerable to his purpose."[3]

---

[3] L'Enfant-Digges-Morgan Papers, Library of Congress.

One of the Commissioners, Dr. David Stuart, wrote to President Washington regarding the sale of lots:—

"Getown 19th Oct.

"Dear Sir: ——I have to observe that the general opinion is that the lots have gone too high. The chief purchasers yesterday and the day before were from the Eastward—You will understand that they are all actual sales excepting about four among the lowest.

"The weather has been much against us. Could we have been on the ground and exhibited a general plan, I believe it would have aided the sale considerably . . .

"I am dear Sir, Yours, etc.

"P. S. The squares on which sales are made are some distance from the President's house."[4]

The President replied to David Stuart:

"Philadelphia Novr. 20th, 1791.

"Dear Sir: I had heard before the receipt of your letter of the 29th of October and with a degree of surprize & concern not easy to be expressed—that Majr. L'Enfant had refused the Map of the Federal City when it was requested by the Commissioners for the satisfaction of the purchasers at sale.—It is much to be regretted—however common the case is—that men who possess talents which fit them for peculiar purposes should almost unvariably be under the influence of untoward dispositions or are sottish idle—or possessed of some disqualification by which they plague all those with whom they are concerned . . .

"Since my first knowledge of the gentleman's abilities in the line of his profession, I have received him not only as a scientific man, but one who added considerable taste to his professional knowledge; and that, for such employment as he is now engaged in, for projecting public works, and carrying them into eqect, he was better qualified than any one, who had come within my knowledge in this country, or indeed in any other, the probability of obtaining whom could be counted upon."[5]

"I had no doubt, at the same time, that this was the light in which he considered himself, and, of course, that he would be so tenacious of his plans as to conceive, that they would be marred if they underwent any change or alteration; but I did not suppose that he would have interfered further in the mode of selling the lots than by giving an opinion with his reasons in support of it . . .

"I have, however, since I have come to the knowledge of Major L'Enfant's refusal of the map at the sale, given him to understand through a direct channel, though not an official one as yet (further than what casu-

[4] Washington Papers, Library of Congress.
[5] Writings of Washington, Bicentennial Edition, Vol. 31, pp. 419-20.

ally passed between us previous to the sale, at Mount Vernon) that he must in future look to the commissioners for directions . . .

"His pertinacity would, I am persuaded, be the same in all cases and to all men. He conceives, or would have others believe, that the sale was promoted by withholding the general map, and thereby the means of comparison; but I have caused it to be signified to him that I am of a different opinion, and that it is much easier to impede than force a sale, as none who knew what they were about would be induced to buy, to borrow an old adage, '*a pig in a poke.*' . . .

"There has been something very unaccountable in the conduct of the engraver, yet I cannot be of opinion the delays were occasioned by L'Enfant. As soon, however, as a correct draft of the city is prepared, the same or some other person, shall be pressed to the execution . . ."

Within a few days President Washington was to hear of further trouble caused by L'Enfant's quarrel with Daniel Carroll of Duddington, concerning which Washington wrote to Mr. Carroll on November 28th. Some days previously to that date the walls of a large brick house which Mr. Carroll was building for his own use on the square bounded by E, F, 2d Streets, and New Jersey Avenue, S. E., were torn down by L'Enfant's orders as the building extended into New Jersey Avenue and an adjacent reservation. This was done in spite of the commands of the Commissioners and the opposition to the owner, the largest property holder in the city. The controversy has been well related by Miss Elizabeth Kite in her L'Enfant and Washington (pages 80-82) and also mentioned in the Commissioners' letter book—

"Daniel Carroll's Case

"In 1790 the cellar of the house was walled up and stood so the winter—March 30, 1791, he signed the agreement subjecting his property marked A. 27th or 28th of June, 1791, he executed a deed in trust to carry the agreement into effect. The original is in the Office at Annapolis where it was lodged to be recorded, but the paper B is a copy of the trust part of that and the other deeds. (B) In the latter end of August a day or two before Major L'Enfant set out for Philadelphia the northern part of the street was run and struck the house about _____ feet. Major L'Enfant (and several of his Assistants then present) told D. C. that the street was originally intended 110 feet wide, but that Major L'Enfant had said to save the building if that would do it, he would reduce the street to 100 feet. Major Ellicott and all the Assistants seem to have been impressed with, and given the idea that a—alteration conveniently could and would be made to leave the house clear . . . Mr. Carroll afterwards hearing the line of the street had struck the house called on Major Ellicott—Major L'Enfant having set off for Philadelphia, and informed him that he intended to write to the President, that if an alteration could not be made with convenience and propriety Daniel Carroll of Duddington might have notice and desist. On which Major Ellicott answered that an alteration might be made without the least injury to the plan and that he would be answerable that Daniel Carroll of Duddington would be safe . . . On Friday the 13th of November, Doctor 'Stewart' and Mr. Carroll met as Commissioners and agreed to meet again the Friday following. After the adjournment Major L'Enfant meeting with Dr. 'Stewart' told him that he had wrote to Daniel Carroll of Duddington, informing him that his house must come down. Doctor 'Stewart' told him that he hoped he wrote in an accommodating manner, the Major said he had and feeling in his pockets said he was sorry he had not the letter with him. Dr. 'Stewart' told the Major the Commissioners were to meet the following Friday and that if Mr. Carroll did not choose to pull his house down, to lay the letters before the commissioners."

"In 1790, Daniel Carroll of Duddington, then a young man of twenty-seven, had selected an eminence and begun building himself a mansion house before the site of the Capital had been decided upon, and it had progressed so far that the cellar had been dug and the foundations laid. In June 1791 the walls were begun and the work pushed forward notwithstanding the fact that L'Enfant had warned him that the site was required for one of the leading public squares and therefore his work would have to be torn down. Later he notified him in writing, for the site was precisely the square marked E on the 'Grand Plan'. It was to be adorned with 'five grand fountains' with 'constant spout of water'. Indeed the spring which was to supply the water for the fountains was the very one that had attracted Duddington to the spot an that made him so persistent in remaining there. November 29, 1791, his uncle, Daniel Carroll, the Commissioner, wrote James Madison as follows: 'The Major wrote Mr. Carroll in very polite terms to take down his house, being built on public ground. Mr. Carroll for answer informed him that whenever it should be deemed an obstruction in consequence of building in that part of the city, it should be taken down, and that he had written to the President on the subject . . .'

"As the Duddington house plays a major role in determining the fate of the Federal city as well as that of L'Enfant the question of its demolition demands a thorough elucidation. Up to the present L'Enfant has been accused of ordering the house pulled down because its walls protruded into the street. A careful examination of the 'Plan' however shows that Daniel Carroll of Duddington had appropriated for his own purposes an eminence that had been selected from the beginning by L'Enfant, and later approved by the President as one of those focal points essential to the symmetry of the City, and whose simultaneous development up to a certain point, along with the central features of the 'Plan' he had urged in the August memorial. It was not therefore a question of moving the house farther back but of its entire elimination from the selected site. In demolishing the house L'Enfant understood perfectly the legal aspects of the case and took care to keep within the law. Thus the foundation, which had been built before the deed of cession had been signed, belonged to the class of improvement for which the Government engaged to pay; what had gone up since the signing of the deed in April, 1791, was at the owner's risk and not subject to indemnity.

"From the first Mr. Carroll of Duddington and L'Enfant had eyed one another with suspicion; each recognized in the other a will that would bend before no obstacle and their interests were diametrically opposed. Thus a clash was inevitable. L'Enfant had sensed from a very early stage in the work that private interests, so strongly combined on the side of the Commissioners with the two leading proprietors of the Federal District, Notley Young and Daniel Carroll of Duddington, would inevitably supersede those of the Nation at large unless the utmost care and attention were given. In the beginning he had attempted to avoid the issue by ignoring it. Later, however, ever fresh manifestations of partiality on the part of the Commissioners had angered him and there soon grew up a mutual distrust and aversion that deepened as time went on. To the President, who had approved the plan of the city, the Commissioners showed nothing but submission, but in reality resentment was felt for avenues and spacious public squares taken from property belonging to kinsmen. As L'Enfant was responsible for the magnitude of the 'Plan' it is quite certain they wished to induce the President to permit important changes that would reduce the extravagant outlay.

"Since his return from Philadelphia in September, L'Enfant had made many trips up and down the country buying different kinds of building material needed for the city, while his overseer, the young engineer Isaac Roberdeau, carried forward the actual work according to detailed directions from L'Enfant.

"In order to complete the purchase of the Aquia Quarries, L'Enfant made a final trip to Virginia starting out the 23d of November. On that day he dined with Mr. Notley Young and accepted a commission from one of the ladies to carry a letter to a relative at the place whither he was going. It was at this time that the demolition of the Duddington house was begun. Two days earlier L'Enfant had written the Commissioners:

"Georgetown, Nov. 21, 1791.

"In pursuance of the measures first taken and of which I took the liberty of informing you by last post, respecting the house of Mr. Carroll of Duddington which may become necessary to have destroyed, he not having acquiesced to proceed himself as requested to the demolishing—In lieu of answering my last summons having set out on a journey—I directed yesterday forenoon a number of hands to the spot and employed with them some of the principle people who had worked in raising the house to the end that every possible attention be paid to the interests of the gentleman as shall be consistent in forwarding the public object.

"The roof is already down with part of the brickwork and the whole will I expect be leveled to the ground before the week is over; this operation facilitating the laying out of that part of the city as is proper to close the process of this and prepare for the next campaign. My wish to avail of the good weather still continuing has induced me to prevail on Mr. Ellicott to remain here a fortnight longer, . . . wishing to take every possible advantage of the season I cannot see [to] the various other objects which demand I should also give an immediate attention, . . . without regretting the want of possibility . . . so as to effect both at once. A complete engraving of the plan and complete drawing and copy of the grand plan are two objects impossible to effect here and cannot be overturned to them unless I spare the grand plan by which the operations here are to be regulated and unless I leave the business here to pursue in Philadelphia objects which I conceive you are most desirous of—the one for the information of the public, the other to be handed to Congress— Neither of these can be done without I can spare the original map which will be wanted here until the work before mentioned is completed, nor can it well be effected without I am in a situation to direct the work a circumstance the consideration of which leads me to accelerate the completion of all that requires my attendance so that work may be mapped out for the hands [so] that [they] may be continuing in employment through the whole winter . . ."

The Commissioners of the District of Columbia replied to this letter as follows:

"Georgetown, Nov. 26, 1791.

"Sir: On our meeting this day we were equally surprised and concerned to find that you had proceeded to demolish Mr. Carroll's house. We were impelled by many considerations to give immediate directions to those acting in your absence to desist.—We must observe to you, that allowing the measure to have been absolutely necessary, and such an one as Mr. Carroll might be compelled to acquiesce in from the terms he entered into, still our opinion ought to have been previously taken on a subject so delicate and so interesting.

  "We are Sir,
   Your obt. serts.
    (signed David Stuart
     Daniel Carroll, Commissioners"

On November 21st Daniel Carroll of Duddington had by letter of that date laid the entire matter concerning Major L'Enfant's action before the President. The President, with characteristic loyalty to the Commissioners of the District of Columbia, stated in his reply of November 28th to Mr. Carroll that he would rather Mr. Carroll had made his appeal to the Commissioners, but feeling that the exigencies of the occasion made it highly important to bring about a speedy settlement of the affair before it should give rise to rumors of controversy in connection with the federal city, he took up the matter in person and proposed two alternatives for Mr. Carroll's choice: first, to have the Commissioners complete the demolition of the building and rebuild it, the following spring, in line with the street, to the height it had attained; second, to let Mr. Carroll rebuild it at his own expense and occupy it six years, at which time it should be removed; allowance to be made only for the value of the walls at the time they were torn down.

President Washington, having heard of the trouble, wrote to L'Enfant as follows:

          "Philadelphia, Novr. 28th, 1791.

"Dear Sir: Your letter of the 21st instant came duly to hand, as did one of the same date from Mr. Carroll of Duddington, on the same subject, A copy of my answer to the latter is enclosed; by which you will perceive I have proposed an accommodation—As a similar case cannot happen again (Mr. Carroll's house having been begun before the Federal District was fixed upon) no precedent will be established by yielding a little in the present instance; and it will always be found sound policy to conciliate the good will rather than provoke the enmity of any man, where it can be accomplished without much difficulty, inconvenience or loss.

"Indeed the more harmoniously this, or any other business is conducted, the faster it will progress, and the more satisfactory will it be.

"Should Mr. Carroll adopt the first alternative mentioned in my letter to him—and there is no pressing cause for taking the building down this winter, the materials will be less liable to injury by standing as they are, and less apt to be stolen, than if they should be taken down before the period shall arrive for re-erection.—

"As there is a suspension at present of the business which took Mr. Ellicott's brother to Georgia, there will be no occasion for his proceeding thither, until he shall receive further advice from me, or from the Department of War. But it is my *earnest* wish, and desire, that he would give every aid in his power to prepare for a large sale of lots in the Spring; agreeably to the sentiments which have been communicated to the Commissioners; and it is moreover exceedingly to be wished, that correct engravings of the City be had, and properly disseminated (at least) throughout the United States before such sale.

"A great pressure of business at this time prevents me from adding more than that I am, &c."

President Washington expressed his views in the matter to Secretary of State Jefferson in the following letter:

"Nov. 30th, 1791.

"My dear Sir: Mr. L'Enfant's letter of the 19th of October to Mr. Lear—Mr. Lear's answer of the 6th instant (the press copy of which is so dull as to be scarcely legible)—in which I engraved sentiments of admonition, and with a view also to feel his pulse under reprehension. His reply of the 10th to that letter, together with the papers I put into your hands when here, will give you a full view of the business; and the Major's conduct; and will enable you to judge from the complexion of things how far he may be spoken to in decisive terms without losing his services; which, in my opinion, would be a serious misfortune. At the same time he must know, there is a line beyond which he will not be that lead him into such blameable conduct, I will not take upon me to suffered to go. Whether it is zeal—an impetuous temper, or other motives decide—but be it what it will, it must be checked; or we shall have no Commissioners, I am, &c."

Again, on December 2, 1791, President Washington wrote to L'Enfant, this time a very stern letter:

"Philadelphia, Dec. 2, 1791.

"Sir: I have received with sincere concern the information from yourself as well as others that you have proceeded to demolish the house of Mr. Carroll of Duddington against his consent, and without authority from the Commissioners or any other person. In this you have laid yourself open to the Laws, and in a Country where they will have their course. To their animadversion will belong the present case.

"In future I must strictly enjoin you to touch no man's property without his consent, or the previous order of the Commissioners. I wished you to be employed in the arrangements of the Federal City. I still wish it: but only on condition that you can conduct yourself in subordination to the authority of the Commissioners, to whom by law the business is entrusted, and who stand between you and the President of the United States—to the laws of the land—and to the rights of its citizens.

"Your precipitate conduct will, it is to be apprehended, give serious alarm, and produce disagreeable consequences. Having the beauty and regularity of your plan only in view, you pursue it as if every person & thing were *obliged* to yield to it. whereas the Commissioners have many circumstances to attend to, some of which perhaps, may be unknown to you; which evinces in a strong point of view the propriety, the necessity, and the safety of your acting by their directions.

"I have said, and I repeat to you again, that it is my firm belief, that the gentlemen now in Office have favourable dispositions towards you; and in all things reasonable and proper will receive and give full weight to your opinions:—and, ascribing to your *Zeal* the mistakes that have happened—I persuade myself under this explanation of matters that nothing in future will intervene to obstruct the harmony which ought to prevail in so interesting a Work.

"With sincere esteem, I am, &c."[6]

On December 6, 1791, L'Enfant had written to the Commissioners of the District of Columbia, giving a full explanation of his reasons for demolishing the house of Mr. Carroll of Duddington. As Dr. Charles Moore has said (for fifty years devoted to the L'Enfant Plan and the Development of the National Capital), if General Washington had been here instead of in Philadelphia, this would not have happened; the integrity of the Plan was at stake, since L'Enfant contended for a prin-

---

[6] Records of the Columbia Historical Society, Vol. 17, pp. 39-40.

ciple, sacrificing his future welfare to the maintenance of the Plan he had made for the Federal City:

"Georgetown, December 6th, 1791.

"Gent: On my return from Acquia where I have made purchase of a quarry ground conformably to what had been agreed at your previous meeting—I received your favor of the 26th Nov. informing me you had given direction to the gentlemen acting in my absence to desist from demolishing a house Mr. Carroll of Duddington was about building.

"Conceiving from this circumstance you supposed these gentlemen were acting of their own accord, or that you must have lost sight of the peculiar circumstance condemning the undertaking of Mr. Carroll of D.—I must here in justice to these gentlemen certify that I had given them positive order for pulling down the house, the removal of which had become necessary and wishing you not to misconceive the motives which had determined me to the measure and which have made me pursue in it with steady activity since my return to this place, I will state to you the following particulars.

"The peculiar circumstances attending the undertaking of Mr. Carroll of Duddington—together with his manifest disposition to contravene his engagement and to oppose the progress of operations—being sufficiently known you could not but be satisfied I acted with propriety on proceeding as I have done. Had that house been one of those improvements the removal of which in complyance with the contract between the individual and the public would have required a provisory estimate of its value, I would doubtless referred the circumstance to your Board and would have suspended the operation until matters had been adjusted between you and the individual concerned—but this not being necessary in the case of Mr. Carroll a different mode of process was expedient and proper and the mode I have pursued, it must be allowed, has been more delicate than his right to expect, having offered him a fair opportunity to oppose—at least to contest an immediate operation. I wrote to him twice stating the circumstances and the obligation I was under 'as charged with the execution of the plan' to proceed to the demolishing of the house in case he should decline or delay availing himself of the alternative I offered him to effect this himself.

"It was him *(sic)* then, if he thought himself wrongly used, who ought to have required the interference of your Board—but it was not my business to call your attention on the matter. Besides I could not at the time have done this with any propriety—since on a former occasion when a foresight of the circumstance in which this house has finally been found to stand—induced me to intimate my opinion of the propriety of using with it as I have done—one of your gentlemen, Mr. Daniel Carroll, declared that if a question was put respecting that business, for the Board to determine upon, he would not here act as Commissioner; as at the moment I proceeded only two of you being available to be called together, Mr. D. Carroll could not consistently with his declaration take up the matter. As a single member [does not] constitute a Board, nothing could have been determined.

"It was necessary and expedient that the measure should be proceeded to with alacrity. It was proper—*as I proceeded to it of right and with as much confidence as in directing a tree to be cut down or a rock to be removed where obstructive to the operation or impediments in the streets.* (italics added.)

"If the way of process 'in any of these cases' a trespass has been made on any of the individuals as injurious, it is to me, not to the persons employed, to whom opposition is to be made—and in every of my steps in regard to the public as well as to the individual rights—complaints from whatever quarter they may come—when founded on reason—have and will ever meet me ready to redress & whenever the matter will be of a nature as to require your interference you will always find me disposed to respect the authority vested in you by law.

"In this instance the magnitude of the object to remove . . . constituted its importance. The novelty of the case has, I conceive, raised your aprehensions and I take account how one of the gentlemen of your Board, close connection of Mr. Carroll of Duddington, must have interested you . . . [in] the event and led you to consider the undertaking delicate and of consequence for you to determine upon.

"After mature consideration you will no doubt have conceived the matter in a more proper light—you will have seen that since effecting the removal was a measure no way hazarded nor contestable, no occasion was for me to refer the measure to your consideration—and as I doubt not you you have as much at heart the speedy advancement of the great work on hand as I have, I trust you will see the propriety of your never interfering with the process of execution, but in case when an appeal to you from individuals may be justly grounded. For it is constant that in other cases it would answer to no other end but that of lengthening the operation in disaffecting the people employed.

"In the present case of Mr. D. Carroll of Duddington it would only have served as a precedent to others to contest every step of the people employed in laying out the city, the progress of which has already been materially impeded in consequence of the strict attention which has been paid in preparing (where ever possible) every convenience to an individual proprietor.

"The building of Mr. C. of D. was erected in contrariety *(sic)* to the plan adopted and throwing it down was doing justice to all individuals concerned in the prosperity within the city and it has been effected without a violation of a right of property; a difference and a wide one too being to be made in the case of that house, from that of touching a man's property without his consent.

"This exposal of the considerations and reasons which has and ever will be made the rule of my conduct, being wholly to convince you that I have acted consistently . . . I hope from this explanation . . . that nothing in future will intervene to disturb the harmony and good understanding which it is desirable may prevail amongst all the concerned in so interesting a work.

"I have the honor to be

"P.S. I have ordered the rubbish to be cleared out of the foundation of the house demolished and directed this foundation should remain for your inspection. As that part of the building having been raised previous to the compact between the public and individuals Mr. C. is entitled to a reimbursement for that part. I request therefore you will settle with him for that foundation which it is necessary should be soon removed." [7]

In the meantime copies of the L'Enfant Plan were made (as we learn later from L'Enfant's Memorials) and were exhibited in the House of Representatives and the Senate chambers, being submitted by President Washington with the following Message:

"United States,
December 13 ,1791.

"*Gentlemen of the Senate and of the House of Representatives:*—

"I place before you the plan of a city that has been laid out within the district of 10 miles square, which was fixed upon for the permanent seat of the Government of the United States.

"Go. Washington." [8]

On the same date President Washington sent another letter to L'Enfant as follows; advising him that he must operate under orders from the Commissioners:

"Philadelphia,
December 13, 1791.

"Sir: I have received your letter of the 7th instant, and can only once more, and now for all, inform you, that every matter and thing which has relation to the federal district, and the city within it, is committed to the Commissioners appointed agreeably to the 'Act for establishing the temporary and permanent seat of the Government of the United States' that

[7] Kite, L'Enfant and Washington, pp. 85-89.
[8] Records of the Columbia Historical Society, Vol. 17, p. 40.

it is from them you are to derive your powers—and the line of demarca
tion for your government is to be drawn by them.

"You may remember, Sir, that the first official notice you had of the
business in which you are now engaged, was from one of these Commissioners—namely, Mr. Carroll; and that a supposed impropriety in his
acting whilst a member of Congress occasioned a suspension, until a
renewal of his commission, after his term of Service in that body had
ezpired.

"Had it not been for this circumstance, all the directions you would
have received on your way to George-town would have been from him.
All you have received since ought to have been from them.

"This is the reason why I have said to you in a former letter, that the
Commissioners stand between you and the President of the United States,
—they being the persons from whom alone you are to receive your directions.

"Were it necessary I would again give it to you as my opinion that the
Commissioners have every disposition that can be desired to listen to your
suggestions—to adopt your plans—and to support your authority for
carrying the latter into effect, as far as it shall appear reasonable, just &
prudent to them,—and consistent with the powers under which they act
themselves. But having said this in more instances than one, it is rather
painful to reiterate it.

"With esteem, & regard, I am, &c

"P. S. Since writing the foregoing letter, yours of the 10th is come
to hand. As you are well acquainted with mine, as well as the earnest
wishes of the Commissioners, to have the work forwarded with all the
dispatch the nature of it will admit, I persuade myself that nothing will be
wanting on your part, or the part of Mr. Ellicott, to hasten the execution.

G. W."[9]

Mr. Carroll, having considered the President's alternative propositions, as above mentioned, accepted the one
providing for the reconstruction of his house by the Commissioners; but when this became known to the proprietors, they addressed a vigorous protest to the Commissioners, who referred it to the President, by whom in turn
it was referred, together with the statement of the case
and other pertinent documents, to the Attorney General.
The Attorney General ruled and it was so decided to pay

[9] Ibid, pp. 40-41.

Mr. Carroll the value of the materials in his house at the
time of its destruction.   The matter was later (June 4,
1792) settled by the payment of L1679 12 sh, 3 d.
($4500.)

The controversy about the Daniel Carroll of Duddington house abated; the Commissioners said nothing more
to him about the house.   They knew they had the President on their side and it seems they now preferred to
remain friendly with L'Enfant.   It seemed to L'Enfant
that he had won his point.   With renewed energy therefore he pushed forward preparations for the work during
the coming winter.   On December 16th he wrote to his
faithful assistant Roberdeau, as follows:

"My dear Sir:

"Your activity and zeal in forwarding your share of the work done in
the Federal City this last season making me hope you will cheerfully
continue giving your attendance throughout the whole winter & see that
all the hands employed do their work with assiduity as far as the
intempery (*sic*) of the season will allow.   While I shall remain absent I
have to recommend to your particular care the following objects: viz.

"To repair immediately to Acquia Creek to see the qurries there
belonging to the public—to have barracks erected thereon for twenty
men on each of these quarries; viz, on the island purchased from Mr.
George Brent & on that rented from Mr. John Gibson of Dumphries. . . .

"The exporting of stone must be begun at once on both quarries; they
must be opened at once all round the island and on the main [land], on
the whole front adjoining to the creek.   The stone must be taken down
as it comes and of any size and in as great quantity as the time will
admit, recommending only that when the rock will be pound sound and
free from staion that blocks of stone be extracted therefrom of the largest size every way as is possible.

"When arrived at Philadelphia I shall send you the particular dimensions of some stone — but without waiting let the hands do the most they
can — when the weather shall prove too severe let them busy themselves
in clearing away the rubble and as soon as often as it moderates let them
set about extracting the stones —

"As to what is to be done in the city, the first object must be building
barracks for 600 or 800 men in four different positions — on the Federal
square or contiguous to it where most convenient for water — for 100

men; on the President's square-do- for 100 men; near the mouth of Rock Creek for 50 men; central to the two grand buildings and at projecting of the intended canal for 100 men; on the grand square above the market barracks for the commissary, store for provisons etc. and opposite for men.—

"The timber necessary for this you may take from Mr. L — wood he having agreed to receive payment for what shall be employed and for a fair valuation thereof. Mr. Burns also proposes to let us have all the wood that will be necessary for the use of the commissary & at 8 s. the cord. This matter I beg you will arrange so that no difficulties arise and no wasting of wood takes place.

"Axe-men must also be kept in constant employment in cutting down and clearing timber from the streets that are now run and where ever the individual proprietors will agree to preserve the trunks of trees, these trunks must be [laid] lengthly way on the side of the street so as to leave a free passage.

"Diggers must also be set about digging on the Federal Square carrying a level across of that part laid out for the building—the area of which must. be excavated to the level of the lowest part of the ground in the ditch as it now stands; wheelbarrows for this will be necessary — Mr. Cabot has taken charge of having a few made. Enquire for them of Mr. Green and apply to the Commissioners for them to hasten the contract for a number which I will require them to procure.

"In all matters which will require supply of money or of provisions send a retuen *(sic)* of your wants to the Commissioners, but if they were absent or that in the execution of this òrder somè delay should appear, let nothing interfere with the work; it must be pursued without interruption. With 40 or 50 men in the city, and twenty-five in the quarries, until I shall write you what further may be done when the season shall be more advanced.

"You will not forget the timber wheel and if you know any person who will be willing to contract for working 100 or 200 wheelbarrows introduce the person to the Commissioners.

"I hope to receive information of what may occur to you of the progress of the work — and will at all times be happy of hearing from you.

"I am, with friendship and regard,

P. C. L'Enfant.[10]

The L'Enfant Plan has as one of its unique features a "square" set apart (at the site of the Pan American Union building), destined for the home of one of the

---

[10] L'Enfant-Digges-Morgan Papers, Library of Congress.

original proprietors, David Burnes, with whom it is said General Washington had his difficulties, and to whom he referred as "even the obdurate Mr. Burnes." The following letter from L'Enfant to Burnes, indicates the friendly feeling between the two:

"Georgetown, Dec. 21, 1791.

"Dear Sir: Agreeable to your request of yesterday the square on the which you desire to erect a house will be marked out so as to enable you to proceed as conveniently and as immediately as you please in laying the foundation. Should the manufacture of the quantity of brick you propose making require more clay than will come out of the foundation you may safely dig out of the street the quantity you want . . . providing you erect all your brick kiln within the area of the square on which your building is to stand.

"This square . . . will border on one of the main diagonal avenues [Virginia Avenue] to the President's palace. It will have a front on part of the square of the palace & will also view on the grand park . . . so that it will be worth your attention to have the house of a proper dimension of fronts and in every respect combined conformably with the plan of intended improvements because you are to consider that the house in helping the advancement of these improvements will accelerate the rise of value of your other property, and besides that it being eligibly situated, well-contrived & with a convenient distribution . . . will enable you to rent it or dispose of it to better advantage.

"As I suppose it will be your wish to reserve the whole of the area of the square upon which you will build, this will be perfectly at your option by your resigning 'in exchange' to the public an area of equal dimensions on the opposite diagonal avenue. . . . I should be glad, Sir, to know your determination on this and if you agree to fix your house so as to make it a contribution to the execution of the proposed improvements I will with pleasure design for you a plan combined with those improvements and will besides attend to the construction & in all parts where the public may derive some advantage from your exertions you may rest assured of being assisted, and that whatever ornamental work will be necessary for the outside . . . shall be effected without incurring you in expense beyond what you shall have fixed upon and as shall be adequate to the object you propose.

"I have the honor to be etc.,

P. C. L'Enfant.[11]

The tactful instinct of L'Enfant became manifest in

---

[11] Kite, L'Enfant and Washington, pp. 100-101.

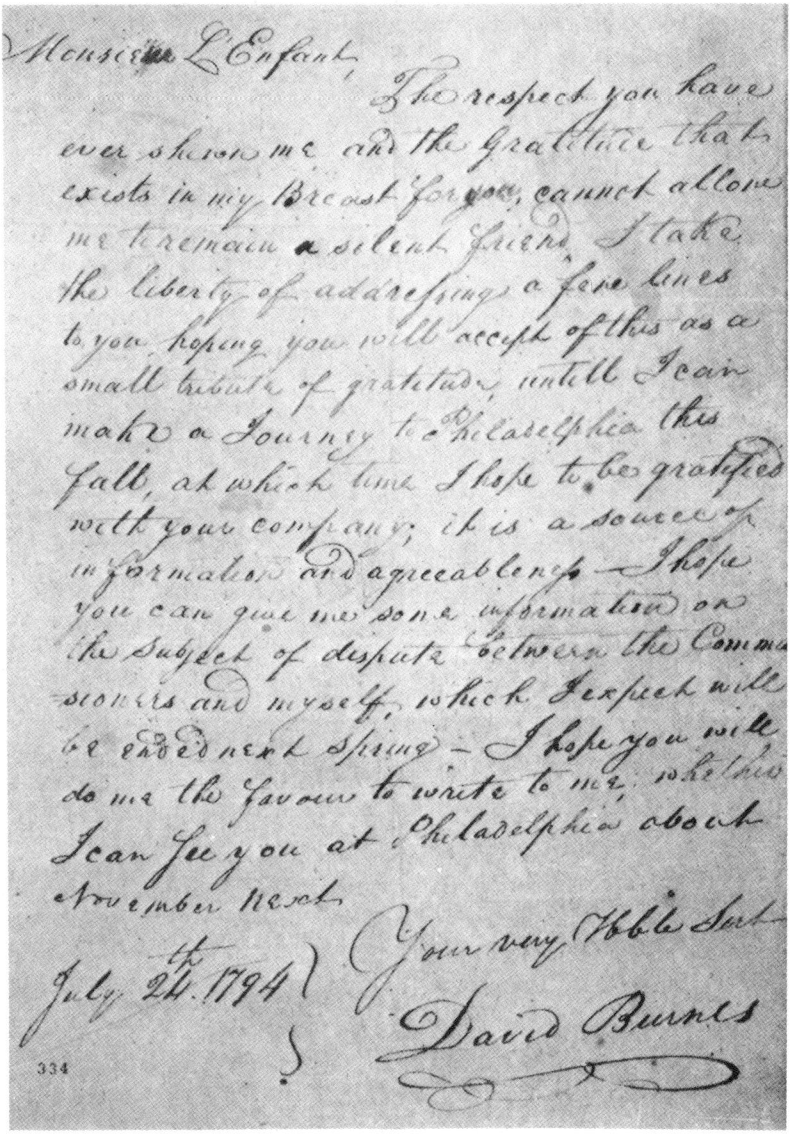

Monsieur L'Enfant,

The respect you have ever shown me and the Gratitude that exists in my Breast for you, cannot allow me to remain a silent friend. I take the liberty of addressing a few lines to you hoping you will accept of this as a small tribute of gratitude, untill I can make a Journey to Philadelphia this fall, at which time I hope to be gratified with your company; it is a source of information and agreeableness — I hope you can give me some information on the Subject of dispute between the Commissioners and myself, which I expect will be ended next Spring — I hope you will do me the favour to write to me, whether I can see you at Philadelphia about November next.

July 24th 1794

Your very Hble Servt

David Burnes

334

Letter of Appreciation from David Burnes to L'Enfant

another instance when it was found the house of another original proprietor, Notley Young, encroached on the Plan for the Federal City. L'Enfant wrote to the Commissioners of the District of Columbia, as follows:

"Georgetown, Dec. 22, 1791.

"Gentlemen: One of the streets lately to be run being unavoidable to strike on the house of Mr. Notley Young and of course render it a nuisance in the city — I have the honor of informing you of the circumstance & to request you may adjust matters with Mr. Notley Young so as to insure the house may be removed when necessary; I see no necessity at present to proceed immediately to the removal — because that house lay on the extreme end of a street and can in no way interfere with the operation of the street; tho in a main avenue leading to one of the principal public squares . . . there is no probability of a speedy settlement taking place — therefore it will be sufficient at present to notify Mr. Notley Young that his house will be subject to be removed at a period which I conceive may safely be fixed at 7 years — postponing to that time the evaluation. . . . as it will be much more to the advantage of the public and equally just to the proprietor concerned to defer this until the time of the removal . . . as the natural decay of the building will diminish its value.

"Should however Mr. Notley Young be willing to engage to rebuild another house in a situation where the aspect may benefit the general improvement of the city, I should be of opinion that in that case it would be policy to settle with him for the value of his house as it now stands, as the public would receive from his new improvement a full compensation for the difference in the money to be paid, if evaluated from seven years hence.

"I have the honor to be, Gentlemen.

"P.S. I have written to Mr. Notley Young on the subject giving him my idea on what I conceive may be his interest to determine upon & should that your arrangement with him may soon take place so as that I may be able to see what proper situation for him in the part of the city where he may pitch upon . . .

P. C. L.

Regarding this letter, Miss Kite makes the following interesting comment:

"One cannot help sympathizing with Notley Young whose buildings and grounds were extensive enough to be valued by the city at £15,000. On January 7, 1792, he wrote the Commissioners: '. . . I had as I thought a well grounded expectation that the Plan would be so ordered as to leave me in an eligible situation with respect to the spot I delighted in, and where I now reside . . . what has happened a few days past, proves it was wrongly placed, for upon opening a street my house is found to be entirely on it.' (Letters to the Commissioners, Vol. 1)"

Then, before leaving for Philadelphia to superintend the engraving of his "Plan" personally, L'Enfant wrote to the Commissioners asking for supplies for the winter work, as follows:

"Georgetown, Dec. 25, 1791.

"Gentlemen: Mr. Roberdeau, on whose activity and zeal I rely in the execution of what is necessary to accomplish this winter, will communicate to you a statement of the business I committed to this care and I have to request you will make provision for the supply of 25 hands in the quarries and 50 in the city which in all will be 75 men kept in employment besides their respective overseers.

"There is an immediate necessity for a number of wheelbarrows and above 100 will be wanted early in the spring.   Therefore I beg you will devise the mode of obtaining that number before the 15th of March next — These wheelbarrows ought to be made light and should be only roughly finished, though substantial,

"I have the honor to be. . . ."[12]

Next we find that L'Enfant addressed a long and comprehensive Report to President Washington "for renewing the work at the Federal City" in the approaching season and giving an estimate of expenditures for one year in the amount of $1,200,000.   Then he stated "this provision will be sufficient for four years Operations and the effect of this expenditure will enhance the Value of Lots to such degree that a more considerable Sale may commence for paying the interest and providing for future expence, securing a sufficiency for commencing instalments to redeem the principal. . . ."   We have here to do with the idealism of L'Enfant that contemplated quite a completely built city before it was occupied and operated as a "Seat of Government."   Unfortunately,

---

[12] Ibid. p. 103.

L'Enfant did not realize the poverty of the Treasury; and the state of mind of national legislators, particularly of the North, who preferred to stay in Philadelphia to moving "to that Indian place" on the banks of the Potomac. Not to endanger the development of the Federal City as best it might, President Washington through his influence succeeded in securing a gift of $120,000 from his State of Virginia for this work and $72,000 from the State of Maryland. This total amount of $192,000, with that received from the sale of lots, enabled him to continue operations in the Federal City without asking Congress for a cent, until the year 1796.

The following is L'Enfant's Report:

"Philadelphia, January 17, 1792.

"Sir: the approaching season for renewing the work at the Federal city and the importance of progressing it so as to determine the balance of opinion on the undertaking, to that side to which it already favorably inclined, require, that exertion should be made to engage in it from the beginning in such a degree of vigor and activity, as will disappoint the hopes of those who wish ill to the business, and encourage the confidence of the well disposed, it becomes therefore necessary to call your attention on measures of most immediate moment to determine.

"Knowing you wished never to be applied to on the subject of business intrusted to the management of the Commissioners, I would decline troubling you at this moment, when other affairs must engross your time; were it not that I consider the commencement of the work next season, will be but the beginning of the grand operations of the plan & conceive a permanent organization of sistem for continuing all future operations to be of absolute necessity and wish it may come from you in the first instance to prevent difficulties, which, (without such organization) will arise in the prosecution of the work & must by intefering with the progress prove constant sources of new importunities to you.

"Wishing then that matters should be determined in such manner, as may insure harmony amongst the parties concerned, and being convinced it would not be safe to rely wholly on the exertions of the managers of the business, I feel a diffidence from the actual state of things to venture further in the work, unless adequate provisions are made.

"I address to you the inclosed statement of work intended with a summary of the expences it will incur, from which you will easily con-

ceive the motives of my inquietude particularly when you will observe . . .
at an hour so near when the work must be renewed, & from the foregoing
considerations it is of the greatest importance not to engage in it but with
powerful means.

"Everything yet remains to be done for establishing a regular mode of
proceeding — no adequate means of supply provided — no materials
engaged proportional to the work to be effected, no measures taken to
procure the necessary number of men to employ the neighborhood of the
city offering no kind of resources at least none to be depended on.

"Assistance wanted must therefore come from a distance, the season
already far advanced, the demand for such hands as might be procured,
will increase in proportion as the winter passing will afford them employment at home, materials will be dearer when an indispensable necessity
for them is known, & provisions more difficult to obtain — no time then
being to be lost and a necessity of seeking additional funds to those at
disposal — these are the considerations which lead me to demand your
particular attention to the enclosed statement of work and estimates of
expences, and sollicite your concurence to the expedient of a loan, which
is offered from Holland — provided that one or more states or the
Commissioners or any competent individuals or company, will be sponsors
— this would at once secure a sufficient supply to engage with vigor, in
the work intended for the year, & continue the plan of operations with
security to the end of the year 1796.

"From the first moment I engaged in the business of the city I have
considered this as the only mode of supplying the demands for so great
an undertaking which could give certainty to the plan.

"When (submitting my opinion to you on the subject) I endeavored to
extend the limits of the city beyond what had first been contemplated
thereby to enlarge the public property therein, my object was not to
secure an adequate supply from a sale of lots, which I ever view and
remain confident will prove insufficient—but to obtain greater means
of facilitating a loan on mortgage of part of the property. lots may
be mortgaged in such situations as will never interfere with the settlement of the city but rather determine it where most essential . . .

"In case of a foreign nation agreeing to build a hotel for their minister
— it would be proper to determine the situation and extent by the
magnitude of the plan of construction intended—since in consequence
of some overtures I ventured to make to the ministers and residents
here on that subject, the idea has been pleasing and some of them have
already engaged to solicit the concurrence of their courts and I conceive that ground being given to them free would prove so advantageous
to the enterprise that I cannot but wish you will soon determine on the
mode most proper for enabling those gentlemen to apply officially to their
restpective courts, as an early acquiessance on their would most power-

fully give confidence to foreigner desirous of purchasing and this together with a loan to be effected and proposed would most certainly decide a pursuit of those grand engagements I have exerted every means in my power to encourage—but none' of which will be commenced by Foreigner or even american associations, unless *some shining progress is made in the grand work* which the publick has to effect—*the continuance of that progress evidently provided for,* and the whole machine put in such motion *as will convince the friends as well as enemies to its success* that it will *be accomplished in all parts proper to secure that superiority of advantage which the various local combinations & novelty of distribution* is intended to procure to the new city over all other now existing . . .

"Full confident I am that you wish to see the whole business conducted with that economy which in great works consist more in a judicious employment of time & application of objects than in the little saving—where procuring a plentifulness of means may accelerate the motion and being not less sensible that your wish is not confined barely to provide accommodation for the government but extends to effect the whole establishment in a manner that shall reflect same to the american Empire—Sir,

"I shall close this letter recaling your attention to the enclosed papers requesting you will determine some permanent establishment for conducting the business & that you will direct the measures most expedient to insure a proper supply.

"In contemplating this object it will be necessary to comprehend the magnitude of the work intended to reflect that it is not merely this or that object which are most necessary or ought to be undertaken first, but to consider that the objects intended have such relation with each other that they cannot be singly effected without great inconvenience and loss by a double handling of objects which a contraction of operation would make necessary, the reducing of a street being necessary to fill up other places worsing *(sic)* or walling here or there to contribute to the advancement of the next, & so on . . .

"to organize a machine so complicated & to insure regular action in all the parts demand coolness and Resolution—& as the means provided are so wholly inadequate, it becomes more interesting to preserve those resource the public property will afford.—

"I am, with respectful submission,
your most humble & most obedient servant,
(Signed) P. C. L'Enfant.[13]

The letter was endorsed on the reverse, Major

---

[13] Received by the Commissioners March 14, 1792. See Letter Book Vol. I, p. 75—Secretary Jefferson to the Commissioners, March 6, 1792.

L'Enfant, with an estimate of the Labor & expences necessary to be employed in the federal city.

"17th Jany. 1792.

The following is the Report of Estimates by L'Enfant:

"Philadelphia, January 17, 1792.

"OPÉRATIONS Intended for the ensuing season in the FEDERAL CITY to which is added an estimate of the expenditure of one year proces & number of hands necessary.

"Number of men

1*st*. To continue clearing the cellars & begin laying the foundation of the two principal buildings and bring these forward to such a stage as they will be safe from injury the next winter. the digers to continue afterward employed in shaping the adjacent grounds.

150   2*nd*. planting the wall of the terrace supporting each of these building & forming the gradual assent to the Federal Square, iether of these must be rised in the mean time as the foundation of the building with which they are connected.

300   3*rd*. wharfing the bank of the potomac to form the end of the canal and from thence to dig & [ ] the canal up to the Federal Square. to effect this in proper season three hundred men will be required four months. the men to be afterwards employed at the other end of that canal on the Eastern branche.

"Number of teams

30 10 4*th*. to Reduce the two streets on the side of the president park and garden to a proper gradation, the excavation of which will be wanted to fill up the warfing & bank of the canal, two objects which must be carried in concert, for this object 10 teams will be wanted and 30 labourer.

200 10 5*th*. to reduce some of the principal streets in such parts as may difuse the advantage thro the various property and bring them to the state of good turnpike Roads. two hundred men and 10 teams will be wanted.

50   6*th*. to build three good stone bridges one over rock creek and two over the canal. that over Rock creek being immediately necessary to engage in to effect a communication with the post Road & for establishing a necessary intercourse will employ 50 men. Filling up the abutment & adjoining warfs will be effected by reducing the post Road. a warf next to that bridge one near the end of the canal on the potomac & another on the East branch at the nearest communication with the Federal and president Squares must be established for landing materials & for an equal encouragement of improvements in

those parts. streets leading to these must be reduced & will serve to the warfing.

60   *7th.* Aqueducts already begun must be continued in various places to convey the water to such places and in such quantity as will be of general use to the city, an object to be done so early as to be compleated before any material improvement are begun for which sixty men will be required.

25   15   *8th.* the transporting of material from the three entry places to various parts where they are to be used will employ 15 strong teams and 10 labourers.

35   *9th.* the quantity of brick wanted in the first instance will employ twenty five men and as many labourers with two teams & drivers but considering the quantity of bricks that will be necessary in prosecuting the building an increasing number of brickmakers will be wanted after the first year.

52   2

10th. two mills must be erected to grind and pound plaster of paris cement and clay, Four horses and six men must attend these mills.

16   2   *11th.* a water mill for sawing various kind of plank will be of great advantage if possible to be obtained in the vicinity, but a number of sawers—ten—must be employed for this purpose.

20   *12th.* tow large scow of a particular construction for the purpose of transporting stone, of large dimensions and two other for smaller stones must be constantly employed and will require twenty boatmen

50   *13th.* the exploring the stone and assisting to load to boats will require thirty labourers.

30   *14th.* twenty stone cutters will be indispensable to work the stone for the building. ten labourers must attend them—and the increasing demand for this wrought stone will require additional number of hands the succeeding years.

80   *15th.* as soon as the materials are collected in sufficient quantity round the buildings, which will not be before the 4th of Jully, the twenty massons must be increased to 40 with the addition of 60 labourers. that number to be increased in proportion to the progress of the building.

1043

16th. the various kinds of iron which must be readily supplied require that tow shops be erected with tow *(sic)* fires for a

5   master and 4 smiths with proper tools & stock.

17 oversees
2 wagon men
3 commissarys
———
1070 men

17*th*. a wheelwright shop must also be established to accommodate a proper number of hands—this and the carpenters are included in the return of number at the canal—for which there will be immediate and constant employment. proper sades *(sic)* for mixing & tempering mortar storing lime &c bing immediately wanted at each place where building is intended.

"there will also [be] wanted shades for brickmakers & to protect the bricks from injury. of weather shops also will be necessary for carpenter, & stone cutters employed in particular work & for other various purposes which must be spedely erected & will require a vast quantity of scantling plank & boards. a yard of which must be established to supply the constant demand for those articles.

"The quantity of lumber that will be wanted is not possible to be stated at this early stage of the business but the magnitude of the objects that will employ that article & the immediate occasion there will be for it, in primary operations, require that contract should be formed to procure an immediate supply of any quantity as can be obtained—

"to purchase so much of the wood as remain now standing within the limits of the city on the best terms the proprietors will agree to part with is very necessary—for though very little of that wood is proper for construction yet most of the straight tress will answer various purposes . . .

"it is necessary to place under the authority of one single director all those employed in the execution, to leave him the appointment or removal of them as he being answerable for the propriety of execution must be judge of their capacity and is the only one to whom they can with any propriety be subordinate—the exercise of any prepondering authority being in this respect to be restrained by the consideration that the good of the object to accomplish is only to be procured by trusting to the attention of one head who having a constant pursuit and the connection of those objects with the whole of the plan to effect.

(Signed) P. C. L'Enfant."

It is generally thought that the trouble concerning the Daniel Carroll of Duddington House was the reason for L'Enfant's resignation from the Washington work in March, 1792, and the reason for the letter from Secretary of State Jefferson terminating his services that month. But a close analysis of L'Enfant's experiences reveals that this was simply a "serious incident" in a chain of troubles to follow. This brings to light the names of

Removing Stone from the Aquia Creek Quarry (Va.) in Recent Years

L'Enfant's assistants Roberdeau and Baraof. There were also Benjamin Banneker; and Alexander Ralston, who helped on the plan for Indianapolis (*q. v. page* 343). We are told by William Tindall in his *History of the City of Washington* (pages 136-138)—

"On Christmas (1791) Major L'Enfant started for Philadelphia to prepare the plan of the city for engraving. He left in charge of operations two young men, Isaac Roberdeau and Balentine Baraof, to whom he gave instructions as to the work to be attended to in his absence. Under his instructions Mr. Roberdeau took twenty-five of the men engaged in the city work to the stone quarry at Aquia Creek. The Commissioners, thinking it more important that the work of digging up the clay for bricks should be pushed during the winter season, requested Mr. Roberdeau to attend their meeting to receive their instructions. Instead of complying with their request Mr. Roberdeau proceeded to Aquia Creek. The Commissioners at the same time directed Mr. Baraof to discontinue the work in the city in which he was engaged, to discharge the hands, settle their accounts, take care of the tools, and sell a horse purchased at public expense. Instead of obeying he went to Virginia to consult Mr. Roberdeau and on returning ordered a supply of bread for the men preparatory to renewing operations. In consequence of this proceeding the Commissioners gave Mr. Baraof peremptory orders to turn over the public property in his charge to Capt. Elisha Williams and warned him that if he presumed to interfere in digging the soil or doing any act on the land as of his own or under any kind of public authority they would order actions of trespass against him. The patience of the Commissioners was now being rapidly exhausted. . . ."

The Commissioners reported their views of the situation and their feelings in the matter, accordingly, in a letter addressed to President Washington under date of January 7, 1792, stating that they would "truly lament if it so happens the last of Major L'Enfant's taste and abilities; but we owe something to ourselves and to others which cannot be given up."

Continuing, Mr. Tindall states (op. cit.):

"After issuing orders to Mr. Roberdeau on January 10th, to turn the public property over to Capt. Elisha Williams, the Commissioners, thinking everything settled for the time, dispersed to their homes. The day following their departure Mr. Roberdeau collected hands and resumed the digging operations. The Commissioners were summoned by express and, making their way to where Mr. Roberdeau was carrying on the work, were informed that he was determined to execute Major L'Enfant's orders in opposition to theirs. On the arrival of mail from Philadelphia he announced that by reason of a communication from Major L'Enfant he held it necessary for his justification to submit to an arrest, which the Commissioners proceeded to cause. He informed the Commissioners that Major L'Enfant had directed him to desire the Commissioners not to have any clay turned up for bricks at the President's House.

"On receipt of information of these proceedings the President both in person and through others endeavored to bring the Major, who was then at Philadelphia, to adopt his views as to the Major's function."

On January 16th L'Enfant wrote Roberdeau giving him directions about taking the "Level of Congress Hill," little realizing that the letter would find his friend detained in prison. Roberdeau did not receive this letter until January 26th. He replied on the following day, informing L'Enfant of what had taken place during his absence, stating further,

"My letters . . . which have gone out with nearly every stage . . . must have miscarried or you would not be ignorant of the lengths by which the Commissioners have proceeded against me."

This information aroused L'Enfant to indignation, and thereupon he sent the following letter to President Washington, impassionately pleading for his friend Roberdeau:

". . . The critical situation to which matters are now brought testifying a disinclination in the Commissioners to facilitate the prosecution of the business in such manner as to enable me to engage anew in it—with much regret do I foresee the various difficulties which must impede the way to a new organization of the whole system . . . feeling myself doubly interested in the success from regard to reputation, and an ardent desire fully to answer your expectations, the confidence which from the beginning of the business you have placed in me enjoins me to *renounce the pursuit unless the power of effecting the work with advantage to the public, and credit to myself is left me.* [Italics added.)

I have the honor to be, etc."

What the thoughts of L'Enfant were at this stage of developments can scarcely be fathomed. He had implicit confidence in "his General" but did not know at the time that President Washington had written to the Commissioners on January 17th, in reply to their letter, as well as one on the 9th, as follows:

"Philadelphia, Jany 17th, 1792.

"Gentlemen:

"I have duly received your favors of Jany. the 7th & 9th—am sensible of the expediency of the act of authority you have found it necessary to exercise over all the persons employed in the public works under your care, and fully approve of what you did.

"It has appeared I think that nothing less could draw their attention to a single source of authority, and confine their operations to specified objects. It is certainly wise to take a view of the work done, the funds for carrying it on, and to employ the best instruments. Major L'Enfant might be an useful one, if he could be brought to reduce himself within those limits which your own responsibility obliges you to prescribe to him. At present he does not appear to be in that temper. Perhaps when Mr. Johnson shall arrive here, he may be able to let him see that nothing will be required but what is perfectly reconcileable to reason & to a due degree of liberty on his part.—

"I will endeavour to procure the information you desire as to Mr. Ellicot.—I am, &c."[14]

The letter above quoted indicates that President Washington still had a sympathetic feeling towards L'Enfant and that he had the hope that L'Enfant would see matters in a proper light and yield to the authority of his immediate superiors, namely the District Commissioners. But doubtless each mail brought news of further trouble in the "Federal City," and on January 18th President Washington wrote to Secretary of State Jefferson, as follows:

"Dear Sir:

"The conduct of Major L'Enfant and those employed under him astonishes me beyond measure:—and something more than even appears, must be meant by them:—When you are at leisure I should be glad to have a further conversation with you on this subject.

Yours sincerely and affectionately,

(Signed) Ge. Washington."[15]

It appears that a complaint had come to the attention of the President that some one was removing surveyor's stakes from lots that had been staked out. It seems that the Commissioners suspected L'Enfant, having so little an understanding of his character as to think that he would stoop so low in an act of criminal retaliation. The latter part of January we find Jefferson sending the following confidential letter to Commissioner Daniel Carroll:

". . . Be pleased to consider this letter as from one private individual letter to another. The conduct of the agents who ought to be subordinate

---

[14] Writings of Washington (op. cit.) Vol. 31, pp. 461-462.
[15] Ibid, p. 462.

is properly viewed here . . . In the mean time the President apprehends that accident or malice may throw down the stakes by which the lots are marked on the ground and thus a whole summer's work be lost. He thinks the attention of one person might be savingly employed in a daily visit to these stakes; and fastening such as may be getting loose or replacing those which may be withdrawn. I have thought it not improper to suggest this to you and am with great esteem,

Dear Sir—"

On January 27th, Daniel Carroll replied that the Commissioners had "employed a careful person with instructions to pay attention in a very particular manner to the posts and marks in the Federal city" and he assured Jefferson that some one would make "daily visits to see that the stakes were kept in their proper position."

Next L'Enfant was accused of slander in connection with the purchase of the stone quarries at Aquia Creek, concerning which Daniel Carroll wrote to James Madison on January 18, 1792. There is another letter in the L'Enfant Papers in the Library of Congress, written by Robert Brent, about that time, to his brother Daniel then in Philadelphia, stating:

"It appears from certificates which have been procured that reports in some measure, about the quarries, came from Major L'Enfant, which from the good opinion I have of him I do not believe . . ."

L'Enfant made written denial to accusations[16] against him, but it had the effect of only deepening the prejudice against him.

Grievances against Major L'Enfant were also brought to the attention of the President by Commissioner David Stuart (a relative of the family and looked upon as Washington's personal representative on the Commission). Miss Kite calls attention to this letter in her "L'Enfant and Washington," page 137:

---

[16] L'Enfant-Digges-Morgan Papers, Library of Congress.

"Among the Washington Papers is an unpublished letter from Dr. Stuart of eight closely written foolscap pages in which the Commissioners' grievances against the Major are given in detail. Some of Dr. Stuart's phrases are interesting. He speaks of 'serious and infamous slanders' having been circulated against them (the Commissioners). He says that 'Messrs. Walker and Davidson had espoused the side of L'Enfant in not giving up the plan during the sales . . .' He calls the talk about the quarries 'malicious calumny'; and says that L'Enfant and Roberdeau had said, or so friends of his had reported a reliable witness to have said, 'that we were *ignorant and unfit.*' 'The spirit of party,' Dr. Stuart elsewhere observes, 'has been so prevalent that it is not surprising that a man of L'Enfant's turn should give implicit credit to every idle suggestion,' and he assures the President that the Commissioners at their last meeting with one voice had determined 'to give up their enviable offices rather than to be any longer subject to his [L'Enfant's]: . . . caprice.' He expresses a hope that the Major can be made happy under other Commissioners, or by being made independent of themselves. In this latter case he greatly fears, so he says, that 'the treasury of the Union will not be adequate to the expenses incurred.' There are also charges against 'the loose and extravagant manner in which the work has been carried on,' and a note of despair about the open spaces provided for in the 'Plan.' 'I beg leave to suggest,' he says, 'that the intended appropriation of ground about the President's house . . . much too extensive . . : It may suit the genius of a despotic government to cultivate an immense and gloomy wilderness in the midst of a thriving city . . . I cannot think it suitable in our situation'."

The President referred the letters and papers concerning L'Enfant that he received to the Secretary of State, and on February 11th addressed another note to Mr. Jefferson, saying:

"Dear Sir:

"If you and Mr. Madison could make it convenient to take a family dinner with me today—or if engagement prevent this—wd. come at any hour in the afternoon most convenient to yourselves we would converse fully, and try and fix on some plan for carrying the affairs of the Federal city into execution.

"Under present appearances it is difficult, but it is nevertheless necessary to resolve on something—

Yrs., etc.

G. W."[17]

---

[17] Writings of Washington (op. cit.) Vol. 31, p. 479.

It appears that (possibly as a result of a conference above referred to) Jefferson then drafted a letter to L'Enfant in the form of an "ultimatum." For in the next letter to Jefferson, dated February 15th, Washington stated:

"Dear Sir:

"Before I give any decided opinion upon the letter you have written to Majr. L'Enfant or on the alterations proposed for the engraved plan, I wish to converse with you on several matters which relate to this business. This may be, if nothing on your part renders it inconvenient, immediately after 8 o'clock tomorrow—at which hour I breakfast, and at which, if agreeable to you, I should like to see you . . .

"You will recollect the communication of Mr. Walker on Saturday afternoon;—from these—those of Sunday differed but little—But as he said Major L'Enfant had declined committing or suffering to be comitted to writing any ideas of his, forasmuch as he had given them to me *before* in a letter, I have looked these over and send the only one I can find in which he has attempted to draw a line of demarcation between the Commissioners and himself . . .

Yours etc.

G. W."[18]

In the meantime Major L'Enfant awaited a reply to the Report he had sent to the President in January, and the absence of such reply held in abeyance a decision as to a course he should pursue. Then hearing that an engraving was being made of his "Plan" without his oversight, L'Enfant wrote to Tobias Lear, Secretary to the President, as follows:

"Philadelphia, February 17, 1792.

"My dear Sir:

"Apprehending there may be some misconstruction of my late conduct and views, as they respect a delay which has happened in the execution of a map of the city upon a scale suited to engraving and being so well convinced that enemies are not wanting through envy or base design of any other nature falsely to represent (more especially at this time) my every transaction as well as the motive by which I uniformly have been actuated, I take the liberty to address to you my ideas upon that subject

[18] Ibid. p. 480.

which at a convenient season I request you will communicate to the President. I do this with more cheerfulness as it is the last letter I propose to write interfering in matters relative to the City until some system or arrangement is formed by the President whereby with certainty I may know in what manner in future the business is to be conducted.

"To obtain this map to which I allude as correct as possible I had some time previous to my leaving Georgetown requested Mr. Benjamin Ellicott should delineate on paper all the work which had been done in the city which being accurately measured and permanently laid down on the ground, I intended to make the basis of the drawing of the remainder from the original plan, and upon a reduced scale for engraving—this was accordingly done; but though I will not say that it was intentionally withheld from me, not having had it in my possession, prevented me immediately on my arrival here to have the reduced drawing begun according to my intention and promise to the President.

"These circumstances and the difficulty of meeting immediately with a good draughtsman and an engraver to undertake the work forced a delay, but a desire to comply with the President's wish in obtaining as soon as possible that engraving, finally determined me to request the assistance of Mr. Benjamin Ellicott, who though not professional in drawing I conceived to be the most proper person to prepare the work in that part [Here note in pencil by L'Enfant.] more especially which himself and Mr. Roberdeau had with accuracy laid down upon the ground—the more to facilitate this I gave him the sketch which you had taken from the former undertaker of the plate, begging him to finish as much as he could in pencil only without the assistance of a large map which I had at that time in use, and by which we together would correct and compleat the whole—I daily attended the progress of the business in all its stages until Mr. Andrew Ellicott gave me to understand that he was ordered by Mr. Jefferson to attend himself to that business in consequence of which he had already agreed with an engraver, this determined me to concern myself no more about it being confident that the meaning of Mr. Jefferson's order to Mr. Ellicott could not be to publish the plan without my knowledge or concurrence, and convinced that it would not be completely finished *without recourse to the large map in my possession.*[19] [Italics added.] I conceived it would be but proper to wait until I was called upon by him to review and correct the whole—In this manner passed some days, in the mean time, having had an application from Mr. Young, publisher of the monthly magazine for a plan of the city upon a reduced scale to place in the next number which indeed I had given him reason to expect, I directed him to apply to Mr. Andrew Ellicott, who upon the application refused his assistance, Mr. Young informing me that his engraver

---

[19] In pencil by L'Enfant: "But by the manuscript stolen they got **all** that was wanted."

would soon be engaged for Mr. Ellicott on the plate for the city, induced
me to go to his house and see how far the draft was advanced. This
draft to my great surprise I found in the state in which it now is most
unmercifully spoiled and altered from the original plan to a degree indeed
evidently tending to disgrace me and ridicule the very undertaking [Italics
added]—inclined as I am to persuade myself this could not be the intention and strange as it may appear that a gentleman to whom in every instance I have conducted myself with the greatest candour, and in whom I
always have confided as a friend should, harbour a design so inconsistent,
as to endeavor to destroy the reputation of one whose contempt for the
little machinations of envy, has left him unguarded against the treachery
of false friends—was it necessary it would not be here out of place to
relate circumstances which in various periods when Mr. Ellicott engaged in the execution of the plan, led me to fear ill consequences
might arise from an apparent desire to suggest ideas of his own, gradually to deviate from the original plan, which would tend to destroy that
harmony and combination of the different parts with the whole, to effect
which had been the chief object of my labour and concern—whither this
inclination to originate, or improve upon my plan, can be attributed to
inattention to the difficulties to be encountered in endeavoring to correct
errors, which such innovasion would necessarily create, or whither drawn
by the allurement of party who are unconcerned in the complete success
of the plan, to their interest. Certain it is that he has been induced
to hazard opinions, and to engage himself more forward to effect objects,
which besides the impossibility to accomplish, he ought the less to have
done, being not willing to reflect upon the conduct of Mr. Ellicott, nor
of any individual farther than a simple relation of facts, from which
conjectures may be formed in vindicaton of my real motives, which are
none other than those arising from an anxious concern for the interest of
the establishment. I shall close this by requesting you for a moment
to think of the consequences that must result from offering to the publick
an erroneous map—laying aside these delicate feelings so difficult for me
to express in points where reputation and honour are most evidently concerned—to all this I should be more indifferent did I not with regret
foresee the gratification to two or three individuals, that would result from
so imprudent a measure, who desire no better foundation for contention
and clamour than the publick appearance of a plan deviating in any degree from that by which the operations in the city have been governed.—
I have the honor to be,

Your obedt. servant,

P. C. L'Enfant"

"P. S. I this day sent to Mr. Andrew Ellicott for the plan together
with other drafts necessary for me to redress the error notwithstanding his
proceeding I was inclined to do to accellerate the engraving. But his

having declined sending me that draft set it out of my power still to effect
the object to my wishes and determined me immediately to address to you
the foregoing."[20]

In connection with the allusions made by L'Enfant
regarding his Plan in the letter above quoted, it is of
interest to quote from an *undated* letter sent by L'Enfant
to Moses Young, Consul-General for the United States
of America at Madrid, which appears in Volume II of the
Records of the Columbia Historical Society,' page 125:

". . . I merely mention the fact of the plunder of my papers, etc., to
make manifest the difficulty of proving how considerable were the quantity
of detail plans of the great project and how the correspondence on the
subject was also lost.

"At that time too the particular plan and copper plates by me prepared for engraving in the month of August '91 in Phila. had (by reason
of the multiplicity of my other avocations at Washington) been unavoidably delayed and lodged in the best place of safely, into the hands
of the President as is shown in documents No. 1. But although thus
protected a number of my drawing copies had been made therefrom
without my knowledge, such as were seen in both houses of Congress
hanging on the Walls in December '91. Others were sent to Europe, viz.
to Portugal and even to Petersburg in Russia. The Commissioners by
means of an agent at Phila. in a surreptitious way procured the aforesaid plan prepared for engraving as shown by document No..., and
having effected the engraving prevailed on the President himself to cause
the publication whereby having obtained the number of copies they wanted
and becoming ultimately possessed of the copper plate they deemed themselves disengaged from the obligation of paying me the value of 10000
copies, which they had before in an affected manner requested of me as
the document No. which No. proves . . ."

Further reference will be made to this letter, which
contains a number of other very interesting matters concerning L'Enfant, in Part II of this chapter on the L'Enfant Memorials and his defense of his Plan.

It seems evident that Mr. Lear communicated L'Enfant's letter to President Washington, for on February
22d he wrote to Jefferson, as follows:

---

[20] Records of the Columbia Historical Society, Vol. II. pp. 144-147.

". . . The plan I think ought to appear as the work of L'Enfant. The one prepared for engraving not doing so is, I presume, one cause of his dissatisfaction. If he consents to act upon the conditions proposed and can point out any radical defects, or others to amend which will be a gratification to him, not improper in themselves, or productive of unnecessary or too much delay, had he not better be gratified in the alterations? This yourself and Mr. Walker can think of. The Plans of the buildings ought to come forward immediately for consideration. I think Mr. Walker said yesterday he (L'Enfant) had been showing the different views of them to Mr. Trumbul.

Yours

Wednesday, 7 o'clock.

G. W."[21]

The same day Jefferson sent to L'Enfant the following letter, which was approved by the President:

"Philadelphia, Feb. 22, 1792

"Sir:

The advance of the season begins to require that the plans for the buildings and other publick works at the Federal city, should be in readiness, & the persons engaged who are to carry them into execution, the circumstances which have lately happened have produced an uncertainty whether you may be disposed to continue your services there. [There is a penciled cross after the first sentence of this letter and a note on the left margin in L'Enfant's handwriting, today scarcely legible, which says: 'The letter to the President of January 17th will show I was not behind in measures to determine a speedy renewal of the work.'] I am charged by the President to say that your continuance would be desirable to him; & at the same time to *add that* [Underlined by L'Enfant] the law requires that it should be in subordination to the Commissioners. They will of course receive your propositions, decide on the plans to be pursued from time to time, & submit them to the President to be approved or disapproved, & when returned with his approbation, the Commissioners will put into your hands the execution of such parts as shall be arranged with you, & will doubtless see from time to time that these objects, & no others, are pursued. It is not pretended to *stipulate* here the mode in which they shall carry on the execution. They alone can do that, & their discretion, good sense & zeal are a sufficient security that those whom they employ will have as little cause to be dissatisfied with the manner as with the matter of their orders. To this, it would be injustice to them not to add, as a motive the more in this particular instance, the desire they have ever manifested to conform to the judgment and wishes of the President. The same disposition will ensure an

---

[21] Writings of Washington (op. cit.) Vol. 31, pp. 482-483.

oblivion of whatever disagreeable may have arisen heretofore; on a perfect understanding being established as to the relation to subsist in the future between themselves and those they employ, in the conduct of the works. I must beg the favor of your answer whether you will continue your services on the footing expressed in this letter; and am with esteem, Sir,

Your most obedt. humble servt.

(Signed) Thos. Jefferson."[22]

"Major L'Enfant."

L'Enfant replied as follows to this letter:

"Philadelphia, February 26, 1792.

"Sir. I received your favor of the 22nd instant; the sentiment therein expressed I have attentively considered, nor can I discover any idea calculated to accommodate those dissentions which so unfortunately have invaded the interests of the Federal city. I am well aware that the season for preparing for the operations of the ensuing summer, if any are intended, has far advanced. Indeed the time in which I conceived they ought to have been in readiness, past. You well know my wishes for arrangement tended in great measure to that object, consequently fault cannot be mine, as my every exertion to accomplish it was impeded by the Commissioners; The circumstances attending these inconvenies *(sic)* have afforded me much anxiety, solicitous as I have always been for the interest of that city; at the same time I acknowledge that I am not a little surprised to find that a doubt has arisen in the mind of your self or the President of the uncertainty of my wishes to continue my services there; the motives by which I have been actuated during the time I have been engaged in it; the continual exertions I have made in its promotion, the arrangement for this purpose which I lately handed to the President, indeed every step I have taken, cannot but evince most strongly how solicitously concerned I am in the success of it, and with what regret I should relinquish it—

"My desire to conform to the judgment and wishes of the President have really been ardent, and I trust my actions always have manifested those desires most uncontrovertably; nor am I conscious in a single instance to have had any other motive than an implicit conformity to his will. Under this impression at the most early period of the work, no attention or politeness as a gentleman has been wanting in me to attain the confidence and secure the friendship of the Commissioners—I coveted it, I sincerely wished it, knowing that without a perfect good understanding between them and myself, whatever exertions I should make, would prove fruitless; and embracing in my mind the immensity of the business to be undertaken, evinced to me the necessity that I should be disengaged from

---

[22] Records of the Columbia Historical Society, Vol. II, pp. 148-149.

every concern, and be devoted wholly to forming and carrying into execution a plan in which I promised myself every support from them, trusting they felt a similar interest in the prosperity and success of the undertaking, and that therefore they would freely have relied upon me in all matters relating to my professional character, and requested from me all the information and assistance in my power to aid them in the performance of their share of the business, which in men so little versed in the minutiae of such operations would have been judicious and might in propriety have been done, without descending from that pride of office which, I am mortified to be obliged to say it, has been their chief object . . . and has afforded me much concern, knowing that the President had always entertained a different opinion of their dispositions, and delicately situated as I was, put it out of my power to assure him that his expectations of these gentlemen adhering to their protestations to him . . . were erroneous, as on the contrary, though apparently acknowledging themselves obliged to me for affording necessary information, on receiving it have uniformly acted in opposition thereto . . . and appear rather to have endeavored to obtain that knowledge from me the more effectually to defeat my intentions . . . The inquietude I feel must continue to the end to impede the business, which will oblige me to renounce the pursuit of that fame, which the success of the undertaking must procure, rather than to engage to conduct it under a system which would . . . not only crush its growth but make me appear the principal cause of the destruction of it . . . seeing there is much stress laid upon the propriety of thir conduct and the motives by which . . . [it] is inspired lays me under the necessity, in justification of my own feelings, to enumerate some instances that occurred. . . .

Thereupon L'Enfant enumerates troubles that he had in the Federal City, heretofore cited, and concludes his letter—

". . . to change a wilderness into a city, to erect and beautify buildings etc. to that degree of perfection necessary to receive the seat of Government of a vast empire the short period of time that remains to effect these objects is an undertaking vast as it is novel—and reflecting that all this is to be done under the many disadvantages of opposing interests . . . the only expedient is to conciliate and interest the minds of all ranks of people . . . by holding out forcible inducements . . .

"If therefore the law absolutely requires without any equivocation that my continuance shall depend upon an appointment from the Commissioners — I cannot nor would I upon any consideration submit myself to it . . ."

"I have the honor to be, etc. etc.

"Thomas Jefferson, Esq."[23]

Jefferson received this letter on Saturday, February 26th, 1792. After reading it he sent it to the President, who the same afternoon wrote Jefferson as follows:

"Sir: I have perused the enclosed answer to your letter to Major L'Enfant. Both are returned. A final decision thereupon must be had. I wish it to be taken upon the best ground, and with the best advice. Send it I pray you to Mr. Madison who is better acquainted with the whole of this matter than any other. I wish also that the attorney-general may see and become acquainted with the circumstances (I can think of no other at this moment to call in) and wish that all th[ree] of you would be with me at half past eight o'clock tomorrow—if convenient at a later hour to be named that I may be at home and disengaged.

Yours

G. W."[24]

What happened that night is related by Miss Kite in her *"L'Enfant and Washington"* (page 151):

"That night the President sent his private secretary, Tobias Lear, in a final endeavor to remove L'Enfant's 'unfounded suspicious' as he said, regarding the Commissioners. This was the 'straw too much' for the overwrought Major. Forgetting for the moment the august personage represented by the friend before him, he waved aside the suggestion with the disdainful remark, 'that he had already heard enough of this matter.' This remark as reported to Washington offended him deeply. When the small group invited by the President came together next morning to discuss the matter so as to arrive at the 'best' decision, they found Washington's mind already made up. The impatience so manifest in Jefferson's note may be considered therefore as the reflection of the President's own attitude. He wrote L'Enfant.

" 'Philadelphia, Feb. 27, 1792.

" 'Sir: From your letter received yesterday in answer to my last, and your declarations in conversation with Mr. Lear, it is understood you absolutely decline acting under the authority of the present Commissioners. If this understanding of your meaning be right, I am instructed by the President to inform you that nothwithstanding the desire he has entertained to preserve your agency in the business, the condition upon

---

[23] L'Enfant-Digges-Morgan Papers, Library of Congress.
[24] Writings of Washington op. cit.

which it is to be done is inadmissible & your services must be at an end.

I have the honor to be Sir,

Your most obedt. humble sevt.

"4 o'clock,   (Signed) Th. Jefferson'."[25]

Feb. 26th, 1792."

As soon as L'Enfant received the above letter from the Secretary of State, he wrote to the President; a parting word to "his General":

"Sir: Having in my last letter to Mr. Jefferson so fully explained the Reasons which urge me to decline all concern in the Federal city under the present system; as these reasons were the result of serious, impartial consideration upon so important a subject, I wish it understood that it is still my resolution. By the letter of Mr. Jefferson to me in answer, I perceive that all my services are at an end. Seeing things are so, let me now earnestly request you to believe that it is with the regret the most sincere I see the termination of all pursuits in which so lately I was engaged, and that my every view throughout was incited by the warmest wishes for the advancement of your favorite object, and that all my abilities were united to insure its success.

"From a full conviction of the impossibility to effect the intended establishment, while struggling through the various difficulties that continually must occur, and which would as certainly prove insurmountable, to late to remedy their ill-consequences; at the same time fearing that by my continuance, you might indulge a fallacious hope of success, by which in the end you must have been deceived, under these impressions do I renounce all concern in it.

"Permit me also to assure in the most faithful manner that the same Reasons which have driven me from the establishment, will prevent any man of capacity, impressed with the same disinterested views, by which in every stage of it, I have been actuated, and who may be sufficiently well convinced of the importance of the undertaking, from engaging in a work that must defeat his sanguin hopes and baffle every exertions—Should this business fall into the hands of one devoid of these impressions, and of course insensible to the real benefit of the public, how great soever his power may be, self-interest immediately becomes his only view, and deception and dishonor are the issue.

"As I am now totally disengaged, and"[26]

[End wanting]

Miss Kite calls attention to the fact (op cit. p. 153), that—

---

[25] Records of the Columbia Historical Society, Vol. II, p. 150.

[26] L'Enfant-Digges-Morgan Papers, Library of Congress.

"Among the Jefferson Papers there is a note of February 28, 1792, relative to the L'Enfant affair in Washington's hand writing which shows that uncertainty had again taken possession of the President's mind. He asks,

" 'Would it be advisable to let L'Enfant alter the plan if he will do it in a certain given time—and provided also we retain the means, if anything unfair is intended, that we may not suff [edge of paper]

" 'Ought anything to be said in my letter to him respecting payment for his past services.—

" 'Should Mr. Ellicott be again asked in strong and explicit terms if the plan exhibited by him is conformable to the actual state of things on the ground and agreeable to the design of Majr. L'Enfant.

Also whether he will undertake and execute with all possible despatch the laying off of the lots agreeable to the plan under the authority and orders of the Commissioners'."

On that same day (February 28, 1792) President Washington wrote a final letter to L'Enfant. As Miss Kite points out, L'Enfant noted in pencil that "The President could not have written this with his own hand. I question if he read it before signing his name." It is the only communication from Washington to L'Enfant not written with his own hand. The letter is as follows:

"Philadelphia, February 28, 1792.

"Sir: Your final resolution being taken, I shall delay no longer to give my ideas to the Commissioners for carrying into effect the Plan for the Federal City. The continuance of your services (as I have often assured you) would have been pleasing to me, could they have been retained on terms compatible with the Law. Every mode has been tried to accommodate your wishes on this principle, except changing the Commissioners (for Commissioners there must be, and under their directions the Public buildings must be carried on, or the law will be violated) this is the opinion of the Attorney General of the United States, and other competent judges. To change the Commissioners *cannot be done* on ground of propriety, justice or policy.

"Many weeks have been lost since you came to Philadelphia in obtaining a plan for engraving, nothwithstanding the earnestness with which I requested it might be prepared on your first arrival—further delay in this business is inadmissable. In like manner five months have elapsed and are lost, by the compliment which was intended to be paid you in depending *alone* upon your plans for the public buildings instead of advertising a premium to the person who should present the best (which would have

included yourself equally) These are unpleasant things to the friends of the measure, and are very much regretted. I know not what kind of certificate to give that will subserve the purpose of Mr. Roberdeau. My conversations with, & letters to you, have uniformly conveyed the idea that the Commissioners stood between you and the President of the U. States; that it lay with them to draw the line of demarkation between themselves and you; & that it was from them *alone* you were to receive your directions. A recurrence to my letters of the 2d & 13th of December, will shew you the light in which I have considered this subject.
"With sincere wishes for your happiness and prosperity,
I am Sir,
Your most obedt. sert.
(Signed) Go/ Washington."[27]

President Washington wrote a long letter to the Commissioners of the District of Columbia under date of March 6, 1792 (See pages 46-48, of Volume 17, *Records of the Columbia Historical Society*), which states in part:

". . . Matters are at length brought to a close with Maj. L'Enfant. As I had a strong desire to retain his services in this business, provided it could have been done upon a proper footing, I gave him every opportunity of coming forward and stating the mode in which he would wish to be employed, always, however, assuring him, that he must be under the control of the Commissioners . . ."

L'Enfant remained silent so far as arguments with President Washington and the Plan were concerned, until 1800, after "his General" had died. In the meantime the L'Enfant Plan was engraved, the question of compensation to L'Enfant came up and he was reimbursed in part; and the integrity of the Plan came into question soon after the turn of the century. These vital matters will be made the subject of Part II of this chapter. L'Enfant answered his critics in three long Memorials (printed in the Appendix), which, while they are a defense of the Plan, give us also many interesting sidelights as to L'Enfant's ideas for the Plan of the Federal City.

---

[27] Writings of Washington (op. cit.) Volume 31, pp. 488-489.

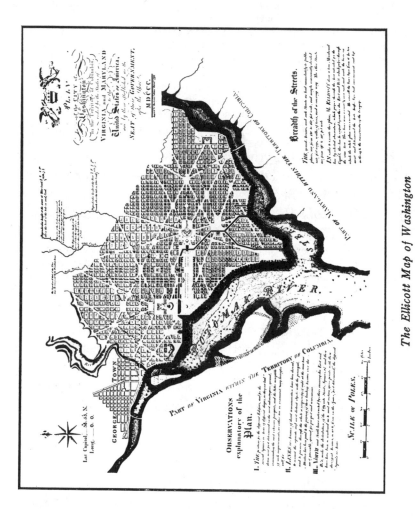

The Ellicott Map of Washington

The L'Enfant Plan Engraved; Compensation To L'Enfant; The L'Enfant Memorials

Part II

Before taking up matters relating to the engraving of the L'Enfant Plan, we should call attention to testimonials sent to L'Enfant in appreciation of his services:

"Georgetown, 9 March, 1792.

"Dear Sir:

"I believe every Proprietor of land within the Federal City except two have signed the letter which I have now the pleasure to enclose. They send their sentiments respecting your return, or rather respecting their wishes on that subject, to Mr. Walker and to the President, by this night's Post—Copy whereof should you wish it, I can furnish you. The Proprietors of land conceive they cannot give you sufficient evidence of their Sense of your services & Exertions in promoting the growth of the City; and they are anxiously solicitous [for] your return, expecting every advantage from your Zeal and Judgment.

I am with esteem and regard,
Dr. Sir,
Your most obedt. Ser.
Uriah Forest."

The letter above referred to, addressed to Major L'Enfant and bearing the same date, reads as follows:

"Geo town 9 March, 1792.

"Sir:

"We find by communications from Philadelphia that there is too much to apprehend, that the City of Washington will lose hte benefit of your *future* (underscored by L'Enfant) Services, — a circumstance which we lament extremely, not only freom regard to our own interests, which we believe no other man, so well qualified to promote by promoting the public object. But from a sense of justice to yourself, for we well know that your time, and the whole powers of your whole mind, have been for many months entirely devoted to the arrangements in the city, which reflect so much honor on your taste and your judgment.

217

"We still hope some mode of accommodation may be devised to admit of your return, on principles not derogatory to your feelings nor injurious to the city — The Commissioners we trust, whatever misunderstandings may have arisen will be very much disposed (for they know and have acknowledged your Talents) to leave you without Control, in all those things in which you would wish to be uncontrolled, and if you will be induced by a knowledge of the high confidence the proprietors repose in you, to stand less on punctilios, we flatter ourselves that the business *of creating* the city, may be conducted to the final completion of the subject by the same talents, Zeal and unwearied industry so much distinguished in the commencement of it.

"At all events, accept this Testimony of our Sense of Your merits and of the obligation we owe you, as persons much Interested in the City of Washington. — We are, etc.

Robert Peters	Wm. King
John Davidson	Wm. Prout
Sam: Davidson	Overton Carr
Jas. M. Lingan	George Walker
Abraham Young	David Burnes
Ben Stoddert	Eliphaz Douglas[1]
Uriah Forrest	

Major L'Enfant.[1]

There is also the letter from David Burnes (*supra* page 190).

As heretofore stated (page 192) L'Enfant had gone to Philadelphia for the purpose of having his Plan engraved. This was the latter part of December, 1791. President Washington wrote to the Commissioners on the subject in a letter dated March 6th, 1792, stating—

". . . It is impossible to say with any certainty when the plan of the City will be engraved. Upon Major L'Enfant's arrival in this place, in the latter part of December, I pressed him in the most earnest manner to get the plan ready for engraving as sooon as possible. Finding there was no prospect of obtaining it thro' him (at least in any definite time) the matter was put into Mr. Ellicott's hands to prepare, about 3 weeks ago: He has prepared it; but the engravers who have undertaken to execute it say it can not certainly be done in less than two, perhaps not under three months.

1 Original letters in the Library of Congress.

"There shall, however, be every effort made to have the thing effected with all possible dispatch. . . ."[2]

As is noted above, President Washington some weeks after telling L'Enfant "to get the plan ready for engraving" put the matter into the hands of Mr. Ellicott. As we have seen (page 205) L'Enfant gave his account of the circumstances that developed in the letter he wrote to Tobias Lear, the President's Secretary, on February 17, 1792, stating—

"I daily attended the progress of the business in all its stages until Mr. Andrew Ellicott gave me to understand that he was ordered by Mr. Jefferson to attend himself to that business, and in consequence of which he had agreed already with an engraver.

"This determined me to concern myself no more about it being confident that the meaning of Mr. Jefferson's order to Mr. Ellicott could not be to publish the plan without my knowledge or concurrence, and convinced that it would not be completely finished without recourse to the large map in my possession. I conceived it would be proper to wait until I was called upon by him to review and correct the whole.

In this manner passed some days, in the meantime having had an application from Mr. Young the publisher of the monthly magazine for a plan of the city upon a reduced scale to place in the next number which indeed I had given him reason to expect, I directed him to apply to Mr. Andrew Ellicott, who, upon the application refused his assistance, Mr. Young informing me that his engraver would soon be engaged for Mr. Ellicott on the plate for the city, induced me to go to his house and see how far the draft was advanced. This draft to my great surprise I found in the state in which it now is, most unmercifully spoiled and altered from the original plan to a degree indeed evidently tending to disgrace me and ridicule the very undertaking. . . Mr. Ellicott engaged in the execution of the plan, led me to fear ill consequences might arise from an apparent desire to suggest ideas of his own and gradually to deviate from the original plan would tend to destroy that harmony and combination of the different parts, with the whole, to effect which has been the chief of my labor and concern. . . ."

"P.S. I this day sent to Mr. Andrew Ellicott for the plan together with other drafts necessary for me to redress the errors which notwithstanding his proceedings I was to do to accelerate the engraving. But his having declined sending me that draft set it out of my power still to the effect the object to my wishes and determine me immediately to address to you the foregoing.[3]

Concerning this matter, Major Ellicott wrote to the Commissioners of the District of Columbia on February 23, 1792, as reported by Tindall (page 148).[4]

"On my arrival at this City, [Philadelphia] I found that no preparation was made for an engraving of the plan of the City of Washington. Upon this representation being made to the President and Secretary of State, I was directed to furnish one for an engraver; which with the aid of my Brother was completed last Monday, and handed to the President. In this business we met with difficulties of a very serious nature. Major L'Enfant refused us the use of the Original! What his motives were, God knows. The plan which we have furnished, I believe will be found to answer the ground better than the large one in the Major's hands. I have engaged two good artists (both Americans) to execute the engraving, and who will begin the work as soon as the President comes to a determination respecting some small alterations.

Continuing, Mr. Tindall states:—

"The result of Major Ellicott's execution of the plan, whatever the circumstances may have been, resulted in its being published to the world apparently as his design. Major L'Enfant's plan contained in the upper left hand corner a title legend giving his name as the author. It also, as previously noted, contained the statement crediting Major Ellicott with the astronomical work incident to the execution of the plan on the ground. Major Ellicott, in his map, omitted Major L'Enfant's name as well as a large part of the explanatory matter, but left the reference to himself as it appeared on L'Enfant's plan, placing it prominently at the lower right hand corner, embracing his name in enlarged letters, in such a manner as upon a casual glance to give the impression, without expressly setting forth such a claim, that Major Ellicott was the author of the plan.

"Ellicott's draft, notwithstanding L'Enfant's charge that it unmercifully spoiled and altered the original, in fact adhered quite closely to the latter. The most easily noted alterations consist in the straightening of Massachusetts Avenue, which in L'Enfant's plan takes a sharp break to the southeast from the point where it crosses New Jersey Avenue, and in the elimination of four or five short avenues which appear in L'Enfant's

---

[3] Kite, op. cit. pp. 141-143.
[4] Tindall, William, Standard History of the City of Washington, H. W. Crew & Co., Knoxville, Tenn. 1914.

plan. It also omits the designation of any of L'Enfant's public reservations except those for the President's House and the Capitol. These alterations, while they may have improved, rather than injured the original, were not such as to justify Ellicott in seeking to obtain public recognition as the author of the design.

"It is evident from the fact that the names of the avenues are given upon Ellicott's map that they were determined upon during the time of its preparation in Philadelphia; for they do not appear on L'Enfant's plan, and Pennsylvania Avenue is mentioned by Major Ellicott, in a letter to the Commissioners written in December, shortly before he went to the latter place, as the diagonal leading from the President's house to the Capitol.

"The work of engraving Ellicott's map was entrusted to two firms, Thackara and Vallance, of Philadelphia, and S. Hill, of Boston. Though both products were referred to generally as the "Engraved Plan," the former was more particularly designated as "The Philadelphia Plate," and the latter as "The Boston Plate." The Philadelphia Plate was about twice the size of the Boston Plate and was much preferred because of the fact that it gave the soundings of the Potomac River and Eastern Branch which were forwarded too late to be incorporated in the other.

"The Boston Plate was completed in time to be exhibited at the second public sale of lots on October 8, 1792, the Philadelphia Plate not being received by the Commissioners until the 13th of the following November.[5]

Concerning a Thackara and Vallance of the "Plan of the City of Washington, 1792," the writer wishes to quote briefly from a letter that he received from the Honorable Ernest G. Draper of the Federal Reserve System, stating:—

"The map entitled 'Plan of the City of Washington' engraved by Thackara and Vallance in 1792 came into my family many years ago as a gift from my Mother, Bell Merrill Draper. Our family on my Mother's side are descendants of Dr. Josiah Bartlett, former governor of New Hampshire and the first person to sign the Declaration of Independence after John Hancock. . . ."

The division of Maps of the Library of Congress had sent to Governor Draper the following explanation of the map, under date of September 27, 1945:

"We have examined the map which you sent for identification on

---

[5] Tindall, op cit. pp. 148-149.

September 21, 1945, and find that it is a copy of the L'Enfant Plan of Washington, engraved at Philadelphia in October, 1792, by Thackara and Vallance.   It has sometimes been referred to as the Official Map of Washington'.   The U. S. Coast and Geodetic Survey issued a facsimile of it in 1888 as its chart No. 3,035.

"A similar map of Washington had been engraved at Boston in September, 1792, by Samuel Hill, but because it lacked soundings, Thomas Jefferson, then Secretary of State, ordered it re-engraved at Philadelphia.   The following, quoted from an article by John Stewart entitled 'Early maps and surveyors of the city of Washington, D. C.' in the *Records of the Columbia Historical Society*, vol. 2, 1899, pages 55-56, gives a bit of its historical background:

"'At the time when L'Enfant withheld his plan, his former assistant, Mr. Ellicott, went to Philadelphia, and, with the assistance of his two brothers, prepared another plan of the city, from a copy he had of L'Enfant's.   He wrote to the Commissioners, February 23, 1792, saying: 'Major L'Enfant refused us the use of the original plan; what his motives were, God knows.   The plan which we have furnished, I believe, will be found to answer the ground better than the large one in the Major's hands.'   This plan of Ellicott's was given to Samuel Blodgett, Jr., to have it engraved at the City of Boston, and it was engraved there by Samuel Hill in 1792; a proof-sheet of it was sent to Secretary of State Jefferson at Philadelphia, who wrote to the Commissioners on July 11, 1792, saying: 'I now send a proof-sheet of the plan of the town engraving at Boston.   I observe the soundings of the creek and river are not in it.   It would be well to know of Mr. Ellicott whether they were on the original sent to Boston.   If not, you will probably think it desirable to insert in this proof-sheet and send it to Boston, addressed to Mr. Blodget, under whose care the engraving is going on.'   Mr. Ellicott, having admitted that he did not show the soundings on his plan, was directed to insert them upon the proof-sheet; but prior to returning the proof-sheet to Boston, the engraving was received by Mr. Jefferson, and his soundings were never inserted therein.

"The explanatory reference on L'Enfant's 1792 Philadelphia engraving in which Ellicott's name is given, was placed there by L'Enfant, who placed his own name in its legend, stating 'By Peter Charles L'Enfant.'   By withholding the legend, and continuing the reference, assistant Ellicott has been honored at the expense of his superior, and confirming that honor by placing the same reference on his own Boston engraving.

"The L'Enfant Philadelphia engraving was first sold at 4 s. 8½ d. and Ellicott's Boston engraving at 2 s. 6 d. showing which of the two was the better."

A careful study of the maps, and considering new information concerning the L'Enfant Plan that has been discovered since Mr. Stewart made the above statement some fifty years ago, causes the writer to call attention to the following.

The name "Peter Charles L'Enfant" does not appear on the Thackara-Vallance Map, but does appear on what we know as the "Original L'Enfant Plan," of which an original pencil draft is preserved in the Library of Congress. It is to be noted that this has the "Explanatory Notes" by L'Enfant in detail, and that no name of streets or avenue are on it. Also, the name "Peter Charles L'Enfant" appears on the map reproduced by the Coast and Geodetic Survey in 1887, and on the Explanatory Notes published by the Gazette of the United States (*supra,* page 163).

The so-called "Ellicott Map" is a version of the L'Enfant Map. L'Enfant was disgusted with it, but it is nevertheless an improvement in this respect in that it straightened a certain avenue, and it contains the names of streets and avenues, and contains also the numbers of the squares. It may be added during the first fifty years of the City of Washington there were fully a dozen of these "versions" of the L'Enfant Plan, notably the McDermott Map, that is "The Tin Case Map of 1798,"[6] the King Map of 1818, which shows the word "Judiciary" (at the site of the present Judiciary Square) where L'Enfant intended the Third Coordinate Branch of the Federal Government should be located. Strangely enough Ju-

---

[6] So named because the District Commissioners sent it to President Adams in a Tin Case on January 21, 1798, who by proclamation confirmed a proclamation of President Washington of March 2, 1797, acquiring 17 public reservations for the Government, but from which the map had been omitted.

diciary Square is largely occupied by court buildings today, although the Supreme Court of the United States has its building near the United States Capitol. Later there were maps showing the development of canals in the city, the location of railroads, and then about 1862 a map showing the location of forts that surrounded the city during the Civil War. Then came the great Highway Plan of 1893, and in 1901 the Plan of the McMillan Park Commission, which extended the L'Enfant Plan to comprise the entire District of Columbia. That Commission restored the L'Enfant Plan for the City of Washington and planned for the needs of the Capital City of the Nation after a century of growth in wealth, power and influence, as will be described in a subsequent chapter.

Hundreds of copies of the original L'Enfant map must have been made, we do not know exactly how many. They were used in connection with the sale of lots and were also sent to the States. Also, as we know from President Washington and as stated by L'Enfant in one of his Memorials, they were sent abroad to interest people in the newly established National Capital. In August 1948, the writer saw a print of the L'Enfant Plan deposited in the Bibliothèque Nationale in the year 1800. Also, the following is an extract from a letter which President Washington sent to the Earl of Buchan, under date of April 22, 1793.[7]

"I take the liberty of sending you the Plan of a New City, situated about the centre of the Union of these States which is designated for the permanent seat of the Government. And we are at this moment deeply engaged and far advanced in extending the inland navigation of the River (Potomac) on which it stands and the branches thereof through a tract of as rich country—for hundreds of miles as any in the world.

[1] Charles A. Skinner, **History of Paterson,** 1919, p. 60, et. seq.

Nor is this a solitary instance of attempts of the kind, although it is the only one which is near completion, and in partial use. With great esteem and respect I have the honor to be, &c."

A statement by L'Enfant concerning maps that were sent abroad is contained in a letter (heretofore quoted, Chapter VII, p. 208) sent by him to Moses Young, Counsul General for the United States to Madrid, stating—

"At that time too the particular plan and copper plates by me prepared for engraving in the month of August '91 in Phila. had (by reason of the multiplicity of my other avocations at Washington) been unavoidably delayed and lodged in the best place of safety, into the hands of the President as is shown in documents No. 1. But although thus protected a number of my drawing copies had been made therefrom without my knowledge, such as were seen in both houses of Congress hanging on the Walls in December '91. Others were sent to Europe, viz, to Portugal and even to Petersburg in Russia. The Commissioners by means of an agent at Phil. in a surreptitious way procured the aforesaid plan prepared for engraving as shown by document No. —, and having effected the engraving prevailed on the President himself to cause the publication whereby having obtained the number of copies they wanted and becoming ultimately possessed of the copper plate they deemed themselves disengaged from the obligation of paying me the value of 10,000 copies, which they had before in an affected manner requested of me as the document No. —, which No. proves . . . ."

Bryan states in his *A History of the National Capital*, Volume I, p. 176:[8]

"From the time the business of having a plan prepared for the engraver was placed in the hands of Ellicott until its completion and the engraver began its execution three weeks elapsed [See letter of President Washington to the Commissioners, Philadelphia March 6, 1792]

"From that drawing the first engraved map of the city was made. It is quite clear from the time taken by Ellicott to get the plan in readiness for the engraver as well as the contemporary references to the matter and a comparison of the engraved plan with the existing manuscript plan of L'Enfant, that Ellicott devised no new scheme. He rather filled in some of the lacking details in L'Enfant's drawing which was at the engravers, and which like the plan that has been preserved was not completely finished. As Washington stated in a letter to the commissioners, Feb. 20,

---

[8] Wilhelmus Bogart Bryan, **A History of the National Capital,** 2 Volumes The MacMillan Company, 1916, Vol. I, pp. 176-177.

1797, 'had it not been for the material which he [Ellicott] happened to possess, it is probable that no engraving from L'Enfant's draughts would have been exhibited to the public,' and adds, 'that many alterations have been made from L'Enfant's plan by Major Ellicott with the approbation of the president.'

"That these were minor alterations is evident from the summary given in a memorial of landowners to the president, dated Nov. 10, 1798, and in a letter of the commissioners, dated March 23, 1802, Doc. No. 157, 7th Cong., 1st Sess., American State Papers. Miscellaneous pp. 330-336, Vol. 1.

"A comparison of L'Enfant's plan and the engraved plan is the best guide now available and shows that the 'alterations' and 'changes' spoken of in contemporary accounts related to details of the general scheme so brilliantly conceived by L'Enfant and not to any essential feature of that scheme."

We come now to the question of payment to L'Enfant for his services, a question that never was settled and because of it the brilliant designer of the Plan of our National Capital was left in want to the end of his days. Indeed when he died he had property valued at $45.00.

It is said to be one of the attributes of a real artist that he gives little attention to money matters (there are of course exceptions), and thus when he left his professional work in New York City to come to Georgetown to make a Plan for the Federal City, in March, 1791, there was no written contract for services between himself and the Government. The first mention of compensation to L'Enfant appears to be in a form the Commissioners of the District of Columbia to President Washington, dated October 21, 1791,—

"From several intimations, we consider the business as resting more on us than heretofore; this is an additional motive for us to wish a clear understanding of the terms on which Major L'Enfant renders his assistance. We therefore requested him today to mention to us the sum by the year, excluding the time past, which would be satisfactory for his service, or if it was not his choice, tho' not so agreeable to us, we would propose the sum. We intended Six hundred pounds, but Major L'Enfant desired to be excused from entering on the subject for the present. . . ."

The next time we hear of the matter is in a memorandum from President Washington found among the Jefferson Papers, dated February 28, 1792 (quoted by Miss Kite in her *L'Enfant and Washington,* as heretofore cited *supra* page 214). . . . "Ought anything to be said in my letter to him respecting payment for his past services."

Then on March 6, 1792, Secretary of State Jefferson wrote from Philadelphia to the Commissioners of the District of Columbia: " . . . It is now proper that he should receive the reward for his past services, and the wish that he should have no just cause of discontent suggests that it should be liberal. The President thinks of 2,500 or 3,000 dollars, but leaves the determination to you . . ."[9]

Thereupon, we find that President Washington, in a long personal letter to his relative, Commissioner David Stuart, wrote the following on the subject:

"Philadelphia, 8 March, 1792.

 " . . . The plan of the City having met universal applause (as far as my information goes) and Major L'Enfant having become a very discontented man,—it was thought that less than from 2,500 to 3,000 dollars would not be proper to offer him for his services; instead of this, suppose five hundred guineas, and a Lot in a good part of the City were to be substituted? I think it would be more pleasing and less expensive. I have never exchanged a word with Mr. Roberdeau since he came to this place, consequently am unable to relate what his expressions have been or what his ideas are; he lives with, and more than probably partakes of the sentiments of Major L'Enfant; unless the dismission of the latter may have worked a change in them which, not unlikely, is the case with both; as I can hardly conceive that either of them contemplated the result of their conduct . . . ."[10]

The Commissioners replied that they had adopted the President's ideas of "five hundred guineas and a Lot in a good part of the City." Thereupon the Commissioners

---

[9] Kite, op. cit. pp. 157-158.
[10] Records of the Columbia Historical Society, Vol. 17, pp. 52-53.

wrote the following letter to L'Enfant dated March 14, 1792:

"We have been notified that we are no longer to consider you as engaged in the business of the Federal City. Notwithstanding this event, we wish to convince you that it is not our intention that your past services should be unrecompensed. You will therefore receive from Messrs. Cunningham and Nesbit of Philadelphia five hundred guineas, whenever it may suit you to apply for it. Besides the above sum, we will make over to you a lot in the City of Washington near the President's House, or Capitol, as you may chuse.[11]

L'Enfant declined to accept the offer, and wrote to the Commissioners of the District of Columbia, as follows:

"Philadelphia, 18 March, 1792.

"Gentlemen:

"I this day received your favor of the 14th instant—informing me you had ordered *five hundred guineas* to be paid to me by Messers. *Cunningham & Nesbit* of Philadelphia, which sum you mention as intended for compensation adding to it a lot which you propose making over to me in the city. Without enquiring of the principle upon which you rest this offer, I shall only here testify my surprise thereupon, as also my intention to decline accepting of it. in testimony of which I hasten expressing to you my wish and request that you will recall back your order for the money & not take any trouble about the lot.

I am

Gentlemen, Your obedient servant.

P. L."[12]

Once more President Washington referred to this matter in a letter to David Stuart, dated April 8, 1792, saying —"Did Major L'Enfant assign any reason for his rejection of the compensation which had been offered to him?"

It was L'Enfant, the gentleman, who kept silent about this question of compensation that he claimed to be due him. He did not wish to get into any arguments with "His General," the Chief Executive of the Nation, and

[11] Kite, op. cit. p. 174.
[12] Kite, op. cit., pp. 174-175.

thus kept silent on the subject until after Washington's death in 1799, as heretofore stated.

Thus the question of L'Enfant's compensation was left unsettled. But it was not the last word on the subject. In subsequent years L'Enfant appeared frequently at the doors of Congress, setting forth his claim in memorials and defending the Plan of the city. In 1800 appeared L'Enfant's first memorial to the President and to Congress stating his claim and asking a settlement. In this document, reported adversely on December 24, 1802, L'Enfant mentions in detail the various items in his bill against the government as follows: "For his labor for one year $8,000; for the profit he had a right to receive from the sale of maps, $37,500; and the further sum of $50,000 to use the petitioner's own expression, 'for prequisites of right in particular negotiations and enterprise.' The total claim amounted to $95,500."

It is evident that the offer made to him in 1792 of about $2,500 was considered entirely inadequate by him and therefore his artistic nature constrained him to decline it. On March 4, 1804, a bill became a law, which in one of its sections authorized the superintendent of the city to settle and pay L'Enfant's claim "In the manner and on the terms heretofore proposed, by the said Commissioners." But as L'Enfant was in debt it seems a creditor secured a judgment and levied on the money L'Enfant was supposed to receive.

The history of the claim apparently was closed by a bill which became a law in 1810, appropriating the sum of $666.66 with interest from March 1, 1792, to pay L'Enfant for services in laying out a Plan of the city. The total amount received by L'Enfant under this Act

No. 112.

APRIL 27th, 1810.

Read the first and second time, and committed to a committee of the whole House, to-day.

A Bill

For the relief of P. C. L'Enfant.

1   **BE** it enacted by the Senate and House of Representatives
2 of the United States of America, in Congress assembled, That
3 the secretary of the treasury be authorised and directed to pay
4 to P. C. L'Enfant, out of any money in the treasury not other-
5 wise appropriated, the sum of six hundred and sixty-six dollars
6 and two thirds, with legal interest, from the first day of March,
7 one thousand seven hundred and ninety-two, as a compensation
8 for his services in laying out the plan of the city of Washing-
9 ton.

A Congressional Bill for the Relief of L'Enfant

was $1,394.20. Most of it, if not all, was claimed by creditors.

We shall now call attention to L'Enfant's Memorials in detail.

THE L'ENFANT MEMORIALS

Due to their length, and the fact that L'Enfant repeats himself several times in describing his Plan for the Federal City, also because L'Enfant, being a Frenchman, became involved in writing in the English language, though for his twenty odd years of residence he had accomplished wonders in trying to master it, we have decided to place the Memorials in the Appendix (A), as they appeared in Volume II of the *Records of the Columbia Historical Society*, by whose authority the writer includes them in this volume. Be it said, however, they are an essential part of the data at hand in describing the L'Enfant Plan for the City of Washington. They are three in number, being dated May 30, August 30, and December 7, 1800. They were written after mature deliberation, that is, eight years after L'Enfant had ceased to be connected in an official capacity with the development of the Plan of the Federal City, and for the purpose of bringing to the attention of Congress detailed information concerning the Plan and the injustice done him in the continued refusal to compensate him adequately for his services.

The originals of these memorials were secured by Henry A. Willard, of Washington, who purchased them at the sale of the collection of autographs of Ben Perley Poore, a well known newspaper correspondent during the third quarter of the Nineteenth Century, and author of the well-known "Reminiscences of Sixty Years," to quote from the *Records* above mentioned (page 72). "All of them [the memorials] are marked by the lines of folding and have the endorsement of official papers. To three of the documents the signature of L'Enfant is affixed, and two are in his handwriting. The memorial dated Philadelphia, August 30th, 1800, and addressed 'To the Commissioners of the City of Washington,' is not in his handwriting and is without his signature, but it contains references to others to which his signature is affixed, one of which is in his handwriting. The memorial dated Philadelphia, December 7, 1800, addressed 'To the Honorable the Senate and the Honorable the House of Representatives of the United States of America in Congress assembled,' and 'paper referred to per memorial December 7th,' and endorsed No. 1, and the 'Statement of the case of L'Enfant, December 11th, 1800' are in his handwriting and bear his signature.

"These facts and circumstances satisfy the Committee on Publication of the authenticity of the memorials and accompanying papers, and justify their publication as verified copies of the originals in possession of Mr. Willard."

The Memorial to the Commissioners of the City of Washington, dated Philadelphia, August 30, 1800:

The reason for writing the Memorial is indicated in the first paragraph,—"A concurrence of disastrous events rendering my position so difficult as to be no longer possible to withstand unless speedily relief be obtained by collecting what yet remains my due . . ." In other words, L'Enfant was poor and without funds, and asks for speedy "relief." The mere mention of it to the Board, he goes on to say, should be sufficient. He then pays tribute to "the departed American Chief," in whose wisdom and honor he confided, and who understood him better than anyone else. Thereupon he states that though he had the ill fortune to have been driven "from the grand Concern in the affair of the City of Washington" sooner than it was possible for the public to appreciate his achievements, yet the absence of this and the changes of Administration, nevertheless "does not the less leave the public Indebted to me."

He goes on to say that by his exertions "the City was at the end made a rich Corporation" in charge of the Commissioners, and while he derived no profit by the transaction, "the immediate result to others has been a great Increase of their wealth from rise of property over a vast extent of territory." And, he states, "if the progress has not been so rapid nor so brilliant" this has been because of a departure "from my principles and particularly for having given way to the seduction of that active Agency of all evil, Speculation." L'Enfant refers here to the deplorable real estate scandal of Morris, Greenleaf and Nicholson, which came near making a wreck of the newly established city had it not been for the noble Washington.

We must bear in mind that L'Enfant had recommended borrowing a million dollars to complete construction of necessary buildings. This would have made the sale of lots unnecessary to acquire funds for public structures, and would have discouraged speculation. Now he points out, "from the Sale of House Lots and the intermissive Supply obtained it has not in seven years lapse enabled the Completion of even one half of the main Edifices."

Then L'Enfant reminds the Commissioners of the promise made to him when he undertook to make a plan for the "Federal Seat" and how subsequently he was deceived "through underhand measures" which led to the disagreement "so destructive of mine and the general Interest." Thereupon L'Enfant cites a series of twelve grievances, whereby he became detached "from the business" and was stripped "also of the fame as has become manifest."—

1st.   By being prohibited to consult "the high authority by whom I acted" and thus preventing "direct communication with me on the subject of the City affairs. (Washington had directed L'Enfant must take orders from the Commissioners.)

2nd.   From the manner my right as author, to the general Map of the City was nullified," first ordering him to having engravings made and then taking the work away from him, "and secretly having had a number of Copies drawn of that Map for private gratification and such as also were seen in the Senate and in the House of Representatives . . .", whereas L'Enfant had intended "presenting those bodies with the Original."

3rd.   For allowing "a disguised personage" to have free access to all his papers, who made copies of them and thereby reaped "reputation and profit" from his labours.

4th.   For placing some one over him in charge of the "Capitol Edifice." It was originally expected that L'Enfant would draw the plans for the public buildings, but he had none ready at the time he terminated his services in March, 1792, and Jefferson thereupon proceeded to hold a competition for the Capitol and the President's House.

5th.   For having been incorrectly represented, in regard to "acting under your Commission."

6th.   By having been deceived by one "highly trusted" who injured his plan by making changes in it.

7th.   For secretly engraving his Plan and making Errors in it "for want of knowledge of my method *of offset of lines where angles fall under a certain degree.*"

8th.   For being tricked in "the revisal of the proofs in printing."

9th.   For "finding my name erased from the title of the Map at the moment of publication and leaving stand on one of my Assistants" and for omitting his name "in all subsequent publications."

10th.   For "the forcible Seizure of particular drafts manuscripts in deposit" which made it impossible for him to publish "the City Plan in my own name."

11th. For being offered "a little Money expressedly as acquit of all obligations."

12th. For "robbing me of the merit and of my fortune," in consequence of sending his Plan to the States and "beyond the Sea."

Then L'Enfant relates the circumstances under which he adopted the "Invitation" of the President to prepare a plan for the Federal City and the instructions given him by the Secretary of State, "placing me Independent," leaving him to understand that his position "should be primary over all employed at the work of the City." He deplores the fact that while compelled to be away from the city at times, "the greater the machination to frustrate my labours." He exerted his abilities to "advancing all matters if Import to the National object," at the great sacrifice to himself, even his health, "by the practice of passing from excessive hard days labour to the no less toilsome of long and whole set up nights destitute of the comforts and means of exigency to such an undertaking and in a clime the like." After his resignation, L'Enfant states, he turned over to the President of the United States his Schemes—"Addressing this first Patron of the Federal Enterprize with the precise of my Ideas and intentions of conducting it," in order that the Commissioners might prosecute the work properly. But while "speculative Villains" took advantage of him, as pointed out in Nos. 7, 8 and 9, above cited, L'Enfant states he withdrew himself, "with the comfort of assurance on that occasion renewed to me, in the name of the President by his own Secretary, that nothing in the business had been but upon the whole entitled me to praise and Insured me the continuance of his particular Esteem and favor . . ."

Thereupon L'Enfant relates the affluent circumstances

he was in while residing in New York in 1790, and of the great loss he sustained through coming to the Potomac to make a Plan for the Federal City. He made claim for—

1. A salary "commensurate with the magnitude and importance of the Object and of the Affairs managed."
2. Payment for the delineation of the City Plan.
3. Proceeds from printing of the City Plan.
4. Additional perquisites resulting from the enterprise.

It appears that L'Enfant was consulted, as he states, in a $1,000,000 scheme to build houses, which was "meant to have been extended to upward double the sum." He claimed this would have "procured me a clear gain of $50,000" as perquisite.

L'Enfant felt he was also entitled to compensation for having undertaken "the Enterprise at the very time of the breaking out of the Revolution in my native Country" as a result of which he suffered loss of his property there, also for many tasks that he performed gratuitously "in a succession of above 22 Years," which "gained me the esteem, and I may say the confidence, of the great late American Chief."

Finally, L'Enfant points out that Secretary of the Treasury Hamilton had offered to provide him "with as many Pounds Sterling as I at time computed of Dollars wanted. His Scheme for which besides enabling the absolute completion of the City Plan gave a greater certainty to the attainment of the political end." It would have made the Seat of Government "a splendid inviting Capital," although it seemed to satisfy some that it stood as "a mere contemptible hamlet."

L'Enfant concludes this long Memorial by saying that he feels:—

"the nation has become more directly in honor bound to compensate my loss and to repay my zeal and trouble . . . that the final fixing of the

Federal Government on the bank of the Potomack, the advantage to result to the Union and the enrichment over an immense tract of contiguous country is in a most particular manner attributable to the vivacity
of my first conception of the business — to the Combination of my exertions beyond my professional line and to the devotedness with which
suffering great reverse of fortune I disregarded all consequences to myself
honestly keeping at my post making head against cavilling opposition until
by a display of the grand intention of my plan and by the manifestation
of power as well as of resolution to effect it the reputation which I
acquired to the Enterprize had in connecting the pride with the Interest
of the Union changed the most influential of the Component States from
Enemies into friends to the Establishment."

The second Memorial is dated—

"Philadelphia, december 7th, 1800
"Memorial to the Honorable the Senate and to the Honorable the house
of representatives of the United States of America in Congress assembled."

In this Memorial L'Enfant calls attention to his services in the Revolutionary War as a Major of Engineer,
"having entered the Service of the United States early in
1776—served without interruption to the end of the war,
and, to great personal sacrifices joining the merit of
wounds received and of hard Captivity endured" and
then continued in useful employment since the peace of
1784.

The rest of the Memorial consists of a repetition to a
considerable extent of the grievances cited in the first
Memorial.

Among the series of questions and answers found in the
second Memorial Question No. 14 is of real interest, in
that it points out that L'Enfant planned for the three
coordinate branches of the Government, namely "the capitol, judiciary and the president's house." "Judiciary
Square" is a feature in the original L'Enfant Map, and
the word "Judiciary" appears at the site so designated today on the King Map of 1818, as heretofore mentioned.

There is a third Memorial of L'Enfant, but it is in the form of a letter addressed by L'Enfant to the Commissioners of the District of Columbia, dated May 30, 1800, with an appendix 20 pages in length. The appendix was discovered only a few years ago "among the records in the National Archives concerning the early planning and development of the District of Columbia. The letter is 19 pages in length and the appendix 20 pages, a total of 39 pages of closely-written manuscript. The papers were in the custody of the "Superintendent of Public Buildings" from the year 1791 and his successors until the year 1925, when many of such records of the Government pertaining to the origin of the National Capital were transferred to the National Archives. The writer used his influence as an official of the Government to have the remainder of them transferred, and early in the Administration of President Franklin D. Roosevelt persuaded the Superintendent of National Capital Parks, National Park Service, Department of the Interior, to have them removed from a "dark room" in the temporary "Navy Department Building" to the National Archives.

Announcement of the discovery of the "appendix" above mentioned was made by Mr. Herman Kahn, Chief of the Division of Interior Department Archives, of the National Archives, during the year 1943. Arrangements were made by the then Secretary and Curator of the Columbia Historical Society, Mr. Newman F. McGirr, to have this document printed in Volume 44-45 of the RECORDS and this was done (pages 191-213). Mr. Kahn stated in his introductory remarks, which will be quoted presently in full, that the letter of May 30, 1800, was sent by L'Enfant to the Commissioners of the District of Columbia, "but omitting the 'appendix' contained in that letter," that the letter of August 30, 1800 (heretofore referred to) is "an almost verbatim copy of his letter of May 30. The author of this volume has examined the letter of May 30, 1800, and verifies this to be true, and he has therefore omitted the letter, although he has included the "appendix" with the Memorials in this volume. The introductory statement by Mr. Kahn reads as follows:

"Among the records in the National Archives concerning the early planning and development of the District of Columbia as a capital city there was discovered some time ago an unusually interesting and significant document concerning Pierre Charles L'Enfant. The document was contained in a volume which had been labeled 'Papers Relating to the Accounts of Various Persons and Firms,' which is a part of the large mass of papers of the 'Board of Commissioners,' the agency that had charge of the affairs of Washington during the early period of its history. These papers were accessioned from the National Park Service as a part of the records of all of the successive agencies which have had supervision over public buildings and grounds in Washington from 1791 to 1925.

"There is no need to repeat here the story of the career of the young French military engineer, Pierre Charles L'Enfant, of his services in the American Revolution, and how he was befriended by Washington and other famous personages of his time. It will be remembered that his abilities were so highly regarded that in 1791 he was commissioned to make a plan for the new capital city which was to be built on the banks of the Potomac. This event was to prove the climax of his career. L'Enfant's impetuous and violent temperament soon led to his dismissal as engineer-in-charge, and although the basic features of his plan were retained, his official connection with the construction of the city of Washington was never reestablished.

"When L'Enfant was first designated to draw up a plan for the future city, no fee or salary had been mentioned, and nine years later his services were still unpaid for. He had several times rejected offers of payment on the grounds that the sums proffered were too small. In the spring of 1800, being is desperate financial straits, L'Enfant began to press his claims vigorously, in the hope of receiving a substantial sum. The first of the lengthy 'memorials' which he wrote on this subject was contained in a letter dated May 30, 1800 (By a very strange slip of the pen, the date which L'Enfant actually put on the letter was May 30, 1780. Not receiving a reply to this letter, L'Enfant sent another letter to the Commissioners on August 30, 1800—almost a verbatim copy of the letter of May

30, but omitting the appendix), addressed to the 'Commissionaires of the City of Washington.' This document consists of 39 pages of closely-written manuscript, the first 19 pages of which are devoted to a detailed and careful statement of the history of L'Enfant's services in connection with the planning of the city of Washington, and the circumstances surrounding his separation from the project. The last 20 pages consist of an 'appendix' in which the architect-engineer refutes his critics, and discusses '. . . the merite of the plan upon which I propose conducting the work of the city to a timely perfection . . .' a discussion which throws considerable light on the original nature of the L'Enfant plan as well as other closely related matters. This part of the letter has never hitherto appeared in print. Indeed students who have written on the origins and nature of the L'Enfant plan have apparently not been aware of its existence.

"Of particular interest in this 'appendix' are L'Enfant's startlingly modern views on the proper role of the architect in large-scale construction projects, as well as on the general status of the architectural 'Science' in this country. The discussion of the manner in which L'Enfant had hoped to make Washington a great metropolis in the space of twenty years is enlightening. The city-planning theories here advanced, especially the idea of scattering small settlements at remote points over a great area criss-crossed with avenues and foot-paths, resulting in a quick growth of the original 'roots' toward each other over the intervening vacant spaces, is characteristic of the boldness of his imagination, as well as of a certain weakness in his grasp of realities which was the source of many of L'Enfant's unhappy difficulties in getting along with his hard-headed contemporaries.

"Insofar as it is possible to transfer manuscript to the printed page, L'Enfant's 'appendix' is reproduced below precisely as it appears in the original. As will be seen, the English leaves something to be desired. At times L'Enfant was almost wholly unintelligible, athough he usually manages to make his meaning quite plain. Occasionally he simply invents words, adding to the pungency of his language."

The "appendix" (See Appendix A, p. 395 in this volume) is another valuable contribution to the available literature on the writings of L'Enfant, and of course, in turn, on the origin of the City of Washington. Through the years past when someone has undertaken to write about the early history of the city, and reference is made to the L'Enfant Plan and matters relating to it, one finds continually the words "possibly," or "probably," or "he may have," by which the writer has attempted to give an interpretation to features of the L'Enfant Plan. This is to some extent misleading and is unnecessary when one undertakes a careful reading of the letters, memorials, and this "appendix" by L'Enfant. They convey a vast amount of information concerning the "L'Enfant Plan."

To supplement the observations by Mr. Kahn, the writer of this volume wishes to call attention to a few additional salient facts concerning the "L'Enfant Plan" found in this "appendix":

It is well known that the L'Enfant Plan is said to comprise an area of fully ten square miles, but we note in the "appendix" that L'Enfant intended to make the city plan much larger; however "the heated humour of some of the disputants was the cause of a contracting of the boundary line, by which not only upwards of 1,000 lots were lost to the public but likewise a very consequent ground for its commanding rise over the east and north entrance of the city . . ."

The "sixteen bases" or centers for settlement were indicated on the L'Enfant Plan as places to be developed and embellished by the States, one for each of them.

L'Enfant planned for a "perfect city" which would have made more progress in twenty years than by struggling along otherwise for a century.

The "miserable regard of penny saving," necessitated sacrificing thousands of pounds worth.

Pursuant to his appeal to Congress for compensation. L'Enfant wrote to President Jefferson, as follows:

"City of Washington, November 3d, 1801.
"Sir:
"The peculiarity of my position and the embarrassement ansuing from

the conduct of the Board of the Commissionaires of the City of Washington in regard to requests and communications made to them rendering the freedome of a direct address to you unavoidable — I hope the necessity will plead my excuse, and seeing the time near approaches when it is presumable- you will wish to Call Congress attention to the State of things relative to this new Seat of Government; I now with great dependance on your goodness beg your consideration of the circumstance with me.

"Noticing that my object with the Board of Commissionaires was to have obtained through their mediation a Compensation for Services and for Injuries experienced at the hands of the Jealousers of the reputation and of the fortune which the planning and Executing of the City of Washington promised to me, it would be useless for me to relate how I became charged of the enterprise and to what extant my agency was Servicable to it — my plans orriginally met your approval and the zeal the Integrity and impartiallity of my management being generally acknowledged especially of those whose property the operations affected, assures me the Service still must be fresh to memory and be remembered as deserving —. therefore passing over my Endeavours to promote the public object, the difficulties subdued, the contrarieties met and all the reasons for the resignation of my agency: the treatment experienced being likewise reminded of by letter to the Board of Commissioners [August 1800] and by two subsequent memorial to Congress [december same year and february 1801 Inst.] the latter together with papers accompanying it remaining with other business of the committee of claim not reported upon I believe I may spare the recital of any of the contents! — but attributing the repulse of my prayer, by the first petition, to misconception of the manner of my engagement and connexion of agency with the Commissionaires, finding they have deceived the dependance I placed in them for Explanation of matters to the Committee of claim, and — unable to account way that Board elluded answering the request and communication to them, and on what principle having themselves advised, and offered their aide to, the petition to Congress, they can have deneyed to the Committee my having any cause for the call on Government I presume the Inclosed paper (A) may with propriety be here offered in explanation of certain transaction, the Injuries from which answing, gave me some right to the expectation but the Board of Comissrs. would have proved more earnest to help an obtainment of the redress and Compensation prayed for.

"Deeming it to be here manifest that the conduct of the Board forbidded the possibility of further call on them about the pending business exciting at the same time a mistrust of the end, and, making my difficulties the greater by thus discouraging what assistance it has been my unhappy lot for many years past to have had to recur to for Sustainance, I forbear more to animadvert upon the proceeding wishing but by this plain exposure of to shew the necessity of the appeal to your and to the Equity of Government.

"Ensuring thus the exact state of thing will be known to you which it seem were kept from former administrations to an hindrance of the hearing of my call on different deportments — what ever be those Interests the Jealousies and machinations, of which I have been dupe and victime they will not be feared where your power is extant. — and allowing the private animosities, as of late years were fostered by parties politique, may yet stimule opposition to affording me a Compensation commensurate to the greatness of objects of national import in which I had a principal — primary and essential agency . . . possible as it is too for some minds not to feel the obligation to repay voluntary Sacrifices or Compensate the deprivation of great promises and of employments of great Expectancy— I nevertheless trust but upon the whole the propriety will be generally acknowledged, of an honorable return being due to honorable acts and for the liberal use I have made of my talents and fortune particularly in the business of the City of Washington as also in other Services constantly volunteered to this Country for these twenty five years past both in a military and Civil employmente to which I might add the merite of wounds of painfull captivity and of exertions, in a mission abroad too, and the close of the revolution war the success of which obtained at a great personal cost to me first of all embarrassed my affairs and never has been redeemed.

"About these military matters: I have, in Jun last given a statement to the Secretary at war *Genal. Dearborn* claiming particular dues and respecting the manner of eventual cessation of my Services as the abituate [sic] Engineer to the United States; of which having beged the representation to be made to you, I only remind here to bring together to your view every circumstances which joined to the absolut destruction of family fortune in Europe concured at almost the same Instant to reduce me here from a state of ease and content, to one the most distressed and helpless! and the only raisonable hope I can maintain of relief from— being in the Justice and libarality with which Government may reward my long Services I will own deed urged me to more minute enumeration of performance, to my own praise and with more reflection perhaps upon the treatment experienced than is congenial to my habit and disposition to have done. and, having thus out of necessity explained upon transactions the most Injurious to the reputation dear to all artists and also upon the most hurtfull to my fortune.

"Now, Ser, permit me to observe as before expressed by the petitions above referred to—that none of the related by me flowed from wish of disgracing anyone, not even those who acted most unfriendly to me, being with much reluctancy that I related particular proceedings and yelded to the Suggestion by the Board of Commissionaires of the propriety of the petition, to the late Congress. — and although the Sum stated by these petitions as the loss by me sustained be an exact nay moderate Compute of the value of the maps taken from me and of other benefits expected and of Right for a first year of the operation of my plan.—observing that I mean not to dictate what should the Compensation be for all that. but mearly by the enumeration of what my expectancy and right were, to invite the Consideration of the hardship of the reverse of my fortune: to render that reverse more sensible I gave the Contrast of the riches I would have now necessarily been accumulating and how these were werested from me by those Speculations and Jealousies which having left nothing possible to have pursued but with dishonor, it is well known made me resign all the Concern,

"Believing that honesty and greatness of the Sacrifices I have made of Enticing prospects universally acknowledged, as that also my care to have ensured first the public advantage in all the bargain and Scheme by me brought within power of effecting carried me to a disregard of myself. — an impossibility then being that in the hurry of so extansive business, whilst Endeavouring my best in all thing I could have watched the usage made of my plans &c &c — or have thought of procuring Surety to the promises' to me so as to be able as in ordinary business to have produced those and made up accounts for Settlement.—I cannot imagine possible that any thing the like be demanded nor expected from me. and — to speak openly — were this in my power to do, I would not think of offering other Support to the claim profered than what I have offered — a Comprehensive view, and general Sum up, of the Interest in the business in which I was employed — Conceiving best consistant with the liberality of unconditional Services and with the Confidence I place in the propriety of my System of plans and of opperation altogether to wait from the Public Sense of the merite of performance the Government award of the Compensation due for all the Injuries of the end.

"Agreable to these Impressions and Sentiments I confine, Ser, to Sollicite your kind consideration of the misfortune depriving me of the necessary to existance, the small remain of hope, till very lately Indulged in, of regaining at least in part, some stocks of Bank, my only having in the country being now vanished away—by reason of Robert Morris taking the benefit of the bankrupt act and the property on which he made me believe to have been secured being found absorbed by treble previous mortgage for Sum each far excedant the worth of that property. — thus for a generous friendly assistance afforded him (on request for only three or four days) — for these seven years past, both Capital and Interest, were inhumanly retained and I necessitated all the while to live upon Borrowed bread the obligations for which at this time to repay Comming with Imperious call and the addition of exorbitant charges for the advance, I must be excused for bringing to notice in this address being indeed what has been determining me to the desagreeable disclosure of my situation and Confidently to request your permission now absolutely to leave the adjustment of the matters of the Subject of this address, to your Benevollance and Justice. —

"Doing this I will no more than express—that I after many heavy pecuniary Sacrifices occasioned by variety of Situations during the revolution war — I since the peace of 1783 was also differently Encouraged and Invited by many Commissions to the free spending of my own, dependant upon promises of regular reappointment with promotion all which ended to my loss and absolut ruin. — that on the particular Instance of my agency to the Entreprise of the City of Washington I have received no remuneration what ever, that — no kind of preconvention were for the Service no price agreed upon for plans, nor the Copy right conceded to the Commissionaires nor to any one else, and that, extanded as was my Concerns and agency beyond the usual to Architects; although by the grand Combination of the new Schems I contributed eminently to the ensurance of the city establishment by which numbers of Individuals and the Country to an immense distance desire a increasing of their wealth I deed by no one opperations nor transactions worked to my own profit.

"Acquainted Ser as you necessarily must have became with managements of the City affairs in which my free exertions were not the least usefull to the promotion of the national object — the merite, and that of originating of the plan you, doubtless, will readily allow to me and certain I am that — for all what I suffered, the only reproach to which I may be liable (in this and business of military description) is my having been more faithfull to principle than ambitions — too zealous in my pursuits — and too hazardous on a dependance on mouth friends — admitting I would deserve reproach if I had imagined every man actuated by liberal honorable views — I nevertheless believe my Conduct in all Instance stand well applauded and Justified by all who knew the Spirite of the oppositions I met and the personages in whom I Confided and — Since Seeing you, Ser, occupying the same heigh Station as the chief under whose order I acted as a Military and at whose Invitation my Services were engaged and by whose Instructions I Conducted in the affairs of the City now become the Seat of Government. — esteeming your dispositions equally as I esteemed his, to be to redress Injuries and to recompense active honest Services — knowing your power is all commensurate to — I for all the reasons I have to lament the decease of that chief, feel reassured that the loss of his good testimonial and promised support shall not opperate my way detrimentally to my present expectancy and that in all respect your Justice will grant me the prayer made.

with great respect

I have the honor to be

Ser

your Most humble and
obedient servant.
P. CHARLES L'ENFANT."[13]

"TO THOMAS JEFFERSON
President of the United States."

No settlement of his claim against the Government having been made, L'Enfant again addressed a letter to President Jefferson, as follows:

"City of Washington, March 12, 1802.

"Sir:

"Under the apprehension of Impropriéty in the liberty I took of addressing you, in november ultmo, but remaining Ignorant whether resting as I decd. requested leave to rest on you for Settlement of the business the subject of two repeated memorials to Congress be agreeable to you: — the difficulties which this uncertainty set me under with regard to the Committee of claims to whom my memorials stand refered since the begining of this Congress (I having consequent to the wish Imparted to you and to the dependance I place in your goodness, beged the chairman of that Committee would delay their proceeding upon) forces on me the necessity to renew the Sollicitation to you.

"From dispositions testified by my last address I promised to myself that such Settlement as I feel entitled to wait from government, might have been effected in some other ways than through a Committee of claims, which (besides, that, I fear from their having once already reported against the memorial) truely to my mind made it a disgracefull reflection that a recompense merited should be made necessary to claim.

"of this, however, Sir, your Judgement best will determine, and I only advert to the circumstance to speak of my embarrassement on the Subject and how seeing the session of Congress fast approaching to its close now add disquietude to the apprehension of having mistaken in the manner of late request to you — well persuaded nevertheless but you will excuse where the Intention was purely to prove my respect and esteem of your natural disposition, encouraged by this hope I have here recalled

---

[13] Manuscript Division, Library of Congress, **Jefferson Papers.**

to your mind all matters before stated — and beg you to believe that the request which I made to you appeared to me proper because more flatering to my embition tŏ obtain my prayer through your Favour.

with great respect
I have the honor to be
Sir — your Excellency
most obedient and
humble Servant
P. CHARLES L'ENFANT."[14]

"HIS EXCELLENCY THOMAS JEFFERSON
President of the United States

P. S. having your Statement inclosed in the late address."

To this letter, President Jefferson replied briefly to L'Enfant as follows:

"Washington Mar. 14, 1802.
"Sir:

"Your letter of the 12th is at hand. immediately on the reciept of the former one I referred it to the board of Commissioners, the authority instituted by law for originating whatever proceedings regarding this city have been confided by the legislature to the Executive, their opinion, which I approved, what that they could only repeat you the offer formerly made with the approbation of General Washington, and they undertook to do this. for any thing else, the powers of the legislature are alone competent, and therefore your application to them was the only measure by which it could be obtained. Accept my respects & best wishes.

Th. Jefferson."[51]

"Maj. Lenfant."

---

[14] Ibid.
[15] Ibid.

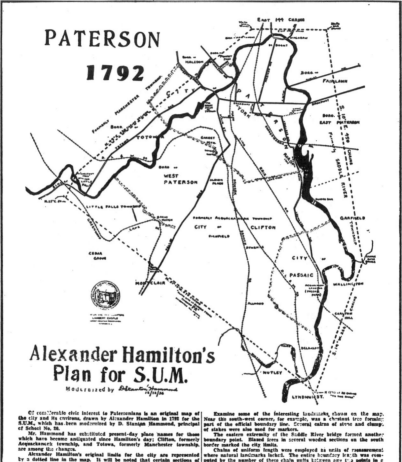

Map of Paterson, New Jersey, 1792

Chapter VIII

*L*EAVING the City of Washington, L'Enfant next
prepared the Plan for Paterson, New Jersey.

On the 15th day of January, 1790, the House of Representatives requested a Report on Manufactures from
Secretary of the Treasury Alexander Hamilton. Hamilton took two years in the preparation of the Report, but
when he did so it was found to be such an able Report
that it came to be regarded a "classic" and has often been
referred to in the years past, since in it he laid the Protective Policy of the United States. It was his most important State Paper. The beginning of the Report reads
as follows:

> "Report on Manufactures, Communicated to the House of
> Representatives December 5, 1791.
>
> "The Secretary of the Treasury, in obedience to the Order of the House
> of Representatives of the 15th day of January, 1790, has applied his
> attention at as early a period as his other duties would permit to the subject of Manufactures and particularly to the means of promoting such as
> will tend to render the United States independent of foreign nations for
> military and other essential supplies; and he thereupon respectfully submits the following report:
>
> "The expediency of encouraging manufacture in the United States, which
> was not long since deemed very questionable, appears at this time to be
> pretty generally admitted . . . ."

The Report is very long, as may be gathered from the
fact that it covers pages 294 to 416 in Volume III of

"Hamilton's Works" by Henry Cabot Lodge. In the Report Hamilton outlined the argument for protection. His broad reasoning rested on the necessity of a proper distribution of agriculture, manufacture and commerce in a government and a prosperous society, but it was many years before this feature of his policy was accepted by Congress.

While preparing the Report, Hamilton became very much interested in an organization which aimed to make the United States industrially independent, known as the Society for Establishing Useful Manufactures (the S. U. M.). It was incorporated on November 22, 1791. The Great Falls of the Passaic River in New Jersey were selected by the Society as a favorable situation for its enterprise, and there a town was established in 1792, named Paterson, after the Governor of the State of New Jersey at that time.

Hamilton was present at three meetings of the directors held in Newark on May 16, 17 and 18, 1792. It was there decided that the town of Paterson should be located at the Falls of the Passaic River. Few houses were there then. They bought about 700 acres above and below the Falls. On July 5th the directors decided to build at once: a mill for spinning cotton, a printing establishment for cotton goods, calicoes, a weaving establishment and a number of houses for the people who were to work in these mills. On the following day they decided 50 houses should be built, measuring 24' x 10', with cellar and garret, and that these houses, together with one-fourth of an acre of land each, should rent for $12.50 a year or sold to any workman for $250, payable in 20 years.

To do all this work it was necessary to have an engineer

and the Society engaged the services of Major Pierre Charles L'Enfant, a friend of both Hamilton and Washington, and who had just completed his Plan for the City of Washington. L'Enfant inspected the ground and resolved on some big ideas, and when he reported them the newspapers stated that "Paterson would be a city that would far surpass anything yet seen in this country."[1] He intended to lay out Paterson as he had Washington, the central point here being a small elevation between what are now Main, Grand and Ward Streets and sloping down almost to where the Erie Railroad tracks now are. The hill was afterwards known as Colt's Hill. From this hill were to be laid out a large number of avenues running to distant points of the future city. The newspapers of the day lauded the prospects of the future "National Manufactory" and the large city to be built in connection with it. It is said L'Enfant's Plan for Paterson comprised six square miles—the Washington Plan comprised 16 square miles. One article which appeared in the newspapers, probably written by Hamilton, took up three columns. It was proposed to manufacture cotton goods, woolens, paper for books and for walls, straw and felt hats, leather shoes of all kinds as well as pottery, and bricks. The land around Paterson became very valuable.

It is evident from L'Enfant's work that when he took up a new task he entered upon it with vim and enthusiasm. In this instance his fertile imagination and sanguine temperament led him to conceive the plan of a magnificent city. It seems to have been his intention also to create an air line road from Paterson to Newark and thence to "New York City" which he regarded a future

---

[1] Charles A. Skinner, **History of Paterson**, 1919, p. 60, et. seq.

metropolis, but fifteen miles distant from Paterson. It sounded big even in the present day of big projects.

A great deal of success was expected to come on account of the wealth and influence of William Duer, the governor of the Society, but there had been trouble in the markets of New York and Duer found himself in jail because he could not pay his debts. Of course Hamilton was greatly disappointed in this. Of all the money that had been promised the Society received only $60,000, which was far less than the amount needed. The banks in New York did not want to lend the Society any money, but finally one of them loaned $5,000 on Hamilton's personal guarantee.

In the meantime Major L'Enfant had been making more plans; he wanted to build a big raceway, running from above the Falls to where Passaic now stands. It was to be a magnificent aqueduct of stone, supported on arches of masonry, along which mills would be constructed and operated, a distance of seven miles. The scheme was regarded impractical, though, as heretofore shown, it is evident that the precarious financial condition of the Society necessitated the adoption of the simplest and most economical scheme. Thus L'Enfant, in 1793, was relieved of his position, by Peter Colt, who undertook to have an ordinary raceway built. But the directors of the Society were anxious to begin spinning cotton and did not care to wait for construction of the raceway. Peter Colt, therefore, put up a small frame mill, in which the power needed to turn the wheels was furnished by an ox. And so it happened that the first mill ever built in the present thriving city of Paterson to spin cotton was named the "Bull Mill." Then work was begun on the big mill, a street was laid out in front of it, named Mill Street, and it has that name at the present day. The big mill did not begin operations until 1794.

In the meantime the Society endeavored to raise more money, as it was badly needed, and the directors resorted to a lottery scheme. Few people wanted to buy tickets, and in Boston and New York a law had been passed forbidding lotteries. The promoters requested the law be changed, but were unsuccessful in this and in consequence suffered great losses on their investments.

Then came a strike—the employes in the bleaching and printing establishment wanted more wages, and the Society settled this by closing the factory. Then the Society tried to raise money by reducing the price of its houses, but no one wanted to buy them.

In the midst of all this the Paterson development became a strong political issue between Protectionists and the Free Traders. Both had its supporters in the Press and acrimonious attacks were resorted to. The Federal Party was influential so long as General Washington was President, but became weak as the century ended, with its consequent effect on the S. U. M. of Paterson, and when President Jefferson was elected in 1801 the Federalist Party went out of existence. In January 1796, the directors closed the big mill and went out of business. Fire destroyed the mill in 1807. About 1811 Peter Colt built a mansion where L'Enfant had intended a "town center." He believed the little town had a future and became one of its enterprising pioneer citizens. The town was incorporated in 1831.

As in the case of the Plan for Washington, L'Enfant

had furnished the ideas for the Plan of Paterson; others were to profit by it.

L'Enfant gives us his views of the situation in a letter as follows:

"Philadelphia, 18 June, 1793.

"Gentlemen:

"Your extraordinary communication of the 8" instant the shortness of which in evidencing the hurry of your proceeding of that day seem no less calculated to keep from me the motives inducing you, made it Indispensable I should call for more particular respecting that business wishing to know the reason which have determined you to direct all the operation in which I am concerned at Patterson to cease — a step the more extraordinary and astonishing to me as I know of no circumstance that could exist which can justify it previous having given me notice of your Intention without first demanding from me such explanation or information of might have enabled you a better jugement of thing. Every of my opperation at Patterson I have constantly combined as best could effect the plan agreed with the former board of Directors of the Society for Establishing Useful Manufactures and which may also have approved by your and especially since your meeting in May last, after the enquiry you had made in the nature of the business to be prosecuted with as also into the actual state of your funds, they having been found fully adequate to the needfull supply, I proceeded ever since in full hope of experiencing no new check in my progress and I was the less apprehensive of what now happen — being certain that an estimate of all expenses incurred since that time if made as you mention to have directed it was evidence that the sum of that expenses have been much less than what you ought to have expected. Considering that of the number of labouring hands which you had yourselves computed I might keep in constant employment until December next, not one half has been enlisted and that no purchase of materials have been made nor required from me beyond what had been before agreed upon *the amount of which had been returned to you.*

"from this you will I hope perceive it is difficult for me to remain satisfied of that *moral certainty* which you mention *that the funds of the society are altogether inadequate to the support of the expense of the plans.* and from the state in which the matter stood, being no less at a loss to conjecture how your judgment of these can establish that *great probability of not attaining the mater.* the request I now make to you for more particular Information will I hope meet your compylance and in

due time occasion the grand meeting of the principals concerned in the
issue of the business.

I have the honor to be

Gentlemen,

Your most obedient and humble servant,

P. Charles L'Enfant"

"the Director of the Society

for Establishing Useful Manufactures."[2]

While the citizens of Paterson, in the early part of the
nineteenth century may have given little credit for the
work done in the immediate years following 1791 towards
the establishment of the S. U. M., nevertheless views on
the subject have changed, as is indicated by the following
extract from an Editorial which appeared in the *Paterson
Morning Call* of June 13, 1942:

"The people of Paterson are celebrating the 150th Anniversary of the
birth of their community as a municipality proudly of the fact that
shortly after the close of the Revolution Mr. Alexander Hamilton, Secretary of the Treasury [in 1792] in President Washington's Cabinet,
realizing that the new nation should prepare itself for the production of
the things its people needed, selected the small hamlet located at the foot
of the Passaic Falls as the site for the manufacturing community of the
Nation because of the tremendous reservoir of water power latent there.

"That was the beginning of Paterson as a great industrial community
and its people are proud of the fact that their forefathers realized the
importance of the task assigned to them by the leaders of our Nation and
have placed the name of Paterson in the forefront of industrial development, beginning in a small way with the cotton industry and progressing
until today our community leads the Nation in the production of air-
planes, the most modern method of travel and which will play the most
important part in the achievement of Victory over the international
gangsters who would enslave the whole world as they already have a
considerable part of Europe.

"The products of Paterson through the years have won world wide reputation for their excellence and gained for it at various times such titles as
'The Silk City of America' because of its silk industry; 'The Lyons of
America' because of its tremendous dyeing industry, named after the
ancient city of France, the reputation of which in the chemical and dyeing industry made it the wonder of the world; and now 'The Aviation

---

[2] From the: Dreer Collection, Sculptors and Architects, The Historical Society of Pennsylvania, Philadelphia.

City of America' because of the tremendous development and expansion
of the Wright Aeronautical Corporation with its principal plant and
numerous branches in the Paterson area. . . ."

Paterson today has a population of about 150,000. A
building of the S. U. M. is still standing; a big Power
Plant near the Falls bears the added inscription, 1791-
1941. It is near the big hill which L'Enfant picked for
the center of the city, and from which streets emanate, as
from a *focal point*. There are numerous parks and triangles to be seen that have a resemblance to the "L'Enfant Plan."

THE ROBERT MORRIS HOUSE

In 1794 Robert Morris employed Major Pierre Charles
L'Enfant to build him a fine palace on the lot on the
south side of Chestnut Street, between 7th and 8th
Streets. When the National Government was removed
to the city of Philadelphia Morris placed his Market
Street house at the disposal of President Washington and
took up quarters at the southeast corner of 6th and Market Streets. In 1797 he went to live in the mansion on
the north side of Chestnut Street, next to the corner of
Eighth Street.

Upon the great palace he was constructing at Eighth
and Chestnut, which never was completed and was allud-
ed to as "Morris's Folly," he is said to have spent about
$30,000, in addition to $9,000 which he paid to the architect, according to Mr. Morris's account books, which
are in the custody of the Pennsylvania Historical Society.
We are told by Thomas Wescott in his *Historic Mansions
and Buildings of Philadelphia* (1877) that the building
was of red brick, ornamented with marble window-

heads, lintels and sills and pilasters, in what might be called the Philadelphia style of interspersing marble with brick in the fronts of houses. In the well-known view by Birch, the building is shown to be of two stories, with a Mansard roof; the doorways, window-heads, and frames were of marble and the porticos and doorways were of that material. According to the representation in Birch's engraving, portico doorways, supported by two marble columns, stood at each corner of the house. There was to have been a large central doorway, the pillars of which are indicated on the engraving. It is impossible to estimate from the picture the size of the house. It was probably from 80 to 100 feet in length facing Chestnut Street and from 40 to 60 feet deep. Very handsome bas reliefs had been prepared for the ornamentation of the mansion by Jardella and other workmen who were brought to the city to assist in the building. Some of their work afterward figured in other buildings.

It has been said that Major L'Enfant first broached the scheme for building a grand house for Mr. Morris at a dinner given by the latter. He said he could do it for $60,000, and upon its being suggested that this sum was enormous, Mr. Morris said he could sell his houses and lots on Market Street for $80,000 and thus be supplied with abundant funds. He owned at that time the house in which President Washington lived, 46 foot front; a lot of 75 feet adjoining, and the house and lot at the southeast corner of Sixth Street, which had a 60 foot front. He sold the house in which the President lived in 1795 for $37,000. The other properties were worth more than enough to make up the $80,000 to which Mr. Morris referred.

The Robert Morris House, Philadelphia, by Pierre Charles L'Enfant. Design Published by W. Birch, 1800

The extravagance of the architect, it has been generally said, was the cause of Mr. Morris's failure. But it is easy to see that the reason was not the cost of the building, which, although it might have exceeded the estimates, was not sufficient to have produced the ruin of Mr. Morris if he had been free from other embarrassments. The enormous land speculations into which he entered with John Nicholson and James Greenleaf were really the cause of Mr. Morris's failure. It was said that the notes of Morris, Nicholson and Greenleaf "were as thick in the money market as autum leaves that were strewn in the brooks of Vallombrosa." The "Company" had contracted to sell 6,000,000 acres of land, much of which was beyond the Appalachian Mountains, which was then the "Frontier of America" but they sold not much more than 100,000 acres. Morris was imprisoned for debt, but in view of his valiant service to General Washington during the American Revolution, was released after imprisonment of about three and a half years. It is said Morris then still owed $3,000,000. He died in 1806 and lies buried in the old Christ Church graveyard, near Second and Market Streets, in the historic Independence Hall section of the city, where the Nation was founded and in which he had such a prominent part.

Robert Morris wrote to L'Enfant at length on the subject of the "Magnificent House" as follows:

"Phila. Septr. 24th, 1795.

"Major C. P. L'Enfant.

Sir:

"I have just now at 2 o'clock received your note dated yesterday. My sole motive for being urgent proceeds from an anxiety to get a roof over the West Wing of the House. I am now paying above £1000 p. ann. Rent, and having sold the House I live in, the owner may want it, before 1 have a place to go into. My intention if the West Wing is covered is to get into it next Summer or Spring, which I know will be impossible if it is not covered this Winter. I am incapable of doing injustice to your fame or fortune, no motives of that kind influenced my Conduct. You gave me assurance six weeks ago that the House should be covered this Fall. I have not the command of my time to look after it myself and therefore depended upon your assurances consequently when I came yesterday and found both by my own observation & by the answers Obtained to questions which I put to Mr. Wallace that there was no chance of getting the whole building covered, I desired to know from you 'to my satisfaction' whether the West Wing could be covered in the time proposed or not, declaring my intention to have it run up with Brick should delay in waiting for marble be likely to prevent the covering of it. To this question you very abruptly told me to ask Miller if he could do his work in time and that a roof could not be put on without the Outside Wall. This answer I think was extremely improper from you to me. I certainly have a right to enquire, to examine and to be satisfied and if you do not think I am entitled to receive satisfaction from you, it is high time to part, my declaration that I would run Brick Walls rather than not have the Building covered is not new. I told you the same thing at the time you assured me it should be covered this Fall, therefore it could be no surprize upon you now. I never desired that you should sacrifice your interest in any respect on my Acct. & if you have done so it has been your own act not mine. I do not wish you to sacrifice any thing to or for me but if I am to pay, I am entitled to every information I may think proper to ask, and I have an unquestionable right to expedite my building & lessen my expense if I choose so to do.—I am therefore determined to have the Roof put on the West Wing as early this Fall as possible, and altho it was not my intention or desire to have the marble you have introduced into this building, yet an inclination to indulge your genius induced me to permit so much of it (before I knew the extent to which you meant to carry it) as seemed to call for the remainder. Had you executed my intentions instead of your own, my family would now have inhabited the House instead of being liable to be turned out of Doors. After all, I prefer that the West Wing & of course the whole building should go on under your directions but with this proviso, that you will positively have it covered this Fall. If not I would rather abandon all the marble and finish with Brick, therefore if you agree, follow it up & get the thing done, if you do not my orders to the builders must be obeyed. I am with sincerity yours &c."

ROBT. MORRIS

In August 1796 Robert Morris complained to L'Enfant that "the delay and accumulation of Expence becomes

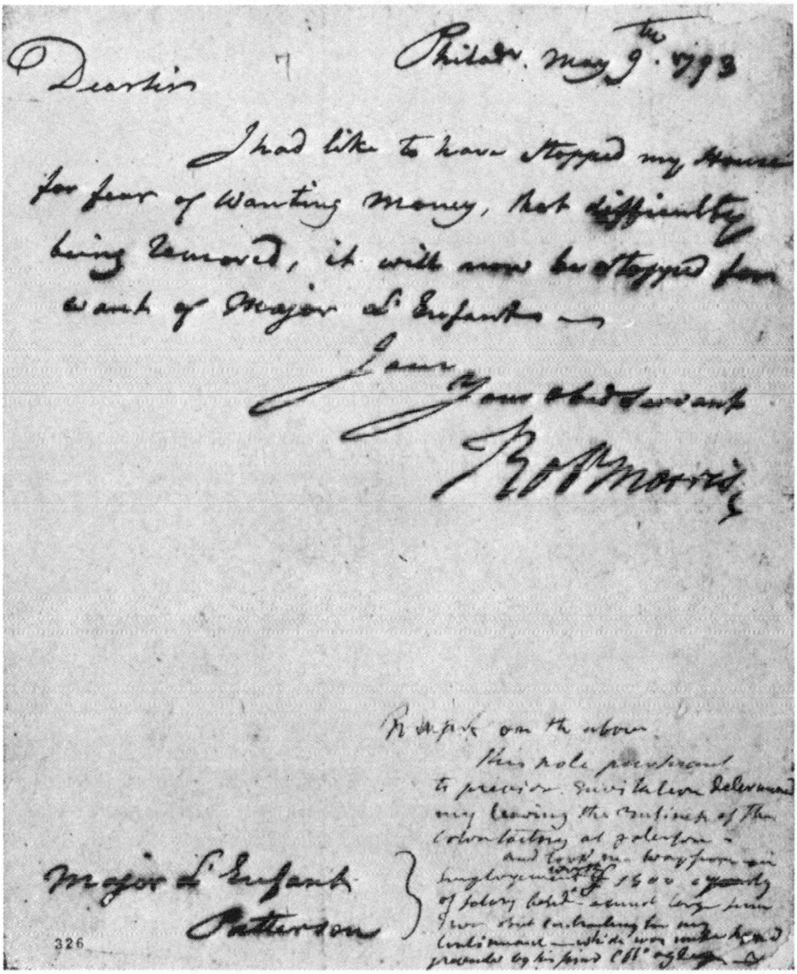

Philada. May 9th 1793

Dear Sir

I had like to have stopped my House for fear of Wanting Money, that difficulty being removed, it will now be stopped from want of Major L'Enfant —

I am
Your obed Servant
Robt Morris

Major L'Enfant
Patterson

326

Courtesy Library of Congress

Letter from Robert Morris to L'Enfant

Promisery Note from Robert Morris to L'Enfant

intolerable." Thus Mr. Morris hoped he could soon get into the house; or else threatened to stop the work.

The house was never completed. The roof was closed and the windows were boarded. Philadelphian's pointed to it as "Morris's Folly".

But L'Enfant bore no grudge against Morris and his unselfish nature manifested itself a few years later when Morris was imprisoned for debt.

Major L'Enfant befriended the financier by loan of bank stocks, and in response to an importunity for repayment, Mr. Morris, on October 18, 1797, wrote:

"I am in as great need as you are and equally desirous of acquiring relief for both, my endeavors shall be increasing and the moment I secure it shall be announced to you with joy and satisfaction."

The Major was a creditor for his services, although he presented no account; and Morris, in 1800, wrote:

"Various circumstances render me little solicitous on the score of his services, but he lent me thirteen shares of bank stock disinterestedly, and on this point I feel the greatest anxiety that he should get the same number of shares with dividends, for want of which he has suffered great distress."

The English traveler Isaac Weld, wrote in the account of his travels through the States of North America during the years 1795-1797, concerning the Robert Morris House:

"The most spacious and most remarkable one amongst them stands in Chestnut Street, but it is not yet quite finished. At present it appears a huge mass of red brick and pale blue marble, which bids defiance to simplicity and elegance. This superb mansion, according to report, has already cost upwards of fifty thousand guineas, and stands as a monument of the increasing luxury of the city of Philadelphia."[3]

OLD CONGRESS HALL

It is possible, even probable, that L'Enfant drew the plans for the enlargement of old Congress Hall in Philadelphia. It is established that the building, then being finished and which had been accepted by Congress for the purpose of holding its sessions there, was too small to hold that body. An addition of about forty feet was added to the building on its southern end, and the internal arrangements had to be changed. It is believed that this work was accomplished under the direction of L'Enfant. Some basis for this belief is to be found in the Journal of William Maclay, one of the first two Senators from Pennsylvania. Under date of May 14, 1789, he mentions a meeting of the Committee for dividing rooms, and also mentions that L'Enfant was present.

Another one of L'Enfant's projects was:

---

[3] Allen C. Clark, **Greenleaf and Law in the Federal City,** 1901, pp. 28-30.

OELLER'S HOTEL

Henry Wansey, in his Excursion to the United States, 1794, writes of it and the Philadelphia Assembly, in that year:

The Assembly Room, at Oeller's Hotel, must not pass undescribed. It is a most elegant room, sixty feet square, with a handsome music gallery at one end. It is papered after the French taste, with the Pantheon figures in compartments imitating festoons, pillars and groups of antique drawings in the same style as lately introduced in the most elegant houses in London. To help my readers to form some idea of the state of polished society there, I must subjoin the rules for regulating their Assemblies, which I copied from the frame hanging in the room. (*Extract from The Philadelphia Assemblies, by T. W. Balch, Philadelphia, 1916, page* 100.)

After the termination of his work on the Plan of Washington in an official capacity, in 1792, L'Enfant returned to Philadelphia to live, for a year or two. While he dwelt in Philadelphia, L'Enfant boarded at No. 4 North Eighth Street, and his name is to be found in the Directory for the year 1794.

L'Enfant's services were called upon to design a residence for John Nicholson and also in connection with another building in Philadelphia as seen from the following letter:

"New York Jan'y the 29, 1787.

"Dear Sir:

"I have received the letter which you did me the honor to write to me dated _____. It would have given me much satisfaction had I been able to comply with your request but the plan mentioned was sent to some of the gentlemen of the society to which it was intended for and never has been since returned to me—what they mean to do with it I do not know but as to it being put into execution is a matter that appears likely not to take place _____ you say, for that the gentlemen of your city are seriously determined upon erecting building similar to that I had proposed here if this should be the case and you so partial to me as to believe my skill might be of service to them I will with pleasure shown a new plan 'a masur' which if agreeable will after all be the best for the one in question was but an imperfect sketch which could be of no assistance to my undertaker but under the immediate direction of the original designer considering that it was made without regard to any particular spot of ground neither combined with relation to any given limits nor consideration of the lott.   monney being the principal which to all motion is most necessary to be considered when projecting any and particularly such building as the one intended consequently this sum which your city propose to laid out in this business I should be glad to known—also what part of the city has been determined upon and what is the out line dimention of the lot proposed—70 or 80 feet front upon 250 dept was the proportion of the draught which I showd to you. I wished to have it fixed on a lot free from all side at least so as to admit of street upon each of its three parallels—the outside of the building I propose to surround with small shops under cover of a gallery the effect of which you are to be better juge than anyone here having seen something similar in the _____ that surround the comedie francaise at Paris or that surround the palais _____ garden—this I conceived would have been not only grand but yet of a pecuniary advantage it being certain that the rents coming from these shops would soon repaid the expenses of the whole building or at least bring a good interest for the money. no city in America being better calculated to admit a building of this kind than that of philadelphia & I hear say now having inhabitants better able to subscribe a sum adequate to the expense I should supose it may be safe for you to influence the mesur and as to assistance on my part should it be wanted it will afford me pleasur _____ 7,000 pounds was the sum to which I had evaluated the cost of the building which I had intended for the city of New York and as I am told the workmanship is at present greatly cheaper in your State than it was formerly I conceive that little more added to that sum would be sufficient to compleat the whole of above mentioned for from the manner I would propose to conduct the work it would prove by much less expense than the common way of doing which in all case is neither safe nor economical and which in this is not even admissible considering that the whole composition of the farming being materially (?) out of the usual way none but the plain work such as the walls and framing of the roofs and floors &c should be done by undertaking.

I have the honor to be
dear sir your most humble obediant
Servant

Mr. W. T. Franklin

P. Ch. L'Enfant" [4]

[4] Printed by permission of the American Philosophical Society, Philadelphia.

Part of Fort Mifflin, Pa.

Photograph by the Author

"Commandant's House," Fort Mifflin

FORT MIFFLIN, PENNSYLVANIA

Fort Mifflin is situated on Mud Island in the Delaware River, one mile below the mouth of the Schuylkill and seven below Philadelphia City proper. The site was occupied for military purposes during and perhaps before the Revolutionary War. The present work was commenced in 1798. The reservation contained about 317 acres. It was designed, with wharves, by Pierre Charles L'Enfant.

L'Enfant was appointed "temporary engineer" to fortify the ports of Philadelphia and Wilmington on the Delaware by order of Secretary of War Knox dated April 3, 1794. An account of the work done is set forth in detailed correspondence published in the *American State Papers,* Military Affairs, Vol. I. 1832 (pp. 82-87). A copy of a part of them appears in Appendix F of this volume.

The writer visited the present Fort Mifflin (now a part of the environs of — south — Philadelphia) in company with Mr. Harold D. Eberlein, author and an outstanding authority on the History of Philadelphia. Mr. Eberlein states that while Fort Mifflin has been restored, work done by L'Enfant is clearly in evidence, as for example the commandant's house, which resembles a French chateau, or mansion — the Petit Trianon in shape — and details of walls of the fort.

Chapter IX

LATER YEARS OF L'ENFANT'S LIFE

L'ENFANT OFFERED A PROFESSORSHIP AT WEST POINT

A S HERETOFORE set forth, L'Enfant spent most of his time from 1800 to 1810 endeavoring to secure payment for his services in laying out the Plan of the City of Washington.

On July 7, 1812, Secretary of War W. Eustis appointed "Peter Charles L'Enfant" Professor of the Art of Engineering, in the Military Academy of the United States at West Point.

In acknowledging the notice of appointment, L'Enfant wrote at length to the Secretary of War by letter dated Washington, D. C., July 17, 1812,[1] giving his reasons for declining the appointment, — "unaccepted but not rejected."

L'Enfant complained first of all about the state of his financial affairs, saying that he had been bereft by the Revolution [both the French and the American] of the whole of his estate, without resources whatever for personal support, and then complained about lack of compensation for his Plan for the City of Washington. Also, he was not well satisfied with his "fitness to the office of Instructor of youths"; he expressed himself as preferring an appointment as military and civil engineer in connec-

---

[1] Original letter in the National Archives; copy, see Appendix G., p. 445.

268

tion with work on harbours, fortifications and the like, for which he considered himself qualified by experience "during the revolutionary war and in the late enterprise of the city of Washington."

Further, he stated that he had not "the rigidity of manner, the tongue, nor the patience, nor indeed any inclination peculiar to instructors"; also, he said, he would have to encounter the difficulty of language. He seemed to prefer trained soldiers through active service to those trained largely through a study of books in "imitation of those of other nations." Also he pointed out that to accept the professorship at West Point would deprive him (by law) from becoming again a military officer, since "none of the staff of the academy shall be entitled to command in the army; it reduces me from the rank of principal engineer, an office to which I was appointed by President Washington in 1793. . . ."

The letter came to the attention of Secretary of State Monroe, and on the same date (17 July, 1812), Monroe wrote to L'Enfant urging him to accept appointment, as follows:

"I have this moment recvd. your letter and have not time to give you an answer on the several subjects to which it relates. My earnest advice to you is to accept the appointment offered you by the Govt. It will deprive you of no claim which you now have, and provide you an honorable station and support. Your creditors have no prospect in your present situation. This appointment may afford some hope. My wish, therefore, is that you accept it. You might write a letter to the Secretary of War and to the President, stating that more active service was desired and—into all the considerations which you think proper, but do not decline this appointment."

With regards, yours,

Jas. Monroe."

Monroe wrote a more detailed letter[2] (personal, in the

2 Original in the Monroe papers, Library of Congress; copy, see Appendix G., p. 449.

spirit and feeling of an old revolutionary fellow) to L'Enfant on July 28, 1812, recommending that he accept the appointment of professor at West Point and suggesting it could possibly be arranged that he rejoin the army; that he would be in the public service; and that by accepting the appointment he would "relinquish no claim." It carried with it the rank and pay of major.

FORT WASHINGTON, MARYLAND

In May, 1813, a British fleet under the command of Admiral Warren and Rear Admiral Cockburn began to blockade Chesapeake and Delaware Bays. Cockburn ascended the Chesapeake and burned Havre de Grace and other towns. From Philadelphia to Richmond most citizens realized that the coast defenses were weak and Major L'Enfant at this time made a report to the President on the inadequacy of these defenses. The National Capital itself was in danger.

On July 25, 1814, just a month before the Battle of Bladensburg, the officer in charge of Fort Washington reported to General Winder the defenseless situation of the post and at the suggestion of the General the War Department consulted Major L'Enfant, who in a written report told of the delapidated condition of the fort and the armament and urged a suitable appropriation for putting it in proper condition for the defense of the Potomac and the Federal City. He spoke of the necessity for an additional number of heavy guns at Fort Washington and an additional fort in the neighborhood, and concluded:

"The whole original design is bad, and it is therefore impossible to make a perfect work of it by alterations."

L'Enfant's Letter of Appointment as Professor at West Point

For two years the City of Washington had stood unprotected. Not a battery or a breastwork was to be found on the river bank except Fort Washington. With all the facts before him, Secretary of War Armstrong argued the utter improbability of a possible force leaving its fleet and marching 40 miles inward. As to the Potomac its rocks and shoals and devious channels would prevent a stranger from ascending it. The City of Alexandria raised $1,500 for defenses, but the matter received little attention. This neglect by Government authorities resulted in the City of Alexandria having to pay the equivalent of $100,000 with which it purchased immunity from attack soon after the burning of Washington in August, 1814.

Only a few days elapsed after the departure of the British when Secretary of State Monroe (who was then also Acting Secretary of War; General Armstrong having resigned) ordered Major L'Enfant on September 8, 1814, to proceed to Warburton Manor) and reconstruct a fort. In accordance with the order of James Monroe L'Enfant went, and the place was subsequently named Fort Washington. The record shows that he used 1,000 pieces of stone and 200,000 bricks, as well as lumber in the reconstruction work. Major L'Enfant designed and superintended the construction of the fort, which was protected by a moat and drawbridge. Handshaped natural stone composed the walls. The original work was begun in 1815 and completed in 1824.

A mound is all that remains of Warburton Manor, then the home of Thomas A. Digges. Here L'Enfant made his home from 1815 until the year 1824. A historical marker indicates the location of the house. After that

Major L'Enfant took up his residence with a nephew William Dudley Digges in Prince Georges County, Maryland, at an estate called Green Hill where L'Enfant died at the age of almost 71 years, on June 14, 1825. For the last ten years of his life he was a dependant.

For many subsequent years the War Department used Fort Washington as a station for troops. In more recent years the fort was used as a place of encampment by the District of Columbia Militia. About the year 1924 the War Department planned to sell the fort, but a group of persons interested in preserving the fort as a place of historic interest, persuaded the War Department not to sell it and Congress agreed to this.

The National Capital Park and Planning Commission received authority to buy the fort as part of what is known as the Capper-Crampton Act of 1930, under which there will be constructed the George Washington Memorial Parkway on the Maryland side of the Potomac River, extending from Fort Washington, by way of Indian Queen Bluff, Fort Foote, and Oxon Run, to the City of Washington, and thence on both banks of the Potomac to Great Falls, which is about 16 miles to the northwest of the National Capital. This Parkway has been in part under construction for a number of years.

There has been considerable discussion concerning work actually performed at Fort Washington by Major L'Enfant. None of the original plans appear to be available. The writer visited Fort Washington in the fall of 1945, at a meeting of The Thornton Society at that place, anod a brief historical sketch of the Fort was given by Lieut. Commander Delos Smith, a well-known architect of the National Capital. Commander Smith pointed out

Plan of Fort Washington, Showing Part of L'Enfant's Work

that records pertaining to L'Enfant's work at Fort Washington are meagre, and evidences of work by L'Enfant still less, since the Fort has been greatly enlarged since his day. However, traces of a ravelin and several ditches are there, which are pointed out as being distinctly work done under L'Enfant's direction. It is to be remembered that, in his letter of September 11, 1789 (heretofore quoted, page 129), L'Enfant, when he applied for the appointment to prepare a Plan for the Federal City, also made suggestions for coastal defenses, and as matters developed,

Fort Washington became one of a chain of forts along the Atlantic sea-coast. Also, as related in Chapter I, designing forts is a technique he had learned from his father.

Mr. Stanley W. McClure, Historian, for the National Park Service, Department of the Interior, made an exhaustive study of the History of Fort Washington, and we quote in part from his Memorandum on the subject dated May 26, 1941:

Subject: The Strategic Location of Fort Washington and the Importance of the Drawbridge in its defense.

"The strategic advantage of the promontory on the Potomac which is known as Fort Washington, seems to have been known to the Indians, long before the coming of the white man into the region. When the English colonists under Governor Leonard Calvert, exploring the Upper Potomac for a location for a settlement, came to the mouth of Piscataway Creek, they found the surrounding heights covered with Indians, to the number of about 500, in hostile array. Although Calvert and his men were able to convince the Indians that their mission was friendly, it was deemed unwise to become established so far up the Potomac, and retreating downstream, the party entered the St. Mary's river and founded the town of St. Mary's [the first settlement in the State of Maryland] on March 27, 1634.

"The land facing the Potomac between Piscataway and Swan creeks, and for some distance to the Northeast, came into the possession of the Digges family in 1717. Mt. Vernon, the home of George Washington, was less than three miles down the Potomac from Warburton, the estate of the Digges'. Washington often visited with George and Thomas Digges and spent his forty-third birthday at Warburton.

"With the establishment of the National Capital in Washington, it was necessary to provide means for its protection on the Potomac. On May 12, 1794, Washington wrote to Henry Knox, Secretary of War, 'The President of the United States, who is well acquainted with the river Potomac conceived that a certain bluff of land on the Maryland side near Mr. Digges, a point formed by an eastern branch of the Potomac would be a proper situation for the fortification about to be erected.'

"Although negotiations began immediately for the purchase of land at Digges' Point upon which to erect a fortification, it was not until April 15, 1808, that three and three-quarters acres of land were purchased there for $6,000. Fort Washington, the name given to the new fortress, consisted of an enclosed star work of stone and brick, situated at the foot of a steep acclivity, the summit of which was protected by an octagonal blockhouse, built of brick and two stories high and designed for musketry. A brick magazine and a brick barracks for one company of men and officers completed the fort. The star work was protected by twenty guns while the blockhouse mounted two lighter cannons.

"Upon the approach of the British Squadron of seven ships under Captain Gordon, on August 23, 1814, Fort Washington was abandoned and the magazine was blown up by Captain Samuel T. Dyson, the American commander. Capt. Dyson was tried by court martial and dismissed from the service for surrendering the fort without having fired a shot in its defense . . . It was abandoned because of the fear of a combined land and water attack.

"Only a few days had elapsed after the departure of the British when Acting Secretary of War James Monroe ordered Major Charles L'Enfant (Sept. 8, 1814) to proceed to Fort Washington and reconstruct the fort. The remainder of the season was spent in clearing the debris and demolishing the old fort, and in beginning work on a water battery. On March 1, 1815, work was resumed on the water battery and in the building of a wharf. Major L'Enfant, however, failed to present a plan of the work as requested by the War Department . . . Operations were suspended on July 8, 1815, and on September 6 Lieut. Col. Walker K. Armistead succeeded

Directions from Monroe to L'Enfant

Major L'Enfant at Fort Washington . . . Additional land was purchased from the Digges'—in all some 52 acres, and a large fort was built, which can be seen today. The amount expended on Fort Washington from January 1, 1815, to December 14, 1836, was $454,103.

"Fort Washington, as completed in 1824, was an irregular bastioned work with a perimeter of 835 yards.

L'ENFANT AND THE GLOVER FAMILY

In his book entitled *With Americans of Past and Present Days,*[3] Ambassador Jusserand stated in the chapter on L'Enfant and the Federal City, page 144, after having mentioned pencil portraits drawn by L'Enfant at Valley Forge:

"Some such pencil portraits by L'Enfant subsist, for example in the Glover family at Washington, and are creditable and obviously true to nature sketches."

The writer had occasion to confer with Colonel Charles C. Glover, Jr., an esteemed member of the Columbis Historical Society concerning this matter, and received from him the following Memorandum, as well as a print of one of the portraits therein referred to and published in this volume:

"February 4, 1946.

"There are in the possession of our family, three pencil sketches of my great grand-father, Charles C. Glover, who was born in Carroll County Maryland, in 1780, and died in Washington in 1827. It has always been understood in our family that these sketches were made by Pierre Charles L'Enfant, although there are no signatures or initials on the drawings.

"My great-aunt, Mrs. A. F. Shriver, who was Mary Jane Glover, and who died in 1918 at the age of 94, told me that her mother, Mary Cocking Glover, who died in 1876 at the age of 87, had stated that these three sketches of her husband were done by L'Enfant, and that he was a frequent visitor at the family residence, 421 10th Street, N. W. It was thought that there were other papers relating to L'Enfant, but these were lost when the house burned many years ago. The present building, which we still own, was erected after the fire.

"The three sketches are quite similar, although there are minor dif-

[3] J. J. Jusserand, with Americans of Past and Present Days, Charles Scribner's & Sons, New York, 1917, p. 144.

Charles Glover

A Sketch by Pierre Charles L'Enfant About 1811

ferences in detail. There is quite a difference in the type of paper used in each one. It would seem that they were done for different members of the family. One is at the present time in my possession, one in that of my sister, Elizabeth L. van Swinderen, and the third belongs to my son, Charles C. Glover III.

"My great grand-father was undoubtedly the subject of these sketches because of the close resemblance to an oil painting of him by an artist of the time, Charles B. King, which is in my sister's possession. My great grand-father was a man of standing in the community. He was actively engaged in the practice of law, had extensive property holdings in the old part of the city, was elected several times to the City Council, and was also a member of the Board of Aldermen. He was active on a committee to promote the building of the Court House, and was a member of a committee representing the citizens to seek legislation from Congress regarding the District.

"In his various activities he no doubt came in contact with Major L'Enfant and was one of several Washington residents who befriended him in his later years."

Mr. Glover showed the writer a picture of the oil painting above mentioned, and noted "the close resemblance." Knowing of L'Enfant's ability as an artist there need not be any doubt as to the authenticity of these sketches.

No portrait of Major Pierre Charles L'Enfant exists. W. W. Corcoran, who knew him best, left a brief description of his appearance, as also Benjamin Perley Poore (quoted on pages 280 and 281).

DESCRIPTION OF L'ENFANT

THE MEDALLION OF PIERRE CHARLES L'ENFANT

The medallion, which appears among others on a bank building in Chevy Chase, was designed by a distinguished architect of Washington, D. C., Leon Chatelain. "When I showed the photograph to Cass Gilbert," Charles Moore, Chairman of the National Commission of Fine Arts said in a brief Memorandum to the Journal, "he thought it was the work of Houdon. Of course a closer examination of the work would disclose that it was not,

Medallion of L'Enfant by Leon Chatelain, Architect

but the general impression given by the medallion is excellent. If L'Enfant didn't look like it, he ought to have done so. In the same manner Daniel Chester French has designed for Harvard University a statue of John Harvard, which has taken its place as the portrait of the founder of the University." (From the Journal of the American Institute of Architects, July, 1928.)

The Honorable Hugh T. Taggart, in his article on *Old Georgetown* (Records of the Columbia Historical Society, Volume XI, pages 216-17) wrote the following:

"Mr. W. W. Corcoran, who lately departed this life in the city of Washington full of years and of honor, and who cherished to the last an affectionate interest in Georgetown, which was the place of his birth and the home of his childhood, had a very distinct recollection of the personal appearance of L'Enfant, the latter having been a frequent visitor at his father's house. He described him to me as a tall, erect man, fully six feet in height, finely proportioned, nose prominent, of military bearing, courtly air and polite manners, his figure usually enveloped in a long overcoat and surmounted by a bell-crowned hat — a man who would attract attention in any assembly. The late John H. Latrobe of Baltimore, who was the son of Benjamin H. Latrobe, at one time architect of the Capitol and at another surveyor of Washington, also had a clear recollection of Major L'Enfant, and his description of him agreed with Mr. Corcoran's. All accounts concur in depicting the major as a man of honorable and high spirit and of great abilities in his profession, but impulsive, and, as General Washington said of him, "of untoward disposition."

In Benjamin Perley Poore's Reminiscences (Volume I, p. 54) we find the following interesting "personal" reference to L'Enfant:

"When Major L'Enfant came to Georgetown to lay out the Federal District he brought a letter of introduction to my grandfather, who had a great deal of trouble in endeavoring to adjust the difficulties between the fiery French officer and the Commissioners appointed to govern the infant metropolis. The Major, who was very imperious, claimed supreme authority, which the Commissioners would not submit to. On one occasion as Mr. Carroll had commenced the erection of a large brick house, which Major L'Enfant found encroached on one of the proposed streets. Summoning his chain bearers and axmen, he demolished the trespassing structure and filled up the cellar, against Mr. Carroll's earnest protests.

"He was a favorite with Washington, but Jefferson disliked him on account of his connection with the Society of the Cincinnati, and availed himself of his difficulty with the Commissioners to discharge him.

"The Major then became unsuccessful petitioner before Congress for a redress of his real and fancied wrong, and he was to be seen almost every day slowly pacing the rotunda of the Capitol. He was a tall, thin man, who wore, toward the close of his life, a blue military surtout coat, buttoned quite to the throat, with a tall, black stock, but no visible signs of linen. His hair was plastered with pomatum close to his head, and he wore a napless high beaver bell-crowned hat. Under his arm he generally carried a roll of papers relating to his claim upon the Government, and in his right hand he swung a formidable hickory cane with a large silver head. A strict Roman Catholic, he received a home in the family of Mr. Digges near Washington, in whose garden his remains were interred when he died."

THE DIGGES FAMILY AND L'ENFANT

The Digges family was related to some of the most notable houses of Great Britain. The records show that

The Grave of L'Enfant, 1825 to 1909

Royal blood flowed in their veins. They had a part in the earliest history of the settlement of Virginia and Maryland.

Edward Digges arrived in Virginia about 1650. He was appointed member of the Council of Virginia and in

The Old Site of L'Enfant's Grave Under the Cedars at Green Hill

1656 was commissioned Governor of Virginia. His eldest son William moved to Maryland about 1680-81 and came into possession of large tracts of land in the Province. From the eldest line of the Digges family in America has descended many of Maryland's most distinguished sons and daughters. Col. Wm. Digges was at once made a member of the Provincial Council and was Deputy Governor during the absence of Lord Baltimore.

Among estates in several counties that he owned was Warburton Manor in Prince Georges County, opposite Mount Vernon. The Digges and the Washingtons were neighbors and friends. It is said a code of signals existed between General Washington and his contemporaries at Warburton; when a signal was received at Warburton a barge would shoot out from its moorings to bring the General across the river. As time passed descendants of the Digges intermarried with a number of representative families of Maryland. Among notable descendants from Col. Wm. Digges was Charles Carroll of Carrollton, Rev. John Carroll, first Bishop of Baltimore, Daniel Carroll, the Commissioners of the District of Columbia, of Rock Creek.[4] One of the descendants was Wm. D. Digges, who lived at Green Hill, which today is in the suburban area of Northeast Washington, called Chillum. When the Government rebuilt Warburton (to be known henceforth as Fort Washington), L'Enfant, who was then living with the Digges' there, found it necessary to seek a new home. He was then an old man, seventy years of age, and the following letter which he received must have relieved him of much anxiety:

[4] H. D. Richardson, **Sidelights of Maryland History.** Baltimore, 1913, pp. 84-86.

"Green Hill,
"February 4th, 1824.

"Dear Sir:

"I duly received your letter by George Gray and have to inform you that it would give me pleasure if you would come up and take your residence here. I have furnished George with what articles you may stand in need of at present; you will also be able to visit the city house at your ease and as often as you may please in order to attend to your business before Congress. I wish you would have all the papers and whatever you may think of any value packed up, so that when you leave Warburton, there will be nothing of importance belonging to me left behind. I shall send my wagon down again in a few days and at that time will send you a horse to ride up. I will also write you again. George Gray will have a list of the principal articles to be brought up. You may rest assured, Dear Sir, that I have considered your situation and know that it has been an unpleasant one; if a hearty welcome to Greenhill will make it more pleasant, I can assure you have it from all my family. As to the Blacksmith he is hired to Mr. Dyer. With compliments to my Aunt and John, I am, Dear Sir,

"Your obt. servt.,

"Wm. D. Digges."

"To Major L'Enfant,
      Warburton
Per George Gray"

William Dudley Digges (1790-1830) married Eleanor, daughter of Daniel Carroll of Duddington and Ann Brent (1791-1864). It was this Daniel Carroll who in 1790 began the erection of a residence south of the site of the Federal Capitol. He was the principal owner of land in the locality and undertook to build a fine mansion, which he called Duddington Manor. Unfortunately, it extended over the line of New Jersey Avenue and L'Enfant in 1791 ordered the walls torn down, as heretofore stated. Carroll was indemnified for his loss for damage done, but it led to the end of L'Enfant's services here in Washington.

Yet it seems the irony of fate that L'Enfant spent his last years in the house of Eleanor Carroll Digges, daugh-

The Digges Mansion, Green Hill

(*The Old Section Near Tree, Enlarged by George Washington Riggs, of The Riggs National Bank*)

The "L'Enfant Chair" Evermay, Georgetown

ter of the man he had offended, and that his death should have occurred there also.

L'Enfant died June 14, 1825, at the age of nearly 71 years, as heretofore stated. At his death it was found that his personal possessions amounted to the value of $45.00,[5]—three watches, one silver and two gold, $30; one compass, $10; two pocket compasses, $2.00; surveyor's instruments and books, $2.00; one lot of maps, $1.00.

L'Enfant's remains lay in the family plot under a cluster of cedars for nearly a century, when, as will be described in the following chapter, they were removed in 1909, given national honors, and taken to the Arlington National Cemetery, where they were placed in a tomb in front of the Arlington Mansion, overlooking the city he planned.

THE L'ENFANT CHAIR

Through the courtesy of Mr. John J. Cunningham, Educational Director of the National Sculpture Society, 1083 Fifth Avenue, New York City, the writer was informed that Dr. A. F. Hopkins, Curator of the Chicago Historical Society, had advised him, by letter of February 23, 1946, as follows—

"I once owned a L'Enfant item, the Ball-and-Claw foot wing chair in which the old gentleman died, . . . The chair had a silver plate inset inscribed with the circumstances of his death. I sold it to F. Lammot Belin and he carried it off to his charming home, Evermay, in Georgetown, D. C."

Mr. Belin allowed the writer to photograph the chair.

------

[5] Records of the Columbia Historical Society, Volume 2, page 123.

NATIONAL INTELLIGENCER

WASHINGTON

SATURDAY, JUNE 25, 1825.

DIED,

On the 14th inst. at Green Hill, the Seat of Wm. Dunbar Diggs, Esq. in Prince George's county, Md. Major PIERRE CHARLES L'ENFANT. Of the age of this interesting but eccentric gentleman, we have no accurate knowledge; but it could not have fallen short of seventy years. We should be glad to have possessed materials for a complete biography of the deceased. In the absence of these, we can state, from general knowledge of him, that he was a native of France, of good family. During our Revolutionary war, he was an officer of engineers, and in that capacity was severely wounded at the attack upon Savannah, and was the last of the wounded taken out of the ditch. After the present government was organized, he was employed as an Engineer in making the plan of this City, of which he is the author, and with which his name ought to be gratefully associated. He thought himself ill remunerated for this service, and, because full justice was not, as he thought, measured to him, he refused to receive what was tendered, and lived a life of sequestration from society, and austere privation, which attracted respect, whilst it excited compassion. Compassion, however, was not what he wanted: his mind was of a cast to be gratified only by receiving that sort of consideration which his talents and high and delicate sense of honor entitled him to. Such consideration he for a time enjoyed, in the rank of a Colonel of Artillery, in planning and superintending the construction of Fort Washington, fifteen miles below this city, the building of which commenced in 1815. He did not remain in authority to finish this work—which, being carried on by him too extensively, it is believed, was put in charge of another officer. He then retired from public employ, and would never receive even what money was due for his services. He was once presented, we believe, by the Corporation of New York, with a square of ground, which he did not accept; and, though poor and dependent, was too proud to put his name to a power of attorney to collect for him a dividend of the estate of an eminent citizen of Philadelphia, who was indebted to him at the time of his death. Notwithstanding this apparent infatuation, he was a man of great scientific attainments, of profound research, and close and intelligent observation. During the last ten years of his life, he was indebted to the frank hospitality of the late Thomas A. Diggs, Esq. of Warburton, until the decease of that gentleman, for a comfortable home; and, since his departure from among us, the grateful task of smoothing the downhill path of the veteran L'Enfant has been cheerfully and most kindly performed by the liberal gentleman at whose house he breathed his last. —[EDITORS.

Notice
of
Death
of
L'Enfant

L'Enfant's Body Lying in State in the Rotunda of the United States Capitol April 28, 1909

Chapter X

*T*HE MOVEMENT to give national recognition to
Pierre Charles L'Enfant terminated in April 1909, in
the exhumation of the body of Major L'Enfant at "Green
Hill." Maryland, placing it in the Rotunda of the United
States Capitol, to lie in state, and its reinterment in the
Arlington National Cemetery. It began many years back
in the history of the Nation. The well-known Washing-
tonian, William W. Corcoran, who knew L'Enfant intimately, the latter having been a frequent guest at his
father's home in Georgetown, wrote in 1884:

> "It has always been my intention, if the Government did not do so,
> to have his remains removed from the garden of the old mansion, to a
> more suitable location . . . I am sure there is not a citizen of the
> United States who would not be glad to see Congress pay this tribute of
> respect to the gallant old soldier who planned this 'City of magnificent
> distances' but which should be called the Garden City of the World."

That same year, 1884, saw the first bill introduced into
Congress asking for an appropriation to be used in the
erection of a monument to Major Pierre Charles L'Enfant. No action, however, was taken. In 1895 another
bill was introduced which demanded the specific sum of
$50,000 to the same end but its fate was in no wise dif-
ferent from the preceding one. Finally came the year
1900, the centennial of the transfer of the seat of Government from Philadelphia to the Federal City, which
aroused a new and deeper interest in the beginning as well

as in the growth and development of the Nation's Capital, and consequently in him who designed and laid out its first avenues and streets.

The movement of the restoration of the L'Enfant Plan and its development so as to adapt it to the entire District of Columbia, by what is known as The McMillan Commission and the Plan of 1901, will be related in a subsequent chapter.

The movement to have the honors of a distinguished citizen bestowed on L'Enfant and his body given a place of honor in the Arlington National Cemetery, was carried out simultaneously.

The Evening Star of April 28, 1909, reported:

"High honors were paid today the memory and remains of Major Pierre Charles L'Enfant, the French Engineer Officer, who under the authority and direction of General George Washington planned the City of Washington.

"The principal ceremony was held in the rotunda of the United States Capitol, beginning about 10:40 o'clock this forenoon.   Central figures in the notable gathering were the President and Mrs. Taft, Vice President Sherman, and the French Ambassador, M. Jusserand.   Surrounding them were Justices of the United States Supreme Court, Senators and Representatives, Members of the Diplomatic Corps, the Commissioners of the District of Columbia, and representatives of patriotic and other Societies . . . The military procession which thereupon proceeded to the Arlington National Cemetery followed along Pennsylvania Avenue ·to Georgetown and thence across the bridge to Arlington."

Reprinted from Records of The Columbia Historical Society, Vol. XIII, 1910:

"THE REINTERMENT OF MAJOR PIERRE CHARLES L'ENFANT

By James Dudley Morgan, M. D.

(Report made to the Society, May 11, 1909)

"The Sundry Civil bill of 1908, contained a small clause which read as follows:

"'One thousand dollars is made available for the Commissioners of the District of Columbia to remove and render accessible to the public the grave of Major Pierre Charles L'Enfant.'

"Congressional action had been sought many times to properly mark the grave of L'Enfant and erect a monument in the capital city; after many fruitless efforts, it was only last year that the members of the Columbia Historical Society, and a few others interested, were able to secure an appropriation; and thus a most fitting and glorious testimonial was given L'Enfant's genius and patriotism on Wednesday, April 28, 1909.

"On April 22, 1909, Commissioner Henry B. F. Macfarland, Dr. James Dudley Morgan, a grandson of William Dudley Digges who befriended L'Enfant and on whose estate 'Green Hill' in Prince Georges County, Maryland, L'Enfant was buried, Dr. William Tindall, secretary to the Commissioners, Mr. George Howard, a grandson of George Riggs, the present owner of 'Green Hill,' drove out to the grave of L'Enfant, arrangements having been previously made with the Quartermaster General's Department of the United States Army to exhume the body on that day after the location of the grave had been designated by Dr. Morgan.

"It was a lonely and unmarked grave more than six feet in length. A graceful, red cedar, drawing its vigorous life from the very earth which enveloped the ashes of the neglected Frenchman, his sole monument for eighty-four years, swaying and whispering with every breeze, carried the inspiration of his genius into never-ending requiem, while its pungent odor served as perpetual incense. 'Nature more generous than man, had drawn over the loney mound a mantle of myrtle, like a pall of perennial green.'

"The work of exhuming the body was done under the direction of D. H. Rhodes, of the Quartermaster General's Department, and of the Commissioners of the District of Columbia. The tall, slender trees which marked the spot where the Franco-American lay, and which had been planted at the head of the grave at the time the body was buried, June 14, 1825, had first to be carefully cut down before the work of transferring the body to a hermetically sealed casket could be begun. A thunder storm interrupted the operations for twenty minutes after the ground had been broken, then the digging of the grave was continued, in silence, for an hour or more. A straight line of black earth, in sharp contrast to the yellow clay the spades had brought up so far, was found at the depth of about four-and-a-half feet. Then the shovel was used carefully, the object being to trace out the line of black earth. As the dirt was cautiously removed, the outlines of the coffin became discernible. The shape was so marked as to prove to on-lookers that the resting place of Major L'Enfant had been found. As the party stood with uncovered heads around the excavation, the transfer of the remains of the famous engineer was begun. A cardinal bird, sitting in a nearby tree, sang almost continuously during the work at the grave.

"Following the sealing of the casket, it was wrapped in 'Old Glory' and conveyed to the receiving vault at Mount Olivet Cemetery where it lay until the morning of April 28, when it was taken, under military escort detailed from the Second Battalion, Corps of Engineers, Captain Michael J. McDonough, commanding, to the rotunda of the Capitol, where it lay in state from nine until twelve o'clock.

"On that day, L'Enfant who drew the plans for our city, was honored by the nation he had served.

" 'Thousands who never heard the Frenchman's name, thousands who have praised the broad avenues of the Capital City, yet knew not whose hand designed them or in whose brain the scheme of the city was born, learned that the name of L'Enfant had been blazoned at the top of the roll on which are graven those illustrious names whose memory will last as long as the beautiful city with which they are linked.'

"The long years of obscurity and lack of appreciation which shrouded the fame of the Revolutionary hero and gifted architect, were rolled away in the Capitol Rotunda, as the Ambassador from France, the Vice-President of the United States and the President of the District Commissioners paid each his glowing tribute to him who may be truthfully called the Father of the City of Washington. And when the thousands had passed around the catafalque on which reposed the casket, draped in the American flag—patriotic men and women, school children who, perhaps, had never seen the name of L'Enfant on history's page—the great casket was lifted by eight sturdy sergeants of the Engineer Corps and borne to the caisson of an artillery gun, and the long-delayed triumphal march which should have been L'Enfant's nearly a century ago, was begun to Arlington.

"L'Enfant's membership in the Cincinnati, for which society he designed the badge and the certificate, was emphasized by two incidents. As the President of the United States entered the rotunda, the blue and silver banner of the society was raised and lowered. After the addresses in the rotunda, Senator A. O. Bacon, of Georgia, inquired of Chairman Macfarland whether any insignia or emblem of the society had been placed upon the casket. Mr. Macfarland replied that there had not been. Senator Bacon then took from the lapel of his coat the badge of the Cincinnati which he was wearing and handing it to Mr. Macfarland requested him to deposit it in the grave with the remains. This commission Chairman Macfarland executed just before the grave was closed.

"The funeral procession was nearly a mile long and most impressive. The streets were lined with spectators, flags were displayed at half mast, and as the cortege passed the rooms of the Veteran Volunteer Fireman's Association, their bell tolled solemnly. Even this-bell has had a varied history. Cast in 1856, for the Northern Liberties Fire Company, it sent out its grim warning until 1864, when the fire alarm went into service. The bell was then lent to Saint Theresa's Roman Catholic Church of Anacostia and for years called that congregation to prayer and praise. Finally in 1895, it was loaned to its present custodians and since then has paid its tribute of respect to many noted ones among the nation's dead.

"In the National Cemetery at Arlington the grave was surrounded by the foremost men of the Capital. With bowed heads and lowered eyes they stood while the Reverend William T. Russell, pastor of Saint Patrick's Church, celebrated the offices of the Church, assisted by James Maloney and Sheldon Fleishell as acolytes. Following the prayers, Father Russell made this brief address:

" 'The State represented by the highest officials of our country and of the District of Columbia having paid its tribute of respect and gratitude to the genius of L'Enfant it is meet that the Church of which he was a member during life should perform her last offices of affection for his memory and of supplication in behalf of his soul. Our National Capital is enriched with monuments to the glorious memory of the heroic souls— Lafayette and Rochambeau—who contributed so generously to the achievement of our independence. Tardy have we been in acknowledging our debt of gratitude to him who planned, the 'City Beautiful.' But at length we have awakened to a sense of justice to him, and to the land which gave him birth. France—Catholic France—was our only ally, when we most needed friends. But for the ready financial aid with which Catholic France replenished our exhausted treasury, whereby our patriots were persuaded to keep the field, and but for the timely aid of Rochambeau and de Grasse—it may well be questioned how long our independence would have been deferred.

" 'This ceremony today reflects credit on the nation which thus speaks its gratitude, and honor on Catholic France and her heroes, who so rightly deserve it. L'Enfant needs no monument of marble or of bronze. The City Beautiful at his feet is the proudest and most endearing monument we can erect to his memory.

" 'But we come not to praise L'Enfant. He is beyond our power of praise. We come to pray for him, that his good works and our prayers may ascend to heaven as the odor of sweet incense before the throne of justice and mercy, and to bless his remains which we trust will rise to a glorious resurrection.

" 'May God grant to him who planned and dreamed the City Beautiful before us, an abode in the new Jerusalem the Celestial City Beautiful.'

"A moment of absolute silence, then three volleys were fired by a detachment of the Engineer Corps and Principal Musician, George A. Wintermyer, of the Engineer Band, sounded 'taps'—a soldier's burial—a fitting climax to the long-delayed honor which that day was paid to L'Enfant.

"Grant me a few minutes to recall some of the many glowing tributes paid to his genius and his faith in the glorious future of his adopted country. He 'forecasted the future.' He laid out a city for 'fifty states instead of thirteen.' He could 'imagine things a century before they happened.' Like many of his kind, he was 'dead long before his dream came true.' His 'services were not for one generation merely, but for all time; neither were they for the United States alone; the whole world may enjoy the beauties of Washington and delight in its charms as one of the greatest national capitals.' 'That L'Enfant's mind evolved the general plan of the present Washington,' said Vice-President Sherman, 'seems beyond the possibility of dispute.' There was no question regarding his 'ability or his taste. These plans which are now universally praised, were laughed at, derided and set aside as being too expensive and too ambitious, at the time they were made; but it is to L'Enfant's adherence to his original idea and his belief in the future greatness of this country, that the beauty of this city is due.' 'To plan this city,' said Ambassador Jusserand in his address, 'Washington selected a French Officer, whose qualities of character and faults of temper, he had for thirteen years many occasions to appreciate; gifted, plucky, energetic, but difficult to handle.'

"Without the aid and backing which the Columbia Historical Society gave and secured, the remains of L'Enfant would not rest in Arlington today. The suggestion of the use of the rotunda of the United States Capitol was made to your president some months ago by two members of this Society, each unconscious until this reading that the other had the same idea.

"It was to Mrs. Madison A. Ballinger and to Mrs. Charles W. Richardson that the appropriateness of the use of the rotunda came. A bereavement in the family of Mrs. Richardson prevented her taking an active part, and it was to Mrs. Ballinger and her husband that we owe the largest part of the success of having secured the capitol for the funeral services. There were many who cooperated and did valiant work; perhaps the names of Messrs. S. C. Neale, W. W. Abell, M. M. Parker, Representative Samuel W. Smith, Senator Isador Rayner and Senator A. O. Bacon, stand out most prominently.

"To but seven others had this honor of lying in state in the rotunda been accorded and each of the others was a native-born citizen:

"Abraham Lincoln, April 19 to 21, 1865.

"Thaddeus Stevens, August 13, 1868.

"Salmon P. Chase, May —, 1873.

"Charles Sumner, March —, 1874.
"James A. Garfield, September 21 to 23, 1881.
"John A. Logan, December 30, 1886.
"William McKinley, September 17, 1901.
"Pierre Charles L'Enfant, April 28, 1909."

"PRESENTATION OF GAVEL TO THE
COLUMBIA HISTORICAL SOCIETY

By Dr. James Dudley Morgan, President
November 9, 1909

"This gavel, made from the root of the red cedar tree which marked the grave for nearly a century of that genius and patriot, Pierre Charles L'Enfant, is presented to the Columbia Historical Society. It is peculiarly appropriate that a society which has worked so unceasingly and zealously for justice to and recognition of a genius who gave up country, home and friends for our cause, should receive as a relic and memento, the heart and root of the cedar tree, which has for generations stood as his only headstone. Erect, ever green, now resting, now sighing with the winds, its growth and strength came from his very ashes; it stood as a sentinel, a constant reminder, as a link with the past.

"Today L'Enfant rests in historic Arlington; an honored grave and pomp are his. And the cedar tree has fallen, but from its trunk and veins this gavel has been made for you.

"The eternal laws of compensation in the end work out all things aright and the 'mills of the gods' though slow, ofttimes grind exceedingly sure.

"With this gavel is also presented the correspondence, clippings and illustrations incident to the life of L'Enfant and the removal of his remains from Green Hill to the rotunda of the United States Capitol and thence to Arlington National Cemetery."

THE TOMB OF PIERRE CHARLES L'ENFANT

ARLINGTON NATIONAL CEMETERY

While in Paris during the summer of the year 1948, the writer had the privilege to confer with Mr. Welles Bosworth, architect, at his beautiful home in the suburb Vaucresson, concerning Pierre Charles L'Enfant, in particular with regard to L'Enfant's tomb in the Arlington

National Cemetery.   Mr. Bosworth presented the following statement, together with a photograph of the competition drawing:

"THE L'ENFANT MONUMENT COMPETITION

"When McKim, Burnham, Olmsted and perhaps others, were defending so valorously the L'Enfant Plan to us members of the American Institute of Architects and to the authorities in Washington, Glenn Brown (a charming gentleman and resident architect of Washington), a great admirer of McKim and all he stood for, was the leading spirit at 'The Octagon.' Deeply interested in preserving the traditions of the colonial period, he worked unsparingly to keep the profession informed of what the government officials were doing to disturb them, and prevented many a project of harmful character from being realized.

"I believe Glenn Brown was among the first who conceived the idea of rescuing the grave of L'Enfant from the obscure Riggs farm, where it was seen so rarely as it was rapidly being forgotten, and having the remains moved to the National Cemetery at Arlington, with an appropriate monument. At any rate, when the scheme was adopted, it was a disappointment to the Commission to find that Army Regulations restricted the prominence of monuments in the cemetery to correspond with the grade of the individual.

"L'Enfant, being only a Major, could not have a monument exceeding a fixed height of seven feet. However, someone suggested that in view of the large number of American architects who had studied at the Ecole des Beaux Arts in Paris, it would be seemly to have a competition amongst them in selecting the architect for the monument. Twenty-five of these men entered the competition—William A. Boring and Austin W. Lord were members of the jury. There may have been others. Whitney Warren was keen about winning it and submitted two designs, very Louis XIV in character, as I remember them. My design was more in the tradition of the pre-Revolution period—of Delafosse.

"The monument was to be engraved and gilded on the oval in front like the pedestal of the Obelisk in the Place de la Concorde, and placed before the public where the view of the accomplishment of what L'Enfant had seen in his imagination could best be appreciated. A detailed summary of his life was to be engraved on the oval at the back.

"I thought it appropriate to make the design as the French architects, such as Gabriel and Migne, were doing at that time. However, Glenn Brown, William Kendall, and Cass Gilbert, who were on the Committee then, asked me if I would be willing to change my view to coincide with theirs—it was that if a monument had been erected to L'Enfant at the

Original Design for the Tomb of L'Enfant by Welles Bosworth, Architect

The Tomb of L'Enfant
Showing Part of the Plan of Washington Carved on It
Arlington National Cemetery

The L'Enfant Tomb, Overlooking the City of Washington

time of his death, by his friends in Washington, it would have been a cemetery monument of that period, colonial in type—a table tomb, with the Plan of Washington on top, and the remains in the ground below. Since this plan seemed to carry out my general idea, I of course was happy to agree with them, and proceeded to make the details, which resulted in the monument to L'Enfant now in place in front of the Arlington Mansion. Glenn Brown took charge of arrangements preparatory to the dedication.

"Mr. Taft was President then, and Monsieur Jules J. Jusserand was the French Ambassador. He took a great interest in the dedication ceremonies, which were given considerable importance. A grand-stand was erected. The President made a fine address, also Monsieur Jusserand, and several others whose names I've forgotten. It was a fine, clear summer afternoon, not hot; a large audience; color, music; and all honors were paid to L'Enfant and Washington, and to Franco-American friendship and collaboration."

"WELLES BOSWORTH
"Paris, August 20, 1948."

At the dedication of the L'Enfant Memorial May 22, 1911, Ambassador Jusserand said in part:

"By the million every year, on ships more and more numerous, immigrants, travelers, tourists, men of business and men of leisure, visit the United States. The majority of them see this land for the first time. Without exception they are struck by its immensity, its resources, the number of its inhabitants, now nearing a hundred million. All of those who visit the Federal City are unanimous in their praise of its beauty, and its exact adaptation to the needs of a great Nation. With the mind of a poet, with the soul of a prophet, perceiving future ages as clearly as if they were the present, a man foresaw over a century ago what we now see, and that man lies under the monument which a generous vote of Congress allows us to dedicate today, Major Pierre Charles L'Enfant."

The monument, whose base is 11 feet long and 7½ feet wide, is of gray Tennessee marble. It has carved on it an indication of the L'Enfant Plan. So the streets and avenues "carve" the L'Enfant Plan into the City of Washington.

On the occasion of the dedication, the Honorable Elihu Root, Secretary of State, said:

"Few men can afford to wait a hundred years to be remembered. It is not a change in L'Enfant that brings us here. It is we who have changed, who have just become able to appreciate his work. And our tribute to him should be to continue his work."

Washington from Arlington, Plan of 1901, Which Restored the L'Enfant Plan

Chapter XI

The Restoration of The L'Enfant Plan
And Its Development Through The Plan of 1901

THE development of the L'Enfant Plan is coextensive
with the development of the City of Washington.[1]
Indeed it could not be otherwise, for the Plan was made
for the city, and its basic features became evident with
every important project pertaining to its development.
Likewise several encroachments on the Plan of L'Enfant
became a source of regret, although this did not become
evident with much concern until the beginning of this
century, when the L'Enfant Plan was revived by the Mc-
Millan Commission.

During many years Washington grew slowly and hap-
hazardly following the death of General Washington in
1799. He had the welfare of the city ever at heart, and
we find that on June 1, 1799, in a letter to Dr William
Thornton, Washington advised that "No departure from
the engraved plan of the city ought to be allowed, unless
imperious necessity should require it, or some great public good is to be promoted thereby."

In 1800, when the City of Washington became the Seat
of Government, there were in the city 109 brick houses
and 263 frame houses, sheltering a population of about

---

[1] In addition to distinguished writers, heretofore mentioned, on the subject of the L'Enfant Plan, there should also be mentioned authors of notable
contributions on the subject written during the first quarter of this century
as Glenn Brown, for many years Secretary of the American Institute of
Architects; Dr. Fiske Kimball; and Elbert Peets, City Planner.

3,000. The two leading structures were the Capitol and the President's House. Pennsylvania Avenue, connecting the two buildings, was laid out in 1796 and for years was a deep morass covered with alder bushes. President Jefferson manifested his interest in the Avenue by improving it and planting two rows of poplar trees on either side. As heretofore stated, it was at the suggestion of Jefferson, approved by Washington, that the classical style of architecture was chosen for public buildings, as exhibited in the Capitol and the President's House, and this style of architecture was adhered to by President Jackson in adopting the classical design for the Treasury Department, the old Patent Office, and the old Post Office Department Building at Eighth and F Sts., N. W.

We may say that with the administration of John Quincy Adams in 1829 and the passing of the generation that knew President Washington, the L'Enfant Plan was generally forgotten. The neglect of the Plan led to departures from it and errors which have been impossible to rectify. The Treasury Department Building was placed directly in the line of Pennsylvania Avenue, thus obstructing the vista from the Capitol to the President's House. L'Enfant had planned this to be an open vista, with the area between Fifteenth and Sixteenth Streets as part of the area for the grounds of the "President's House." (Likewise on the West side of the White House part of the grounds were sacrified for the State, War and Navy building along Seventeenth Street.) The Smithsonian Building, begun in 1846, projects into the Mall area. At about the same time gardens were established at the head of the Mall near the Capitol. A half century later these proved to be one of two great obstacles in the

Incomplete Washington Monument, 1875
(Showing Also First Building of the Department of Agriculture, on the Mall)

restoration of the L'Enfant Plan. The other obstacle was the removal of railroad tracks from the Mall that had been placed there soon after railroads entered the city, from the year 1835. In 1846, in accordance with an Act of Congress, the portion of the "Ten Mile Square" located in Virginia, was ceded back to that State.

A further difficulty manifested itself through the neglect of the L'Enfant Plan when disputes arose as to street boundaries, and the integrity of the Plan was questioned. This happened in three particular cases that came before the Supreme Court of the United States. The need for accurate data inaugurated researches into the history of the long-neglected L'Enfant Plan, directed

by the Attorney General. The Court published in 1887 a
picture of the L'Enfant Plan as changed by Ellicott and
a portion of the Dermott map in its report on the case.
Also, the Coast and Geodetic Survey Office completed a
reproduction of the L'Enfant Plan as we have it today,
and printed an explanatory statement on the map as follows: "A tracing for preservation and reproduction has
been completed of the original manuscript plan of the
City of Washington which was prepared by Peter Charles
L'Enfant in the year 1791, under the authority of President Washington."

Instead of a great avenue and formal treatment of the
Mall, as was originally proposed by L'Enfant, the devel-

*View of Uncompleted Dome of the Capitol, and of Canal at Foot of
West Side of Capitol Hill, About 1861*

opment of the Mall took on an informal treatment beginning about 1853. The L'Enfant Plan had provided a location for the Washington Monument, that is an equestrian statue of General Washington, at the intersection of the Capitol-White House axes, but when the cornerstone of the Washington Monument was laid in 1848 it was located about 123.17 feet south and 371.6 feet east of the point of intersection of these axes. This has had to be taken into account in the location of all future buildings on the Mall.

In 1860 Washington was still a comparatively small and undeveloped city, with a population of 61,122. But the people were soon aroused to intense excitement because of the strife between the States. When the Civil War began the eyes of the Nation were turned on Washington. The city increased in population to over 100,000 in a few months' time and was the center of great wartime activities. Thousands of soldiers came to the city in response to President Lincoln's call for volunteers. Washington became an armed camp. Schools, churches, and public halls were turned into hospitals to care for the sick and wounded. A chain of forts and batteries was erected about the city to protect it, and by October, 1862 there were 252,000 soldiers encamped around Washington on both sides of the river. Several great improvements were made to mark the development of the city, notably the construction of the Washington Aqueduct, supplying the city with water from Great Falls, about 16 miles up the Potomac. Then too, the United States Capitol building was completed in 1863, by order of President Lincoln, as we see the building today. This work was begun in 1850 when the United States had expanded from the Atlantic to the Pacific, with 31 States in the Union, and additional room was needed at the Capitol for the 62 Senators, (that convened in the old Supreme Court Chamber), and the 232 Members of the House of Representatives that were crowded in the present Statuary Hall. The Capitol was enlarged according to the plans of Thomas U. Walter by adding the Senate and House of Representatives wings, making the Capitol 751 feet long, constructing a new dome and placing thereon the Statue of Freedom, by Crawford, at a height of 288 feet above ground.

The year 1870 marked the beginning of a new and effective movement for the development of the National Capital. Washington was then a city of 109,199.

In this connection, the following information recently received by the writer from Mr. Abram Garfield, of Cleveland, architect and former member of the National Commission of Fine Arts, son of President Garfield, is of real interest. It is a quotation from the "Journal of James Abram Garfield, Washington, D. C., May 14, 1873," mentioning in particular the L'Enfant Plan:

"The city has grown wonderfuly since I first saw it, and I shall be glad if it turns out that the improvements are not being over done. I am afraid they are undertaking too much and that the pressure of taxation will fall too heavily upon the citizens. . . . I have great respect for the ideas of Major L'Enfant, the engineer who laid out the original plan of Washington City. It must have required no small power of imagination to see the future city in the wild woods of his day."

In a subsequent statement in his Journal, President

Garfield also made vigorous objection to the fact that the railroads were allowed to cross the Mall.

Great efforts to relocate the National Capital in some other city, preferably farther to the west, were made by some who were familiar with conditions in Washington. St. Louis offered to spend several millions of dollars for the erection of public buildings. Congress settled this agitation by appropriating $500,000 as an initial sum for the construction of the State, War, and Navy Building.

By an Act of Congress approved February 21, 1871, a Territorial form of government, consisting of a governor, a Board of Public Works, and a legislative assembly, was created. Alexander R. Shepherd, better known as "Boss" Shepherd, a native of Washington, was appointed a member of the Board of Public Works and later Governor of the new Territory.

Great projects were placed under way for the development of the city. One hundred and eighty of the 300 miles of half-made streets and avenues were improved, and nearly all the thickly settled streets of the city were paved with wood, concrete, or macadam; 128 miles of sidewalks were built and 3,000 gas lamps were installed. A general and costly system of sewers was begun. Old Tiber Creek was filled in, and the greatest nuisance of Washington thereby put out of sight. Scores of new parks were graded, fenced, and planted with trees and several beautified by fountains. A special park commission was appointed for this work. It planted 6,000 trees, and a movement was thus begun which has given to Washington one of its most characteristic features. Today there are more than 125,000 trees along street curbs because of the custom that has prevailed to plant trees along curbs

Court of Honor, Looking West; Columbian Exposition, Chicago, 1893

when new streets are opened for traffic. Many of the small triangles planned by L'Enfant had become rubbish heaps and were transformed into beautiful reservations, planted with trees and shrubbery. There were soon more paved streets here than in any other city of the country, and President Grant, in his message to Congress, said, "Washington is rapidly becoming a city worthy of the Nation's Capital." All these improvements put the city in debt about $20,000,000 and Governor Shepherd was banished from the city. But real estate increased 65% in five years and the improvements made possible an increase of 120% in the population from 1870 to 1890.

In 1893 the World's Columbian Exposition in Chicago,

Court of Honor Looking East, Columbian Exposition Chicago, 1893.

had a great effect on art in the United States. It stirred the whole world by the production of beautiful and impressive groups of buildings, so arranged and coordinated as to create the sense of unity in the whole composition. It achieved what L'Enfant had visualized in 1791, that is the relation of public buildings to their landscape settings. The use of landscape effects in the White City along the shores of Lake Michigan, of canals and basins, statuary and paintings, all contributed to impress the public and to lift people to new standards and ideals of achievement. It marked the beginning of a new era in civic development. A most remarkable result of the aesthetic achievements of the World's Columbian Exposition was the influence it had on the architecture of several national expositions which were held at the close of the nineteenth and the beginning of the twentieth centuries. It was to have a lasting influence on our National Capital.

During the Convention of the American Institute of Architects in Washington in 1900 Mr. Frederick Law Olmsed, Jr., read a most interesting paper entitled "Landscape in Connection with Public Buildings in Washington" (Papers relating to the Improvement of tht City of Washington, Senate Document No. 94, 56th Congress, published by the Government Printing Office, 1901), which he concludes with this significant paragraph:

"Here is a plan not hastily sketched, nor by a man of narrow views and little foresight. It is a plan with the authority of a century behind it, to which we can all demand undeviating adherence in the future; a plan prepared by the hand of L'Enfant, but under the constant,

Railroad Tracks Crossing the Mall at Sixth Street, Washington, 1900

Site of the Lincoln Memorial, 1910

Model, Plan of 1901; Showing Existing Conditions

Model, Plan of 1901; the L'Enfant Plan Restored

Arlington Memorial Bridge Development, Plan of 1901 (Showing the Lincoln Memorial, Arlington Memorial Bridge, The Parkway and the Water Gate, All Carried Out)

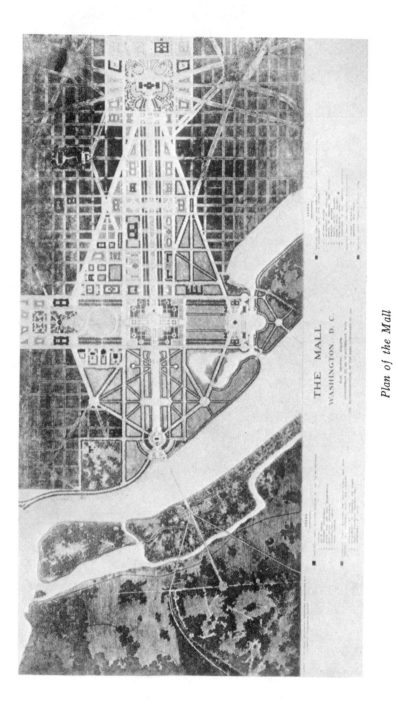

Plan of the Mall

direct, personal guidance of one whose technical knowledge of surveying placed the problem completely within his grasp, and who brought to its solution the same clear insight, deep wisdom, and forethought that gave preeminence in the broader fields of war and statesmanship to the name of George Washington."

Following the centennial celebration in the year 1900 of the establishment of the Seat of Government in the District of Columbia, a movement sponsored by the American Institute of Architects resulted in bringing the leaders of the World's Columbian Exposition to the City of Washington. These consisted of Daniel H. Burnham, Chief of Construction of the World's Fair held in Chicago, chairman; Charles F. McKim, architect; Frederick Law Olmsted, Jr., landscape architect; Augustus Saint-Gaudens, sculptor. Dr. Charles Moore served as Secretary of what became known as the McMillan Commission, named for Senator McMillan, of Michigan, who on March 8, 1901, secured the adoption of a Resolution by the United States Senate, to provide for the preparation of plans for the further development of the National Capital.

The Plan of 1901 reasserted the authority of the original Plan of L'Enfant, extended to meet the needs of the Nation after a century of growth in power, wealth and dignity, and also marked the path for future development. A great many of the improvements in Washington during the past 49 years have been executed in accordance with the Plan of 1901.

The McMillan Commission made a thorough study of the needs of the National Capital, visited a number of leading cities in Europe, and then decided first, that the

Dr. Charles Moore
(1855-1942)

*Member of the National Commission of Fine Arts, 1910-1940; and
Chairman, 1915-1937*

January, (15—350) WEDNESDAY, 15. 1902.

Called at Corcoran gallery this morning on way to Capitol. Special Meeting of Committee. Read the Preliminary Report to Committee. It was approved unanimously. Went to Corcoran Gallery with Senators McM. and Gallinger to meet President. When he saw me he came through the knot of people and thrust out his hand in the old way. He fell foul of the small model of Monument, saying it looked like fussy work. I expostulated but he insisted until Mr. McKim took him to see the pictures of the Monument. Then he frankly acknowledged his error and took back all he said. Senator McM. asked me who a black-bearded man was. I didn't know and asked Cortelyou, who said it was the new Asst. Secy of Navy. "You better tell the President that," said Senator, "for he just asked me." Had long talk with Secy. Root about War College and Mr. McKim's suggestions as to location of buildings. Showed Lincoln Memorial pictures to Secy. Hay, who was very much pleased with them. Secy Hitchcock liked plans. Said Rond of fountains surpassed those at Versailles. Explained plans to Senators Clark of Montana and Foster of La. Mr. Burnham came in evening; was much pleased. We went to Cosmos Club and talked till after midnight.

Courtesy University of Michigan

Extract from Diary of Dr. Charles Moore

L'Enfant Plan of 1791 should be restored; and, secondly, that it should be adapted to the entire District of Columbia. They then employed numerous artists, who portrayed the ideas and recommendations in the form of perspectives, plans and other drawings, also two great models, showing present (1900) and "Future Washington." They were published by the McMillan Commission in a report entitled, "The Improvement of the Park System of the District of Columbia" (Senate Report No. 166, Fifty-Seventh Congress, 1902) edited by Charles Moore, while Clerk to the Senate Committee on the District of Columbia.

One of the artists, William T. Partridge, architect, who was in charge of the "Washington Group" was employed as consulting architect by the National Capital Park and Planning Commission, upon its establishment in 1926, and has been most helpful in the development of plans for the National Capital.

The plans prepared by the McMillan Commission and for grouping of public buildings. It is regarded by many the best Report on city planning published in this country. It marked a most important epoch in the development of the National Capital, since it revived and made possible the carrying out of the original L'Enfant Plan of 1791, adopted by President Washington and Secretary of State Jefferson for the Federal City but which had been neglected for practically three-quarters of a century. Henceforth, unity, orderliness and beauty were once more to become the watchwords. Champions of the Plan of Washington asserted themselves amidst opposition by

Tribute to Charles Moore, 1937

vested interests. The city planning movement in the United States soon followed.

As has been mentioned heretofore, there were two outstanding difficulties that presented themselves which interfered seriously with the possibility of carrying out L'Enfant's Mall Plan, namely the removal of existing railroad tracks that crossed the Mall; this was achieved by Mr. Burnham in conference with President Alexander J. Cassatt of the Pennsylvania Railroad Company, almost immediately. It was agreed, with the help of Congress and the Baltimore and Ohio Railroad Company that a Union Station would be built in Washington, as well as a tunnel to connect with trains to the South. The second obstacle, regarded in 1901 to be much simpler, involved the removal of the Botanic Garden from the Mall, and was not achieved until some 25 years later. Thereupon plans were carried out for completing the Mall between the Capitol and the Washington Monument, a mile in length, as we see it today.

During the succeeding decade after publication of the McMillan Commission Report of 1901 little more in the way of progress in planning was made. A few monumental building projects were carried out, such as the construction of the Pan American Union Building, and the headquarters building of the Daughters of the American Revolution. The Corcoran Gallery of Art and the Library of Congress had been completed during the previous decade. The Senate and House of Representatives Office Buildings were completed in 1908, as also Union Station, which Mr. Burnham planned as a monumental gateway to the National Capital. The McMillan

Commission went out of existence on the submission of its Report.

President Theodore Roosevelt, as also the Honorable Elihu Root, Secretary of State, and Hon. William Howard Taft, Secretary of War. both cabinet members at the time, became champions of the Plan of 1901, and the controversies that arose in defense of the Plan is an interesting story in itself. It should be stated that next to the restoration of the Mall Axis the greatest feature in the Plan of 1901 was doubtless the provision made to extend the axis from the Washington Monument westward three-fourths of a mile, and there locate a Memorial to Abraham Lincoln. The scheme was thought out while the members of the McMillan Commission were spending an evening on the Pincian Hill in Rome, as the writer was informed by Dr. Moore. Much opposition prevailed in those days to locating the Lincoln Memorial—there in a swamp "where it would shake itself down in loneliness and ague" as was said. Yet the project was so well carried out and the city grew so fast that by 1930 a million visitors a year passed the Lincoln Memorial, and in 1940 fully 2,000,000. The Arlington Memorial Bridge, the Watergate, and the Rock Creek and Potomac Parkway entrance were made parts of this composition, which was completed in recent years.

On January 18, 1909, President Roosevelt appointed by Executive Order a Council of Fine Arts, consisting of 30 artists, but Congress denied the Council their traveling expenses. Thereupon, on March 21, 1909, President Taft abolished the Council and Congress soon after, on May 17, 1910, established the National Commission of Fine

The Lincoln Memorial, Dedicated 1922

The Lincoln Memorial, Looking East Toward the Capitol

Arts "to consist of seven well-qualified judges of the Fine Arts."

The first project to come before the Commission was the design and location of the Lincoln Memorial and in this the Commission reaffirmed the site selected by the McMillan Commission of 1901 in Potomac Park on the banks of the Potomac, in connection with a Memorial Bridge and a Water Gate. The Commission was regarded the "custodian of the Plan of 1901." Dr. Charles Moore, who had edited the Report of the McMillan Commission, became one of the original members of the Fine Arts Commission and its Chairman in 1915 for a period of 22 years. He served on the Commission for nearly 30 years, until 1940, and died two years later at the age of 87. Dr. Moore was succeeded as Chairman in 1937, by Dr. Gilmore D. Clarke, Dean of the College of Architecture of Cornell University, and well known City Planner of the United States. During those years Dr. Moore had the counsel of distinguished members of the Fine Arts Commission, who were his fellow members, and it is generally admitted that it is largely because of their painstaking zeal that the City of Washington developed into the beautiful city that it is today. For many years this Commission had also attended to park and playground developments and highway problems.

However, in 1926 Congress established the National Capital Park and Planning Commission "with the duty of preparing, developing, and maintaining a comprehensive, consistent, and coordinated plan for the National Capital and environs" including traffic and transportation problems, plats and sub-divisions, highways, parks and parkways, playgrounds, and other elements of city and regional planning, with authority to cooperate with similar "commissions" in Maryland and Virginia. This includes planning for the Metropolitan Area of Washington and coordinating it with the city proper. The present Chairman is Maj. Gen. U. S. Grant III (Retired), grandson of President U. S. Grant. According to recent reports the population of Metropolitan Washington is approximately 1,500,000.[2]

Some traffic engineers criticize the L'Enfant Plan as being unsuitable to an "Automobile Age" and thus would seem to regard the "checker-board" system of streets and squares preferable to the Plan of L'Enfant. On the other hand it is to be noted that the L'Enfant Plan provides park reservations, circles for the location of monuments (not for cannon as proposed by Napoleon III, who relied on the military and police to maintain order, in the development of Paris under him by Baron Haussmann), and wide streets, as well as radial avenues that make "distant points easy of access," based on the principle of the hypothenuse of a triangle. Also, considering the progress made in the means of transportation during the past 50 years, who knows but what fifty years hence some other form of conveyance, in addition to travel by air, will be invented to supersede the automobile at least in part. In the evolution of things certainly such an invention can be expected, while the City of Washington by that time will have grown to be a city of 2,000,000 inhabitants, including the metropolitan area. The City of Paris, which in Plan is much like the City of Washington, has

---

[2] Upon the expiration of the term of office of Maj. Gen. Grant, in 1949, the Commission elected the Honorable William W. Wurster, Dean of the Department of Architecture, Massachusetts Institute of Technology, as Chairman.

4,000,000 inhabitants today, with scarcely any underpass in it.

Criticism has also been made of the fact that, while the City of Washington has been termed "The City Beautiful," there are slum areas in our National Capital that are a disgrace to the Nation. True enough, and a disgraceful one within the shadow of the United States Capitol. But this is because of the neglect of the L'Enfant Plan during the Nineteenth Century. Originally, to repeat, L'Enfant had sixteen "districts" in mind, to be developed one for each State at the time; if today our 48 States would each assume responsibility over the development of a section of the City of Washington (as Ohio did some years ago in helping to get rid of the appearance of a disgraceful Ohio Avenue), the slum conditions would soon be removed from the city, and *every* part of it would be clean and beautiful as L'Enfant originally intended.

Nevertheless in all this, attention should be called to the fact that Congress has enacted legislation that will remove these bad spots in time, but the progress is slow; it comes under the direct supervision of the National Capital Housing Authority and of the National Capital Park and Planning Commission. For instance, alley dwellings—among them remodeled barns of the old days —are to be abolished soon, and there is also the District of Columbia Redevelopment Land Agency, which will provide for low rent housing. These projects are being advanced as rapidly as Congress provides funds for them.

The National Capital Park and Planning Commission, in connection with its study of highways and traffic problems, has given particular attention to the L'Enfant Plan. The methods and features of L'Enfant's plan, which included the reports and correspondence between L'Enfant and President Washington were given, in 1930, intensive study by William T. Partridge, consulting architect of the National Capital Park and Planning Commission, as heretofore mentioned. Mr. Partridge's findings and his review of the features of the plan, which are still possible of attainment, constitute a notable contribution to the research in this field, and we quote at length:

"A study of L'Enfant's Plan, as well as a careful reading of his descriptions, shows the effort made to model his design to the existing topography. * * * He reiterates again and again in his letters that this plan of his was 'original' and 'unique.' In a letter to Jefferson requesting some Old World city maps he deprecates any copying and asks for this information only as a means for comparison or to aid in refining and strengthening his judgment.

"In order to investigate how far the existing conditions of the site for the Federal City dictated the plan of present Washington, a topographical map of the terrain, as existing at that period, has been carefully prepared from old maps and descriptions and an attempt made with an open mind to follow L'Enfant's procedure. All printed transcriptions of L'Enfant's reports have been altered by their editors in the effort to interpret L'Enfant's strange English, a fact leading to misinterpretation on the part of trained architectural commentators dependent solely on these printed transcriptions. * * *

"There has come down to us only a single manuscript plan which students have accepted as the original design and on which they have based all their comments. This drawing depicts only an intermediate stage of the plan. The first plan was much altered by L'Enfant himself at the request of President Washington, but by a careful study of internal evidence of the later drawing the designer's masterly original may be restored. Existing documents tell us that not only were considerable changes made in the plan by order of President Washington, but alterations in the layout were also made by L'Enfant's successors, all of which disturbed considerably its skillful symmetrical fitting to the irregular topography. * * * It is the writer's conclusion that L'Enfant did exactly what he claimed—devised an original plan, entirely unique. He arrived at his parti only after a careful study on the spot of the best sites for public buildings, allocated in the order of their importance, and located with consideration of both prominence and outlook. He tied these sites together by means of a rectangular system of streets and again connected them by means of diagonal avenues. The principal avenues followed closely the existing roads.   Additional avenues were extended to the 'outroads' or city entrances and were laid out primarily for the purpose of shortening communication — an engineering consideration.   L'Enfant mentions that the diagonal avenues would afford a 'reciprocity of sight' and 'a variety of pleasant ride and combined to insure a rapide Intercourse with all the part of the City to which they will serve as does the main vains in the animal body to diffuse life through smaller vessels in quickening the active motion to the heart.'

"The similarity of the angles of the two principal avenues (Pennsylvania east from Eastern Branch Ferry to the Capitol, and Maryland east, from the Bladensburg Road entrance to the Capitol) which followed closely for some distance the existing roads, doubtless suggested the radial pair-avenue idea.   This was entirely accidental and the outgrowth of existing conditions.   The system of a rectangular-street plan with radial avenues is not only borne out by the mention he makes himself in his descriptions but was followed by Ellicott in his drafting of the plan for the engraver.

"Our artistic, hasty-tempered genius refused to give Ellicott any documents or any information. * * * Space and time do not permit an excursion into the squabble over this engraved plan.   Changes were made in reduction to the proper size of the plate.   These changes led to violent protests on the part of L'Enfant, although in later years his memorial states that the changes were not so very damaging. * * *"

A most important part in the work of transforming the City of Washington culminated in the great Public Buildings Program of 1926, adopted during the Administration of President Coolidge, who took up the matter with Dr. Moore in its earliest stages, and he in turn with the members of the Commission of Fine Arts at numerous sessions.   The outstanding result of this Public Buildings Program was the purchase by Congress of the entire 70 acres south of Pennsylvania Avenue, between the Treasury Department and the United States Capitol, and the development of the "Triangle."   Congress had specified in the Public Buildings Act of 1926 the requirement "of providing suitable approaches to said buildings, and beautifying and embellishing their surroundings as nearly in harmony with the plan of Peter Charles L'Enfant as may be practicable.   Said buildings shall be so con-

The Mall and Monument Gardens, Plan of 1901

View of the Mall, Today, Looking from the Washington Monument To the Capitol

structed as to combine high standards of architectural beauty and practical utility * * *"

Of L'Enfant and his Plan for the National Capital, Dr. Charles Moore, a member of The Commission of Fine Arts for nearly 30 years, as heretofore mentioned (from May 17, 1910 to January 18, 1940), of which he served 22 years as Chairman, and all told nearly 50 years of his life towards the development and embellishment of the National Capital, stated:

> "L'Enfant planned a city with every adornment and every convenience then known to man. He provided for needs of recreation, of learning, and of religion . . . [there were to be] radial avenues, water effects, and such disposition of public buildings as creates an ensemble in which every part has organic relation to every other part."

In recognition of what Dr. Moore accomplished towards restoring the Plan of the City of Washington, the dignified and elegant lines designed for it in 1791 by Major L'Enfant, the French Government bestowed upon him, in November, 1928, the distinction of Chevalier of the Legion of Honor.

By the Act of March 4, 1929 (45 Stat. p. 1694), an Act to enlarge the Capitol Grounds to include the Mall area between the Capitol and the Washington Monument, the completion of the Mall development was assured. Instead of a central driveway, as had been recommended by L'Enfant the change made by the McMillan Commission for two roadways on either side of a *tapis vert* 300 feet wide was adopted. To quote Daniel H. Burnham, this provides "an unobstructed vista between one of the great Domes of the world and one of the great monuments of the world."

Among other important projects included in this Pub-

lic Buildings Program were: the completion of Union
Station Plaza; the enlargement of the Capitol Grounds
with provision for an additional House of Representatives Office Building; a United States Supreme Court
Building; the Arlington Memorial Bridge and Water
Gate; the completion of the Tomb of the Unknown Soldier; the Restoration of the Arlington Mansion; and the
construction of the Mount Vernon Memorial Highway.
This work continued well into the decade from 1930 to
1940. Thereupon a National Defense Program was begun, and while this was under way the City of Washington grew very rapidly. In 1940 the population of Washington had increased to 663,091, an increase of 36.2 per
cent during the decade. It was reported to be the fastest
growing city in the country. By November, 1941, the
population was 770,000 and on September 1, 1942, the
city had a population of 962,000. At the present time the
City of Washington is one of the twelve or fifteen cities
of the country having more than a million inhabitants.

The expansion of the business of the Government during World War II created a great need for office space and
by 1945 the Government occupied 35,000,000 square feet
of office space for some 250,000 clerks occupied in ten
great Departments of the Government and numerous
"agencies" such as the Federal Works Agency, the Social
Security Agency, and the like, which are like Departments in themselves. What a remarkable growth from
the four Departments and 137 clerks that were here in
1800, when the City of Washington became the Seat of
Government!

A "Post War Building Program" to meet the needs of
permanent buildings is now proposed. Both the Na-

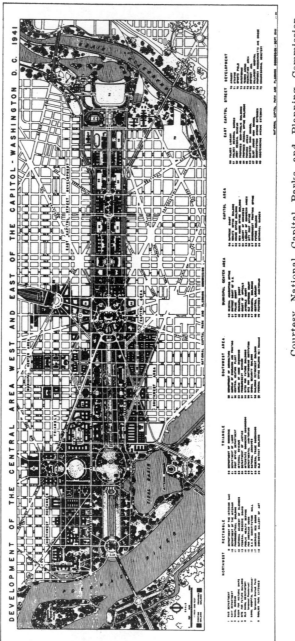

Courtesy National Capital Parks and Planning Commission

Proposed Plan for the Development of East Capitol Street

tional Commission of Fine Arts and the National Capital Park and Planning Commission are looking forward to an ever greater and more beautiful National Capital. The ideals of L'Enfant for a unified, well-ordered and well-articulated city are being realized, and it is to be made the occasion of a great celebration in 1950, the Sesquicentennial of the Establishment of the Seat of the Federal Government in the District of Columbia.

Chapter XII

THE INFLUENCE OF THE L'ENFANT PLAN ON OTHER CITIES

*I*T IS manifestly impossible to give an account of all the cities that have benefited in one way or another by adopting features of the Plan of our National Capital. But it is certain that among the millions that have visited the City of Washington in the past 150 years, especially during the past half-century, there have been many individuals that have been inspired by what they have seen in "The City Beautiful" and have endeavored to improve their own "home town" accordingly. Since Washington is not a commercial city, our National Capital is, of course, different from most cities, and to adapt the L'Enfant Plan *in toto* has never been expected.

But there are certain features of the Plan that can well be adopted by all cities and towns, such as wide streets, park areas, reservations and even monumental buildings in relation to their landscape setting; also Zoning.

It is to be observed that the City of Washington is a city of "Standards" and in this respect the achievements of the National Commission of Fine Arts, during a period of 40 years, and the National Capital Park and Planning Commission for a period of nearly 25 years, with the cooperation and endorsement of the Congress, the President, other officials, organizations and leaders in civic life, are reflected in the beauty of our National Capital today.

There are a few cities in which the L'Enfant Plan as

338

Air View of Detroit, Michigan

such has had a conspicuous part and has been adapted accordingly. A brief account of them follows:

DETROIT, MICHIGAN

Detroit has been described as a city substantially built upon rising ground; its streets are broad, well paved and shaded with trees. There are several fine public parks.

Few know that the city plan of Detroit had its prototype in the L'Enfant Plan. Yet this is a fact, and the story has been well told by the late Dr. Charles Moore, a resident of Detroit for fully fifteen years and a resident of the City of Washington for about 50 years.

The following is an extract from an article entitled "Augustus Brevoort Woodward — A Citizen of Two Cities" by Charles Moore, read at a meeting of the Columbia Historical Society and printed in the RECORDS (Volume IV, pp. 114-127):

"By the act of January 11, 1805, Congress set off from Indiana territory the territory of Michigan; and provided that the new government should begin on the 30th day of the ensuing June. According to the form of government established in the Ordinance (of 1787), it became necessary to appoint a governor, a secretary, and three judges; and after selecting for governor, the Revolutionary soldier, William Hull, of Massachusetts, President Jefferson named as the combined legislative and judicial body, Augustus Brevoort Woodward, Frederick Bates, and John Griffin, all of Virginia . . . (Woodward lived in Alexandria).

"As he approached the site of the town founded by Cadillac, a hundred and four years before, there was much to impress him that he had come to a land of Frenchmen and of Indians . . .

"Finding temporary quarters with his colleague, Judge Bates (who had been the land commsisioner), Judge Woodward awaited the coming of the Governor, General William Hull, of Massachusetts, who, with Stanley Griswold, the Territorial Secretary, arrived on July 1st. To the Governor and Judges the people presented a plan of a new Detroit, which was to be a duplicate of the old one. Imagine the consternation of the Frenchmen, and of the Scotch and the Irish traders as well, when the gentleman from Washington frankly informed them that he would have none of their plan.

He had not lived in Washington for nothing. What if Old Detroit covered an area scarcely greater than four city blocks—was not land to be had even without the asking; and why throw away such an opportunity? Here on the banks of the Detroit should arise a new city of wide streets and avenues diverging from common centers, with reservations and parkings and all the beauties that L'Enfant had borrowed from Versailles to make beautiful the nation's capital. Away with St. Antoine and the St. Anne for street names. The main thoroughfare should be named for the President of the United States, Washington; and Adams, Monroe, and Madison should be honored, and the great north and south avenue should be called Woodward, not because that was the judge's name but because the thoroughfare ran woodward! Then, too, propensity for the classical names must be observed; and so we have the Campus Martius and the Grand Circus, which remains to this day. Thus it happened that Detroit, although a century older than Washington, was laid out according to a sectional map of the capital city, which Judge Woodward had brought with him. Unfortunately, fires, and other causes have somewhat disturbed Judge Woodward's original design; but in its main features the City of the Straits is a counterpart of the federal city. One difficulty, however, remained to be conquered. None of his colleagues presumed to dispute the plan which the energetic judge prepared, but of which French residents each laid claim to a lot fronting the river, for it had been their custom to secure a water front, however narrow, and to extend their ribbon-like farms back into the endless forests. So the judge, nothing loath, hied him back to Washington; and by the expenditure of the modest sum of $300 on wine for Congressmen, he secured the passage of an act granting 5,000 square feet of land to each of the 121 inhabitants of the old town who were thought to be entitled to a share in the division."

BUFFALO, NEW YORK

Extract from an article entitled The City of Buffalo, by Jane Meade Welch, Harpers Magazine, July, 1885, pp. 202-03.

"In her many diagonal streets, all radiating from a common center, Buffalo, as I have heard, bears an intentional resemblance to Washington. But where is the Capitol? queried one of the newer settlers lately. It is not to the credit of Buffalo that she has as yet perpetuated by neither statue nor memorial, save in the name of

Air View of Buffalo, New York

a single street, his fame who not only first predicted her commercial destiny, but what is almost unparalled in the history of cities, selected her exact site and laid out in the then wilderness at the foot of Lake Erie a city on a scale commensurate with his inspired belief in her destiny. As agent for the Holland Land Company, Joseph Ellicott in the year 1804 completed the survey of the broad streets, diagonal avenues and public squares, some of which are today included in her extensive park system and all of which form adequate approaches to the newer suburbs of the Buffalo of 1885 . . .

"Joseph Ellicott was the brother of Andrew Ellicott, then Surveyor General of the United States, who was appointed by General Washington to survey the boundary line of the 'Ten Mile Square' provided for in the Constitution of the United States, and which became the District of Columbia, and who assisted L'Enfant in his work of preparing the Plan for the National Capital."

INDIANAPOLIS, INDIANA

Indianapolis, capital city of the State of Indiana, was founded in the year 1820, when the legislature of the State approved the site, which was intended to be in the center of the State.

Alexander Ralston, who helped in the survey of Washington, D. C., as assistant to Pierre Charles L'Enfant, was appointed to complete the survey of the new capital city. He received the appointment from Judge Christopher Nicholson, who had come from Maryland to make his home in the then far west.

Thus it is that Indianapolis has wide streets and several radiating avenues, intersecting at the central plaza,

Courtesy Fairchild Aerial Surveys, Inc.

Air View of Indianapolis, Indiana

known as the circle, and in the center of which was placed the Governor's Mansion. But some years later a new site was selected for the Mansion, and now there is located in the center of the plaza the Indiana Soldiers and Sailors Monument.

As in Washington, the intersecting avenues took the names of States of the Union. But in Indianapolis only one square mile was surveyed.

"It is a well-known fact," relates Mrs. Laura F. Hodges in her article *Early Indianapolis* (Volume 7, Indiana Historical Society Publications, 1919) "that the design employed by L'Enfant influenced Ralston in his survey of Indianapolis,—the scheme involved, as it does, a circle in the center with radiating avenues and streets intersecting at right-angles. Completing the survey, Ralston left the settlement, but returned in 1822 for permanent residence . . . Here he lived until his death in 1827. He was buried in Green Lawn Cemetery."

The legislature moved to Indianapolis in 1824. It was then a "capital in the wilderness." The town grew slowly, but in a few decades it was realized that the surveyors had made one mistake—the one-square-mile proved to be too small. Indianapolis became a south-central "crossroad" of the West, and by 1910 numbered about 250,000 inhabitants; and today numbers fully half a million.

MEDELLIN, COLOMBIA

Medellín typifies the eternal spring of Tierra Media. The town lies in a beautiful valley some thirty miles wide and twice as long. Looking down from a plane, you see along the sloping side of the valley the estates and country houses of the wealthier Antioquenos, with rolling lawns, swimming pools, tennis courts, and formal gardens. Down on the flatter land are the small farms, neatly culti-vated and divided by long rows of tall waving bamboo trees which resemble the Lombardy poplars characteristic of the French countryside.

Medellín, Colombia, down at the lower elevations of Tierra Media, is likewise approaching planning with vision and thereby developing what promises to be one of South America's most lively and beautiful cities. Medel-lín's is an unusual program, the result of citizen action through the efforts of an especially effective group known as the Sociedad de Mejoras Publicas, or the Society for Public Betterment, led by Ricardo Olano, a retired indus-trialist. Nutibara Hill, rising high in the center of the valley of Medellín and overlooking the city, has been purchased by the municipality and is being planted with trees. The low area west of the city is being drained, streets are already laid out, the new facilities for the city's two universities are being planned. These projects are the result of the efforts of the Sociedad de Mejoras Pub-licas.

Contribution of private land for public uses seems to be much less painful in Latin America than in the United States. Citizens of Medellín, Colombia, through an or-ganization called the Sociedad de Mejoras Publicas, aroused interest in the idea of building a parkway along each side of the River Medellín, which was in the process of being channelized. The owners of the land adjoining the river were so attracted to the plan, which included other features as well—parks, university, etc.—that they have given to the city a right-of-way, some two hundred

Courtesy Pan American Union

Medellin, Colombia, General View

Courtesy Pan American Union

Plaza de Berrio, Medellin, Colombia

feet on each side of the river, over a length of thirty-five miles — absolutely free. With Ricardo Olano, one of SMP's leaders, I drove over a portion of the boulevard (only a small section is complete) and, seeing the site for the development, I could understand why the beauty of the riverside inspired the owners to cooperate with the plan. In this case, it would have been difficult for even the most hard-boiled North American property-owner to refuse to contribute his share of land. This is just one example of the lesser degree to which mercenary standards have taken hold in Latin America than in the United States.

The city of Medellín, one of the most progressive in Colombia, has its own housing department, formed by municipal legislation in 1925. Small houses are built for about 800 pesos ($400 U. S.) and rent for as low as five pesos ($2.50 U. S.) per month. Where families can prove the existence of a steady income, houses are sold on a twenty-five year payment plan, but with the ruling that the house cannot be sold again other than back to the city. A total of 344 houses had been built up to November, 1941, under legislation which though in effect since 1925, was unusued up to several years ago. Municipal authorities wish to maintain a construction program of about one hundred houses a year in order to prevent the further building and continued use of substandard dwellings, as the city becomes more and more industrialized.

I have said that Medellín, Colombia, is growing rapidly and doing so according to a plan. The outstanding planner there has been not a professional planner at all but a lay citizen, Ricardo Olano, a retired industrialist. Thirty-five years ago he was sufficiently impressed with the plan of Washington, D. C., which he saw in the Library of Congress, to return to Medellín to introduce the idea of planning for the future growth of the city. Ever since, he has worked to promote planning for Medellín and other cities and has been an active and effective leader in Colombia in this field . His accomplishments make an interesting story.

A unique citizen's group called the Sociedad de Mejoras Publicas, or Society for Public Improvement, has been Olano's chief instrument in the education of the public for forty-three years. Through it he has urged many towns to make master plans and form similar affiliated groups. In order to discuss the problems of the cities of Colombia he promoted the first national planning conference of that country. His work with S. M. P. has produced a community spirit that is making Medellín one of the best planned cities of the West Coast. This community endeavor has made possible the construction of Medellín's Art Building, financed with a $65,000 fund collected through public subscription. S. M. P. is also responsible for the opening, twenty-seven years ago, of the city park, the Bosque de Independencia, and today maintains a large nursery for growing trees, of which they have planted ten thousand throughout the city. S. M. P. has likewise shown public-spirited courage and vision in acquiring for the city, through private contribution, both sides of the Rio Medellín for parkway purposes. Nutibara Hill, rising above the city in the midst of the valley of Medellín, is being planted by S. M. P. under the personal direction of Olano, and a restaurant is planned for construction on the hilltop. Olano told me how his organization has shamed the public into cooperation by

Courtesy Government of Australia

Air View of Canberra, Australia

branding in the press anyone who resisted contributing his share to civic improvement as an *hombre estorbo*—a stubborn obstructionist. Since no one wants to be an *hombre estorbo,* property owners who oppose a particular project generally relent under the pressure of public opinion.

In 1917, Olano held S. M. P.'s first national Congress in Bogota, and since then Congresses have been held every two or three years. Olano and the S. M. P. have worked with an interesting Comision de Cultura Aldeana (Commission for Village Culture) to study the planning and improvement needs of small villages. Studies include Sections on education, literature, health, agriculture, etc. Today Olano's ambition is to see a complete garden city built in the valley of Medellín according to highest planning standards. His studio, set in an orange grove on his small farm near the city, has walls covered with many maps—an air photo-map of Washington, maps of old Mexican towns, and of modern European cities—but that of highest importance to Olano is the map of the tiny village where he was born, back in the Andes beyond Medellín.

Few citizen groups can be found in Latin American cities to compare with Medellín's Sociedad de Mejoras Publica for effectiveness in meeting local problems, but I did find other examples of citizen action in Lima, Santiago, Buenos Aires, and Sao Paulo.

Extract from: Cities of Latin America—from pages 7, 93, 106-107, 147, 176, 177 by Francis Violich, Reinhold Publishing Corporation, N. Y.

CANBERRA, AUSTRALIA

Another city whose Plan is based on the L'Enfant Plan is that of Canberra, capital of the Commonwealth of Australia. Like our own federal district, the District of Columbia, the establishment of the Seat of Government in Australia was imposed by the Commonwealth of Australia Constitution, Act of 1900. The Seat of Government Acceptance Act of the Commonwealth was brought into force by proclamation on January 22, 1910, and the control of the Territory was officially assumed by the Commonwealth on January 1, 1911. "It was the will of the people, expressed by their acceptance of the Consti-

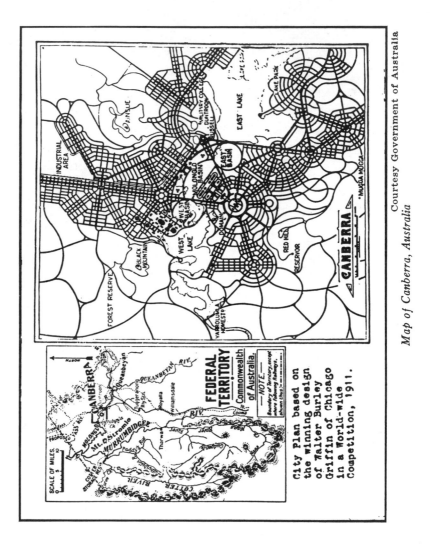

Map of Canberra, Australia

tution, that the Commonwealth Government should be master in its own house free from any dominating parochial influence with respect to matters of administration or legislation."

The site of Canberra was selected after exhaustive investigation had been made of other possible sites for a Capital in New South Wales, within the limits imposed by the Constitution. It was located in accordance with the Constitution Act of 1900 that the Seat of Government "shall be in the State of New South Wales, and be distant not less than 100 miles from Sydney," also that "Such Territory shall contain an area of not less than 100 square miles."

The design for laying out the site of the Capital City was obtained as the result of an international competition held in 1911, when Mr. Walter Burley Griffin, of Chicago, was awarded the first prize. Development has since proceeded on the basis of his plan. As described by Kenneth Binns, General Editor of a *Handbook for Canberra*:

"The plan, as originally drawn, is regarded as being of marked distinction and originality. The author made skillful use of the excellent features presented by the site for effective planning. These consist of the scenic background of the Australian Alps; local mounts affording terminals to vistas and sites for future monuments; hills and spurs providing appropriate sites for public buildings and also terminals to main thoroughfares; the Molonglo river and its valley traversing the City site, and rendering possible the formation of a chain of large water basins as a valuable and striking central feature in the ornamentation of the City which, as already mentioned, lies in a large amphitheater.

"It will be noted that the main focal point of the plan is Capitol Hill, from which all main avenues—200 feet in width—radiate. Through Capitol Hill also passes the main City axis, projected north-easterly from the summit of Red Hill to that of Mount Ainslie, and this is traversed at right angles by the parallel water and municipal axes from Black Mountain to Mount Pleasant. Balanced and symmetrical planning is based upon these three axes, and the various areas are bound together by a well-devised system of main routes.

"The governmental group is located and balanced on the main axis on the south side of the river, and forms a large and beautiful park sloping from the higher elevation of Parliament House to the central river basin, with an open vista along the axis terminated by the Australian War Memorial, the white mass of which will be seen in effective contrast against the dark wooded slopes of Mount Ainslie. The zoning principles of the plan provide for complete separation by the river of the national and civic centres. The civic focus is placed on an eminence—Vernon—on the northern side, being approached from the south by a wide thoroughfare crossing the ornamental waters over a high-level bridge. The University site lies to the northwest between the Civic Centre and Black Mountain and the industrial area is located at the extreme north of the City, adjacent to the railway route to Yass.

"Residential suburbs are conveniently disposed on both sides of the river, shopping provision being made in these groups for local retail requirements only, the main commercial development being designed around the Civic Centre.

"It will be seen that the allocation of areas has received careful consideration, and that the whole design gains in firmness by orientation of the plan on the main axis, which, by crossing the river valley at right angles, secures a reasonable degree of symmetry, at the same time allowing variations that add interest to the plan without any sense of confusion.

"The design admits of easy and indefinite expansion into new suburbs, as may be required by future growth, with no appreciable difficulties in regard to engineering services, and the maintenance of the high standard of town-planning and arrangement for all related purposes which are embodied in its conception . . . . . .

"Up to the 31st of December, 1920, when his association with Canberra ceased, Mr. Griffin had made progressively minor alterations in the evolution of his design for the City, as the result of further study and practical experience in adapting it to the site."

Canberra (accent on the first syllable) was occupied officially as the Seat of Government in 1927. It is 200 miles south of Sydney, and during the past 30 years has grown into a flourishing city, "a city with noble buildings, fine thoroughfares, splendid far-stretching vistas and glorious gardens." The climate is ideal, about like that of the City of Washington. Its population in 1943 was 13,000; estimated by 1949, 25,000. The adaptation of the Plan of Canberra from that of the L'Enfant Plan is obvious from a comparison of the two plans.

OTTAWA, CANADA

Under date of April 16, 1946, the writer received a letter from Mr. Edouard Fiset, Assistant to Monsieur Jacques Gréber, Consultant of the National Capital Planning Service, Department of Public Works, Ottawa, which reads in part as follows:

"The National Capital Planning Service, which is charged with the preparation of plans for the development of Ottawa and the National Capital Region, is interested in the basic natures and scopes of such regulations as are enforced within the City of Washington, D. C., in the control of factors effecting the planning and development of the Capital City . . .

"We are particularly interested in securing copies of regulations and rules which are applicable throughout the City of Washington and its environs generally in the control of its development and planning from the physical and aesthetic viewpoints, and would seek your advice and aid in securing same for us or advising us of the sources to which we should address ourselves in the fulfillment of our objectives . . .

"It is appreciated that the foregoing request has a wide application and may involve considerable inconvenience on your part, but we are encouraged to seek your guidance and assistance from the most courteous reception of his recent visit to you with Mr. Jacques Gréber, for which we would express deep appreciation and would thank you in advance in anticipation of your further favours."

As above indicated, both M. Gréber and Mr. Fiset were in Washington and visited the writer, who explained to them the merits of the L'Enfant Plan of 1791, and told them briefly the story of the development of the City of Washington since then. They also conferred with Major General U. S. Grant III (Retired), while Chairman of the National Capital Parks and Planning Commission, which Commission has charge in particular of planning for "Future Washington" taking in the metropolitan area, in

cooperation with similar Commissions in Maryland and Virginia, as heretofore stated.

In the spring of the year 1948 a delegation of leading citizens of Ottawa, and adjacent regions, was brought to Washington by M. Gréber to see the City of Washington. They were much impressed by it, as is indicated by the following letter which the writer received:

Federal District Commission,

Ottawa, Ontario, May 10th, 1948

Dear Mr. Caemmerer:

On behalf of the members of the National Capital Planning Committee information tour to Washington on the 19th of April, I want to express our thanks for the reception given us by you and your associates.

Our visit to Washington was the most important part of our tour of the United States, because we have always looked upon the City as the model of a National Capital. We are just beginning the work of development of Ottawa as a National Capital, and an understanding of the methods by which Washington achieved its present state is most helpful . . .

Yours sincerely,

Grenville W. Goodwin, Chairman,
Information Committee,
National Capital Planning Committee.

It should be added that Monsieur Gréber is an authority on City Planning and well acquainted with the L'Enfant Plan. He is Inspecteur général de l'Urbanisme,

Plan for Ottawa—Hull and Environs

Paris. He told the writer it is his desire to see features of the L'Enfant Plan adopted in Ottawa, and the National Capital Planning Committee is now at work endeavoring to bring this about. It is their desire to make Ottawa "the Washington of the North."

Statuette of Pierre Charles L'Enfant
Courtesy of The Sons of the Revolution in the State of New York,
Headquarters, Fraunces Tavern, New York City

THE MAJOR PIERRE CHARLES L'ENFANT
MEMORIAL ASSOCIATION

In the year 1927 the Major Pierre Charles L'Enfant Memorial Association was organized, for the purpose of securing for the City of Washington through an appropriation from the Congress "an appropriate and fitting Memorial to the Planner and Creator of the Federal City." Numerous patriotic organizations cooperated in this worthy project, as well as a great many distinguished and patriotic citizens. Among them is the Major L'Enfant Chapter of the Daughters of the American Revolution. The Inaugural Meeting was held at Fraunces Tavern, New York City, January 17, 1930, at which His Excellency, the French Ambassador to the United States, was speaker, and also former Congressman Hamilton Fish, Jr., a representative of the Society of the Cincinnati, and of the National Society, Sons of the American Revolution. At this meeting the bronze statuette of Major L'Enfant, by Clark Noble, sculptor, a picture of which is here shown, was presented by the Society of the Cincinnati on behalf of the Major L'Enfant Memorial Association to the Sons of the Revolution in the State of New York. The statuette is 18 inches high and has a black marble plinth. It will be noted from the picture that the sword, which extended down the length of L'Enfant's left leg to the boot top, has been broken off,—probably by some sightseer.

PIERRE CHARLES L'ENFANT MEMORIAL FOUNTAIN

In the year 1949 the National Sculpture Society expressed their interest in securing an appropriate memorial to Pierre Charles L'Enfant in the City of Washington as a feature of the Sesquicentennial Celebration of 1950. The matter was taken up with the National Commission of Fine Arts, and the Commission recommended a memorial fountain. Honorable Clifford Davis of Tennessee introduced H. R. 4274, "A bill authorizing the erection of a memorial fountain to Pierre Charles L'Enfant in the city of Washington," on April 14, 1949. It is one of the pending bills of the Congress.

Conclusion

In the conclusion of this work the writer feels a brief statement should be made concerning plans for the forthcoming Sesquicentennial Celebration, which in the year 1950 will mark the one hundred and fiftieth anniversary of the establishment of the Seat of the Federal Government in the District of Columbia.

We have noted that following the preparation of the L'Enfant Plan of 1791, efforts were put forth to begin building the City of Washington by the laying out of streets and avenues, the construction of residences, and in particular the erection of suitable buildings to house the Federal Government, namely the United States Capitol, the President's House, and a Federal Office Building. It was hoped General Washington might have lived to see it, but he died December 14, 1799. After nine years, on November 22, 1800, President Adams opened the second session of the Sixth Congress in the City of Washington, in the small north wing of the old Capitol Building, which housed the entire legislative establishment of the Government at that time. There were then 16 States in the Union, with 32 Senators and 105 Members of the House of Representatives.

In addressing the Congress, President Adams said in part—

"I congratulate the people of the United States on the assembling of Congress at the permanent seat of their Government, and I congratulate you, gentlemen, on the prospect of a residence not to be changed. Although there is cause to apprehend that accommodations are not now so complete as might be wished, yet there is great reason to believe that

363

this inconvenience will cease with the present session.

"It would be unbecoming the representatives of this Nation to assemble for the first time in this solemn temple without looking up to the Supreme Ruler of the Universe and imploring His blessing.

"May this territory be the residence of virtue and happiness! In this city may that piety and virtue, that wisdom and magnanimity, that constancy and self-government, which adorned the great character whose name it bears, be forever held in veneration! Here and throughout our country may simple manners, pure morals, and true religion flourish forever . . . ."

To commemorate this event, the Congress of the United States, by Act approved July 18, 1947, created the National Capital Sesquicentennial Commission. Under the leadership of Mr. Edward Boykin, Director, a comprehensive program has been planned. Great emphasis is being placed on the outstanding achievements of the developments of the City of Washington during the past 150 years. Appropriate recognition will be given to Pierre Charles L'Enfant for providing the Plan of 1791 for this beautiful city. It is also proposed to have a "Symposium on George Washington" which will portray important events in his life and in the development of the city. The distinguished dramatist Prof. Paul Green, of Chapel Hill, North Carolina, has offered to write it. The Washington Monument Grounds are to be appropriately developed to honor the "Father of Our Country," being one of several features in the city plan to be carried out soon. The President of the United States, who is Chairman of the Sesquicentennial Commission, is to address the Congress, the same as President McKinley did in the year 1900, which marked the Centennial Celebration, and as then the Governors of the several States and Territories of the United States are being invited to participate in the event; also foreign nations.

What the City of Washington will be fifty or a hundred years hence can scarcely be comprehended. Paris, which the City of Washington resembles so remarkably, was considered to be a "Giant City" in the year 1482, when it had a population of 200,000 that is after being in existence fully 1,500 years from the time of the Parisii in the days of Julius Caesar, as Victor Hugo relates so vividly in his "Notre Dame de Paris." It was not until about the year 1850 that Paris had a million inhabitants, which number, however, has increased to fully 4,000,000, including suburbs, at the present time. But what shall we say of the City of Washington, which numbers 1,000,-000 inhabitants after an existence of but a brief period of 150 years! Washington is today, in comparison, a youthful city, yet it is regarded "the center of the democracies" and has become a World Capital. It differs most from Paris, perhaps, in that in Washington great public, as well as private, building projects are constantly under way. Thus may the City of Washington ever be an inspiration to the millions of both this country and foreign countries who will come to see our National Capital in future years.

Finally, it should not be forgotten that "the City of Washington is your city and mine," and it is today what the people of the country, through their chosen representatives, have made it. This will apply to the development of Washington in future years. The appearance of a capital city, the center of government, reflects the pride of a Nation to a considerable extent, and to reassert the words (page 435) of an arden champion of the Plan of Washington, the late Senator McMillan, "Nothing is too good for the United States Capital."

Washington and His Family, With the Plan of the City of Washington Before Him. Painting by Savage, 1796.

Appendix

APPENDIX A

THE L'ENFANT MEMORIALS[1]

The originals of these memorials are the property of Mr. Henry A. Willard of this city, who secured them by purchase at the sale of the collection of autographs of the late Ben Perly Poore. Mr. Willard has kindly permitted them to be copied for publication in this volume of the transactions of this society. Their verification seems to be conclusively established. All of them are marked by the lines of folding and have the endorsement of official papers. To three of the documents the signature of L'Enfant is affixed, and two are in his handwriting. The memorial dated Philadelphia, August 30th, 1800, and addressed "To the Commissioners of the City of Washington," is not in his handwriting and is without his signature, but it contains references to others to which his signature is affixed, one of which is in his handwriting. The memorial, dated Philadelphia, December 7, 1800, addressed "To the Honorable the Senate and the Honorable the House of Representatives of the United States of America in Congress assembled," and "paper referred to per memorial December 7th," and endorsed No. 1, and the "Statement of the case of L'Enfant, December 11th, 1800," are in his handwriting and bear his signature.

These facts and circumstances satisfy the Committee on Publication of the authenticity of the memorials and accompanying papers, and justify their publication as verified copies of the originals in possession of Mr. Willard:

To the Commissioners of the City of Washington

PHILADELPHIA *August 30th* 1800

A concurrence of disastrous events rendering my position so difficult as to be no longer possible to withstand unless speedily

---

[1]From the Records of the Columbia Historical Society, Vol. 2.

relief be obtained by collecting what yet remains my due: I trust the simple mention of the case will justify an application to your Board and wih Instance on the Subject of my late Concern in the affairs of the City of Washington.—

I confided in the wisdom and honor of him whose patriotic views in giving birth to the Federal Establishment he knew my Zeal & Exertions were great to have forwarded, but at the present juncture, and since left with you Gentlemen to mourn the departed American Chief, thus at once missing the friend, and principal dependency in my cause, and of course became censurable for too great a confidence and liberality it will not be expected I can any longer forbear claiming Redress for Injury when the feeling is rendered so acute and the Consequences distressing.

I indeed have indulged the hope that—though an ill Star would have me be driven from the grand Concern in the affair of the City of Washington too soon for the merit of my labour there having been made perceptible to vulgar Senses—still the all comprehensive mind of its founder having adopted my Ideas and esteemed in the development of early attempts the promise of complete success would at this moment have acknowledged but the attainment (be it of only the leading object) for all the changes of Agency that have been does not the less leave the public Indebted to me.—

In the first place he knew, that—to my exertions your Commission owed the acquisition of means over commensurate with the Work to have supplied and by an oeconomy of which (on principles as were suggested) the City was at the end made a rich Corporation—he knew that—I derived no profit by the transaction while the immediate result to others has been a great Increase of their wealth from rise of property over a vast extent of terirtory, and if this Increase has not continued in a progressive ratio—if the business has proved more Complex than expected— if the progress has not been so rapid nor so brilliant and the resources were soon done away, reflection could not fail but convince him how these disappointments were invited by a departure from my principle and particularly for having given way to the seduction of that active Agency of all evil, Speculation,—he knew my early fear of the result when seeing the Interest that had already worked to disable your Commission of its means at the first stirred up disturbance of my operations combining with Jealousy to render loud the cry against keeping me powerful in the direction.—he had seen how suddenly after my retreat the City property being depreciated to an excessive low rate actual Bankrupts, Land and Stock Jobbers became the forestallers of the major portion and well approved and safe mode of accellerating public Improvements being renounced the growth of the City left a chance of Caprice was retarded through grumbling Interest and a Swindling Scheme of Lottery and to these facts the repeated call by your Commission made upon Government for assistance concurring in proof of the promised by Speculation Contract, he surely must have allowed but the apprehension of the consequences of which I had warned were not chimerical when besides it is seen that with all the prduct from Sale of House Lots and the intermissive Supply obtained it has not in seven years lapse enabled the Completion of even one half of the main Edifices.—

The Remark here reminding of the promise upon wch I engaged in the planning of the Federal Seat, of the Subsequent agreement with your Commission and how ungraciously when a thorough understanding of my plan being presumed and the execution thought facile, these were deceived through underhand measures which in the origin recognised inconsistent being in the proposal to me also Insulting Compelled my resignation. were I now to particularise grievances—that of the breach of the engagement to me respecting those edifices doubtless would be ranked high for having destroyed an essential part of the combined division of the City and thereupon if it were asked whence arose the disagreement so distructive of mine and the general Interest—recollecting how some of the esteemd friends of the enterprize in acknowledging the superiority of my Scheme at the same time confessed a regret at my standing so conspicuously the Agent of its success, it would easily be explained how the illiberal Sentiment rallying round all the inimical and the speculative Emulated the working to detach me from the business and to strip me also of the fame as has become manifest.—

1st. From the ascendancy of those friends and period at which exercised, persuading upon the high authority by whom I acted the discontinuance of accustomed familiar and direct communication with me on the subject of the City affairs whence followed an unshakened disturbancy of the best approved of my measures and abuse consequent also to your Commission refusal of explaining the object and denial of redress of private injury done by the mistake.

2ndly. From the manner my right as author, to the general Map of the City was nullified, first inducing my consent to an essay engraving, and next hindering it by taking the principal hand away from the work and secretly having had a number of Copies drawn of that Map for private gratification and such as also were seen in the Senate and in the House of Representatives wherein they had been hastened through opposition to the promised honors of myself presenting those bodies with the Original.

3rdly. From the deception of employing near me of a disguised personage who rendering himself serviceable gained free access to all my papers and so honorably acquitted of his Secret Commission gathering all by transcription and chalk out of Manuscripts and Drawings as to have at the opportune moment secured all that could serve to others to reap reputation and profit from my labours.

4th. From the Invitation given to a particular Individual, a copiest of my own plan, bringing him forward as original proprietor, by which was seen superceding me in the direction of the Capitol Edifice one of repute for having betrayed a trust deserting his duty to me on an occasion before and to the utter disappointment of a public object.

5thly. From the incorrect representation of my disposition when saying that I declined acting under your Commission — whereas well avered that no terms ever were offered to me on wch to have obtained my sentiments and that I myself made advances which remained unanswered proposing a mode of adjusting different and for the organization of the business, for the Security of my Agency in wch I simply wished the agreement mutually binding to respect and observance, a precaution well justified from prior violation.

6thly. From the Conduct of one highly trusted but on whose dependency on particular patronage made him connive with all the inimical and Contentious· besides when free from my Control his deviating from the agreed with me in the execution of my plan and injuriously too to all property by having rendered numbers of it incapable of improvement wch by my combination were made the most advantageous.

7thly. From the assumption altogether of the property of my plan, again secretly engraving, wch engraving incorrect in part being given for guide of operations has been misleading all succeeding Surveyors whose innocent Errors for want of knowledge of my method *of offset of lines where angles fall under a certain degree,* necessarily must have atchieved equal mischief as where the mistake has been malicious.

8th. From the tricking proceeding on my discovering of the above when after I generously permitted the completing of the engraving and had even lent manuscripts drafts as were said wanting for correction—those manuscripts were detained and I refused the revisal of the proofs in printing.

9thly. From me finding my name erased from the title of the Map at the moment of publication and leaving stand on one of my Assistants,—a proceeding too plainly descrying by what Mind dictated, for need being of remark upon as besides the petty policy proved itself also by the careful omission of my name in all subsequent publications pamphleting and other more unstable accounts of the City Establishment.

10thly. From the forcible Seizure of particular drafts manuscripts in deposit and of other abstracts papers and effects likewise Stealhed away from my Agents and out of my own quarters when in my absence the disturbances consequent to the combined arrest and false Imprisonment of that Agent laid all open to plunder, and by which I was bereaved of the possibility of effecting an intended publication of the City Plan in my own name.

11th. From the hearty and pressant manner of a tender of a little Money expressedly as acquit of all obligations the rejection of which commended by feeling of a better due was no less determined by discovery at the very time of the abusive dealing as stated No. 3, 8, 9 and 10

12thly. From the extention of the wrong in having contemptuously of the assurance given me in primary instances but the publication of my plan was meant to be limited multiplied the emission in rapid succession to each other, and disposed of the prints not merely through the United States but over all Country beyond Sea thus spreading the fame of the enterprize robbing me of the merit and of my fortune by making the great proceed the enrichment of them who have no title to it except it be as expert Agents of Villainy.

If pausing here and to shorten the disgraceful Catalogue the question were to turn upon what has been my own conduct—I conscious of no wrong at my hand done would simply reply but my endeavours were uniformly to the purpose of the enterprize,

and the System of my Process likewise the best calculated
(known of) to have within the appointed term raised the City
a fit Capital for this vast growing Empire and capable of receiving the Government—

Further—I would give to consider—that the Invitation to me
to the Potowmack was in words as follow viz—To undertake
there the execution *of the President's intentions*—that next his
Instructions came *through the Secretary of State* placing me Independent [which Instruction it will not be unimportant to
notice had (either through inadvertency or for some purpose)
made my position at the first instance most perplexing and deli-
cate]—I would give to consider that the apprehension of the
mischief attendant to all dispoint or jealous directions made me
the first Solicitous of a proper Union of agency, and that it was
in testimonial of concordant disposition and to determine my
undertaking the plan of the City that I was assured of the direction of the two main Edifices the Site and Configuration of which
constituted essentially the base of its divisions—I would give to
consider—that being agreed my agency should be primary over
all employed at the work of the City, and that work all over to
have been conformable to the Plan—for all what I could do
afterward inviting your Commission at its part [to provide and
organize all the Branches of Administration] it having slighted
the call and disclaimed owing an immediate attendance questioning whether the foundation of a new City had at all been the
intention of its appointment the Consequence was that much of
what ought to have been its care necessarily devolved on me to
perform under the particular confidential Instruction of the
President. I lastly would give to consider that—thus eventually
made to act a principal part in transactions of first Interest to
the Federal Establishment (otherwise foreign to my agency)
successful and approved in every Step and proposal made by me,
I on the adoption of the grand Idea of the plan having been en-
joined a prompt execution conformably to—the Scruple then with
your Commission preventing an active cooperation, it became
incumbent on me resolutely to endeavor those things of which it
would not make a particular business and when necessitated to a
disagreeable exertion of authority to trust on, and avail of, the
support afforded me as in few instances I did cautioning the
delinquents and pursuing the right course of my operations.

To contrast my proceeding with the treatment which I met in
return—it also would be seen that the greater the machination to

frustrate my labours, the more regardless of personal consequences, I exerted abilities advancing all matters of Import to
the National object abetting no party meaning the advantage of
all and that—if my occasional absence (necessitated by variety of
distant avocations) was opportunate to disturbances and arrest
of my measures, these disturbances and arrest having constantly
subsided and been receded from as I drew near again to the place
—all can only be proofs additional but every of my directions
must have been considerate, Judicious, Proper, and not as some
would have had it believed running Counter to regulation and
Convention with them from whom I derived the power—it would
be seen that notwithstanding the discouragement also of incon-
siderate hurrying on of most intricate opperations, of the un-
timely call of marking out Lots for Sale and other similar indis-
creet orders which besides the uselessness of were effectedly given
more to perform than by human power could have been devou-
ment to the business made me cheerfully endeavour the utmost,
overlook all Inconveniences repressing the Sentiment of the Injury to me Intent and to do Justice to every call commit my
health by the practice of passing from excessive hard days labour
to the no less toilsome of long and whole set up nights destitute
of the comforts and means of exigency to such an undertaking
and in a clime the like.

Thus it would be seen that left alone and having had to conquer the prepossession of people the primary affected by the operation of my plan, actively subduing difficulties and under a
surcharge of care the mind engaged in the framing of a plan
novel, extensive and varied in its ramifications, my agency extending also to ministration relative to Concessions of territory
(that which I gained to the public being above three fourths over
than the first sought after besides other detached acquisitions of
as much moment and advantage) the entire Scheme of the Federal Establishment was secured, most eminently to my preseverance in the business till the main bases of the plan were
immutably fixed and a portion of the whole of the division and
Improvements so began as needed for a regulation to the end.—

By so liberally facilitating the execution of the plan Independent of me being visible I was diminishing my own Consequence
in the Concern with your Commission—I knowing of no new
Legislative act to have Rendered the continuance of my Agency
in union with your Commission more Incompatible in 1792 than

had been from 1790—here may be remarked the ungratefulness of the management at issue being then when all matters were by one set in a good way that the cry against my so continuing began to be heard and that in unison, those long born vexations (before cautiously mitigated), were boldly redoubled and with so insufferable unprecedented Indignities that no longer abiding to compact the transaction as also as in the foreging numbered, shewed clearly the Mastery of an inimical envious Genious over both your Commission and the chief on whom depended the reorganization of the directive whom by preventing them the consideration of my proposals for—at last left nothing honorable for me to have done but the resignation which followed.

Resolving on the resignation, the Contrast again of my Conduct would Shew others ruled by petty policy against the better knowledge of things converting the reasons of my abandonment as best could sooth up the concerned in the event to a passive endurance of this mischief—biassing the public in belief to me injurious by whispering round but I failed in the respect due to the president of the United States and wished to have placed myself above your Commission, the ingenuity of which Story helped first in dissuading the Citizens of Washington from remonstrating on the business by address as they intended to the President an act which would have been a manifest of the esteem which I left being me, too clashing with the purposes of blotting all traces of my agency for admitting doubly handling in order also of precluding the better disposition of the chief and create distrust in me mistating to him my Sentiments, and to me representing him ill inclined thus casting the odium of particular doings on sides rendered of difficult access, were tricks ably managed but which for all that failed in the intent of exciting me through mistaken anger to uncivil demeanour toward any.—it was seen to the contrary that—not only due respect to Office but right esteem of person all along actuated me, and so much so that at the moment previous to my resigning (and against the advice of all that surrounded me) I gave fresh proofs of to the President of the United States—addressing this first Patron of the Federal Enterprize with the precise of my Ideas and intentions of conducting it—loyally giving into his honor my Schemes to enable your Commission the proper prosecution of the work began advising such ways and means as I knew were attainable and warranted the most safe and Expedienfal—after which when the whole business with me was closed, manifesting none but my anxiety still for the good of the City—feeling strong in the integrity and honor of my past Services against the Shafts of speculative Villains contemptuous of them all, I simply invited attention on the singular doing respecting the publishing of the City Plan as Explained Nos. 7, 8 and 9 and withdrew myself, with the comfort of assurances on that occasion renewed to me, in the name of the President by his own Secretary, that nothing in the business had been but upon the whole entitled me to praise and Insured me the continuance of his particular Esteem and favor— the sense of mentioning which warranted me the sincerity of.—

Having yielded in this honorable manner to the Jealousies of the same which the complete raising of the City to a Splendour and greatness worthy of its name must have acquired.—were it necessary more to illustrate the merit of the Sacrifice I could for the Satisfaction of those whose estimation of a concern may chiefly attach to the weight of base Coin from which to deduce profit or loss—produce data from which to appreciate the loss to my fortune consequent also to the failing of the promise upon wch I engaged in the planing of the City of Washington.

Giving to compare my actual distressed Condition with the affluent circumstances of, in 1790.—however may be said of the disastrous events Surveyned in Europe and of the robberies which I in the interim experienced on other hands of my saving here having contributed a share of the reduction—it would be easily demonstrable but the Invitation to the Potomack and subsequent engagement there were ye primary causes by necessarily having diverted my attention from the turning of my family affairs in Europe and also—that having forced by removal from a place (New York) where I stood at the time able of commanding whatever business I liked, the chances all were missed there by which I might have retreaved from difficulties—as what I elsewhere since I endeavoured proved unavailable or rather added to —owing also to tricking not altogether foreign to what I experienced in the Federal Enterprize—obvious therefore but the Inducement for hazarding my all in that Enterprize must have been the contemplation of a full compensation, here leaving a part what is claimed by the circumstances of loss and expence of the removal as necessitated.—if only inquiring into the advantages promised by, may be set down that.

1st. Of a Salary to my Agency commensurate with the magnitude and importance of the Object and of the Affairs managed.—

2ndly. Of payment for the delineation of the City Plan on an estimation expected such as the Sentiment of a work of genious alone alone can suggest and—differencing the production of the artist from that of the mere artisan or virtuoso, making also the price comport with the benefit in the end to result to the Nation.

3rdly. Of the proceed from the printing of the City Plan or an equivalent for being taken away the property thereof.—

4th. Of the great additional perquisite necessarily to have devolved to me from the agency.—

What those perquisites would have come to—this would be well deducible from observing that on the adoption of my plan, proposals already from Particular Companies placed under my immediate agency the errecting of Houses to the amount of $1,000,000 only for a first operation meant to have been extended to upward double the Sum and for my trouble in directing whch besides what would have come from an Infinitude of other detached fabricks, very liberal offers had. been made and such as (exclusively of the right on public account) had procured me a clear gain of $50,000 on first start of the business and upon failure of which brought on as has been the Compensation due by Government follow from all such Concerns having been made the Consideration in the planning of the City—the object of the first authorization of my Steps enticing those private ventures having been principally the obtaining from the ventures themselves a loan of Money for the public work the carrying on of which they considering of essential mutual safety in the Enterprize made the loan be agreed with them for, at a moderate rate of 5 pct. and to an amount at once equal to the computed expences of five years of all projected operations—by which mean the grand machinery of my plan was to have been set in motion raising, as if it had been magically a ready built City out of the Earth, thereby to have secured at all chances the most of the looked for, by the Shares of property whilst it had enabled the quiet prosecution of the political object saying the expences to the Nation since out of the Lots nót built on when the loan reimbursement once effected would have remained a surplusage of great means and Income to the City itself.

Whether the measure mutually failed from having been kept back waiting my going out of the agency—or whether it was dissuaded from by alluring Interest such as I wished to have restrained—being only reverting to the principle of the negociation that I bring the disappointment up to the list of Services left un-requited—reflection must easily satisfy how the prospect in such an agency and the being hurrying on to a beginning of the Enter-prize at the very time of the breaking out of the Revolution in my native Country made me lose the hearing of its Summons and taking away from me the leisure to have saved property revertible to me there, caused me the loss—a loss since the event of which I could only be heartened against the fear of want here by reckon-ing upon a great due (at least of gratitude) for a long series of Services, mostly gratuitous and which for having in a succession of above 22 Years, gained me the esteem, and I may say the con-fidence, of the great late American Chief were not a little encreas-ing my Security in the concern taken at his Invitation, in the federal business my expectation from which as expressed cannot but be still as sanguine as it was at the moment of the adoption of my plan, or more over I would give to consider that my belief in a full acquiescence to the terms and manner of the provisions negociated as above stated was consequent to my having seen every other interfering proposal, to mine dismissed and one par-ticularly noticable for having come from *the* Secretary of the Treasury A: Hamilton himself which it is observable if it had prevailed still would have placed me within a Sphere of larger perspective than what I otherwise embraced—Speaking of the *Secretary's Intention* to have provided me at once with as many Pounds Sterling as I at the time computed of Dollars wanted.

His Scheme for which besides enabling the absolute completion of the City Plan gave a greater certainty to the attainment of the political end, than the most timorous of the Interested to its success could well have questioned—here to take away the won-der of the dismissal so far as I myself witnessed of the trans-action ascribing the mistake to the temper of some of the primary consulted who precluded the president's own Judgment of the merits of the proposal the circumstances may be well appealled to as one of the many Instances when to my knowledge the dear-est Interest of the City of Washington was sacrified through the passion and weakness of its most esteemed Supporters and the Infatuation of some whom wishing the Seat of Government stand a mere contemptible hamlet had rested better satisfied with giv-ing great name to small things than with having in reality those things done which were to have reflected an immortal honor on

the nation, and rapidly raised that Seat a splendid inviting Capital—the Influence of whose character surprizingly discernable in
the opposition met while pursuing matters, the Injunction to me
to effect which had been positive and reiterate, betrayed no less
personal ill will causing those Injunctions to me the more Imperious in proportion as bereaving me of the means I was
tricked into a necessity either to have metamorpohesed myself
an Insignificant impotent employer or renounced all concern in
the business the latter of which must have been expected from
me better than that I could with honor at Stake at the issue of an
Enterprize wholly of my own Scheme have descended from my
Post insensible of a greater due and that I would covetously
stooping to Insult and breach of agreement have committed myself to becoming the pliant tool for middling Speculators to have
worked the destruction of the very riches by my labour to your
Commission procured and so that on the Event of the Enterprize
missing its end, I must have stood the apparent reprehensible
cause.—a chance which for being now happily evaded still will
not be believed out of the Intent of those who have advised or
advocated that beggarly system of Oeconomy to which your
Commission has been reduced being incredible how other but
raking Schemery and Enemies to the politics and glory of the
great patron founder of the City, can have opposed more provi-
dent arrangement and at the hazard of losing all, dared so novel
and vast a work without a guide at least with none that could
feel his repute and honour engaged to the success

Could them whose Influence was so prevalent be at all the
City friends—these insidious flatterers and courters of my exertions—it must be seen that watchful of the progress and Jealous
of the Success, they provoked the resignation of my concern out
of conceit of abilities to have themselves overtaken again my
ways and advantaged of all by me brought within power of effecting, and the facts and deductions to be drawn from all in the
foregoing recital speaking of the wrong I suffered all the pretence
of this having been perpetrated out of good wish to the City,
would not make that wrong less it would not diminish the evidences of the abuse of my property nor would it embellish the
hideousness of the motive for the use make of people who under
me were necessarily trusted with all my Ideas and Intentions,
to say but these people did not so aid the business as might
be imagined or that such promotion as in No. 4 (related) was

only meant as a screen to the preferment of more reputable con-
current.

Be those persons who superceded me and who in rotation may
have expelled one another either mere would be thought Architects or truly bred up to the profession and learned and able
practisers—if they followed the paths chalked out by me or
stepped from it, the result as the City shall rise will shew which
of presumptuous ignorance or of true Judgment has been their
guide and as I shall sincerely more lament the errors than Jealous the success—declaring here that I am far from the Idea of
even reproaching them who have benefited of my stripping and
that I neither pretend challenging an explication of the conduct
of Superiors simply yielding, and with much reluctance too, to
the hard necessity of unfolding the unhappy situation of my
affairs and to what owing—I have particularized heads of grievances, and offered a comparative of Conduct in order that a right
Judgment may be formed of the Errors and of where may lay.—
and how the estimation of which you Gentlemen whom I now address I trust will be satisfied of the ground upon which I promised to myself—but the Man whose mind I esteem was too great,
and whose heart was too good to have partaken of the Intention
of Wrong would not have failed at this Juncture for causing a
redress proportionate to all what my fortune, and fame have
suffered.

Claiming such redress I question not but your Commission has
itself all along holden the honor and Justice of the American
Nation for Engaged to—and therefore hope that you Gentlemen
actually in Office will view the foregoing as properly submitted
to their consideration and left to be acted upon as in their own
joint wisdom shall be deemed most consistent—I remaining well
certain that divested of all prepossessions and selfish regard—
as a body actuated by no Interest but that of doing good—the
merit of all circumstances will be generously weighed and that
if—incompatible as I apprehend it may be with your charge be
to do that ample Justice which is my right to expect—if the matter should need be referred to Government you will (without re-
fraining from affording what redress and relief may be in the
power of your Commission) make it a point on the first convenient opportunity in an official way to call the Government
attention on the state of the business—

Could the opportunity soon occur I would anticipate much

from your Individual good Commendation. Indulging in the per-
suation but the propriety and merit of all my acts and directions
in respect to business of the City of Washington has long before
been rendered sensible to you Gentlemen in the prosecution of
the Enterprize and that—however renouncing the System of operations by me set in train you have attained the principal of the
end for which I contended—you will feel the attainment short of
what I aimed at but not the less for that adding to the debt of
gratitude to me for—you will feel how by being secured in the
object, the nation has become more directly in honor bound to
compensate my loss and to repay my zeal and trouble and you
will that the whole due may be appreciated, and discharged with
credit to the nation as readily acknowledging, and as doubtless
would have done him in whose praise I made my pride,—that the
final fixing of the Federal Government on the bank of the Potomack, the advantage to result to the Union and the enrichment
over an immense tract of contiguous country is in a most particular manner attributable to the vivacity of my first conception
of the business—to the Combination of my exertions beyond my
professional line and to the devotedness with which suffering a
great reverse of fortune I disregarded all consequences to myself
honestly keeping at my post making head against cavilling opposition until by a display of the grand intention of my plan
and by the manifestation of power as well as of resolution to
effect it the reputation which I acquired to the Enterprize had
in connecting the pride with the Interest of the Union changed
the most influential of the Component States from Enemies into
friends to the Establishment.

With due Respect I have the honor to be

[Endorsement.]
Mr. L'Enfant':
Memorial
delivered by
Jno. Langdon
21 March
1801
Sess
2 Cons.

Philadelphia, decembr. 7th, 1800.

Memorial to the Honorable the Senate and to the Honorable

the house of representatives of the United States of America in Congress assembled—

Respectfully shewing that, I your memorialist—Peter charles L'Enfant—major of Engineer in the revolutionary war, having entered the Service of the United States early in 1776—served without interruption to the end of the war, and, to great personal sacrifices joining the merit of wounds received and of hard Captivity endured — having remained an inhabitant of the Said States, and a freeman of the City of new york by Special honorifick patent continuing usefull in various public employment since the peace of 1784—but without any pay, and at my own expenses having performed many Services through encouragement of promises of regular reapointment with preferment consistant with my acquired title to—waiting that and, on the occasion of the first of the act fixing the permanent Seat of government on the bank of the potomack I having also been Invited there and charged of the devising of a Scheme for the establishment of a City, I consequently afterward, upon the adoption of the whole of the plan by me proposed became a principal in the direction Jointly with the Commission by law Constituted—further giving to Consider that I your memorialist proceeded on that Service as I had done many before with more promptness to act than care of Stipulating Conditions or of procuring legal Substantiating to all the promised in the end—the mournfull event of the loss of the great chief and first President of these United States by whose choice and Confidence I had been honored depriving me of the friend and principal dependancy in my cause—the whole in the following submitted claim from the Equity of your honorable house to be generously considered.—

The terms of the Invitation to me to the potomack having simply been these (viz)—to undertake there the President Intention—and next on the Connecting of my agency with the Commission—the Supremacy over all the employed being Conceded to me the Commission also having left it to me—to devise to Suggere and to bring on all Sorts of arrangement or matters of Intersct to the enterprise—this great Confidence and responsibility too to—answer, whilst at the Same time the required and the expected from me at once at the on Set of the business enlarged its difficulties and the Scheme of enterprise for its novelty excited a faning of Interests—will doubtless well Satisfy your honorable house—how laborious was my task and that an active resolute exertion of abilities alone Could forward that business and in the midst of a world of Intrigues and of Contrarieties have well preserved the mind free for the Combinations of a plan So peculiarly adapted to circumstances and so varied as is that of the city of Washington.

Noticing these Intrigues because at first and so long as uncertainty attended by labour having been moderated—the disguise was thrown off as gradually as by a loyal and generous display and communication of my every Intentions and ends, I diminished my own Consequence by rendering my own plan possible to other to execut Independant of me and—it having been then when—agreably to the President desire and after urged on by the Commissionairs themselves—a begining had been made at all points and when—Supply was Insured to all adequate (at least by me brought within reach to have been so Insured) that a cry against maintaining me so able in the agency became to be heard.—there upon will I pose—leaving it to the wisdome of your honorable house to define the reasons—to Judge of the wrong and how to me hard and mortifying that—when my agency had thus far been availled of and after so active and successfull —when by all acknowledged to have been to the best of end directed to the satisfaction and advantage of the people owners of the territory of Columbia and also—that my every Step and measures had met the approval and been given the support of the great patron of the establishment whose personal glory the grand end Concerned—the Enemies of that Entreprise and Speculators coalised with the Jealouses of the same which a complete raise of the city to a splendor and greatness worthy its name and the capitol of a grand Empire must have acquired—Should have found Supporters and have become so prevalent and so irresistible as has proved from the wrought on necessity of a departure from my System of general Economic of management to the end of compelling the relinquishment of my concern.

on the resulting abuses and to confine to what directly affected me.—to the evil of Injury to my fame and to that of the destruction of my fortune—having been joined that of a disappointment also of a preferment to an office particularly made my dependency at the first, of the late raising of fortifications and at the succtssive variance ini the reorganisation of the department of Engineers—mentioning that merely to Shew whence and how different ways a victim of my Confidence liberality and zeal in my public Concerns—the Integrity also of the views in all my aspirings having kept me from an over pursuit, in the meanwhile Sunk my every resource under deceptive prospects and Encouragements and—of this Integrity and of its Consequences, the ready resignation I made of my grand Concern in the affairs of the City of Washington affording conspicuous uncontroulable proof — on these will I rest, deeming it unnecessary more to enumerate Instances when disinterestedness and a Sense of the honorable to do, has been the predominent through my Several atchievements for fame—I maintaining the hope that—twenty three years of attachment to these United States, the free Spending of my own in Services not altogether unprofitable to them—having born evidence of my Constancy to principle and gained me the esteem as it had merited me the Confidence of the late chief and first president of these United States will be recommending me to the Indulgence and favour of your honorable house, especially at so auspicious a juncture as that of its first Seating in the city of Washington—when the circumstance naturally is to recal to mind or to prompt to Enquiry to known—by whom was the establishment first framed.

Encouraged by this persuasion in here Stating the object of this memorial to be to Submit to the Equity of your honorable house—certain cases of Infraction of my rights and due, with other Injury Sustained at the close of my Concerns in the affairs of the City of Washington (all in abuse of the generosity and loyalty of my conduct.—referring for particular to the Subjoigned paper No. 1. I your Memorialist confidently pray for redress and for Compensation.

also and to the end that my Scheme of the City establishment may become better understood—referring to the Commission itself for Explanation of the proprietie of the novel way of division and to Shew the practicability (agreable to my Intention) with ease to have Completed the work within the period by the act limited.—this as will Satisfy of the fore-cast of my combinations and of the weight of the charge and care at the Setting on of so great a work under opperation, being to enable the proper valuing of the plan and the merit of my direction.

farther I shall not take up the time of your honorable house but to express regret that, the Interests that have been so detach me from that business Should have also dissuaded its prosecution on the System by me laid down and to the admission of Ignominous

lottery Speculation and of other destructive of the city property—
which by dissabling the Commission from that great mean for
Suprly that had been through my exertions first created—has
left the growth and population of the city a matter of chance at
the hazard of missing the main object of its foundation and as
necessarily caused its actual Insufficiency and will keep it long
yet before it can afford any thing like the promised by me or
Suitable for a Seat of national Councils and Government. not at
the Same time questioning—but that in parting from my System
the principals, managers or others respectable characters Influential to an opposition to me were all actuated by Justifiable
motives though differing from the policy that rulled me.—I well
account how likewise in an Entreprise so novel a misconception
may have been of the proper for an efficient prosecution of the
design—how honest minds unsuspecting of the end, can have
been persuaded to the worst of expedients and how also Subaltern
agents, over officious, may have atchieved much to my Injury—
only therefore lamenting the mischief of a coersion of the best
Intentions I shall here pass silently over the arts and machinations by which I became a victim of my zeal and of my respect for
and Confidence in the high authority by whom I acted—this indeed too long and too disgraceful for recital being besides unim-
protant, Since it would not alter facts nor could niether add nor
diminish of the Injury to Indemnify.   ·

having given the Commission full minute relation of facts and
of management as have been in above of the loyalty of my conduct
which Joined to the Stock of its own Information will Enable
the gentlemen now in office themselves to explain (if that Should
be necessary) on points both delicate and grievous to me to remind of—also having there upon obtained the assurance of those
gentlemen disposition to Support or aid the prayer I have no
made—I not only rely on their Sensibility of an Indemnification
being due to me for loss consequent to deprivation and Infraction
of certain of my rights as also for other Injury—but that—their
own Experience through a long administration—their knowledge
of the State in which I found and of that in which I left the local
of the City of Washington—both as have Satisfied them of what
begining I made and what were the difficulties by me Conquered—
will press out an honorable avowal that—for all the change the
agency have undergone and however deviating from the principle
of the work by me began the chief of the ends for which I con-

tended is now attained—Such an atainement glorious as may be to the Commission Still Short of what I aimed at, is not the less attributable to me and in a high degree too deserving of a munificent acknowledgement for.—being well certain that them who wittnessed my actions, if they be but disinterested men, will all agree that—the Success of the City of washington was first Insured by the reputation which I gained to the entreprise—by the quick Conception of the proprietie of its local—by exertions and Combinations uncommon to my proffessional line and—by the de votedness with which, whilst I Suffering a great reverse in my family fortune I still persevered in unprofitable labour and at the end resolved, the Sacrifice also of my prospects in that Entreprise to a reconciliation and harmonising of parties and Interests that opposed the progress..

I indulg therefore the hope that to the regard of all circumstances upon which my prayer is founding the pressure of my necessities will be conclusive from Seeing me come forward in the mortifying attitude of Supplicant before your honorable house at a place and on a day too as the present when reflection alone must Convince that—if I had but been permitted the execution of the City plan, the brilliancy of the Success by bringing me all triumphantly over the Jealouses would now have gained me the honor of a free unanimous vote in Expression of the Satisfaction at the Service.

feeling the differenc of the Situation and humbly Submitting my case to your honorable house I your Memorialist remain with profound respect

the Honorable the Senate
and the Honorable the house
of representatives

most obedient
most devoted and
humble servant
PETER CHARLES L'ENFANT.

Note referred to on pàge 12 of the Exposition

With respect to the tales that "I withheld from the commissioners the plan and the information in my possession relative thereto" the following questions and answers must naturally occur, viz.

Question. 1.—What right could the commissioners pretend to my plan or to those informations relative thereto?

Answer. none whatever.

Q. 2.—Did they ever ask this of me?

A. never.

Q. 3.—Why did they not?

A. I presume because I was not paid for & was not obliged by any promise to have done more than I did.

Q. 4.—Did they not receive the plan from the president and the information which he chose to give to them?

A. they certainly did.

Memorandum

If I had retained anything improperly, the president was the only person to whom I was accountable.

Q. 5.—Did not the commissioners forcibly take possession of a manuscript of my plan, together with notes of my directions to surveyors, which I had lent on trust to one of the persons employed by them after I had left the business?

A. They absolutely did so.

Q. 6.—Did they not in a surreptitious manner procure and cause my plan to be engraved at Philadelphia?

A. They did so.

Q. 7.—When they thus procured the engraving did they not know that I intended to have published it? and had they not themselves engaged of me 10,000 copies?

A. They undeniably did know & had so engaged.

Q. 8.—Was I not justly entitled to expect from them the price for those 10,000 copies that I might have got by a sale to others?

A. I believe there can be no doubt of it.

Q. 9.—Was it not therefore doing me a wilful injury to sell the engraving for their own account or purpose at a reduced price thereby depriving me of my price and of the right to the exclusive privilege of publication?

A. It was.

Q. 10.—If they had had any right to it would they have resorted to so shameful a mode of procuring it?

A. I believe they wd have taken a more legal way.

Q. 11.—Did not president Washington declare the engraved plan to be the determined plan of the city and that he would not permit it to be deviated from?

A. He did so declare.

Q. 12.—Was not the president bound by every principle of honor and justice, as he had previously promised to the proprietors not to depart from the original, by me in the first instance laid out?

A. He certainly was.

Q. 13.—Was it not by thus binding himself as also by promising the execution in the way I proposed that he obtained the assent of the landed proprietors to the partition of the building lots & obtained besides the several parcels of land purchased for the use of the U. S. at so low a price as 25 pounds per acre?

A. This is a well known and an undeniable fact.

Q. 14.—Can it therefore be doubted that the engraved plan is agreeable to the original *lines of the grand divisions* of the city? that it is correct with respect to the distribution of the sites of the capitol, judiciary and the president's house—that it is also correct in the course of the canal and that no alteration can be made in any of those things?

A. This cannot be doubted and I certify that it is absolutely so.

Q. 15.—What then are the alterations. Were there not several lines of avenues suppressed from the original design; and did not this suppression cause a derangement in the lines also of some of the right angled streets?

A. There were some such alterations but these were made by myself at the recommendations of the president & of the secretary of state, Mr. Jefferson, as early as august 1791 before I prepared tht map for engraving, and at the request of the original proprietors of one particular section of the city. And all the proprietors know that altho the drawing laid before them at their general meeting was declared to be approved by the president, it had not his final approval until after the above alterations were made and only on the date aforesaid.

N. B.—No other alteration could possibly be effected except the change of property from hand to hand, that is to say, that some squares were struck out which were intended to be reserved as public property and have permitted to be sold to individuals—this producd a change in numbering the lots and could not be justly called an alteration in the plan.

P. CHAS. L'ENFANT

No. 1
paper referred to

per memorial to—the Honorable the Senate (decembr. 7th) and
the Honorable the House of representativs
of th United States &c.

Particular Statement of Cases referred to per memorial and
the Circumstance under which offered having been explained
leave now to be Considered as are in the following numeral heads
respectfully Submitted (viz)

1st.—of Injury done to my fame as an Artist—by multiplied
Spurilous publication of my plan of the City of Washington, in
abuse of a permission first by me granted in *obedience* to the
president own desire for an essay engraving with his prior assurance that no copying from would have been allowed.—next by
hinderance of publishing a Correct map in my own name the
materials for which, Such as manuscript,. drawing notes of
grounds level and measurements &c. all were through Some
authority laid hold of and detained from me. lastly — by the
Singular policy—of suppressing my name from the title of the
maps as emitted and that likewise of preventing the mention of
in pamphlets and other the most notable public relation that
have been of the Columbian establishment and to the end (manifest) of depriving me of the honor of becoming known as the
Original designer.

2dly.—of the resulting Injury to my fortune—by deprivation
thus of the proceed from Sale of my own work—to the number
of upward of 15,000 Copies on a moderate computation from
the difference of the Engravers hands—from the variety of Sizes
plates, also from the extent and population of country and places
where have for these nine years past been disposed of here and
in Europe and mostly Selling for from tow to three dollars each.
—whether or not such be the number out, at least from 15 to
20,000 Copies are but the raisonable to be taken into view as
the probable quantity that would have Sold of the right maps
at the time of first Interest and Curiosity as had been excited
by my exertions at the Commencement of the enterprise—therefore being easily to estimate the difference now to my fortune
Seeing the mischief obviously owing to my Condescension in
obedience to the President of the United States—I cannot doubt
but my rights to a Compensation will here be readily admitted.

3dly.—of Injury likewise to my fortune and fame—owing to
transgression of promises, particularly respecting the tow main
Edifices, the Capitol and presidency palace.—the erecting of

both which after my own designs had been a primary Condition
to my engagement to planing the City.—to whose peculiar division those Edifices were in Configuration essential to have exactly corresponded.—whereas the unjust recant from the promised—the injudicious departure from what I had began through
management of people either ill Intent or Incapable of fitting
the plans to the Circumstances of the Site for—has ruined the
most estimable part of the Scheme which for the originalness
of the thought in its whole Connected would have raised the
City of washington to an unrivaled splendour.—an Injury to my
fortune thence arising from the loss of the very designs Sketches
minute of the Intended Edifices and of preparative for other
and for the *aqueducs,* the *bridges,* the grand *dock* and *Canal* &c.—
all precious memorandum for an Artist to have preserved and
all destroyed or diverted away from my own quarter and out
of othr offices under favour it is believed of disturbances in my
absence excited—the last Instance of which (when while I was
abroad on business with the president my beginning of the
foundation of the main Edifices was arrested and other operations too prevented, that were waited for by me and necessary
to my perfecting the general plan) determined the abandone-
mnt of the whole of my Concerns to the Commission.

4th.—of the Injury to my fortune owing to heavy expences
and loss consequent to removal from a City (New York) were
prior Successful entreprise had placed me able of commanding
great business and where I not only missed great chances of fortune by absense but absolutely lost a property in lots of ground
worth $5,000 (for which it was Sold) through contrivance of
Some malevolent avaricious men amongst the Corporation of
that City who made me appear as having renounced the grant.

5th.—that at the end,—those Jealousies and Speculations
Contradictory to my System Caused me the loss of a bargain of
$50,000 a Sum of right perquisite accruing from particular Com-
pagnies Entreprises of building in amount at first place of
$1,000,000 and which Intended to double that Sum with an In-
crease of the benefit to me, being to have been planed and conducted in concert and to the advancement of the public part of
Improvements were Consequently to have depended on my direction.—on which—

it may be remarked that—in order for giving certainty to
the whole connected Entreprise (no provision having been made

for by law) I had been from the begining and while planing of it authorised to the organisation of Such compagnies, and with the double object of by their meaĥs procuring advances of money, which at my Invitation they had offered to an amount at once equal to the whole Computed want for five years of opperations—for the paving of Streets—for the grand canal and—for other usefull and pleasurable Improvements which it made part of my System to have progressed far in, before making any great Sale of lots even before building of houses.—the Contract proposed hath afforded all the necessary money on a Simple Interest of 5 per Cnt. without any premium, on the Security of the City property itself—and to have been gradually reimbursed either by giving houses lots or Cost, at the choice of the borower and begining only after ten years, So that the houses lots enhanced in price by progress of Improvements clearly would have answered (what I meant by that property) to have Saved altogether the Expense of the City establishment to the nation— a Scheme of bargain the most Equal in advantages to both Sides of the Concernies—the which hath m'et the mind of the president and his approval too (apparently at least Judging fom the dismissal of all Interfering proposals and namely of one coming from the Secretary of the treasury [*Mr. Hamilton*] all which making the negociation Complete So far as in me depended— maintain me in the hope but the missing of the promised by the bargain, as related to myself with those Compagnies, especially when it is reflected on the cause, will be admitted as a grievance properly recorded amongst Injury Intitling me to Compensation.

6th.—that besides that the esteem of the character and my personal dependancy in the late President dispositions had commanded an early unreserved communication of my plans and the display of the machinery for Execution (so much to my Injury since abused of) other raisons Joined as forcibly Inducive that—no beforehand bargain—had been possible for the work of those plans nor no Sallary Could have been well determined for my agency nor direction of a work so varied and unprecedented —before Some previous begining and an understanding of the whole magnitude of the objects of pursuit had been for an appraisement of the labour and Computing with that too the advantages ensuing to the nation from the grand Combination of the plan.

thus the matter more than once all considered with the late President and on particular occasions too when the Commissionaires questioned what would be the price of my services they having acquiessed in the observation on the propriety of a postponing of the determination on the subject—it was by all well understood that an allowance proportionate to a gross estimate of the hole expenditure is the due, in all great entreprise to the Architect Conductor, Independently of payment for plans and of other gratifications—and being agreable to Such common usage that the Compagnies aforenoticed did offered me the $50,-000 clearly the public part of the opperations to have gone on upon a pace with the private ventures—the Commissionaires themselves must have felt had at least Intitled me to Some thing Similarly gratifying as allowance for the general direction Since that direction Could not possibly have embrassed less than it at first did—because upon a fast progressing of at one and the same time all the main parts of the City was depending my promise and Engagement to them to have raised it a City to all Intent and purposes by the time by law prescribed for the removal of Government.

7th.—that being charged with the execution of the president of the United States Intentions I could not have thought of bargaining before hand, nor of asking for written Instructions or directions as 1 might well have done if I had been the Simple agent of the Commission—that thus—Insecure myself—but Engaged to an Insurance of the political end of the Entreprise as well as to the Safty of the ventures in it, and urged as I were besides from all sides and by Injunctions too the most positive and recidive from the president and from the Commission; to a premature begining and progress in all what I proposed—having So confidently and So laboriously worked to gratify Impatient desire and been left no leisure, for thinking of the end to myself,—when it is considered that that end proved so abusive that it would Seem as if I had only been valued as a convenient tool for levelling difficulties and be handled at every ones wish till the way made certain for other, the trowing of me aside had become expedient for reaping reputation and profit from my labour—Surely it cannot be otherwise but manifest (and as I promised it to myself) that the great chief patron of the establishement whose immediate and Confidential agent I was—whose approval and Support hath Encouraged me in all my

pursuits—being himself too honorable and too good to have encouraged doings against his own Sense of the proprietits or with
an Intention of the resulted wrong—knowing how much I suffered and that I Submitted to all out of respect for and Confidence in him—would not have failed on the present occasion from
befriending me and have of his own movement procured a redress every ways proportionate extending the esteemation of the
Indemnification due to what a few months of longer Continuance
in the business must necessarily have all secured to me.—an estimation which how high so ever may here bring the Sum to Indemnify—none who have a knowledge and understanding of the
nature and proprieties of all the performed will Consider any
way above the merited nor Could it indeed be deemed so by them
who may be judge of only the labour and fatigue—the tow first
seasons of tryal of which all who withnessed will allow Committed me to more than the human frame and mind would be
Capable of long Sustaining

8.—and lastly that—the Cases offered here for Consideration
—are not Cases merely of a missing of gain or of depprivation
the causes of trivials embarrassment momently felt—but cases of
real loss—of disappointment of absolute dues—of right dependency and of abuses altogether the cause the active cause of my
total ruin—the cause of the total extinction of my resources in
this Country and likewise of the loss of inheritance in my native
—being the fact that being Invited to the entreprise of the city
of washingon at an Epoch of revolution when the occurences in
my native Country proved the most destructive of any that have
been to Individuals rental estate took away from me the possibility of exertions to have Saved mine and that whilst my attention necessarily diverted from the turning of my family fortune
caused the entire ceasing of the Supply from parents whom did
afforded to all my need both during the late war and till that
time in this Country—it so proved that also the necessary abandon or neglect of all private Concerns that could have divided
my attention from the City of washington—were jointly the
cause that—(on the vanishing of the grand prospect of fame and
fortune by which I had been allured to the Entreprise) I was left
without any thing on which to depend for Sustainance—since
which vain though ardous my exertions were to retrieve—the disappointment also of the waited for employment in my line of
engineer exausting all my having and the assistance of my

friends too—has plundged me in to an abyss of difficulties the
endurence of which I have only been heartened to till this day by
the reflection that I am deserving of better end.—

Closing here and Conscious that all in the foregoing is Strictly
the true and precise exposition of facts and of their unhappy
Consequences—pledging myself to that—it is nevertheless not
upon the exciting of a sensibility of the wrongs which I suffered
that I found my hope now in the Equity and munificence of the
American national representation—my Encouragement so to
hope from them rather deriving from a Confidence in their just
sense and well appraising of the greatness of my Entreprise of
at once creating a City to be the Capital of so vast an Empire
and that in the Estimation of the national advantages therefrom
to derive, they will allow me my Share of the merite.

whatever be the room for petty criticism as out of zeal to
excuse the actual Incomplete State of thing seem bent to Shiff
off the blame on me by affectingly reproving the extensiveness
of the plan and novelty of the distribution of the City of washington—fearing not the malignancy of such fault finder nor that of
Jealouses where I have the approbation of my own mind for all
what I did or Intended doing—relying on the honor of the Commissionaires themselves—in referring to them for the explana-
tin of the Intention and conditions upon which my plan was
framed and to tell how far they have Conformed to or deviated
from—here I will rest upon the presumption of its being visible
to all woll dicerning mind—

that the actual Inconveniency and difficulties under which
Government will have for a while yet to Continue at the City of
washington—are not the fault of the System of the plan of
establishment nor Imputable to any of the management of the
projector but—to the contrary that it is the natural necessary
consequence of a departure from the rull of conduct first by
me traced and Entirely the fault of the abandonement of the
works by me began—nothing of which therefore can any wise
diminish of the merite of original Intent nor make those great
advantages (as after all soon or later, must result to the United
States, the less attribuable to the well Conception and grand
Combination of my Scheme. upon which it may Suffice to remind

that the first gain, from my labour has been that—of an Immense property over and above the wanted for defrayment of
the whole work of the city—that to me is equally due the great

Increase of the wealth of all the Indigenous Individuals of the territory of Columbia as likewise will be the progressive enrichement of an Extensive Surrounding Country whilst manufacturers and mechanicians will be benefited various ways whose genius and arts in all the respective relations the vast opperations of the plan of the City were calculated for, and can not but yet by suscession of time greatly advance to a rivalling of European Superiority.

thus to the recall (as per memoranda) of my military Services •and Suffering in trying time of difficulties and hazard—being to be joined the recollection of many of my atchievements and endeavours to an advancement of the genius for liberal arts and Sciences, I trust—that allowing me the merite of having been a zealous and primary promoter of a Spirit for great entreprises through the United States—the Consideration will be that— *I in no Instance worked to my profit* and that having had on all occasions the Glory and Interests of these United States at heart—my exertions as respect to the terriory of Columbia were no Confined to the machinal drawing of plans nor to the Stupid overseeing of men

therefore Safely here leaving off the Consideration of grievances—if such as are in the foregoing numbered were possible to be denied the redress and compensative prayed for—Still would I not renounce the expectation of a full Equivalent to that —in an other way on the Simple appraising of the merited by my Services and performances

relying upon this it is that I here confidently Supplicate that redress and Indemnification may be—for the Injury done to my fame by anonymous Spurious publication of my plans—and for the wrong to my fortune likewise owing to deprivation of the proceed from the Sale of my own work—from that of the learning by my labour and for other loss and Sacrifices the result of my zeal confidence and liberality.—testifying at the same time my position now became such as to render me pressing for a determination—it being absolutely upon what power I may obtain for a restoration of my former having that now depend my Existence—I remmain well persuaded but the prayer will be granted in all points answerable to my long dependency on the Honor the Justice and Equity of the American nation.—

P. CHARLES L'ENFANT

[Endorsement.]
Leg:
2D: 6TH CONG:
No. 1.
Statement of the
Case of M. L'Enfant.
Decemr. 11th,
1800.

APPENDIX TO PIERRE L'ENFANT'S LETTER TO THE COMMISSIONERS MAY 30, 1800
With an Introductory Note
BY
HERMAN KAHN[1]

Among the records in the National Archives concerning the early planning and development of the District of Columbia as a capital city there was discovered some time ago an unusually interesting and significant document concerning Pierre Charles L'Enfant. The document was contained in a volume which had been labeled "Papers Relating to the Accounts of Various Persons anr Firms," which is a part of the large mass of papers of the "Board of Commissioners," the agency that had charge of the affairs of Washington during the early period of its history. These papers were accessioned from the National Park Service as a part of the records of all of the successive agencies which have had supervision over public buildings and grounds in Washington from 1791 to 1925.

There is no need to repeat here the story of the career of the young French military engineer, Pierre Charls L'Enfant, of his services in the American Revolution, and how he was befriended by Washington and other famous personages of his time. It will be remembered that his abilities were so highly regarded that in 1791 he was commissioned to make a plan for the new capital city which was to be built on the banks of the Potomac. This event was to prove the climax of his career. L'Enfant's impetuous and violent temperament soon led to his dismissal as engineer-in-charge, and although the basic features of his plan

[1]Chief of the Division of Interior Department Archives, the National Archives, Washington, D.C.

were retained, his official connection with the construction of the city of Washington was never re-established.

When L'Enfant was first designated to draw up a plan for the future city, no fee or salary had been mentioned, and nine years later his services were still unpaid for. He had several times rejected offers of payment on the grounds that the sums proffered were too small. In the spring of 1800, being in desperate financial straits, L'Enfant began to press his claims vigorously, in the hope of receiving a substantial sum. The first of the lengthy "memorials" which he wrote on this subject was contained in a letter dated May 30, 1800,[2] addressed to the "Commissionaires of the City of Washington." This document consists or 39 pages of closely-written manuscript, the first 19 pages of which are devoted to a detailed and careful statement of the history of L'Enfant's services in connection with the planning of the city of Washington, and the circumstances surrounding his separation from the project. The last 20 pages consist of an "appendix" in which the architect-engineer refutes his critics, and discusses ". . . the merite of the plan upon which I proposed conducting the work of the city to a timely perfection . . .," a discussion which throws considerable light on the original nature of the L'Enfant plan as well as other closely related matters. This part of the letter has never hitherto appeared in print. Indeed, students who have written on the origins and nature of the L'Enfant plan have apparently not been aware of its existence.

Of particular interest in this "appendix" are L'Enfant's startlingly modern views on the proper role of the architect in large-scale construction projects, as well as on the general status of the architectural "Science" in this country. The discussion of the manner in which L'Enfant had hoped to make Washington a great metropolis in the space of twenty years is enlightening. The city-planning theories here advanced, especially the idea of scattering small settlements at remote points over a great area

---

[2] By a very strange slip of the pen, the date which L'Enfant actually put on the letter was May 30, 1780. Not receiving a reply to this letter, L'Enfant sent another letter to the commissioners on August 30, 1800, consisting of an almost verbatim copy of his letter of May 30, but omitting the "appendix" contained in that letter. The letter of August 30 has been printed in Columbia Historical Society, *Records,* vol. 2, pp. 72-90.

cris-cross with avenues and foot-paths, resulting in a quick growth of the original "roots" toward each other over the intervening vacant spaces, is characteristic of the boldness of his imagination, as well as of a certain weakness in his grasp of realities which was the source of many of L'Enfant's unhappy difficulties in getting along with his hard-headed contemporaries.

Insofar as it is possible to transfer manuscript to the printed page, L'Enfant's "appendix" is reproduced below precisely as it appears in the original. As will be seen, the English leaves something to be desired. At times L'Enfant was almost wholly unintelligible, although he usually managts to make his meaning quite plain. Occasionally he simply invents words, adding to the pungency of his language.

The Appendix, pp. 19-39, of L'Enfant's Letter:

Having in the foregoing sheets been minutely exact in the relation of that part of the menagement of the affairs of the city of washington the most Immediately affecting my fortune and also in enumerating transactions evidencible of Intended Injury to my reputation—although feelling secure against the malignity of envie from consciousness of Integrity in the discharge of all my dutys and contend I have the approbation of my own mind for all what I deed I am no seeker after vulgar praises—I think that since I have been reduced to the necessity of myself commending my own acts—a digression now touching the merite of the plan upon which I proposed conducting the work of the city to a timely perfection become an essential appendix and also to confute railing criticism such as daily reach to my hearing, which, out of zeal or may be to excuse the mistakes that have perevented the city from yet affording the desirable to a seat of government, seem in spirit bent to shift off the blame on me, condemning the grand sisteme of the novell distribution of the plan adopted

Idle talkers and busy brain peuple as i at best take to be those fault finders who can pretend Ignorance of the conditions upon which that sisteme was framed and presume to Juge of thing the Intention of which the understand not—I will here remind —that it was the Injudicious retraction from the condition first approved which determined my abandonment of the entreprise and (as in witness whereof stand many of my letters to the late president) because I was convinced of the Impracticability of it subjected to a direction differently organised than what I had

been made to calculate upon and—that I was unwilling by my
continuance in the business to have nourished expectations of
success which I no longer could see nor feel in my power.

having uniformely, on every occasions, contended against, even,
the esteemed geographical merite of the Seat of the city and
against notions entertained of the means created by the partitioning of the ground property—I never admited merite in the former
but on a distant view and merely as an eucouragement to great
exertions and looked on the later as no more than as a mean of
procuring money on credit and—hence arrose my decided opposition to the early auction sale of house lots, I deeming it had
been more consistent in the first place to have made present of a
few of those lots to entreprising people for them to have immediately builth upon than even to have parted with a single one at
the high price at which I myself raised the first sold.—in my
endeavour to gain to the public a property in house lots extensive as it were, I deed not, could not, have expected the valu equal
to the expenses of my projected opperations but meant to have
raised it more than adequate to the defryement by husbanding
the whole till the season had come for reaping out of it, according to circumstances and, without destroying nor impoverishing
the stock, the luxuriant growth of which I made certain by borrowing of a Sufficiency to have in the first tow years, changed
the whole face of the city ground, from a savage wilderness in
to a compleat heden garden—the happy thought of which both
had met the President own mind and determined me to the
peculiar and novell distribution of the city on the enlarged scale
adopted—the proprieties of which and expediency of the mode of
portioning lots (by me proposed somewhat different from what
took place) were to have facilitated the sale and Improvement
of Individual property of preference, and, to have confined speculation to the building of house only and at such place too as I
might have appointed, without by that having of the least impeded such marchantyle establishment as has taken place on the
east branch.—a combination of management the departure from
which has not merely ruined the great end of the plan but—moreover—has been an Infraction of the compact with the orriginal
owners of the territory—on which regard I own to them and to
my self in truth to declar that—however the deed of conveyance
left the disposal of the public share of house lots discretionary
with your commission, the property had been asked of them as a

funding from which to have defryed the execution of my plan—
the disply and the adoption of which at the general meeting of
the concerned was conditional of the concession made and—that
besides not expecting the precipitate hammering down of that
property niether so partial parting with as has been at the pris-
ing of pawnbrokers, themselves the buyers—all sale money together with the borrowed on the credit of that property was ex-
plicitly engaged to, and only to, have supplied the work of a
great dock and navigable canal, the regulating, paving of all
main streets and the shaping and beautifying every public area—
my promise of effecting all which in proportionate progress too
at a same time across each differents properties to the equall
benefit of all, alone had persuaded on, the general transfer and
subsequent division thereof—nothing of the public edifices being
to be understood for included—because these as being by law directed your commission all along called thier own Separate concern and that—besides the particular provision afforded by the
State of virginia and that of Mariland there had been quarry
ground very extensive by me purchased for—the proposed manner of exploring [exploiting?] which, as it would have enabled
the supplying of all private demands both in the city and the
neighbouring towns, was to have defryed not only its own expences but likewise that of the labour at those edifices, for which
in adition of all that, greater facilities could have been procured,
had but only your commission lent an hear to proposals or been
somewhat active in courting Such grant as the establishment act
authorized the acceptance of—and seeing the neglect on that
head niether could be supposed to have been owing to a depen-
dence on my personal exertions nor can Imply, the property in
house lots to have been expected in Sufficiency for the Supply of
those edifices also—for if so had been the calculation then Indeed
most the conduct of the gentlemen first in commission be declared to have been at variance with thier minds—being a fact
that though careless about all matters of thier own particular
concerns they had been wondrously vigilant, through proneness
of manifesting authority and power, in opposing my every exertions and that so earnestly deed they opposed and crossed the
Steps for the general partitioning of the city land as all most
made the whole of the people, the best inclined to, at one time
recant from and so nearly so, that however upon the President
himself Interfering the partition finally was acquiessed in, the

heated humour of Some of the disputant was the cause of a contracting of the boundary line, by which not only upward of 1,000 lots were lost to the public but likewise a very consequent ground for its commanding rise over the east and north entrance of the city and for other advantages which made it Important to the perfecting of my plan.

but to return to In what manner the whole of the territory (limited as it is) might have made a city in fact:—adhering to my sisteme of branching out settlements from remote corresponding situations—Independently of linking together the Executive Palace and the Capitole, as Intended by the compagnies already mentioned (who were to have builth up one quarter part of the north Side of federal avénue up to half way of Independence Road) sixteen bases or rather Roots of distincts establishments were to have been Soon planted which would now be as many pleasing hamelets equidistant of but from three to four furlong, being intended one at each grand Intersect of avenues, the area by which formed was destinated, one for each Individuals States, Intermediary to which again (consequently at about tow furlong only apart) allotements were made for Societies both learned and religious to have formed establishments of their own.

were it possible for any of the states to have refused Comming in to the Schem for errecting commomerative monuments of their own philosophie and military atchievements in the conquest of liberty—I will that I trusted on the spirit of the people at large —expecting that in each States there could easily have been fund Citizens of patriotism not so extinct yet but that they may have been Induced to speculate on that proposal, and so that by forming a number of compagnies could have been effected that which the apostacy in some councils or the poverty of some States might have prevented—thus at least Speculation had turn to some good and the honor of the country—a beginning of some thing had ensued and had it been of only one or tow houses at each different Spots, these belonging to separate communities the rise and range like trees in a young orchard that it first occupy but a few feet of the soil would in Jealousy of each other and by circumfuse Spreading vividely have made the shade contigous all over

the sacrifice of a few lots as premium according to the hazard of private venture in building at certain places appointed as also —the spending of borrowed money at the levelling planting the avenues with trees and making footways from settlement to settlement, railling in the Intervals by large block of the vacant property without avariciously minding whether or not private lots intermixt be thereby advantaged—att that far from extravagant would by the opperation have proved of grand calcule— money thus sown (before the sale of house lots) had been making sure of a twentyfold harvest, adding to which—the appropriation of upward of an hundred lots scatered all along upon the edge of the city boundary for the habitation of whole family of labouring people with vegetable gardens and fields for the rearing of catel & &—besides the object of hastening a plinty and cheap market—those families so housed had been Inducing the migration from other places soon to have carried the population over the whole ground—being constant that all settlement thus began back—especially facilitated by numerous Short cut way, avenues in every directions, had faster progressed toward central points and down the river Shore than ever will from the Shore to the center or can from iether of these points extend backward where no great Inducement is.

that the beginning being made on the eastern branch has Impeded the establishment over all the rest need no demonstration and every one agreeing that the houses there and those scatered at other extreem are of no convenience to, nor capable of, harbouring the followers of government—with what Intention, let me ask it, was that seven years of labour and all the resources wasted about matters no wise aiding the object of the city fundation—if policy ,a policy which I must acknowledge is with me of difficult comprehension, forbided making the Individuals states parteners in the entreprise or the forming of compagnies after my own Intention—what was so seducive about those great forestallers of the city property as that they must have been advantaged and could not be constrained by contract to have erreced a number of house Intermediary of and in the vicinage to both the public Edifices where the most ought to have been exerted and with co-operation too on the part of your commission who easily could have had by this time, all the principals streets completely paved ready for hous the building of which it would have Invited, and who would at least have formed a small town of traders mechanics and taverns, central to the whole.

this I had Strenously insisted upon should have been Sat about even before beginning any of the main Edifices, upon

which I remonstrated that time was wanting for opperations,
which were requisit previously to determining upon those Edifices plans—to have computed the reciprocal level to be given to
every abutting avenues as also to have by the Squaring of the
Surrounding area Solved the variant angles of the Sights in fault
of which no given height for bassment nor the module for the
architecture were possible to be with any due affinity to the
immense plan of these areas

had those Instructions been attended to, the Edifices surely
would not stand, as now do, ridiculy sunk in on the declivity
of hills—for the Sight from good round distances must have convinced that, even, the Submit [summit?] where I meant placing
those Still wanted a considerable raising, at both places, before
fitted for the bases of any stile of buildings and the discovery
being to have satisfied but the little malice of moving those bases
a few paces out of the Site by me Staked out for, is to work
more to the Injury of the city than can reflect disgrace on´ me.
I would presume—them in authority then, would not have been
so Spitefull as to have drawn upon themselves the ridicul and
blame as deserved for having given in to advices So evidently
a mocking of thier own understanding of the business in management.

pointing out the errors of the site of both Edifices (that of the
executive especially being upward of twenty feet idly sunk) may
be Joigned the mistake of the plans in thier whole out lines un-
fitting the Shape of the respective areas and which (as must be
the case with all counterfeited prdouctions) not the better for
being altered from the model consulted, Shew in the choice of
desing no mind of the convenable for the proposed use of iether
of those edifices—the one hardly the suitable for a gentlemen
country house wholy Inconsistent for a city habitation in no
aspect present that majestick of outer ordinance nor inward distribution becoming the State Residency of the chief head of a
Souverain people and the other—for being a more estimable Imitation of the Suitable for a residence place being equally Improper considered as a basilick consecrated to the august representation of the people, the architecture of which ought to [?]
with respect, and consequently in Stead of a pretty Should be of
a massy Sullen, a the Same time grand aspect, the distribution
present no oppening as should to a place of free resort, niether
is calculated for that protecting the all accessible Sanctuary of

national councils as in all popular government is at time requisit—and were all this to be deemed no deffect, even then, the
whole composition as it is of too Slander a Module (if at all of
an architectural like division) for having not sufficient large
mases nor boldness of profile and being to laboured never can be
of good aspect—as although at present it may appear great, it
will necessarily loose and decease in proportion as the neighbor-
ing houses by raising will bring the Size and Shape of the open
are around to an eyed comparaison

giving my sentiments as one who feel for the Injury done to
the Intention of the plan of the City and who cannot but have a
desire of Stimulating to Such correction as yet is possible—I
will import what Struck my mind at a moment Survey of the
Capitole, which is that—although narrow I take to be the Intended central body, Judging from the place of the wing that
is up—the main of the north front may well bo brough forward
double and more of the distance Intent, and with lofty massy
grouped columns exausted on a projecting padron and so as to
render the height of the wings together with the whole South
front but only the 3/5 of the projecting body exausting in proportion the dome upon a plain Socle [sic] changing the church
like form of that which I understand is proposed—by this Small
alleration gaining room on the whole front for raising the ground
So as to mask the kind of Stereoble [sic] of the wings with good
accordance with what is done, it would nearly restore the primi-
tive given level of people Square and as I may assert will soon
or late be fund necessary for a proper regulation of all depending
declivities and raise to be given to abutting Streets and avenues
—I taking the occasion here to renew a warning often repeated
that none of the height at the crossing can admit of being lowered and that unless the long Stretching levell be preserved and
the declivities as by my orriginal direction and in the manner
Indicated in my notes and sketches, be Scrupulously observed
and determined before tinking of filling up or digging down any
the by-streets—better would be at once to return the whole
ground back to the plougher for maize and tobacco planting

having remarked before but the beginning first of the city at a
central point was to have facilitated every other part of the business, I will further observe that however reduced in means and
confined to small doing, your Commission might easily have
formed such a town of trader and mechanics as mentioned, by

only having fixced its own Individuals habitations at or near about the head of the grand triangle formed by tow of the leading avenues to the Capitole and Executive place, appropriating for a term of years for the use of each a number of reserve lots and doing the like for every principall employed having fixced every offices stores and all stationary work shops, at wide distances, principally builth up at corners, and planted trees and made good the principals streets within the precinct of that triangle the vacant lots in which would have become the better Saleable for this arrangement which by offering a neat convenient ready levelled place for buildings had attracted Speculative Settlers and without question would by this time have rised the city to what I myself meant when I proposed errecting my own quarter at the Spote mentioned and for the prompt accommodation of all round which, I by way of preliminary directed the oppening and clearance of the avenue at the time purposedly denominated the post Road.

unplaisant as by comparison the Situation may appear—that nor the fear of distance from landing places Should have prevented the whole body of the administration there—it would have Shewed its Impartialty—and if partialty must have rulled it would have been but wisdom to have bestowed the most on those situations the less likely of benefitting by a natural course of opperations, by establishing itself there, your Commission would have at once conciliated the good will of Funkstown, Rock creek, carroll borough and events [?] Jaring Interests—and to what ever common way calculation could bring the expences in some kinds of transportation at the Stores—to minds comprehensive of the great whole of the plan, the manifold of object by that arrangement to have been imperceptibly advantaged must have proved a great gaining in the result.

by necessitating a constant going in every direction whether for Spending the Social after noon or for transacting morning little business—the paths beaten through all avenues would to the eyes of all visitors best have depicted the grand feature of the city plan and Satisfied of the proptrties of the triangled division then can the Inspection of a map or the hunting through copice wood he Indicative Stone to a place—the ride over accidentally to have discovered a variety of Situation more pleasing and convenient for houses than are describable, building would have raised where the owners of the ground themselves

can as yet have no Ideas—at all events it would have manifested
a disposition earnest to the business and which must better satisfied the orriginals proprietors of the territory, of Every thing
having been exerted (as far as in your Commission power was
left) to give thier remaining property all that Equall chance of
Sale which had been promised them

Inconsiderable at beginning, the Establishment nevertheless
necessarily becoming the general rendevous of all the curious
and people for business—a class of wanderer Industrious pedler
all would soon have become Sedentary there and—by way of making the place attractive also to the opulent idler, the Instituting
of some kind of diversion rural sports, collecting the neighbouring fairs, and shaking off of that rustiness of doleful habits
giving to old gentry round, a taste for the enjoyment of great
metropolis, would have been but preparing for the time coming
that would have turned the former Industry to market Supplying, while the crowd of visitants attracted enriching the place
thier Continuance easily could have been Induced by having
caused some taverns fitted up in a Stile accommodating to different character of guests—with all surrounding shaded grove,
garden, baths &c and as in short to have afforded more than the
mere manger for man and horse.

ludicrous as some critic would call this Idea of management
I for all that feeling no blush in avoing my Intention to have so
conducted—more over venture to assert but it would have proved
as certain or lively a way of effecting the timely establishment
of the city, and—had your Commission pursued it on, on that
Sistime, its chances of Succes were greater than I could have calculated upon—those calamitous seasons which successively drive
thowsands of people out of Jealous metreopolis having disposed,
on the first years, a vast numbers to have become citizens of
Washington but whom by themselves or agents upon viewing the
plan were dissuaded through disgust at the death like aspect of
all about it

on other hands your Commission might have helped the business by making itself a little busy with neighbouring affairs,
about the potomac canal expecially who Should have been completed four year sooner, being to be reminded how with a view
of drawing Supply that way I myself in order to Enable the
compagnie used of some Influence in persuading upon the dutch
agent the purchase of the remainder of its shares—the oppening

of severals new roads—an Interesting part of my project likewise should have been long ago effected—and the going on of all these matters in and out of the Columbia territory which were to contribute to the Interest of the city would seem clearly to have claim to more attention that what has been bestowed on—the advantages and dissadvantages of activity or neglect respecting those points were early by me Expounded and at, even, the first of my Communication to the President on the subject of the city affairs, when I also Suggested a mode of altering the Eastern post road, which alleration I repeatedly since urged on—demonstrating the Inconveniences of the traveling as the greatest Stopage to pleasurable Junts to the city of Washingon, which with so great an Interest to have Invited, it may be wondered at that no petition from the citizens nor no remonstrances by your commission to government, ever Joigned in the Endeavour to have given an early and proper Start to a grand Improvement of all main Roads through the United States—what partial mending has of late taken place, haing had no better effect than filling the pokets of contractors—the ordinary result of all similar half measures, the prime allowance for which insufficient to the well perfecting of anything, make all works be kept on agoing, only, by calling for more and for more again, constantly dissappointing the end, and so that deceiving the expectation of them who Subscribe to the Subsidy, with all well computing mind the doing are reputed theft under the Specious name of Economie

disputing not, but in all matters depending of states jurisdictions any proposals of measure tending to advance the Interest of the city of Washington, must be opposed by rivals commercials places—allowing but offten Intrigue will even arrest the best Intentioned in the federal legislature—I would not for this have suffered the apprehension of Insuccess be an hinderance to making proposals—I would in case of rejection again and again have renewed those in differents shape and through various agency's would at least by the publishing of plans well demonstrative of the advantage Intended to the community at large, have exerted to the awakening of friendly Interest some where, and of such as must have excited the back yeomanery to a closer and earlier attention to the new market oppening.

thus and thus alone I deed conceived that be a combination of efforts and with an active prosecution of great and small thing at one and the Same time making private and public works help one another—with a mind watchful of every occurrences abroad that could have been taken advantage of—realy might in Seven years time the city have been settled at its principal points, with all the Splendid intended Improvements perfected, and those advantages of the geographical Situation realised which so much extolled by the friends to the establishment when wanting the passing of the act, if—rendered nulties has been owing to the Inconsistancy of those friends own tempers—being well manifest that having caused the business to proceed on the contrary tack from the first by me started on—undecided has been the course and that thier Improvidency causing every season to pass waiting a Scanty and uncertain Supply—Spiritless and timorous in all pursuit each concerned naturally tinking more of his loved self than he could feel for the fame of the entreprise—none of the money expended can possibly have been applyed to the best of purpose nor to public advantage.

real Economie in an Entreprise of such Extant and of works so varied, would have been that of a beginning made by as many points as possible, and knowing how often and when timely to Shift off part of the hands from one to an other work, successively, according as the case at some places may have called for numbers or rendered the attendance of the many troublesome—with this talent of directing the handling of men, and of materials, quickly and seasonably, it would have been fund that half dozen of buildings can well be carried on and completed at same time and with the very same hands that would be necessary to keep all that time in employ at the single undertaking and with this other gaining that all necessary wasting (or the bad work that is to ensue from the Endeavour of Saving in the single case) will easily be avoided and the better in proportion to the number of buildings carried on—Industrious Inteligent masters builder, well enough endeavour savings of that sort but only in a small, and not allwaise the proper, way and so far merely as that saving may come to their pockets—else the compass of thier comprehension never extend beyond usual practice—and especially in case of public entreprise the supply for which is dependent on agents, the more of those masters are in employ who have each a separate object to attend the greater the missaplication of means, and the difficulty to prevent it—because each undertaker must necessarily pull a particular way and each will constantly pretend the greatest want and endeavour to persuad is work of greater Importance than that of all the other—and as to believe that any, even, of the most conscientious of those undertaker will alter from his mode of opperation and take care whether it will Serve or Injure others matters Intended, it would indeed be knowing little of mans avaricious disposition, on which may be remarked that—all labourers by the. task or otherwise—all masters builders, and mercenary Aorchitects (all them who un-dertake have a joint Interest quite the opposit to that of con-ducting in respect to the advancement of any next works, the rendering of that next of greater expense rather will be the calcul of profit to the trade and mechanic tho' in opposed branch-es all conceive as being of one general association—from whence may be deduced way all mercenary will bear an antipathy to the well bred up Aorchitect, under whose quick eye decitfull doing can not so easily be made to pass for good as may to the Self conceited knower.—an apprehension in its effect so greatly beni-ficial that wherever the Science is understood and merite distin-guished not only the right of the artist is to see to the correct execution of his project, but likewise to obtain that execution the better to the Interest of the Employer all people and thing em-ployed are wholy Subordonate to the Architect, and as often plans require the joint Jugement of different genious in that case and in all Entreprise of some magnitude Severals will be con-jointly employed with a principal and more advantages result than the Saving, would be, of the Indemnification to them, tho' that may come high according to a proportion with the cost of the Entreprise and the estimation of the merite of the artists so Employed.

having before hinted upon the primary causes of the disuniting of my agency from the connection with your Commission and Stated the wroung which I suffered as the result of venal specu-lation united with Jealousie—hoping, here, that I have not been understood So as, iether directly or Indirectly accussing any of the geneleman who now are nor who have been of your commis-sion as having themselves been actuated by such passions but that to the contrary it will.have been seen that I traced to others sources the Errors of hte conduct toward me—Simply giving my conjecture but the want of experience in work of this nature as in the entreprise with the commission having made miscon-ceive the propriety of my whole Sisteme of opperation, rendered the gentlemen, first in office, more Susceptible of being misleaded by the ill designings—knowing how often those matters which to my own experience required time and a particular mode of process would be by Some represented as of quick easy prosecution while the most Simple and facile were given to consider [?] a magnifier of the atoms in the way—I well accounted how by embarassing the Jugement the flatering courtesy of all the hunters for favours, and for employ, succeed in persuading against my Sisteme. it was no more then than what has been the fate in other pursuits and as indeed will be seen on all Stages where the worthless, placid carriage and babbling, over thwart the meritorious. (mountebank there are of all profession and them especially coming from afar off, master of learning (gotten in the by-lane of great Schools by waiting on the whole of Same great patron or by arguing with the valet, waiting in the anti chamber of ministers) those people who can take Side each way as the wind blow, all full of honor and trampling under every honest principle, will every where make friends.—but to confine to the business in consideration with your Commission, observing but the more Ignorant the more prone to Criticism his likewise the soonest ready to any undertaking—these and all virtuoso designers (even of the most liberal education at best themselves but superficials in thier acquirements) puffed up with a smattering of art and Sience will dare what the most able and Consummated experienced Artist could but only with dread and with disgrace attempt. and the reason being clear that it is for want of the sense to see or to feel, the certain inexplicable constitutive of the good and Beautiful in all production of arts, that, there are so many who think they can Imitate, and, so many medlers in the pursuit, it being daily Seen how the Sience of the architect is disgraced, by plans mongers and men who can take pride at the most Shamfull mistakes which they Impudently Style, Improvement upon thier model—the case of all such undertakers being that they must necessarily for execution relay on the Skill of the masters worksmen and however each in his particular branch may be expert, no one, anywhere, being to be fund a master of the whole, to Squash would only Stain and Infect me—I would have rested on my own Conviction and on the presumption of its being visible to all well appresiating minds—that the Inconveniences gouvernement may be Set under from the actual state of thing at the city are Solely ascribable,—to the subversion of my orriginal measure—to the Speculative maneouvre by which your Commission funds itself deverted of those means and riches created at the Sweat of my own brow—which together with having permitted lotterys on a schem of pick-pocket Interest, gave way to an Infinitude of combination and calculation upon the protraction and even arresting the most essential part of the entreprise, the consequence of which reduced your commission to the miserable regard of penny saving while the difficulties worked, necessitated its sacrificing thowsands of pounds worth for a ten shilling procuring a kind of Economie from which it can not be Surprising if after the Sacrifices made and the expences of all the gotten by, nothing could be effected of the establishment any ways to a proportion to what I promised—being rather obvious but the flood for migration has been barred and that if the sources of the future greatness and riches of the city are not wholy drained, the Streams for having been given a roung course becoming difficult to bring back—the work of a century will hardly now be Sufficient to raise the city of Washington to that Splandor and credit which twenty year time may have gained to it, had its establishment been but only prosecuted till this day conformably to my Sisteme and plan.—

P. CHARLES L'ENFANT

To the Commissionaires of the City of Washington.

APPENDIX B

To General von Steuben

Charlestown, May 24, 1779

My General,

After marching 29 days I finally arrived in Charlestown, which I was very much afraid I could not reach on account of the enemy's approach; so far we had only an alert; the English came near this town toward dawn, and left with the same speed with which they had approached it, after summoning the city to surrender, which it almost did. That day was spent in conversation, a sign of weakness on both parts, the one behind the fortifications trying to save time, and the other to seduce the enemy. The latter almost won, but thanks to the commander's firmness and a small number of men, the voice of honour and duty was heard, patriotism won, and each citizen became a soldier, went on the fortifications and would not hear of any bargain, save by arms. All the day long, the enemy who had been hidden in the woods near the town stayed there without any attempt at reconnaissance, and all was quiet in both camps when General Pulaski, whose infantry had arrived, entered the city at 10:00 a. m. He was sent in the evening to reconnoitre the enemy, with a few volunteers with him, was turned back, his infantry broken by the British cavalry. Colonel Coather who comanded it, was killed with 75 men and 4 officers, the rest wounded or prisoners. Lt. Colonel Bendak and 18 men alone escaped with the General and a few officers, came back to town pursued by the enemy. Major Endger had gone away without giving any notice at the doors and gave the alarm by his return; our sentries fired and made him a victim of his carelessness.

The next day, the enemy retreated toward _____ ferry, 10 miles South of the town, crossed the river, and camped on Jongh Isl. where we had already burned Fort Johnson and the barracks, fearing the enemy would take possession of it. It would have been a pity to sacrifice a single man there as this fort was not important for the defense of the roadstead. After coming on the island, the enemy did not attempt to establish

411

itself on what was left, and moreover found itself very weak, for we have 4 armed warships and 2 gallows; he crossed Jongh Isl., leaving only part of 300 men without artillery, 10 or 11 pieces of gun including 2 of 9, which proves that they had planned only a small operation on that town they believed to be helpless. They were mistaken, and could have been still more so if General Lincoln had not been 3 or 4 days away from the town. They were much superior in number, their position made their strength a double obstacle to their retreat, with their flanks between two big rivers defended by our gallows and warships, having in front of them an enemy well protected and covered by a respectable artillery.

In war, an army may be inferior in number but strong by its position. We were protected by our warships, artillery to which the enemy would not have answered, as he could not fight on four sides, and move easily in the midst of inaccessible swamps. Here is, my General, all what happened since I arrived in Carolina.

At present, the enemy who marched on Beaufort road has camped 15 miles from Charlestown, where General Lincoln was before he lost ground and went back 10 miles, to camp 21 miles from here.

I do not know the reason for this maneuver, but in spite of the apparent calm, this serenity doesn't reassure me, and I fear we have lost our chance, for, though the English seem to want to avoid an encounter, we might lose if it was to take place, and then our situation would contrast badly with the one in which we could have followed the enemy in the trap he set for us; our superiority would have been greater than by going back to Savanah and putting a distance of 130 miles between our army and his without any other aim but to pursue him after he has devastated everything and put us in the impossibility to subsist, and to watch the loss of both Carolinas, being compleely helpless to prevent it.

I must finish this long epistle, planning to tell you about myself in the next mail. I do not know anything positive. The Marquis, however is quite pleased; as for me, I must appear to be so, since I am major of two regiments. Colonel Laurence has at my arrival made me the agreable offer of the greatest part of the one he was hoping to raise when the enemy was approaching . . . but he is going away and I am afraid . . . (illegible) . . . the

first one would have been more effective if one had given the . . .
on the fortifications we had to defend with four guns . . .

I am with respect, my General, your most humble and obedient
P. L'Enfant

Many pleasant messages to Henry and Waken des Epines and
(illegible)

Charlestown, July 6, 1779

To General von Steuben

You probably expect, my General, some interesting details,
because the position in which the enemy was when I wrote my
second letter on June 2 may have led you to believe that we were
out of this period of inertia, and that things would at last work
in our favor. But nothing of the kind happened. Our raid on
Jongh Isl., served only to show the enemy our lack of decision
and the poor intelligence of our two generals. One has to live in
America to realize what disorder and neglectfulness are pre
valent here. Indeed these two capital military sins reach such a
degree, they look more like virtues that everybody thrives to attain.

Anyway, after the enemy retreated on Jongh Isl., our city
troops, under the orders of General Moultay, went down on
James Isl., on June 1st at 11 a. m., four hours too late, as it is
their praiseworthy custom. They had taken their arms at midnight and sailed onl yat 10 o'clock, in the middle of a great confusion caused by the lack of ships and the absence of a tide—
this factor had been overlooked, as of little importance, and yet,
on that account, our galleys were not able to leave the creek before the next day. Our passage on Jongh Isl. could not be protected and we could not attack the enemy in the rear while General Lincoln, helped by our galleys' fire would have attacked the
800 men fleet of the Regulars, to cover Stoni river. He did it,
at 8 a. m. on Sunday, but without any news from General Moultay or the galleys, so this attack so badly planned only caused
him to lose some men, and taught the enemy what he wanted to
know—intelligence that helped him, and made him decide to send
his troops across the ferry, leaving us in charge of his post; we
heard of his departure only 36 hours later, and quite by chance.
One of our dargoons, who very likely was trying to desert, approached the enemy by night and found out he was gone. For-
tunately he came back to tell us of his discovery. The news had

escaped our advanced posts, and yet these always brag to be constantly near the enemy; they had not been so since 36 hrs apparently, and yet it is the only time where they could have made a sudden attack.   But in spite of these mistakes, we are victorious, we have chased the enemy, at any rate we have to admit that we did not oppose his retreat, which he did as leasurely as could be imagined, since we did not interfere with him since our appearance on the island, except for our galleys, which having not been of any use to us on Sunday, received the order on Tuesday, to burn a bridge which unfortunately did not exist but that our big scouts had aimed at, as they did at the enemy's lines, where after the engagement, they were positive they had left many men in the ditches.   After the enemys' retreat no lines or ditches were found, but only two meriocre redoubts nobody had spoken about, and for good reasons, because our troops did not get out of the wood more than 4 or 500 feet.   Our artillery did a little damage.   We can be assured the English hold no grudge against us, and we are as quiet as in peace time.   Though they are less than 40 miles away, we are dismissing the greatest part of our militia.

As for my own affairs, all I can tell you is that if I did a foolish thing in America, it was to come to this province, where I stay rather by lack of means than by lack of will to go away.   It is indeed the worse place on the continent since war has begun, and the one in which toryism is the most domineering; business is bad and people discontented.

In the middle of all this, General Provot's conduct is inconceivable; I don't know how his expeditions will be received at Great Britain's court, but his campaign cost him lots of men, and ended by capturing only 17 or 1,800 negroes, a little equipment and nothing else—a regular pirate's expedition, and not the one of a general who seemed ready to conquer everything on these shores, where a few poor fellows only are victims of the army's unruly conduct rather than of an invassion, which has amounted to nothing for either side.   I do not know if he is planning to spend the sumer in Beaufort, I don't suppose he will, judging by their movements.   If they go back to Florida they will be less advanced for the opening of the coming campaign than they were for this one; our Virginia troops having arrived we can start before they do, without fearing for this city, where 2,000 men and the bourgeoisie (?) guard it while our army goes forward and keep the enemy in check, preventing him to move

without risking to lose St. Augustine, on which we cannot march
to soon; at any rate, I think this should be the first aim in the
renewal of the campaign, for as long as we let the enemy keep
this shelter, we cannot hope to save this state from destruction
as we are not in the possibility to maintain troops in all important points without heavy expenses and losses that will dis-
hearten the population, which is already too prone to ask for neu-
trality in order to save what is left of its possessions from fire
and looting. The richest landlords of these provinces have been
ruined, not only by the loss of their products, but also by so many
hands taken away from them, without which they cannot repair
damages which they will feel for a long time to come. They are
responsible for much of it on account of their neglect to forestall
the enemy and their lack of enthusiasm for the common cause,
which, though touching them now in their personal interests,
does not urge them to seek a just revenge, but seems to encourage them to tie their chains anew and accept a dishonourable
bondage.

We are expecting everything from the General Assembly which
is to meet on August 15, lucky if it does n't bring trouble and dis-
cord where union must reign.

My paper is at an end and this will keep you from receiving a
longer epistle, leaving me just enough room to ask you for the
kindness with which you have always honored me.

I am with deep respect your very humble and obedient servant,

P. de L'Enfant

Colonel Laurence being here, I am resolved to wait until he
makes the last attempt for the conscription of his corps, for
which he still has the same intentions regarding me—

(four illegible lines, with mention of Col. Ternant)

To M. de Gérard

Charlestown, Aug. 8, 1779

Monsieur,

According to the certainty given to me by M. de Brétignie, of
the majority of the corps he was expecting to raise in this province, I was obliged to give up my commission of captain of engineers. I was not supposed to hold two positions and chose that
one, thanking him. Colonel Laurence at my arrival offered me
the corps of negroes that he was about to raise, but at this time
everything is changed and I am most puzzled and take this op-

portunity to take advantage of the offer you have honored me with, to help me if you could.

There should not be any obstacle, I have never asked anything from Congress, neither for my promotion, nor for any gratification; I have hardly asked what was due to me in a few occasions. I have very high expenses, and received no indemnity for coming from philadelphia to this province; I find myself here in a very awkward position, expenses are exorbitant; I hold no title with which I could demand a gratification from the province. Foreign trade is so poor that it is impossible to get any money from Europe unless you sacrifice your entire fortune.

The campaign, which may begin any time, will put me in an embarrassing position if I don't receive an answer from Congress, to whom, a réquest presented by you will probably receive a favorable answer. Moreover I do not think my claim is erroneous; if it appeared so, I could justify it by some facts doing me credit. I am just asking the simple ratification of a title I should have held since the continental regiment of M. de B[rétignie] was created, and whose liquidation, though at its beginning, should not deprive me of a rank I was counting on and for which I resigned my position.

Here are, Sir, the motives that make me call on your good intentions toward me, and that will add to the gratitude and thé veneration I have for you.

I am with deep respect your very humble and obedient servant,
P. de L'Enfant

There is nothing new since we took our quarters. The English are still in Beaufort, where they had their ships come from Savanah; one of their frigates, the "Daphne" has been cruising in front of this city for 3 days; a raid on Georgetown is feared but we are in no condition to oppose it, and unless Congress takes a little more interest in this province by sending troops, I fear that it cannot hold the enemy in check or organize a good plan of attack. The city is full of grumbling people, everything is lacking, money has no value, one readily gives 36 dollars for a silver gourd.

One cannot support oneself for less than 17 or 20 dollars a day, without servants or horses; these cannot subsist, and they die in the streets where they go to get some food. You can judge of the discouragement experienced by a foreigner who, even with a fair income, can hardly subsist a month.

Such is my present position and I see no remedy; I cannot even leave this province for lack of means. I have still less because of the fact that I am receiving no pay on account of the confused position in which I find myself.

Whatever my commission will be, it can only be in the infantry, as I cannot, for good reasons, serve in the engineers, here or in the North.

Since I now have some hopes with the light troops that are going to be organized, I implore you to see that my fate is decided on before the beginning of the campaign if it is possible. I would like to have a special letter of recommendation from Congerss to the Assembly of this province and to the General in Chief. With this I fear no obstacle in view that . . . (a few words illegible)

To General von Steuben

Charlestown, Aug. 8, 1779

My General,

The uncertainty I am regarding M. de Gérard being on this continent prevented me from mailing him directly the letter I take the liberty to send you; I beg you to forward it to him with a word to remind him of my request which I hope won't meet with any hindrance. It would be very unfortunate if I could not count on it, as I have been obliged to resign from the engineers corps, give up my title for the one of major in the infantry, at a time when M. de Brétignie's business was taking a turn to the best and when there was no doubt as to his behaving like a sensible man; he would probably by now have a regiment and would be truly respected. But if these two factors have escaped him by his fault, it would be cruel that I should suffer by it and be obliged to beg for a position by an indirect voice . . . It is impossible for me to earn a living as I cannot get the salary of a major without a commission; therefore I am counting upon your help with Congress.

You know, my General, that I never had any other claim but my merit, I flatter myself that you do me justice, I have asked for nothing, the little I have I owe it to you; you know me enough to be assured that I am grateful.

I thought I knew human nature but though I have acquired some knowledge, often at my expense, I did not see deeply enough into it. There is a type of person whose "lightheartedness, always agreeable, appears natural and sincere, and had, if not completely convinced me, at least partially persuaded me of its uprightness, but it is only a varnish, more dazzling than substantial, which cannot stand daylight and the slightest scrutiny without showing a number of serious flaws," and that the straigthforwardness and frankness of your nature could not let you suspect or even less discover. You can, my General, easily apply these thoughts to their proper objective.

There is nothing new here, lots of people are still getting into mischief. Besides that, everything is all right. The General Assembly began a week ago. They seem to agree about raising an army, but I don't know how they will go about it, nobody cares to pledge one'self and the population is in no condition to stand a forced conscription without running the risk of not providing a living for these troops without the work of the farm hands.

As for the negroes, a corps of workers is going to be raised, one cannot do without them, for in this army a white man is not expected to fell a tree. This conscription cuts short the hope I had about Colonel Laurency's corps, as it is difficult to take many negroes away from the residences. So I see, at my expense, the truth of the saying "he who courts two women doesn't enjoy any"; if not indisputable, at least this truth can be applied to me. After having counted on two "majorités," promised to me, only a name remains, and nothing substantial with it. Yet I do not despair, and since I cannot doubt that you will show some interest in me in this circumstance, I dare to hope this negociaion will succeed.

I hope to receive news from you any day, and hear that your health is as good as mine—which has not always been so, when shortly after Colonel Ternant's departure I thought I was leaving this world.

Will you, please, my General, try to have my business taken care of before the campaign starts again, which will not be before two months. This would suit me very much on account of the experience I have with light troops question which is going to be settled. My fate, which is being decided by Congress will enable me to reach my goal; I would also like to have a special recommendation from that body to the Assembly of the province and to General Eichy.

I am with deep respect, my General, your very humble and obedient servant,

P. de L'Enfant

If the Minister of France has gone, I beg you to do everything in your power and send this letter for him to M. Alker who is in charge and whose honesty I can count on to replace the Minister in this case.

From Charlestown, December 24, 1779

To M. le Baron de Steuben

My general

If you are in a position to see the minister, I beseech you to present to him my respects and tell him of the desire I have to go to philadelphia to introduce myself to him but my wound is an obstacle. I had from M. le Comte d'Astier some pleasant promises and if, contrary to my former stand, I should now ask for a promotion, which is due me, it is only because of his wise advice and because a higher rank would make a great difference to me in Europe where I was asked to do my utmost to join some letter to it.

If you have any connection with Congress, whatever may be their intentions toward me, surely they must send me their decision here, favorable or not. I hope the President cannot refuse at your request to send me a private letter, in consideration of my present condition.

The expectation in which I have been of receiving news of you has just been completely disappointed by the arrival of Colonel Ternant, by whom I was hoping, but in vain, to receive an answer to the letters I had the honor to address you, and especially the one sent by Captain Roberts; its contents was rather interesting to me as I was pledging my word that you would help me and transmit to the French Minister the one that I had put into your package, but which he did not receive—at least to judge by the two letters he honored me with, of the 24th of August and the 12th of September in which he tells me of his departure without mentioning anything of the one which in his absence I would have addressed to Mr. Alker, Consul of France—as I did not wish to annoy you. But, depending upon the friendship you were good enough to bestow upon me up to my departure, I hope that my separation from you has not altered it, and that you take enough interest in me to help me in this circumstance, with the agreable prospect I have—when you and the minister have given me the certainty of a position, for which I first showed only dislike, and which I now look for only after your advice which has always been Law for me—you know that my aim has never been to owe any title to the (illegible) you have never seen me envy at that price honor and position—the little I have, I think I have deserved, and I have asked for nothing that was not due to me—the minister, who will have told you that I have been advised to return to France, will convince you that if I had aspired only to my temporary well-being, and only looked for a fictitious glory, I should have, beyond doubt, seized the opportunities coming to me here; perhaps I shall be blamed for not having done so; I could have claimed a treatment like the one given to Captain Touzard, which certainly should not have been refused me, with my three years of service, a wound depriving me of the use of a leg, and the mention of my services during the day of October 9 by which I can flatter myself to have deserved as much as the ones who made more show of their zeal and whose schemes made them more successful.

But such is the fate of arms, if out of thousands of daily mistakes of the enemy—chance makes us profit by one in several campaigns—one of a grossness which could not escape even the less discerning eye, Success, whatever be the cause, attracts fortune and honor—often refused to unhappy worthiness with a false appearance of justice—these are not complaints, but only thoughts, in which jealousy has no part. I do not pretend to diminish the merit of those who reallly have some—but I would like to cover with the worst ridicule the ones whose gross schemes uphold their pride, and who gather the fruit due to real worthiness, whom he robs of it, and often forces it into submission.

Truly, my general, it is distressing to think that the ones who bestow favors, lavish them at random, but it is inconceivable that people who are in a position to see and distinguish worthiness allow themselves, by an unfortunate weakness, to be seduced by words, or grant on very ordinary considerations recommendations and certificates which, having a greater weight than rank, were the voice by which the truly worthy man was hoping to make himself heard, a voice that is snatched away from him, compelling him to the hard necessity of soliciting some rank which will not honor him much.

As for me, though just now compelled to replace by two

crutches the use of my leg, I could hope in this condition for a furlough from Congress more than anyone else—yet I am determined to stay and do not want any other reward than to be put in a position to deserve again, if I were fortunate enough to hope that you will help me to realize my desire. I would be happy if in the midst of your affairs you gave a moment to mine, and would speak in favor of the commission that I should have held since the first of last May. It is not a favor that I am asking from Congress, but a debt which I hope they will acquit, begging them by you to grant me as sole reward a position giving me a special function—if my zeal during three years, my services, my wound, can speak in my favor, these are the only voices by which I wish to be heard, and nothing will be wanting in my happiness if I owe it to you—

There is nothing very interesting here, the enemy is still holding its positions, and has established its various quarters in the neighborhood with small posts everywhere, reaching nearly to Beaufort where we have nobody, neither troops nor civilians, the latter having all abandoned the place. We hold our quarters by the same method as the enemy and his "surete de jeux" is real only by our weakness, which prevents us from undertaking anything against these small units, against which one could not do anything except in force, although isolated and cut off from each other, on account of the difficult creeks and rivers which are obstacles holding both armies within the limits of their own camps

Of the three French frigates left in Charlestown roadstead, two have just been bought by the State of South Carolina and the third one, *"La Chimere,"* will soon sail for France.

I am, with respect
Your very humble obedient servant
P. L'Enfant

APPENDIX C

Major general Baron de Steuben
Philadelphia

Paris, December 28, 1787

My dear general,

It is with the greatest satisfaction that I inform you of the success of the Cincinnati in France. The difficulties that could have stood in the way of allowing that order into France, where it is not the custom to admit any foreign order, have been removed and His Majesty, in his Council, has permitted his officers to wear it along with His Kingdom's other orders, wishing in that way to give the Americans a proof of the friendship which he desires to maintain with them.

I have written to General Washington a letter of which I send you a copy; I should like to have it translated well and published in the gazettes; you might persuade General Washington of this. I think it would make a good impression—

The order of Cincinnati is commented upon in France with more warmth than is the Cross of St. Louis and I receive every day reports on that subject.

The eagles are being made—see to it that the subscription is successful in philadelphia. I have made arrangements but to carry them out money is necessary—

I have the honor to be, my general, your very humble obedient servant

L'Enfant

I expect to leave again for America during February

Receipt signed by L'Enfant in West Point, on Oct. 15th, 1783 for $302 69/90, received from General McDougall, for the purchase of the diploma and the dues for the medal of the Cincinnati Society.

To his father and mother   From New York, Sept. 10, 1787

Being in the impossibility to interpret the cause of the silence which I was expecting to get an answer, I can only entreat you

you are keeping, in spite of the contents of my last [letters] to earnestly [to write] and trust your health is good.

The packets, leaving Havre de Grace every six weeks, give you a good opportunity to do so. Comptois, my servant, who arrived in France last May, and of whom I had asked news of you, did not even write me. Should his silence make me conclude that you were good enough to pay my debt to him? This circumstance makes your silence still more mysterious.

M. Leclerc, to whom I wrote by all possible opportunity, M. Detouches, nobody answered me. Surely you would not suppose that my coming return to France would make your writing unnecessary; when I wrote in February I only mentioned the uncertain hope I had to be able to leave America during September. So five mails have come since, by which you could have written.

My business (les affaires) is not finished yet, not nearly so; I fear it will never be concluded to my satisfaction. However, as I do not want to make up my mind without ground for it, I must still be patient. So be sure to write me, and encourage M. Leclerc to also do so. Write in duplicate, and though I sent word to you by Comptois to send all my letters in care of M. le Marquis de Lafayette, or of [M.] de la [Luzerne] (?), to avoid any inconvenience write me by the mail and pay for the postage, or no letter will go through. I also think I must warn you to be more careful in sealing letter that must travel so far; most of the ones I received from you were open, or had been put aside as notes of little consequence. The surest way is to have them countersigned, you have the opportunity to do this and it will save you the price of postage.

I have the honor to be, with respect, my dear Father and Mother, your very humble, obedient servant and son,

P. Ch. L'Enfant[1]

[1] By courtesy of The Historical Society of Pennsylvania.

Major L'Enfant reported his return from France to General Washington by letter, as follows:

New York, April 29, 1784

Sir:

I take the liberty to inform your Excellency of my arrival at this place after a passage of 43 days from france which I left on the 16th of march last after having finish'd every thing respect-

ing the society. the Diploma is engraved and many prints of it
already drawn together with a number of stamps of the Bald
eagle or sign of the association exceeding by more than *two hundred* the number for which I received the money issuing from the
subscription which took place previous to my departure from
america, those given to the french being included, the die for the
medal is the only thing wanting, but will be sent after me.

a letter which I had the honnour to address to your Excelency
in janary last will have acquainted you with the particulars of
my first steps to bring to a proper issue the matter trusted to me;
with his most christian madjesty Kind reception, and graciouse
assent to the wearing in his Kingdom the marks of an association
already Beheld as one of the most recommendable among those
formed on similar occasions and of which the Basis established
pon a characteristick Republican principle will leave to poster-
ty a respected monument of fraternity, and a glorious testimony
f a national and reciprocal union, never a token of honor even
the most illustrated in the different kingdom of Europe could
have fixed more tht attention, and been received with more gratitude than that which is Bestowed by the american army on that
of france. I will soon furnish your Excellency with proofs abundantly. sufficient to vindicate my assertion, and could have done
it at this moment had not the numbers of letters I am the bearer
of, been to voluminous to be sent by this opportunity your Excellency will percive by thier differents contents what sensation
the cincinnati has caused in france and petition coming from
different persons who had the laist share in the last contest with
great Bretagne; and I am apt to belive that tho' the limited
numbers of foreigners the american army has resolved to admit
into their Brotherly association seems to leave no Room for
adtitional members, yet the rank and distinguished merite, as
well as the eminente services Rendered to the United States, will
be worthy of particular consideration and will move the society
in favor of some gentlemen whose name can not but reflect honnour on the society, of this numbers are the captaine of the Roial
navy who Rank or colonels in the armys, and some land officers
whose particular Right are mentioned in the petitions formed in
their behalf by the Counts d'Estaing and de Rochambeau. as for
what concerns the officers who acted conjointly with us under
the comand of general Count d'Estaing and who were not personally named in the Resolve relative to foreigner, as it could not

have been the intention of the society to cast any reflections upon gentlemen who nobly hazarded thier lives and shed thier blood on many occasions and of whom the galante Behaviour even in the much unfortunate attempt deserved the praise and gratitude of america, I thought it my duty to attend the purpose of the resolve as nearly as possible and construing its meaning to give to the world a publick testimony of the american army's fraternal friendship and gratitude towards the french, I looked upon these gentlemen as having been tacitly comprehended under the more usual denomination as expressed in the Resolve of the cincinnatus, who said all the general and colonels who served america in the armys under the commande of general counte DeRochambeau, your Excellency sensible how prejudicial such a forgetfulness would have been to the chief aim of the resolve, will I hope approve my conduct towards those gentlemens to whom 1 presented the marques of the associations as being directed by special command from the society it self.

previously to the day appointed to distribut the order of the Cincinnati general count de Rauchambeau communicated to the lands officers the King his permission to their acceptance of it, and after the Reading of your Excellency official letter together with the included copie of the institution of the society those gentlemen being assembled made a motion to cause a sum of money to be layd up by voluntary subscription the amount of to be thrown in to the funds of the general society.—Being acquainted with their intention, I opposed it objecting as freely allowed to foreigner, and that the american army had not meant to comprehtnd the french in the assessment required only from her continental Brethren. but they insisted upon supporting their motion by interpreting to its advantage the article of the institution which leaves a door open to donation even from personnes not reconised as members of the society, and arguing from this that it would be a Breach to the law of the association to oppose thier donnation they informed me of thier having unanimously agreed to compleat a sum to the amount of 60,000 Livres and deliver it up to me, which notwithstanding thier instances I refused to accept previously to my reciving more particular direction from the general society to Whom I informed the Count de Rochambeau I should transmit thier intention at the first general meeting and it as been agreed that until thier desisive Resolution the sayd should be deposited in the hand of the treasurer of his

army, after that matter had been setled in that way, al these
gentlemen assembled again on the 16 of janary last the day
appointed for thier being admited amongst the cincinnatus; on
that morning I waited first on vice admiral count Desting and
after having presented him with the marques of the association
I procided from his hotel to that of the count DeRochambeau
were al those gentlemen were waitting and they being these invested with the order, the cermony inded with al Elegant Entertainment at which, toast suitable to the occasion were drink.
until the compagnie divided,—that very day I dispatched the
same included in letters, to the marin officers who were absent
from paris and whose answer I shal have the honnour to communicat to your Excellency.

As for what regards the french in the continental service the
marquis de la fayette being at paris at the times of my arrival in
that town I delivered up to him your Excellency dispatches, and
he will have appointed you with his prociding towards them, I
am only to mentione some particular, which are that although
from the terms of the association we did not think our selves
Hotorised [authorized] to forme a regular assembly yet many
petition having been made from gentlemen of our association we
formed a iomity to examine their particular pretention and
some of them, being juged deserving to be distinguished from
among the others, we agreed that they should be recommanded
to the general society, and the marquis de la fayette as Chief of
the commity is to communicat this resolution to your Excellency.

having also considered the advantages which Would result
from a regular corespondence with our Brother in america we al
Expressed our wished to obtaine from the general society the permission to name a president and to forme a society similar to
that of the respective lignes of the Continental army,—upon
what it as been agreed to hotoraise [authorize] me to informe
your Excellency with our prociding and to solicite the general society to comply with our demands Requiring al so that three of
their representative be admitted to set in the general assembly—
living to your Excellency to choose amongst those who are stil in
america—whaitting for your Excellency ansuerd to this account
of my proceding in france[2]

I have the Honnour to be etc.

P. S.: the name of the officer of count desting army which were
considered as comprehended into the resolve are

the marquis de Vaudreuil lieutenant general
de Bougainville brigadier, eschef descadre
Count Aartur Dilon Brigadier Commandant in second in
his army at savana
de seting [Stedingk] suedois Colo. idem
Marquis de Rouvray Colo. idem
[2]Edgar Erskine Hume, *General Washington's Correspondence concerning The Society of the Cincinnati,* The Johns Hopkins Press, Baltimore (1941), pp. 146-149.

.

APPENDIX D

THE SKETCH MAP OF 1791

The most important of these transfers from the Toner collection is a manuscript map of part of the District of Columbia, erronerously labeled "Unfinished plat of Mt. Vernon estate." It may have been made at the request of George Washington by Peter Charles L'Enfant.

This map, which is without title, author, date or scale, is 41 5/8 inches wide and 26 3/4 inches high. It shows the shoreline and the drainage before they were modified by man and indicates by hachures the topographic features of the site of the portion of the city of Washington south of Florida Avenue. Ten of the original houses in the present District of Columbia are shown, nine of them by small red squares. The locations of these houses appear to be indicated with more precision than on any other maps that have been preserved. No names are given, but the houses appear to be those of Robert Peter, an unnamed neighbor, John Davidson, a resident of the present LeDroit Park, Benjamin Oden, an unnamed neighbor, Daniel Carroll, William Young, the Widow Wheeler, and the Widow Young.

The map also shows that the northernmost of the two Bladensburg roads entered the city at Florida Avenue and Seventh Street, N. W. Florida Avenue is not shown as a street, but a tinted line at or close to its site indicates ha his was to be the outer limit of the Federal Capital. The portion of this line from Rock Creek to the Reedy Branch of Goose or Tiber Creek at Seventh Street, N. W., follows the Bladensburg Road.

A system of streets, squares, and circles is drawn upon the map, but no names are given. The streets are shown by single dotted lines. The legend lettered upon the map reads as follows: "All the Lines coloured red, are finished and those coloured yellow are intended to be compleated this Season." The map is drawn upon Whatman paper, whose watermarks demonstrate that it was made between 1770 and 1794.

It is not likely that the map was made by Andrew Ellicott,

since he was engaged from February to August, 1791, and for some time thereafter, in surveying and marking the outer limits of the District of Columbia. Ellicott gave L'Enfant "kindly assistance," however, perhaps including the outlining of the Potomac water front and of Rock Creek and the Tiber. Ellicott's map of the city proper, published by Thackara & Vallance in 1792, was evidently based in important part upon this manuscript map. This might be the map which L'Enfant directed Benjamin Ellicott to make some time between December 25, 1791 and February 17, 1792, in order to "delineate on paper all the work, which had been done in the city" (Records Columbia Hist. Soc., vol 2, 1899, p. 144; Elizabeth S. Kite's "L'Enfant and Washington," Baltimore, 1929, pp. 103, 140). It appears more likely however, from the use of dotted line on this map for streets and the reference to the "map of dotted lines" in the letter from L'Enfant to President Washington dated Georgetown, August 19, 1791, that this map was made in the summer of 1791 by or under the direction of L'Enfant. In this letter L'Enfant refers to what he was doing as being in response to the President's direction. He then says:

"The inspection of the anexed map of dotted lines being sufficiently explanatory of the progress made in the work will I hope leave you satisfied how much more has been done than may have been expected from hands less desirous of meeting your applause . . ." (Records Columbia Hist. Soc., Vol. 2, 1899, p. 38).

Moreover the map displays certain features which are said to be characteristic of L'Enfant's plans at this time. The streets and avenues which radiate from the Capitol and the White House are focused upon the front and back entrances of these buildings rather than upon the centers of the edifices. Some of the streets which come into squares in the city reach the squares at one corner and depart from them at the corner diagonally opposite.

The map suggests that in August, 1791, the only circular park that was planned was Thomas Circle at Fourteenth Street and Massachusetts Avenue. The rectangular parks shown are 12 in number. They are located on the sites of the present Patent Office, of the Public Library, of Judiciary Square, of the Pennsylvania Avenue market and part of the Mall to the south, of Farragut Square, and of McPherson Square. Parks which were not laid out were planned at Pennsylvania Avenue between Eighteenth and Nineteenth Streets, N. W., at Connecticut Avenue between M and N Streets, at hree poins on New York Avenue, between Twelfth and Thirteen Streets, at Eleventh Street, and at Fifth Street, respectively, and on C Street, N. W., between New Jersey Avenue and First Street. The map also shows that it was L'Enfant's intention to extend Judiciary Square northward to H Street.

The streets and avenues which had been laid out prior to the making of this map were Pennsylvania Avenue from the Capitol to Rock Creek, Massachusetts Avenue from New Jersey Avenue to Sixteenth Street, Sixteenth Street from the White House to Florida Avenue, New Jersey Avenue from K Street to the Anacostia River, Delaware Avenue from K Street to Washington Barracks, Virginia Avenue from the Anacostia River to the site of the Washington Monument, Maryland Avenue from the Capitol to Washington Channel. New York Avenue from the Naval Hospital to Florida Avenue, Louisiana Avenue from the site of the Washington Monument to Judiciary Square, North Capitol Street from the Capitol to V Street, South Capitol Street from the Capitol to Anacostia River, East Capitol Street from the Capitol to Fifteenth Street, N. E., West Capitol Street from the Capitol to the site of the Washington Monument, Eleventh Street, Ninth Street, Eighth Street, and Seventh Street from Florida Avenue to Washington Channel, Fifteenth Street from K Street to the Tidal Basin, Seventeenth Street from K Street to B Street, N. W.

Eighteenth Street from M Street to B Street, N. W., Twenty-fourth Street from Rock Creek to I Street, Eighteenth Street from Florida Avenue to New Hampshire Avenue, G Street from New Jersey Avenue to the Potomac River, F Street from Delaware Avenue to the Potomac River, and K Street from Florida Avenue to Rock Creek.

One of the most important features of this map is that it shows Massachusetts Avenue as an essentially straight line, lacking the angle in the eastern part near the present Union Station, which is shown upon the familiar L'Enfant Plan of 1791, and reaching the neighborhood of Rock Creek farther north than on the L'Enfant Plan. Accordingly, since L'Enfant seems either to have made the manuscript map which the Library of Congress has now identified, or to have caused it to be made, he must be credited with initiating certain of the major changes in the L'Enfant Plan which have occasionally been attributed to Andrew Ellicott or some other of L'Enfant's successors.

Extract from: Report of the Librarian of Congress, 1930, pages 164–167:

APPENDIX E

Called at Corcoran Gallery this morning on way to Capitol. Special meeting of Committee. Read the Preliminary Report to Committee. It was approved unanimously. Went to Corroran Gallery with Senators Mc. M. and Gallinger to meet President. When he saw me he came through the knot of people and thrust out his hand in the old way. He fell foul of the small model of the Monument, saying it looked like fussy work. I expostulated but he insisted until Mc. McMillan took him to see the pictures of the Monument. Then he frankly acknowledged his error and took back all he said. Senator Mc M. asked me who a black-bearded man was. I didn't know and asked Cortelyou, who said it was the new Asst. Secy. of Navy. "You better tell the President that," said Senator, "for he just asked me." Had long talk with Secy. Root about the War College and Mr. McKim's suggesions as to location of buildings. Showed Lincoln Memorial pictures to Secy. Hay, who was very much pleased with them. Secy. Hitchcock liked plans. Said Peterhof fountains surpassed those at Versailles. Explained plans to Senators Clark of Montana and Senator Foster of La. Mr. Burnham came in evening; was much pleased. We went to Cosmos Club and talked till after midnight.

(From Diary of Charles Moore, pertaining to the Plan of Washington.)

TOPICS OF THE TIME
Civic Improvement a Phase of Patriotism

There is something enkindling to the imagination in the plans for the improvement of the city of Washington, as described by Mr. Charles Moore in The Century for February and March, and as illustrated by the accomplished artists who have made their drawings under the direction of the Congressional Commission. The more these plans and pictures are studied, the more thorough, the more magnificent, the nobler, do they seem. It is a part of the good fortune of the republic that men of the taste and large-mindedness of Washington, Jefferson, and

L'Enfant shaped the city at the outset, and that its "improvement" should have come, in he ripeness of time, into the hands of an expert commission of the trained ability and moral force of Burnham, McKim, St. Gaudens, and the younger Olmsted. All honor to Senator McMillan for his share in bringing this great scheme to its present flourishing condition, and to the Presidents and secretaries and other officials who have so wisely and enthusiastically coöperated to bring about results the accomplishment of which will enjoy the approval and support of the intelligence of the entire country.

The "old Washington" is not without the attraction given by a fine and liberal ground-plan and the presence of public buildings adhering, under the influence of the city's founders, to the classic style of architecture. The new Washington will certainly compare favorably with any modern capital. Two of the city's existing public monuments are of such transcendent nobility that, being accented by their new surroundings, architectural and landscape, the whole impression will be unique in its magnificence and beauty: we refer to the great white shaft of the Washington Monument, and to the Capitol itself—the most imposing structure of the modern world.

To the devotee of art no new building can ever appeal with the poignant beauty of the ruin that crowns the Acropolis. In its pathetic dilapidation it remains the supreme and unapproached masterpiece of architecture. Nor can any later dome put to shame that which greatened from the brain of Michelangelo. The Capitol at Washington is not in rivalry in our thoughts with the imperious associations of Athens and Rome, or with any of the creations of the ancient world or of the Renaissance. We speak of it in comparison with the finest accomplishments of European art, since the great days, in its power, by reason of its commanding position and of its own lines and masses, to impress the minds of men. Its technical faults, whatever they may be, are lost sight of in its soaring, its imaginative proportions.

The good work planned for the capital city will give new impetus to the advancing tide of civic improvement now passing over the United States. It will be the pleasure of The Century Magazine to do its share in popularizing and extending the movement by a number of articles on various phases of the subject, accompanied by illustrations of a particularly attractive sort.

To us this great esthetic movement appeals as being, in essence, a phase of patriotism.

Moorelands, Gig Harbor,
Washington.
Washington's Birthday, 1939

Dear Mr. Delano:

Nothing would please me so much as to meet the members of the Commission of Fine Arts around your table on March ninth. Like unto a certain pervasive personage who came into a celestial gathering, as reported in the first chapter of the Book of Job, I have spent many years going to and fro in the earth, and am now only returned from going up and down in it; even from the Strait of Juan de Fuca to the cactus covered wastes of Mexico. But alas, unlike Satan, I have not the gift of omnipresence, and therefore cannot present myself at your assemblage of lords of the Fine Arts.

I trust that you will have with you Olmsted to recall the days of the Senate Park Commission of 1901, and of its successor, The Commission of Fine Arts. The memory of the friendships of those times furnish a picture gallery finer than either of the World's Fairs of this year can offer. Loyalties then established continued so long as life lasted. Loyalty to the nation to whose service willing allegiance was given as a patriotic duty. Loyalty to the inspired plan of Washington and L'Enfant, who by faith had the assurance of things hoped for and the evidence of things now seen. Loyalty to the spirit of that architecture on which Jefferson relied as, "the laying out of money for something honorable, the satisfaction of seeing a proof of national good taste," as contrasted with, "the regret and mortification of erecting a monument to our barbarism, which will be loaded with execrations so long as it shall endure." Loyalty to the plan of 1901, modestly devised and recorded by true artists as the necessary culmination of an original design so comprehensive as to fit "all times, however remote." Loyalty to fellow members with respect for one another's opinions, a meeting of minds uncurbed by parliamentary forms—and invariably ending in amicable accord.

All of this I saw and in it I had some part—the part of an appreciative layman among creative artists; at times perhaps, the part of adapting Commission conclusions to existing situations. Often those conclusions were arrived at around a dinner table at the Century Club in New York, rather than at the formal meetings in Washington.

In carrying out the conclusions of the Commission, the Chairman, like Saint Sebastian of the pictures, was subjected vicariously to the arrows of vituperative slurs and sarcasms by some Diocletian of the Congress; but found consolation in the duties increasingly placed on the Commission by the Congress of its own initiative. A President of the United States complained to Elihu Root that the Chairman was arbitrary. Bu he carried out the advice of the Commission as to the location of the Arlington Bridge. A Secretary of the Treasury seeking a compromise on the Great Plaza plans laughingly said that evidently the compromise meant agreeing with the Commission. He accepted the compromise. All of which goes to prove Charles McKim's dictum—one can compromise anything but the essence.

Looking back over two decades, I doubt if it would be possible to crowd into twenty years more pleasure than has come to me in association with the successive members of the Commission and those persons with whom the work has brought contacts.

The development of Washington will go on so long as the Republic endures. The problems of the future will be multiplied and will be different from those of the past. Charlatanism always is a menace, and it is no less charlatanism when it pervades the field of education in the Arts. The remedy lies not in words but in good design, faithfully carried out; with the firm conviction that beauty alone gives perpetual life. You cannot go wrong or be inadequate if you follow the advice given to me by Senator McMillan half a century ago.

"Remember, Washington is the Capital of the United States. Nothing is too good for the United States Capital. When a problem is to be solved, see that the most competent men in the country are called to solve it—and then see that their advice is realized."

On that foundation the Commission of Fine Arts was established and has been maintained. Under its guidance it must have continued and increasing usefulness to Washington and the nation.

With warmest personal regards and best wishes to you and
your guests and with renewed regrets, I am
    Cordially, faithfully and confidently
                        Yours

                                Charles Moore

APPENDIX F

MILITARY AFFAIRS
FORTIFICATIONS, PHILADELPHIA, AND WILMINGTON, DELAWARE.

Instructions to Peter Charles L'Enfant.

SIR:

In pursuance of the directions of the President of the United States, you are hereby appointed a temporary engineer for the purposes of fortifying the ports of Philadelphia and Wilmington, upon the river Delaware.

You are therefore immediately to proceed in the execution of this business, under the general directions of the Governors respectively of the States of Pennsylvania and Delaware.

The following is an extract of the estimate on which the appropriations of the fortifications have been founded:

For Mud Island and Philadelphia, - - $11,913 82
For Wilmington, - - - - - - 3,000 00

The proportions of expense therefore must not be exceeded. But every thing now undertaken must be completed and be considered as the parts of a more general, perfect, and permanent plan, to be hereafter executed; provided the sum now appropriated should prove insufficient, which is highly probable.

It is presumed that the completion of Fort Mifflin, at Mud Island, will be considered as the first object to be undertaken in Pennsylvania. The works to be erected at Wilmington, in the State of Delaware, will also require immediate attention in order to be put in a train of execution.

It will be perceived, by the lowness of the estimates, that the parapets of the works to be erected are in general to be of earth, or, where that cannot be obtained of an adhesive quality, the parapets may be faced with timber and filled in with earth. A parapet, however, formed of tenacious earth, is conceived not only to afford a solid defence, but even to be durable, provided it be properly sloped and sodded inside and out, and sown with

437

a species of grass called knotgrass, so as to bind the sods and earth together.

Your judgment will decide where to have embrasures for your batteries, and where to fire en barbette, and also where to have the common garrison, and where the new carriages to fire en barbette, at present used on the sea coast of France.

You will also direct what part of the works shall be protected by palisadoes and what by fraizes.

It is conceived to be essential that all batteries which are erected on islands or points of land at a distance from support ought to be protected by redoubts or other enclosed works, and that such redoubts ought to be secured by a block house, where the garrisons, which in ordinary cases will be but small, ought constantly to reside.

In the construction of the redoubts, or enclosed works, they ought in the first instance to be constructed so as to contain a respectable garrison, suppose five hundred men, and casements ought also to be contemplated in the construction, although they will not now be erected.

It has also been contemplated in the estimates that the magazines should be formed with timber, and five or six feet thick on the roof, so as to resist a heavy shell. This thickness is independent of the earth which may be placed over the timber. These magazines ought to be well ventilated, so as to be entirely free from dampness, and of a size to hold one hundred and fifty rounds of powder for each piece of cannon.

The spots at which magazines of this nature should be fixed will require great judgment, so as to combine security against all enemies, either open or subtle, and against common accidents.

A reverberatroy furnace, of the best construction, in order to heat balls red hot, must be erected for each battery.

These are general ideas, but are not to constrain your own judgment, excepting as to the limitation of the expense, which, as before mentioned, must not be exceeded.

The choice of the ground on which the batteries and works are to be erected, together with all the combinations and effects dependent thereon, will rest upon your judgment under the directions of the Governors.

All the plans must be accompanied with sections and elevations, so that a complete judgment may be formed thereof, an estimate of the expense must also be formed of each work, and the number and size of the cannon intended must be specified. One copy to be given to the Governor, and one transmitted to this office, to which also you must weekly report your progress.

Your requisitions for labor and materials must be made upon —————, who is appointed by the Secretary of the Treasury to account for the sums to be expended at Philadelphia, and upon —————, who is appointed for the same purpose at Wilmington.

Given at the War Office of the United States, this 3d day of April, 1794.

H. KNOX, Secretary of War.

Copy of a letter from Major L'Enfant to the Secretary of War.[1]

PHILLADELPHIA, April 19th, 1794.

SIR:

Much consideration being requisite in combining a fortification, especially when the safety of a capital city is the immediate object, I cannot but wish for time to mature my ideas on the subject; and seeing what grand system of defence the protection of a fort on Mud Island will require, and, independent of which, a stand at that spot can give no kind of security, your opinion being to determine my process, the following notes I conceive necessary to facilitate your judgment of the principle on which to direct my labor.

First, Viewing the situation proposed, I find, that however spacious as the fluid surface appears to be, the breadth of the ship channel is sufficiently narrow, and can be absolutely commanded over by the cannon from Mud Island; that batteries erected at A, under the defence of a fort B, —would play right down the stream over the width of the river; that they would batter in front, every vessel coming up, and do more damage, in proportion, to the crowding of sail. No position would be safe to stand by them, and the batteries easily covered from the land side, the garrison being perfectly secure, the fort may be expected to make a steady defence. But that its defence should be effectual in stopping a navy, on this I will observe, that the great object of an expedition rendering of no consequence the loss to which a daring attempt may expose, a fort standing alone may easily be passed; and, as a variety of circumstances would

---

[1] From American State Paper, Military Affairs, Vol. I, 1832. pp. 82.

here occasion some additional forts, to render the attempt to force the pass impracticable, it becomes a question, whether some other position in the river may not be found more eligible to make the establishment? But, until I shall have acquired all the information I need to support an opinion in the affirmative, looking upon Mud Island as the spot determined upon, the only method I see of making it answer the object, would be, to take advantage of a bank, to erect a second fort at C, the defence of which would co-operate with those of Mud Island, as may easily be seen on the small sketch of the river to which these notes have reference; that bank only three or four feet under water, easily to be wharfed, no inconvenience being to result to the current with which this bank runs parallel, the measure would prove most beneficial, and the trust which I place in its effects makes me desirous it may be first attempted.

The situation also, D, would be important to secure as well those at G, E, F, where batteries under the cover of Red Bank, and of another post at H, would much annoy a shipping engaged with the forts, as was experienced last war from a battery at F; protecting one another, these batteries would see down the river as far as would the defence of Mud Island, and of the fort C; they would procure a cross fire all the way, but especially above the forts; there it would become such, that no vessel should ever venture through, especially as having first to steer close between the two fires A a nd C; these different batteries successively to be passed should leave no safe position to repair a damage sustained.

With this, the greatest possible security would be ensured to the city of Philadelphia, and without n eed of chevaux de frise, an expedient which once might have been commendable, but which, for having in a manner succeeded, should not, however, be thought necessary at this time. In no case whatsoever, I would not advise the sinking of any of them, being well convinced, that more embarrassment would ensue to trading navigation, and more injury be caused by the necessary alteration whirh it would occasion in the bank and current, than there can be benefit derived from; all considered, every such means are mere expedients and contrivances, subject to accidents in their accomplishment at the moment when danger is near, and they are too precarious a protection for a nation to rest its safety upon, and ought never to be made a consideration in the delineation of a plan for fortification, the grand object of which should be to ensure perfect security, with a little trouble, and with as few military as possible.

All kinds of forts, and most particularly one as intended, ought then to be made capable of self-defence, and should be so situated as to check alone the progress of an enemy, in a country especially where militia being the main body to muster from, much time is required before troops can be assembled and marched. Too much attention cannot be paid, to make all fortifications capable of standing against a vigorous attack, and whenever this cannot be done, it is better not to have any, as by becoming useless they must prove greatly prejudicial.

Guided by these reflections, and considering that the defence of a pass on which the safety of the city of Philadelphia depends, is of an importance, as must make the expense attending the accomplishment of an effectual plan to defend it, a trivial consideration, although, endeavoring to restrain the works, as may be first begun, within the limited sum granted by the Government, I could not, in viewing the situation of Mud Island, confine my labor immediately to the contriving of a figure for a work, the combination of which, I perceived, demanded a previous investigation of the particular circumstances of the opposite shore, and some reflection on the manner of attack possible to be carried against; independent of which consideration, any fortifications as may be erected there, will ever stand a mere mock of defence.

Far remote from the sea as that situation is, it is certain, that no attack will ever be made, unless it is a very determined one; and, viewing the precedent of the manoeuvres of an army by a circuitous march to take possession of Philadelphia, cannot establish a probability of such an attempt being renewed under the present circumstances of the country, all grand operations must now be first directed toward gaining the pass for shipping, which, consequently, would determine an operation against the defence of Mud Island, or of any other situation in the river, on a very different principle than was once carried on there in 1777. Taking, however, that expedition under consideration, the result of my inquiries about, and the observations I have made on the proprieties and inconveniences of a stand so circumstanced, convince me, that in addition to the work above mentioned, as necessary for the defence of the ship channel, others will be wanted to cover and protect these.

The cover of a regular fortified post, to command over Province and Carpenter's Island, will be wanted sufficiently spacious to admit, as the occasion may require, a good garrison, and made strong to support regular approaches and hinder them from being carried directly against the forts on Mud Island, where they may still easily be advanced on the island below, which is but the consolidated part of the same mud bank on which the fort would stand.

The small sketch may show the situation where this post should be fixed, the figuration of the work being left undetermined until a proper survey of the country round has been obtained—whether in the manner of a horn, or crown work, must depend from the manner of the establishment on Mud Island, which it must cover, and by which it ought to be defended.

Some difficulties will be, to continue the work on the island a regular one, the solid part being too narrow to admit of square forts, whose line of defence it would render too short; an inconvenience would also arise from crooked lines, these being always defctive, for a situation easily to be surrounded, as half of the circuitous line must inevitably be seen in the flank and rear. Wishing to avoid this inconvenience, and to procure a larger front of fire over the channel, I would determine upon the position of the battery as at A, which will show the advantages of that direction over that of the old forts, the remains of which cannot be any way serviceable but my making use of the materials.

N. B. The defect of that old fort, not only lay in the configuration of its line of defence, which, as General Duportail well observed, are too short for mutual protection, but its situation is altogether so ill judged as to be enfiladed from every point from whence an attack is the most likely—a disadvantage in no manner remedied by the improvement proposed by that officer, who surely did not see the situation with a proper attention, or he must have observed, that no part of the addition which he planned would have been more secure than the old; no work, indeed, would be possible to contrive making the old one serve, which could be made a stand even against a few gun boats in the west channel; necessarily then, rejecting all idea of connecting any new work with the former one, I would establish the forts and batteries back of the wall now standing, making this serve as a cover, until the work is sufficiently advanced to mount the batteries, after which it would be pulled down, making the stone serve the construction of the principal forts.

As to what relates to the construction of the batteries and forts, the island being mostly overflowed and of a soft clay bottom, it will necessitate to some expense to lay on a solid base in logs framed in the manner of a grate under the whole, with a kind of upright framing to receive the platform; observing that, however temporary the object of the batteries now to be made may be, the time of which they may be of use, perhaps distant, may render them then out of repair, and consequently useless, or that being ever so near at hand, a defect in the superstructure being to accelerate their destruction, their object would be unanswered, and the confidence placed in them being disappointed, the sparing of proper materials and of the labor should, in both cases, be dearly repaid by the loss of valuable lives, and the disasters attending a weak resistance.

I have the honor to be, &c. &c.

P. CHARLES L'ENFANT.

———

Copy of a letter from Major L'Enfant to the Secretary of the Treasury.

PHILADELPHIA, *September* 15, 1794.

SIR:

After all possible exertions on my part, to progress the fortification at and near Mud Island, and however attentive I have been in confining the extent of my operations to the limited sums assigned for, it is with the greatest concern I am to inform you that those means, by proving too small, have long since forced me to relent of the progress; they are at present so far exhausted, that, unless you can procure a sufficiency of supply to continue the work for two months longer, the whole must stop before any part is brought to that state of perfection necessary to be guarded against winter, and answer to some object of defence.

In endeavoring to obviate the consequent injury which I saw must result rfom leaving what is done in a state still imperfect, and apprehending no new supply could be procured, since last supplementary sum obtained has itself proved much less than what I had been led to expect from General Knox's own promises,

I determined upon an expediential step, that of soliciting, through the Governor of Pennsylvania, the necessary assistance from the State. This measure, and the information I gave to a committee of the House at their visit on the island, and at two subsequent meetings on the business, determined a report agreeable to my wish—a sum of *six thousand* dollars they granted as an advance, leaving the manner of repaying it to the next Legislature to determine upon, and also referring to t he same, the consideration of what would be proper to do respecting the cession of the island to the United States. This was the purport of the bill this committee proposed, and, on another part having obtained the concurrence of some of the members the least disposed to favor federal measures, I judged that but little opposition would be made to the bill; in this hope, however, I have been frustrated by the sudden adjournment of the Legislature, who confined their labor to the consideration of the few bills which the Governor, *in haste of leaving town with the militia,* pointed out as the most essential for them to pass. Left by this disappointment in the same dilemma of difficulties as had induced my applicaion, the prosecution of the business solely now depends on what you can do, and in soliciting you to give me immediate directions, I must beg, before you determine on the arrest of the whole of the operations, that you will consider the consequences, giving a due attention to the particular statement, herein enclosed, of the actual situation of the several parts of the work that is engaged in conformity to order of April 27, and 29th ultimo.

I have the honor to be, &c. &c.

P. CHARLES L'ENFANT.

(From American State Papers, Military Affairs, Vol. I, 1832, pp. 82–87.)

APPENDIX G

City of Washington, July 17, 1812.

Sir:

I received the Honor of your notification dated the 7th instant that I have been appointed professor of the art of Engineering in the Military Academy of the United States.

Appologizing now for delay of the answer I beg you will indulge me some time longer answering you; that the terrifying review of the state of my affairs impel me to pause and most seriously to reflect. Indeed the sudden unexpected mark of the President's esteem of my talents excited in my breast a conflict of sensations more felt than easy to describe.

Bereft as I have been by the revolution of the whole of my present estate, in Europe, without resources whatever for personal support, existing, but in constant apprehension of imperious call from auditors, I with fortitude resigned to my fate. I rested quiscently in some respect content that the veil covering over the transactions which also robed me of my fortune and of my labor in this country must worn out the ————— of that veil will discover the ignominious policy which has thrown me down so helpless into the mire, that it will expose the malignity of the mind, the unfeeling heart of those who could machinate the suppression of my name from record, to deprive me of the name of the original projector of the plan of the City of Washington, and who caused me to remain the idle spectator of the efforts which have been made to prevent the proper execution of my plan. and being not one of those who to better their circumstances will abandon their rights, or who will accept of any office looking at the emoluments not at the responsibility which attach, I have more cause to be cautious of what consequences may follow from too hasty acceptance or rejection of the appointment notified. nevertheless, Sir, believe me that I rejoice at the manifestation of a disposition to restore me to a life of useful activity, and it encourages the hope which it authorizes that in order to enable the performance of whatever duty you may think fit to order me on—some means or

445

others *will have been previously determined upon*—if not for an absolute satisfaction at least for arrangement suitable to the stand of the claim I have depending, with regard to due remuneration of the hope I have been made to sustain in the affair of the establishment of this site of government. Honestly imagining, I cannot well be desired out of this place and sent on as it were to *confinement more dismal* at a distance which would hinder me the possibility of availing of what chance time may offer more favorable to the attainment of an extensive undeniable right. and the next consequence would be the exposure of my person to arrest and to persecution for debts in amounts far greater than possible to repay in *20* years time by the saving out of the salary of any office whatever, and think too would follow the impossibility for reason of the continued cause of vexation of mind, to give due attention to duty.

On other record, Sir, I am not so well satisfied of my fitness to the office of Instructor of youths. I candidly will avow I would prefer any other commission—on a station more accommodating to circumstances of affair of this place, or likewise more in the line of my former habit of real works both as military and civil engineer, distinctly in works of the *harbour,* or *camp, fortification,* in those of defense and of attaque of fortified places as the war now may require. and in all which the experience of service during the revolutionary war and in the late entreprise of the city of Washington I presume to think give me an advantage over untried men and some right too over upstart doers, but which experinece is by no means a recommendation to the professorship in an academy, because by long habit of pursuit of real work, every able practitioner will have formed judgment and method of process very different from the doing of that thing that are done by way of experiment for eexrcise in a school.

Further, sir, I have not the rigidity of manner—the tongue— nor the patience, nor indeed any of the inclinations peculiar to instructors. I am not fond of youth. I am adverse to the society of those self important talkative temperament whose vanity for what little they remember from the reading of works, make them talk at random about every subject and on matter and thing which they often do not understand and which so frequently make fools be mistaken for genius.

besides I would have to encounter the difficulties of language and that of a memory not remarkable for rententiveness of technical terms and speaking the true I have no reverence for the name of modern academicians nor do I believe in the utility of this military academy as many people affect to believe, who would have every institution made a pageant of imitation of those of other nations. I really see inconveniences and more ill than good to result from. I do think, especially since there is a small standing army, that a proper organization of the diffeent corps of which that army is composed may afford at all time of *peace* or of *war* more convenable way of instruction for young military and more efficient because on service more real than that of education in the best administered academy. and having uniformly on many occasions publicly expressed these my sentiments I surely deed not coveted the Honor of a professorship.

truly, Sir, I hoped that if my past services were deemed meritorious, I would have been replaced in a military situation. and I can not but be very much mortified at seeing I am *put out of the way of sharing* in the danger and of participation to the glory of the field of action war which is now opening! as very different from placing me in the army the appointment notified *disqualified me!* the law providing that "none of the staff of the academy shall be entitled to command in the army." moreover, it reduces me from the rank of principal engineer, an office to which I was appointed by President Geo. Washiington in 1793. it also subjects me to the caprice of inexperienced young officers, *some of them pretty old men,* of the actual corps of engineers! and it makes me a subaltern to one of the academy professors whose functions are by no means of military nature, who has the rank of Col. a simple teacher of natural and experiemental philosophie, which of all the different branches of military education is certainly the less necessary tho not altogether to be dispensed with.

Not however of disposition disputative about rank nor embitious of title, I am only desirous of the proper authority and power to direct in all matter and thing of my competency or may best insure advantage to the United States and to secure myself against the possibility of new contraditions, similar to those which—political animosities—base personal jealousy, cowards, rancor. the little malice of fools, and the speculation of avarice, excited against the best of my exertions in former employment.

and with regard to what I have before said about dues to me for the loss I have been made to sustain by deprivation of the emoluments from the sale (made here and in Europe) of the map of the City of Washington and to which I was justly entitled.

I question not, Sir, that the President and your self will consider the satisfaction of this due is of as much interest to the reputation of the american name as it is of Importance to me

with due respect,

I have the honor to be

Sir

your most humble and

obedient servant,

P. ch. L'Enfant

The Honbl. Eustis,　　　(City of Washington, July 17, 1812. P. C. L'Enfant states his reasons for delaying

Secretary of War.　　　answer to his letter of appointment—will want more time to answer it definitely.)

Original in *Records of the War Department,* Office of the Secretary of War, File L-145 (6) 1812, The National Archives.

17 July, 1812

Dear Sir:

I have this moment recd. your letter and have not time to give you an answer on the several subjects to which it relates. My urgent advice to you is to accept the appointment offered on you by the govt. It will deprive you of no claim which you now have, and provide you an honorable station and support. Your creditors have no prospect in your present situation. This appointment may afford some hope. My wish therefore is that you accept it. You might write a letter to the Secretary of War and to the President, stating that more active service was desired and cite all the considerations which you think proper but do not decline this appointment.

with regard yours,

Jas. Monroe.

(Original in the Manuscript Division, Library of Congress)

Washington, July 28, 1812

Dear Sir;

I have read your second letter and had much communiation over your subject, and now write you this in the spirit and feelings of an old revolutionary fellow soldier and friend. I must speak to you without reserve. I leave town tomorrow for a fortnight, and shall not be able to see you before you decide on a question that is highly interesting to you.

Since I had the pleasure to see you here two years back, I have done all that I could to promote your interest on just principles. I have wished that your claim which has been so long before Congress might be fairly examined and disposed of finally, but I have seen many obstacles to it. Some think that it is not one which Congress ought to sanction, others that if just the value attached to it, is altogether unreasonable from those considerations and a delicacy to you, it has remained suspended. If you accept it, it is probable, in case you wish a more active employment you may obtain it. I see no reason to doubt that you might obtain the permission of the President to join the army in the same rank, and to serve with the army instead of acting in the closet, especially when the army takes the field. By accepting the place offered you, you will be in the publick service, and it may be possible to transfer you from one station to another, especially when you qualifications are considered. But in your present situation, having no connection with the army, or publick, it is impossible.

By accepting this place you relinquish no claim. on the contrary you put yourself in a better situation to pursue it with effect. By rendering service to the country you increase the value of your former services, at least to yourself, as you will bring them more into view; and by making new acquaintances you will interest others in your welfare.

What objection can your creditors have to your accepting this office, or any other, for from the evident indisposition to grasp it, and an equally evident one to reject it, I am led to impute the indecision and delay to those causes only. Whether you will ever succeed in obtaining a favorable decision, is in my opinion very doubtful. I do not think that you ought to calculate on it, at the same time I am far from dissuading you from pursuing it. I wish you on the contrary to do it, since you think the claim just and are so much interested in it.

The appointment offered to you is an honorable one. The rank and pay of major, with professional duties which you can discharge, or soon may with credit and advantage, is an honorable station. It is a comfortable assylum and independence for life. It was, I am satisfied, intended for you as such. You have been so long out of the public service, in the civil engineer department, and other proper obtained place, that it was impossible to do better for you. Indeed you are the only foreigner in the country for whom as much could have been done. If you reject this appointment I have no hope of seeing you in any other that provides you an honorable support. None as I presume. In your present situation you can do nothing for them. Everything that improves it, however little it may be, improves their prospect.

I give you the advice which I should not hesitate to follow myself, in similar situation, which is to accept the office. It is a beginning and may lead to something better. Honorable rank and pay in advancing years ought to be cherished. In accepting it you give a proof of your attachment to the country. I would disdain to advise any one, especially an old revolutionary friend, to do a thing which was not honorable and praiseworthy. I think the course before you is so. I therefore repeat my earnest advice to you to pursue it, by accepting the office in question. I beg you to be assured of my best wishes for your welfare.

Sincerely yours,
Jas. Monroe.

(Original, Manuscript Division, Library of Congress)

APPENDIX H

Potowmack,   Fort Washington, 23 June, 1815.

Sir:

The distracted state of affairs at this place owing to the conduct of men who speculate on the subversion of the works and whose incessant struggle in opposition to my management and their brutal treatment of the people and insulting language to me go to discourage and ·to stop the prosecution of the work could only be contervaited by a resolut pursuit of honest doing, and consistency of my attendance with the labouring hands, all which prevented the means and leisure for an earlier reply to the Honor of your letter of May last and so absolutely has placed me under the necessity now, however much defident I am of the propriety, of addressing to you the following sheets not only in bad handwriting but in a raged shape of notes of an intended report such as you directed me to make on several special questions—persuading myself nevertheless but that on consideration of all circumstances you will indulgently pass over the deffect of form and of diction I will hope your perusal of explanation on the principal points of your enquiry and shall be happy if they be found deserving of your notice in any communication which you may think to make to the President on the subject.

with respect your most obedient and humble servant,

P. Ch. L'Enfant

The Hon.   works of Fort Washington.
A. J. Dallas,   Acting Engineer Officer of the
                           Works at Fort Washington.

Secretary of War.

P.S.

Summary of the principal matter referred to in the following sheets.

1st. on the plan of the work and what will be the quantity of land required for them

observation on the circumstances of the situation of the fort.

2. with what assistance of men from the army and at

451

what expense—answer, none at all. Explanation of
the assistance received.
3. what will be the requisite time and expense to complet
the work with or without men from the army
.remark on the information which I myself want in
order to answer that
some remarks on the conduct of the contractor
A B, & c.

———————

I, with respect to the plan of the work contemplated and
what quantity of land will be required for them?

The hurried on beginning of the range of the batteries over
the River Road—prevented the previous drawing of plan—neither
was I allowed time to have made such survey of the land around
them, as I wished—this alone would have taken up several weeks
to make, and the near stand of the Enemie urged on the employment of all my time as the raising of such barrier as was
practicable in season to oppose a renewal apprehended of the
conflict which had just then ended. nor was I ever since at
leisure to have lay down anything upon paper more than on
scrap, all near memorandum sketch, of what I proposed and
which all sufficient for my regulation of day work could not be
set in order for a proper show plan without the aid of clerk and
of copist draftsman whom I had not.

With respect to the quantity of land that will be required—
I never intended any extension of fortifications beyond the
height of the ground of the old fort, and no further than on
the end of that height east northeast of the blockhouse. at
the same time an enlargement of the limits of about 3 or 4
acres on that side is very desirable which would secure part
of a commanding ground over the little valley near the old gate
on the Road from the fort to Mr. Digges, house. this enlargement
I say is only very desirable, but whether granted or not on other
sides all round the fort, the whole of the shape of the Hill is
indispensable to obtain, to wit: on the south down to the meadow
ground; on the northeast; on the west; and on the northwest
down to the river edge, part of which is now nearly warfed at
the expense of the United States for the landing of materials.

all this enlargement taken together with the 9 acres of the
survey made in the year 1814 for the old fort will not exceed
the quantity of 22 or 23 acres and possibly may be something less.

I did not (indeed I never had the hour leisure to have) run the several lines of this desired adition. I looked on that of no immediate importance because the converse of the several lines of the contemplated bound will be better determined by what will be the shape of the counterscarp of the divers front of the fortification and that front on the land side were left undetermined until now for reasons as will be found herein after explained.

here in the first place I beg it to be remarked that the very first view I had of the situation and state of the old fort, almost a ruined camp by the blowing up of the powder magazine and the burning of all the combustible afterward by the enemie, was had on a hasty visit by call there on attendance with the President and Secretary of War. I then had but only a few hours (much disturbed) for judgment of what best could be done. the position and extent for the batteries where I proposed them and other essential work for their protection met with full approbation as likewise deed all what I exerted to do from that time to the time of the close of the war.

in second place—on accepting the commission habitually regardless of my own security, convenience and interest, I eagerly ventured the contribution of my feeble abilities to an insurance of the safety of the site of government at an eventful turn of warfare which threatned it of total destruction, in so doing I endeavored to forget and really expressed very painful feeling of the manifold injury which my fortune and fame have been made to sustain for this that I was in an eminent degree instrumental to the establishment. again I could not think of stipulating conditions for a service invited by the President of the U. States. on imparting my ideas of plan I simply asked and I was readily granted the permission of the reserve of those ideas in order for the better perfection of them—in short I was given the liberty to pursue what methods of process experience had thought me to be the most certain. and above all I was assured that I should not be in any degree dependent nor subject to the control of the military in what line I had long before created to rank.

now more on the reasons why I wished the liberty to reserve my plan, the following amongst others were—

that Warburton point, whereon the fort stands, although of a strong aspect from the river, and nearly insulated by deep

ravines on the land side, is nevertheless totally dominated by
ground within reach of musket shot and from distances to most
favorable to an enemie approach. besides that the uneven broken
surface and the center where the old fort stood encased between
two arms sloping from the steep hill on the rear and the narrow-
ness of the flat at top of that Hill, also the want of space at
every other point, the most proper to have fortified. all this
rendered the undertaking most ungrateful and prudence dictated me not to fix precipitately on any conclusive line, for the
connection of the work began. and surely great difficulties must
have been apprehended in this especially by men of science from
seeing the hasty erection of great range of batteries as aforesaid. therefore it can not but be well sensible to those who are
capable of judging of the matter that it would have been indiscret
in the extreme to have bounden any by the drawing of show
plan to the execution of thing which the natural bad contexture
of the ground itself also might have prevented or which in the
wholetogether viewed with a military eye could be susceptible
of melioration, but this only by long study of the fort, and, by
constant attention step by step of progress of operations which
made me discover more plainly the possibility of leaning back
the direction of lines of fronts and of the projection of angles of
the several sides of the fort. within narrower limits and at the
same time in a way certain to cover the part dominated or seen—
from eminences, at distances without.———

the success of my endeavour to this effect, if only I will be permitted to continue the work on the principle of its begining gave
me the full confidence that thing can in some measure be effected
to accomodate to the viscicitude of event and at much less expense
than some may imagine provided, however, that the speculation
of *contractors* will not stand in the way of my management.
the great end of which has constantly been to bring all the
essential part of the contemplated fortification to a state of
advancement such that if the fort is to be left unfinished it may
be so left in a shape capable of resistance not merely against
some such *burlesk* of an attaque as that which caused the late
abandonment of the old fort but absolutely also capable of sustaining days of siege at any further occurence of war—occurences
which for all the contrary opinion of people who have the happy
faculties of seeing or of believing everything just as their affec-
tions or interest led them to hope or wish,—I fear most likely

may soon ensue from a renewal of the contest between the great
potentate of Europe which should it end in the restoration of
the superannuated sistem of Legitimate Souvering necessarily
must bring back the late invader of that show with more powerful and better combined forces supported by a coalition of
Souvering interested finally to decide the question that free
popular government be permitted to exist any more. hazarding
the expression of this sentiment for that, that it excited me to
redoublement of my efforts since the eventual return of peace
and on the presumption to that it will continue to be the policy
of government to pursue precautionary measures for the better
security of the country and of this district in particular—the
following will explain what has been the work, its difficulties
and the progress made in the advancement of the plan.

at first moment of the enterprise several temporary parapets
of heavy earth were raised for the protection of better intended
work, and with proper caution of what attempt the enemy could
have made to disturb them. At the same time considerable
difficult digging were affected preparatory for foundation of
solid structure, all this was expediently begun at several detached
places, in order for acceleration of progress by leaving the inter-
jacent ground to be more securely afterward acted upon.—all this
preparatory work both in nature and extent, had been determined
upon on relayances on promises and assurances given and often
repeated—that the requisit aid and all needful materials, stone
in particular, previously engaged were ready to have been supplied immediately as I wanted. but by these promises and assurances as often as made I was deceived. the contractor would
never bring any thing in time, neither in quantity nor quality
suitable. This neglect rather speculation of the providing department, and in the meanwhile an unusual rainy season caused
the destruction of immense part of the ditches dug ready for
mason work. They were all filled up by the caving of the bank.—
also an extensive waterbattery when nearly established became
ruined but this however altogether owing to the workmen having
been arogantly taken away by the contractor A. B. and an overseer together with number of labourers likewise enticed away
by offer of higher wages to other business of that contractor's own
private concern. thus solid work were in the first instance
hindered, and besides that the first master managed so badly
and so visibly to enhance his gain and to disgrace me, that all

his part of the structure erect could only be permitted to stand as monument manifest of the treachery of that contractor, a circumstance which obliged me to stop progress. and although after repeated remonstrances on the subject to the A. g. master, I obtained another master mason and this later one now in employment truly has been more attentive to business, better disposed and I believe more honest still absolutely dependent of the contractor, both for his men and for materials his hands were soon tied by distress of every necessary. the most of time unfit for employ and nothing better than the rubish of street pavement mear balast of ship instead of stone were frequently forced into his work,—in short every contrivance which avarise and jealousy could suggest were resorted to to hinder the doing of better work than at first—and but little work therefore could be done before the setting in of winter.

during that season, unusually severe, I did not allow myself one single hour Rest from labour, the precariousness of the state of the work and the enemy headquarters in the vicinity imposed on me the necessity of endeavoring ways against stormes and first to have better arranged matter for an early renewal of grand operations! in order to do this I requested only the constant supply 30 men and six or seven horse carts. but though small was the request, I was left without one single hand and never could obtain more than 15 to 20 until the middle of March. so that I was unable to have effected any material objects. The insufficiency of force of hand and of carriage it will easily be imagined prevented the stop of the rapid degradation of earth parapets, even large portion of high ground untouched, draped down and the incumberence thence of every excavated part between such that so far from being ready as the return of spring as they had been at the later end of the fall all the ditches cut for foundations had to be dug a new. and again, when cleared of the incumberences exactly as had been before the case, the materials were kept back by the contractor new injury ensued and caused an excessive redoublement of labour at proportional additional expense without any advancement of business.

nevertheless by preseverance in the pursuit of my method of process to the astonishment of many I had sufficient ground ready for beginning of solid foundation and as early as on the 10th of March masons were at work. from that time to this day notwithstanding frequent stop by continued frost and occupied by delay of the supply of stone, a considerable extent of rampart, the escarp of one of the principle batteries (calculated to mount 16 or 18 guns), has been raised up to the level of the platform together with the wall of the counter escarp, altogether measuring between 3 and 4 thousand perches of stone, partly stone procured *from the demolition* of the old fort.

This an immense work considering it was done by not above twelve hand, half of them prentice boys and carried on in a new methode of layer, deserves to the master mason Mr. *Owlitha Laws* credit for his zeal activity and attention to my directions. and this I must say here that it gives me pain to see a man who labored hard not receive his due and obliged to give one half of his profit to the man who placed the supply, at the same time that the contractors who do nought but contriving to scheme his gain by stopping the progress of the work set the government at double the expense of the real cost of the work.—it is painful also to see the overseer of labourers (the overseers were paid last Saturday; the labourers were only promised pay on the next week to the first of the month) and that when they ask and would be contracted to have bill or certificate of the due to them, this even is refused. all these things are strange but I only mention fact, and it does not belong to me to envestigate into the cause.

it will be seen from the above that I had no more than 20 hand at most in the later end of the winter, that number gradually increased toward the middle of month and till the first of appril since which they organized bodies that do not exceed on day of the longest muster 96 men, white and black, three overseers and 16 or 18 horse carts with an overseer also. Never was I believe an enterprise of such magnitude engaged in and conducted with so small forces and so ill provided of all other necessaries.

for all this if I may hope the approbation of the government I will applaud myself. For that by arduous perseverance in my pursuit I surmounted the difficulties encountered. and it shall ever be to me a pleasing remembrance that the rapidity of my first progress of the entreprise has been in a great degree owing to the free volunteer aid and contribution principally of the citizens of Alexandria also from Washington and Georgetown. this spirit of voluntary services, however, did not last nor could it be expected it would have lasted any longer than so long as their apprehension of danger stimulated it, and paying here just

tribute to the merite of the citizens at the same time I am under
necessity further to observe, but the cession of volunteer aid
left me destitute of power at a moment when I needed greater
force of hand to have preserved the work from the destruction
which awaited it during winter and from other cause in the
above states.

had that unfortunate circumstance been guarded against, which
it would have been but wisdom to anticipate, had the government in first instance made adequate provision for the support
and constant employment of 1 or 200 hired dabourers and workmen and had the contractor acted more honestly and the supply
of materiel been more punctual, better and more plenty than
has been, then indeed instead of the bases of only one batter
erect I would certainly have had ere now, as I promised, the best
half of the whole of the contemplated plan of the fort completed.

what has been the provision made by government if any I was
never informed of that, consequently I presume it will not be
expected I could have regulated or limited operations so as not
to exceed the amount of the provision. in short, I may simply
set on to work and recomended all possible expedition in the most
suitable way for the immediate protection of the place and for
its security hereafter, which could only be done by setting such
hasty temporary work as I have done on a system susceptible of
the transformation of that work into solid and permanent structure *such as I now prosecute* on . with respect to what assistance
of men from the army and at what expense?

I never received any such assistance, and none of the army
expenditures are at all chargeable to any work of my direction.
I truly at the time 'when the volunteer services of the citizens
were about to cease wished them replaced by army men and I
then suggested the propriety of employing *1* or 200 of them who
were for a while stationary in or near the District of Columbia.
but I could obtain no determination on the subject—only late
last December a small detachment I believe of Col. Oreel's regiment on its pasage was ordered to the fort but before fixing
quarters it was called back, the officers had never reported themselves to me and that men were never employed by me; consequently the expense of the movement of that nor of any other
corps of the army cannot justly be charged on account of the
work of the fort and very different from being indebted to the
army for assistance I could well charge the ordnance or quarter-

master department with the amount of assistance which I was in a manner forced to give them relative to transportation of 38 guns of 32 or 33 pounds, the dragging of which only from the landing place up the ground of the fort employed in addition to soldiers of the garrison.

above 30 of my own labouring people, 12 oxen and 8 horses during the space of more than six weeks at interruped days, owing to the badness of the ground the unfitness of carriage and the want of proper machineries to have lifted up the weight out of the mire where the pieces were frequently left at half way (six weeks of labourers time 40 men at $10 per month besides rations and 12 oxen at 15 sometimes 20 dollars a day)

This employment of labourers certainly cannot be esteemed part of the business of the building of the fort, it did not aid but much to the contrary it greatly arrested the progress by distracting the hand from their usual labour. there were number of other similar instances which would be tedious to relate. and until this day and from the beginning of the month of March last, I have been obliged to detach from the work about six carts and several hands every day to do the business of the contractor A.B., who thereby secured to himself the expense of causing materials and other necessaries to the place where wanted.

more I presume it will on investigation of items in their several accounts be found that both the contractor and quartermaster have charged under a general head of expenditure for fort Washington, numbers of matters (such as the carriage of firewood and of provision to the garrison, such as the transport of gunpowder and the fitting up of a temporary magazine and many other things not chargeable to the work of the Govt.

it will also be seen that a temporary barack erected in december last and the repair of the old block house fitted up for officers quarter, although on ground assigned for by me, were works done by the contractor A.B. in a manner independent of me. and this must be clear from the circumstance that I was not called upon to certify his bill of charge for that and he would never tell me the amount—and truly these were business of the quartermaster department to have ordered and which were in no respect part of the govt.

now if casting off out of general accounts all such items of Matter and things not chargeable to the work of the fort—if also a just deduction is made of all over charge of material—just on the one point—lumber, four or five large rafts of which after being paid for were made to disappear. but above all if reducing the charge for stone which in the employment failed allways short in quantity of the quantity said to have been shipped on the carrying vessels and which contractor A.B. would never allow me to have perched at the landing, this just reduction and other proper reduction also of the speculative errors made in the sum of the measurement of mason work done—all this undoubtedly will shew then the *real* expenditure of the business by me directed was considerably less than the sum made apparent by the manner of the contractor and quartermaster accounts.

3. what has been the real expense of what is done and what will be the requisite time and expense with or without the assistance of men from the army?

having never had access to books of accounts of the contractor nor of the quartermaster and the persons who at different times acted as their clerks at the site of the work, keeping but only a very confused account even of the expense of the hands in pay and of their subsistence, none hardly of the tools nor of other things, and of having never been able to obtain even information whether materials by me requested were supplyed in part, in full, or how much over—all this renders it impossible for me to tell what has been the expense both of men, tools and materials employed at the work done. and surely it must be sensible to every understanding that without the knowledge of what has been the expense it is impossible to form any manner of comput of what will be the requisite to complet the work.

with respect to the idea of carrying on work with the assistance of men from the army to the exclusion of other—I must be explicit, *that cannot be done.* Soldiers whatever the discipline may compel them to do can at best only be useful in part of the work similar to that of the rugged construction of camp fortifications —at the same time the assistance of 40 or 50 men such as the artillery companies at the fort can daily detach as fatigue party will be desirable and will be of some advantage, provided that in the meantime I may be allowed the constant employment of *100* or *150* waged labourers, say from 50 to 60 white men and from 40 to 50 black organized as I now have in several bodies under distinct overseers with a supply wanted of 50 wheelbarrows together with from 15 to 20 one horse carts and six two-horse carts including oxen carts which later will soon become inconvenient to up. with this force of hand and of carriage if well assured, I will certainly be able to progress work fast as respect to the digging and levelling of ground.

but with regard to massons, stone cutters, carpenters, smith and all the hord of those mechanic journey men as will soon wanted, the number of any of them cannot yet be told because it will depend of what quantity and kind of materials will be at hand for them to work—and

that what ever may be the promise of contractors, what ever may be the penalty they may be subject to in case of failure— they never can be safely depended upon— indeed it would here carry me too far to describe the varieties of winding ways which avaricious, *dishonest avaricious* men, can safely pursue in effect- ing their own aims of plunder in business of the nature and extent as the one under consideration—and saying this much I do not mean to charge men on mere suspicion—suspicion is no ground for accusation, only of one thing I am apprehensive of is that a man so law minded as to offer a bribe may well be found disposed to accept of one and accepting too for the worst of purpose.—will you, said that man to me, if you but only will let me manage affairs as I have been permitted to manage them in former public employment, *only tell me what money you want* it shall be afforded, the profit to me will be immense.— if this is not offering a bribe I will acknowledge myself ignorant of the meaning of that word. repeated proposals of similar tendency were made, as for instance, requesting the building of vessels which finding I would not give lesser for them to be berth at the expense of the U. S. the man told me but if you only let me berth them they shall at the end of the season be yours , in short the men proposed making a present of them to me pro- vided I would not oppose his employing the public workmen and the public timber at them.

the least which may be fairly said from these proposals, cer- tainly is that the profit of these men is not altogether confined to the rightful percentage on his advance or on the cost of object he procure and that upon the whole the profit he aim at is worth making sacrifices of some of the amounts. all this I respectfully submit for consideration and will only express the wish that some way of procuring materials may be resorted to as I deem it practicable and certain would be more safe and more economical than putting the whole in the power of one contractor. and also that some arrangement should be made with the master mason for carrying on his work by day labour or on agreement with him for such part as may be done by measurement but all independent of contractor.

unless some such arrangement is made and provision also offered for regular payment of the labourers hand, indeed it would be really committing myself to far to dare fix the time on the requisite expense for the completion of the contemplated plan or for any of its part.

P. Charles L'Enfant,

to the Hon.   the acting eng. and Director of the work
the Secretary of War.   of fort Washington

Trinity Parish Herald,
October and November, 1947

L'ENFANT AND ST. PAUL'S CHAPEL

By Margaret Elliman Henry

When Lafayette came to this country in 1777 he influenced eleven of his friends to come and have a share in the advancement of the cause of freedom. One of these young soldiers, perhaps the most gifted and most versatile, was Pierre Charles L'Enfant. He had been born Aug. 2, 1754, in Paris, City of the Arts. His father was an historical painter of military subjects to the Crown, some of his designs still surviving in Gobelin tapestries. At an early age the boy was articled to learn the profession of architecture and engineering. Here we have his background and training. His gifts were later offered freely to his adopted country, where his influence is as yet unrealized.

L'Enfant signed articles in Paris to become an officer for service in the United States in North America. With characteristic impatience he preceded Lafayette by several months, and arrived here in the midst of the War of Independence. Through a Resolution of Congress he received a commission as 1st Lieut. of Engineers, and served for five years of "baptism in life and death." He shared the rigors of the winter at Valley Forge, a bond between him and his Commander in Chief. In 1779 he was in the campaign in the South, was wounded in the assault on Savannah, taken prisoner, and exchanged in '82. He was promoted to the rank of Major, and honourably retired from army service in 1784. He must have had some connection with West Point, probably as engineer, as there is a panoramic painting of the Reservation made by him about 1782. At the request of Lafayette, Washington sat to L'Enfant for his portrait, an outline sketch which has not survived. L'Enfant was over six feet in height, "of a good nature," and possessed great enthusias, imagination, and personal charm, which endeared him to the more restrained and conservative Washington. His devotion

463

and ability also drew him to Washington, who favored the young officer, twenty-two years his junior.

At the conclusion of hostilities, Major L'Enfant, then 28, wished to visit his father in Paris, but before his departure he was commissioned by General Washington to execute the Golden Eagles, the emblems and delicate enamelled insignia of the Society of the Cincinnati, composed of Washington's staff. These were his idea and design. His original drawings are in the archives of the Society in New York. A diploma after his design was also to be engraved in Paris. L'Enfant knew he would return to America, and doubtless spent his few months in Paris not only in executing his orders, but also in preparing himself still further in the arts of peace, the contribution he burned to make to American architecture. When he returned to New York in 1784, he immediately established himself as an architect and engineer. He was a well-known officer of the Army, and had many friends and connections.

In 1786, at 31 years of age, he was called upon by the Vestry of Trinity Parish to undertake a work for St. Paul's Chapel. Trinity Church was still in ruins after the fire of 1776, and St. Paul's was serving as the Parish Church. They wished a suitable decoration to go above the altar of St. Paul's, concealing the back of the Montgomery Monument. This handsome Italian monument, ordered by Congress and purchased in Paris by Franklin, had crossed the ocean three times before it was finally erected in the East portico of St. Paul's, where it was visible from within through the translucent, hand-hammered glass of the great East Window. The result of L'Enfant's work was the carving of the great Shekinah, or Glory, which focuses all eyes on the altar, as he intended it should. The design is inspired by Old Testament symbolism, Mount Sinai and the Tables of the Law, Jehovah (in Hebrew), in a Triangle surrounded by rays, representing the Deity, and a background of clouds and lightning, suggesting the power and majesty of God. There are several such "Glories" in French churches, but none so soaring, so inspiring. It fulfills the purpose indicated in Didron's "Christian Iconography," emphasizing the supreme holiness of the altar, the Throne of God's Presence in the Great Sacrifice. During the rectorship of Dr. Dix, its beauty and meaning were obscured, by dark and muddy overpainting, making it more menacing than inspiring. But now that the original gold and white have been restored by the work of the ecclesiastical architect, the late Thomas Nash, no one can fail to see its meaning. It is a symbol of the Church of the Ancient Law, leading to the Altar of the Incarnate Christ, the Church of the New Dispensation, the Law of Love. L'Enfant worked on St. Paul's for two years, eventually glorifying the whole church. He added the graceful garlands on pulpit and Clerk's desk, and the curving Communion Rail, giving to the strong, dignified architecture of the Classic Revival that touch of delicacy which, we are told, is an essential element of true beauty. McBean's design might have been too severe without his loyal additions. Religion should also have grace. As William Hindley, in his monograph on L'Enfant, says, "He added to St. Paul's that glory which makes it the finest Church edifice in this country." He was devoted to this noble place of worship, admired its "virility" and "Americanism" (not remembering it was British-built), and was greatly influenced by it. We know that an unemotional Vestry acknowledged its indebtedness to him, and testified that his work had given universal satisfaction.

L'Enfant was next entrusted with the task of converting the old Jacobean City Hall into Federal Hall, first Capitol of the young Republic. New York hoped to retain the seat of government, and wanted something very splendid. For his elaborate and symbolic plan L'Enfant was offered a Testimonial and ten acres of land near Provost Lane. This he declined. Ten years later, when in financial difficulties, he appealed for suitable compensation and was tendered $750. which he again declined. This fine and historic building was torn down, alas, in 1812, but a model may be seen in the Museum of the City of New York. Then came his greatest opportunity to exercise all his gifts. He was commissioned by Washington to plan the new Federal Town by the Potomac. His plan iincluded the avenues, circles and squares which are still the glory of the city, also a site for a Cathedral, where the National Cathedral now stands. When his plans were engraved he was only 37. The plan was worthy in imagination and prophetic vision. He stimulated Washington to enlarge the size of the area to make it "proportioned to the greatness which the capital of a powerful empire ought to manifest." But he exceeded the appropriation and refused to submit to the authority of the Commission, and finally was told his services were at an end. He was offered $2,500. and a lot near the White House but refused both. He had the weaknesses of his virtues, artistic sensitiveness, impulsiveness and pride, a soaring imagination impatient of restraint, which resulted in his being poor and humiliated much of the time. His commissions in Philadelphia, notably the Morris House, where he again plunged into extravagance, his plans for Fort Mifflin on the Delaware, where he was temporary engineer, and his design for Government House on Bowling Green in New York, do not especially concern us here. Mr. Hindly thinks he had some part in the design for the spire at St. Paul's, also that he made the draft for the second Trinity Church. He left no autobiography, however we know he worked in and around New York after Federal Hall was completed. He was a hundred years ahead of his time so inevitably never received his due of recognition.

We find strong evidence of his return, about 1820, to his first love, St. Paul's. The city had overgrown the suburbs where the church had been built amid fields and orchards. Now the fire laws had to be enforced and this called for exits from the galleries at the East End, leading to the Broad Way, which had now come of age. The General Theological Seminary, begun in the library, a small room at the North East corner off the gallery, had moved elsewhere because the four iron stoves in the corners of the church did not send sufficient heat up to their eyrie. Those corner rooms and the sacristies below them must be sacrificed to make room for stairways and general exits. We see how effectively the problem was solved. In the small space of the original sacristies, now vestibules, were built graceful spiral staircases, easily ascended, compact yet ample, with no evidence of being an afterthought, and with a delightful curve to the balustrade, which ends in the snail characteristic of L'Enfant. We find identical newel posts in houses around New York which he designed about this time. What more natural, almost inevitable, than that he should be asked to undertake this small, but important, work. Surely here we detect the touch of his genius, his loving care.

What must have been his feelings when his old comrade Lafayette, now 71, almost his own age, was welcomed back to America in 1824, and landed in New York, where he received a tremendous ovation, and a gift of $200,000 from the Government? The reverberations of this welcome, and the report of an Oratorio in his honour given at St. Paul's must have reached L'Enfant in Virginia. He was broken in health and spirit, befriended by a noble Virginia family the Digges, then living in Prince George County. When he died a year later they buried him in their private burial plot. His personal effects, a few surveying instruments, books and maps, were valued at $45. He has since been reinterred in Arlington, and given an imposing monument, upon it a tracing of his plan for the City of Washington, which in letter and spirit governs the development of the Capital today. But his imperishable legacy is the service in beauty, Old World tradition, the good taste of the French, the intertwining of the mutual love of liberty, the free and generous giving of himself and his abilities to the land of his affection and adoption.

APPENDIX J

NOTABLE QUOTATIONS FROM THE WRITINGS OF
PIERRE CHARLES L'ENFANT
AND OF OTHERS CONCERNING HIM

To facilitate it, the *abatis* were set on fire that afternoon by the brave Major L'Enfant and five men, while exposed to heavy volleys of musketry from the garrison. . . . (Page 58)

From Lossing's Field Book of the Revolution, Volume II, p. 531—

L'Enfant at the Siege of Savannah, October 9, 1779.

───────────

A medal is a monument to be transmitted to posterity. . . . (Page 72)

From a letter by L'Enfant dated June 10, 1783, addressed to Baron von Steuben, concerning a medal for the Society of the Cincinnati.

───────────

The plan should be drawn on such a scale as to leave room for that aggrandisement & embellishment which the increase of the wealth of the Nation will permit it to pursue at any period however remote. . . . (Page 128)

From L'Enfant's letter of application to President Washington to make a plan for the Federal City, September 11, 1789.

───────────

I would reprobate the Idea of imitating and that contrary of Having this Intention it is my wish and shall be my endeavor to delinate on a new and original way the plan the contrivance of which the President has left to me without any restriction soever. . . . (Page 146)

From a letter of L'Enfant to Secretary of State Jefferson, dated April 4, 1791, requesting from him maps of "Old World" cities.

───────────

I am happy that the President has left the planning of the

468

Town in such good hands and have no doubt it will be done to general satisfaction. . . . (Page 147)

> From a letter of Secretary of State Jefferson to L'Enfant, April 10, 1791, sending maps as requested by L'Enfant April 4, 1791.

Whenever it is proposed to prepare plans for the Capitol I should prefer the adoption of some one of the models of antiquity which have had the approbation of thousands of years; and for the President's house I should prefer the celebrated fronts of modern buildings which have already received the approbation of all good judges. Such are the Galerie du Louvre, the Gardes meubles; and two fronts of the Hotel de Salm. (Page 149)

> From letter of Secretary of State Jefferson to L'Enfant, dated April 10, 1791, sending maps as requested by L'Enfant April 4, 1791.

After much menutial search for an elligible situation, promoted I may say from a fear of being prejudiced in favour of a first opinion I could discover no one so advantageously to greet the congressional building as is that on the west end of *Jenkins heights* [*Capitol Hill*] *which stands as a pedestal waiting for a monument.* . . . (Italics added) (Page 152)

> From L'Enfant's report to President Washington June 22, 1791.

Since my first knowledge of the gentleman's abilities in the line of his profession, I have received him not only as a scientific man, but one who added considerable taste to his professional knowledge; and that, for such employment as he is now engaged in, for projecting public works, and carrying them into effect, he was better qualified than any one, who had come within my knowledge in this Country, or indeed in any other, the probability of obtaining whom could be counted upon. . . . (Page 175)

> From a letter of President Washington to David Stuart, Nov. 20, 1791.

For we well know that your time, and the whole powers of your whole mind, have been for many months entirely devoted to the arrangements in the city, which reflect so much honor on your taste and your judgment (Page 217)

From a letter written by the "Proprietors" to L'Enfant March 9, 1792.

. . . . A tall, erect man, fully six feet in height, finely proportioned, nose prominent, of military bearing, courtly air and polite manners, his figure usually enveloped in a long overcoat and surmounted by a bell-crowned hat—a man who would attract attention in any assembly. . . . (Page 280)

Description of L'Enfant by W. W. Corcoran, as reported by the Honorable Hugh T. Taggart, in the Records of the Columbia Historical Society, Volume XI, page 216.

If General Washington had been here instead of in Philadelphia this would not have happened [demolishing the house of Daniel Carroll of Duddington, partly built, because it extended over the building line]; the integrity of the Plan was at stake, since L'Enfant contended for a principle, sacrificing his future welfare to the maintenance of the Plan he had made for the Federal City (Page 182)

Statement by Dr. Charles Moore

Tardy have we been in acknowledging our debt of gratitude to him who planned the "City Beautiful." But at length we have awakened to a sense of justice to him and to the land which gave him birth. . . . (Page 295)

He laid out a city for fifty States instead of thirteen. He could imagine things a century before they happened. Like many of his kind, he was dead long before his dream came true. His services were not for one generation merely, but for all time; the beauties of Washington and delight in its charms as one of the greatest national capitals (Page 296)

From a Report by Dr . James Dudley Morgan to the Columbia Historical Society May 11, 1909.

To plan the city, Washington selected a French Officer, whose qualities of character and faults of temper he had for thirteen years many occasions to appreciate; gifted, plucky, energetic, but difficult to handle. (Page 296)

From an Address by Ambassador Jusserand at the Reinterment of Major Pierre Charles L'Enfant, Arlington National Cemetery, April 28, 1909.

Few men can afford to wait a hundred years to be remembered. It is not a change in L'Enfant that brings us here. It is we who have changed, who have just become able to appreciate his work. And our tribute to him should be to continue his work." (Page 303).—Secretary of State Root at the dedication of the Tomb of L'nEfant, May 22, 1911.

Federal City, June 1, 1799

—"No departure from the *engraved* plan of the city ought to be allowed, unless imperious necessity should require it, or some great public good is to be promoted thereby."

George Washington to Dr. William Thornton, Miscellaneous State Papers, Page 336.

APPENDIX K

BIBLIOGRAPHY

L'Enfant and Washington, by Elizabeth S. Kite; Records of the Institut Français de Washiington. The John Hopkins Press, Baltimore, 1929.

Report on the Improvement of the Park System of the District of Columbia (Plan of 1901), edited by Charles Moore, Government Printing Office, 1902.

The Writings of George Washington, George Washington Bicentennial Edition, 1932, Government Printing Office.

The Diaries of George Washington (4 vols.) by John C. Fitzpatrick, Houghton Mifflin Company, 1925.

With Americans of Past and Present Days, by J. J. Jusserand, Charles Scribner's Sons, New York, 1917.

Records of the Columbia Historical Society, Washington, D.C.

Reminiscences, by Ben Perley Poore (2 vols.), Hubbard Bros., Philadelphia, 1886.

Sidelights of Maryland History, by H. D. Richardson, Baltimore, 1913.

The City of New York in the Year of Washington's Inauguration, 1789, by E. V. Smith, 1889.

History of New York, by Martha Lamb, 1881.

St. Paul's Chapel, by Rev. Morgan Dix, S.T.D., New York, 1866.

Histoire de la Participation de la France dans l'Etablissement des Etats Unis, Henri Doniol (5 vols.), Paris, 1886.

Documents of the American Revolution, John Durand, New York, 1889.

United States Revolutionary Diplomatic Correspondence (2 vols.), by Francis Wharton, Government Priting Office, 1889.

Beaumarchais et son Temps, par Louis de Lomenie, Paris, 1850.

Beaumarchais et les Affaires D'Amerique, Jules Marsan, Paris, 1919.

Beaumarchais and the War of Independence, E. S. Kite, (2 vols.), Boston, 1918.

Records of the Common Council, City of New York, City Hall.

General Washington's Correspondence concerning the Society of the Cincinnati, by Edgar Erskine Hume, Johns Hopkins University Press, Baltimore, 1941.

History of the City of Washington, by William Tindall, Knoxville, Tenn., 1914.

Greenleaf and Law in the Federal City, by Allen C. Clark, Washington, 1901.

A History of the National Capital, by W. B. Bryan (2 vols.), The MacMillan Company, New York, 1916.

Early Philadelphia Architects and Engineers, by Joseph Jackson, Philadelphia, 1923.

American Colonial Architecture, by Joseph Jackson, David McKay, Philadelphia, 1924.

A Manual on the Origin and Development of Washington, by H. Paul Caemmerer, Washington, 1939.

Outline of Town and City Planning, by Thomas Adams, Russell Sage Foundation, New York, 1935.

Essays in the Earlier History of American Corporations, by Joseph Stancliffe Davis, Harvard University Press, Cambridge, 1917.

L'Art Français aux Etats Unis, by Louis Réau, Paris, 1926.

History of Paterson, New Jersey, by Charles A. Skinner, 1919.

Lossing's Field Book of the Revolution, Harper & Brothers, New York, 1860.

Greek Revival Architecture in America, by Talbot Hamlin, Oxford University Press, New York, 1944.

Cities of Latin America, by Francis Violich, Reinhold Publishing Corporation, New York, 1944.

INDEX

A

Adams, President John, 363.
Adams, President John Quincy, 306.
Agreement between the Government and the Proprietors, 143.
Alexandria, City of, 134, 152, 272.
American Institute of Architects; Journal of the, 279, 280; 314.
Amphitrite, The, 34, 35, 37, 38.
Appendix to L'Enfant's Letter of May 30, 1800, 395.
Appendix A—The L'Enfant Memorials, 367-410.
Appendix B — Letters concerning L'Enfant's experiences in the Revolutionary War, 411-421.
Appendix C—Letters concerning his services for the Society of the Cincinnati, 422-427.
Appendix D—The Sketch Map of 1791, 428-431.
Appendix E—Extract from Diary of Charles Moore, and concerning the McMillan Commission, as well as the Plan of Washington, 432-436.
Appendix F—Reports concerning fortifications, 437-444.
Appendix G — Letters concerning L'Enfant's appointment as professor of Engineering at West Point, 445-450.
Appendix H—Report by L'Enfant concerning Fort Washington, 451-462.
Appendix I—L'Enfant and St. Paul's Chapel, 463-467.
Appendix J — Notable Quotations from the Writings of Pierre Charles L'Enfant and others concerning him, 468-471.
Appendix K—Bibliography, 472-473.

A (second column)

Aquia Quarries, 178, 187, 199, 203.
Arlington Mansion, 302, 335.
Arlington Memorial Bridge, 325, 335.
Arlington National Cemetery, 291, 297, 298.
Artist of the American Revolution, 66, 134.

B

Baltimore in 1790, 132.
Baltimore & Ohio Railroad Co., 324.
Bunneker, Benjamin, 199.
Baraof, Balentine, 199.
Bartlett, Dr. Josiah, 221.
Beaumarchais, Caron de, 31, 33, 37, 39, 41, 47.
Belin, Hon. F. Lammot, 288.
Binns, Kenneth, 353.
Bonvoulier, Archand de, 27, 28.
Bosworth, Welles, architect, 297, 302.
Botanic Garden, 324.
Boykin, Edward, 363, 364.
Brandywine, Battle of, 43, 44.
Brent, Robert, 203.
Brown, Glenn, 298, 302, 305.
Bryan, W. B., 225.
Buchan, Earl of, receives L'Enfant Plan, 224.
Buffalo, New York, 341.
Bulfinch, Charles, 123.
Burnes, David, 190.
Burnham, Daniel H., 319, 324, 332, 334.

C

Canberra, Australia, 351, 352, 354.
Capital City, location of the, 134.
Capitol, The, in 1800, 306, 363.
Carroll, Daniel, District Commissioner, 171, 203.

475